The American Revolutionary War was a conflict that Britain did not want, and for which it was not prepared. The British Army in America at the end of 1774 was only 3,000-strong, with a further 6,000 to arrive by the time that the conflict started in the spring of 1775. The Royal Navy, on which the British depended for the defence of its shores, trade, and far-flung colonies, had been much reduced as a result of the economies that followed the Seven Years War.

In 1775 the problem facing government ministers, the War Office, and the Admiralty was how to reinforce, maintain, and supply an army in North America that grew to over 90,000 men while blockading the American coast and defending Britain's many interests around the world; a problem that got bigger when France entered the war in 1778. With a 3,000-mile supply line, taking six to eight weeks for a passage, the scale of the undertaking was enormous.

Too often in military histories the focus is on the clash of arms, with little acknowledgement of the vital role of that neglected stepchild – logistics. In *All At Sea*, John Dillon concentrates on the role of the Royal Navy in supporting, supplying and transporting the British Army during the war in America. Because of individual egos, other strategic priorities, and the number of ships available, that support was not always at the level the British public expected. However, without the navy the war could not have been fought at all.

John Dillon joined the RAF in 1963 and, after some years as an apprentice and a Cranwell Cadet, he flew as a navigator on Vulcan bombers. He left the service in 1976 for a 30-year career in computers. Early retirement in 2005 was an opportunity to study for a history degree at Reading; a First was followed by an MA and a PhD. His previous books (both with Helion) are *'Allies are a Tiresome Lot' The British Army in Italy in the First World War*, and *Battalions at War. The York and Lancaster Regiment in the First World War*. John and his wife live in Berkshire where retirement allows time for his photography, military history, and travel.

All at Sea

Naval Support for the British Army During the
American Revolutionary War

John Dillon

 Helion & Company Limited

Helion & Company Limited
Unit 8 Amherst Business Centre
Budbrooke Road
Warwick
CV34 5WE
England
Tel. 01926 499 619
Email: info@helion.co.uk
Website: www.helion.co.uk
Twitter: @helionbooks

Published by Helion & Company 2019
Designed and typeset by Mary Woolley (www.battlefield-design.co.uk)
Cover designed by Paul Hewitt, Battlefield Design (www.battlefield-design.co.uk)

Text © John Dillon, 2019
Maps by George Anderson © Helion and Co, 2019

Front cover: View of the attack on Bunker's Hill, with the burning of Charles Town,
June 17, 1775. Hand-coloured engraving by John Lodge after James Millar. (Anne S.K.
Brown Collection)

ISBN 978-1-912866-67-0

British Library Cataloguing-in-Publication Data.
A catalogue record for this book is available from the British Library.

For details of other military history titles published by Helion & Company Limited
contact the above address or visit our website: http://www.helion.co.uk.

We always welcome receiving book proposals from prospective authors.

Contents

List of Maps

Acknowledgements

I must start by acknowledging a debt to three historians whose monographs from the 1970s are fundamental to the topics covered in my book: David Syrett, Norman Baker, and Arthur Bowler. In researching my book I had the benefit of the internet, a facility denied earlier historians. My work would have been enormously more difficult were it not for the work of those who scanned all 11 volumes of the Naval Documents of the American War, some 15,000 pages. The ability to download these to a laptop at home, along with relevant articles in the *Mariner's Mirror* and the Navy Records Society, puts me in debt to those who made these documents available online from the different archives.

Duncan Rogers of Helion deserves my thanks for continuing to support me by publishing my third book. Jacqueline Reiter was a patient and understanding editor and any remaining errors in the text are my own. George Anderson, who produced the maps for my previous books, did another admirable job of turning an amateur's sketches into usable maps.

Lastly, I must thank my dear wife, Susi for her patience and support during the last couple of years; there must have been times when my excuses for not doing other jobs were wearing a little thin.

Introduction

The war that is the backdrop to this book has been variously labelled 'The American War of Independence', 'The American Revolutionary War', and even the 'First American Civil War'. What became an American war for independence from Britain did not start out that way. The original protests against taxes imposed by Britain were just that: they were protests. There was no intention to start a war with the mother country, but actions can have unintended consequences. From the standpoint of British ministers, the American colonists were subjects of the Crown, goaded by extremists (usually referred to as Rebels) into insurrectionary and revolutionary acts against the legal sovereignty of Parliament. The British did not want a war with the Americans, nor did many of the colonists want to see a conflict that would hurt trade and hand power to those who many saw as troublemakers and firebrands. In a bid to recoup some of the costs of the recently won Seven Years War, and to make the colonists contribute towards their ongoing defence costs against possible future French aggression, the government in London imposed taxes on the colonies. In their attempts to impose and collect these taxes the British ministers, 3,000 miles away in London, demonstrated their lack of understanding of the independent nature of the American colonists and their unwillingness to accept the imposition of taxes in the same docile way that a farmer in Lincolnshire might. As the situation deteriorated, the British found themselves in a war that they were unprepared for, while looking over their shoulders to see if the French were about to take advantage of London's little problem.

American society in the early 1770s was very different from that in Britain; only five cities had more than 10,000 inhabitants, and they were all seaports – Philadelphia, New York, Boston, Charleston, and Newport, Rhode Island. Unlike the British, Americans were predominantly independent, self-sufficient farmers and tradesmen living in small villages and hamlets; their frontier spirit held little regard for central authority. Back home, the British lived in organised towns and cities and they worked either on the land or in the new industries, not moving far from their place of birth and regulated by local and central government authorities whose right to tax them was largely accepted. The two societies were very different. David Syrett commented that 'revolutionary America was to the British government the unknown viewed by the uncomprehending'.[1] The independence of the Americans and the distributed nature of their communities and society posed a problem for the British government in their prosecution of the war; it was not enough to capture and occupy a town in a country that had no one political or economic centre; this was a country of backwoodsmen and farmers spread over a vast area. The independent nature of the Americans also meant that there were divergent views among them as to the need for a conflict with Britain. Many (particularly wealthy merchants and traders) were Loyalists, and did not want hostilities to damage their businesses. In addition, not all British people agreed with the need to go to war with the Americans; some, like the Howe brothers (who would lead the army and the navy in the early years), had strong connections and sympathies with the colonists and did not want to leave behind a legacy of bitterness. Hugh Bicheno trenchantly commented that it was a war in which 'a sympathetic Whig general [William Howe]' had half-heartedly directed 'a professional British Army in operations against an ever-changing band of miserably supported amateurs led by one [Washington] who, in England, would have been considered a Tory'.[2] The possibility that the British might make war on their American subjects was one that the French also kept under observation. In January 1775, before hostilities had broken out, the French *chargé d'affaires* in England wrote to Paris: 'The progress of the rebellion required a more extensive plan and the question was to determine whether or not European England would wage war against American England'.[3] Major-General Howe was not the only senior commander to have reservations about fighting the Americans; Admiral Keppel had proclaimed that 'he was ready to do his duty but *not in the line of America*'.[4]

After the initial shots were fired at Lexington and Concord, the British became trapped within the confines of Boston. The Rebels controlled access to the town as well as the surrounding high ground, with the result that the British troops were cut off from local supplies and were dependent on their home bases, 3,000 miles away across the Atlantic. The army became, and would remain, utterly dependent

1   D. Syrett, *The Royal Navy in American Waters 1775–1783* (Aldershot: Scolar Press, 1989), p.312.
2   H. Bicheno, *Rebels & Redcoats: The American Revolutionary War* (London: HarperCollins, 2003), p.xxxix.
3   *Naval Documents of the American Revolution* (henceforth NDAR), Vol.1, p.383, Garnier to Vergennes, 19 January 1775.
4   Navy Records Society (NRS), *The Rodney Papers, 1763–1780*, vol.2 (Aldershot: Navy Records Society, 2007), p.233.

on the sea for all their needs, which had to be coordinated via a communication system reliant on wind and sail, a journey that frequently took six weeks in each direction. On 5 October 1775, General Howe acknowledged receipt of a letter sent to him on 2 August[5] (about eight weeks in transit) while, in another example, on 31 May 1780, Admiral Rodney (in the Caribbean) wrote to the First Lord of the Admiralty to say that he had 'not been honoured with one word [...] since I left England [in December 1779]'.[6] The slow communications had an effect on the conduct of the war as both London and New York were always out of step with each other; the clerks in London who were trying to provision the army were never sure of the location of the troops, or the number of mouths they were trying to feed. The problem was further exacerbated by the failure of the British to appoint an overall commander for the American and Caribbean stations.

The history of the British involvement in the war is usually written from the viewpoint of the army and most of the milestones are associated with the actions that involved the troops; Lexington, Concord, Bunker Hill, Philadelphia, Charleston and Yorktown. Against this backdrop, it is easy to overlook the role of the navy and to assume that America was the primary focus of the government and the Admiralty throughout the conflict. Once the French joined the war in 1778, America became of secondary significance. The maintenance of a fleet in home waters to deter a French invasion made the Admiralty face the dilemma of how to best use its limited number of ships between the Channel and North America. Additionally, Gibraltar had to be held because of its strategic position as gateway to the Mediterranean; convoys would have to be sent to relieve the Spanish siege of the Rock and London could not ignore the defence of the Sugar Islands in the Caribbean. These islands were far more important, commercially, to Britain than the American colonies. After the entry of the French, America became much more of a backwater than American myths of their struggle for Independence would have us believe.

Given the distance from Britain, the slow communications, the limited number of ships available to the navy (many had been put in 'ordinary' following the Seven Years War), and the reducing importance of America as the war progressed, how was the army provided with all that it needed to remain a fighting force? This account will not attempt to be a 'guns and drums' history of the war, many actions will get no mention and those that do will only be described in limited detail – those wishing to read more on the operational side of the war will find some admirable studies in the bibliography. The aim of this book is to give more

---

5   The National Archives, Kew (henceforth TNA), CO 5/92, ff.211, 306.
6   NRS, *The Private Papers of John, Earl of Sandwich* (henceforth SP), vol.3 (London: Navy Records Society, 1935–36), p.214.

focus to the vital, but often overlooked, role of the logistical services that supplied the army, as well as the various ways in which the navy supported the troops on shore. Naval support was not just admirals and ships but included the Admiralty, the Victualling Board, the taking on of responsibilities for transport and feeding of the army from the Treasury, the contracting of ships for the transport of provisions and troops and the cooperation in combined operations – what we now call amphibious landings. There is little glamour attached to the logistics services, as Bowler accurately stated: 'In the study of warfare, logistics and military administration have been neglected stepchildren'.[7]

When the war started, the troops in America received their provisions from the Treasury, boots, leggings, shirts, tents and bedding: all that was necessary to maintain an army away from home. At that time, the army commissary would have been able to buy food and hay, as well as procure fresh water, from the local area. The troops would also have been able to move relatively freely between locations. Once the war started, the local supplies dried up and the army was trapped in Boston by a hostile population and militia. From that point on, the troops became utterly reliant on the sea for their supplies and for freedom of manoeuvre. As the conflict grew in size, and troop numbers increased, the Treasury found itself more and more unable to cope with the administrative task of supplying an ever increasing army. The navy had processes and departments in place for supplying ships around the world with food and other necessary provisions, as well as clerks who were experienced in putting out contracts for victuals and transport shipping. However, they were reluctant to take on the added responsibility of providing these services for the army, although the Treasury were keen for them to take on the work. By 1778, the problems had escalated to the extent that the provisioning of General Howe's army was approaching crisis point. Although the Treasury wished to offload the responsibility to the navy, there were obvious differences between victualling ships at home and an army 3,000 miles away. In the case of the navy, once the Victualling Board had let contracts for beef, pork, butter etc., this was loaded aboard the appropriate warships in British naval ports, sufficient for the ship's crew for three to six months. Once at sea, the ship could replenish from another vessel, or in a foreign port. With the army in America, the problem was of a different order. As we will see in subsequent chapters, the army was poor at providing the necessary information on the number of mouths to be fed, especially when they took in Loyalists and refugees, and this information took weeks to travel home by sea.

7   R.A. Bowler, *Logistics and the Failure of the British Army in America, 1775–1783* (Princeton, NJ: Princeton University Press, 1975), p.3.

While the problems involved in supplying the army take up the early chapters of this book, the navy also had to support the troops operationally. Joint operations require good commanders working effectively together. The later chapters demonstrate how events in America were not helped by poor relationships between some of those commanders (not all of whom had been selected on merit), and the number of roles that the navy was expected to perform with an inadequate number of ships. The availability of sea transport, escorted by naval warships, provided added mobility to the army giving commanders the opportunity to surprise the Americans with successful supported landings at Kips Bay, Philadelphia and Charleston.

In the important role of maintaining an effective economic blockade of the American coast to cut off the trade of the colonists, and their access to arms and ammunition, the navy was less successful. Following the Seven Years War and British naval supremacy over the French, the British public and politicians expected to hear of naval victories, but that required admirals of a more determined stamp than those sent out to command the American station.

Once the French entered the war in 1778, the British Navy (which politicians had been slow to mobilise) found itself reacting to French initiatives. As long as ministers in London, together with the King, insisted in pursuing the goal of returning American colonists to their allegiance to Parliament, as well as looking over their shoulders to France, the Admiralty was forced into a policy of 'defending everywhere;' America, the Channel, Gibraltar and the Caribbean. In the end, although the army's supply needs were provided for, the navy let the troops down when they were besieged at Yorktown. Between them (and for various reasons), Admirals Rodney, Hood, Graves and Digby failed to meet the country's expectations off Chesapeake Bay in September 1781. The following year Rodney did defeat the French at the Battle of the Saintes, re-establishing British naval supremacy, but too late to save Cornwallis at Yorktown, and the loss of the American colonies.

1

'Revolt, hostility, and rebellion'

In 1763, Britain and France signed the Treaty of Paris, bringing an end to the Seven Years War. Having consolidated its empire from India to Canada (recently won from the French), and demonstrated that the British Navy was the pre-eminent force on the world's oceans, Britain could settle down to expanding its international trade and its nascent Industrial Revolution. However, the war had been expensive and there would be the ongoing costs of protecting far-flung trading posts and colonies from rival trading nations, especially the recently humiliated French. One of those costs was associated with the need to station British troops in Canada and New York against the possibility of future French ambitions in North America. How these troops were to be paid for was to be more problematic than British ministers anticipated.

Prior to the war, the colonists had been left to pursue their own expansionist aims and economic growth without too much interference from London. A policy of 'salutary neglect' had shielded them from the onerous taxes paid by British subjects.[1] With the growth of the national debt and the need to increase taxation at home, some measures to raise revenues in the American colonies to cover the cost of their defence seemed reasonable from a London perspective. Ministers estimated that upwards of 8,500 men would be needed to protect Canada and the trans-Appalachian west from French ambitions. As well as the troops, 26 naval ships – the largest naval detachment outside home waters – would be needed to patrol the east coast of America and guard against possible French moves.[2] The British government's various tax initiatives over the ten years following the abortive Stamp Tax (1765) provided a focus for colonial resentment and a 'cause'

1 N. Philbrick, *Bunker Hill: A City, a Siege, a Revolution* (London: Bantam Books, 2014), p.23.
2 P. Padfield, *Maritime Supremacy and the Opening of the Western Mind: Naval Campaigns that Shaped the Modern World, 1588–1782* (London: Pimlico, 2000), p.221.

of the subsequent rebellion. It would be facile to claim that taxes were the only motivation for the events that led to American Independence, a point well made by N.A.M. Rodger: 'It is hardly possible to sum up in a paragraph the issues which sustain the historians of half a continent'.[3]

Founded by men and women who had left the Old World to escape religious and political persecution, the coastal colonies prospered and expanded westwards. Apart from Britain's insistence that the colonies obey the Navigation Acts (passed in the 17th century and requiring colonial trade to be carried in colonial or British vessels and via British ports) and pass no laws which clashed with those of England, those living in America were free to make their own laws, impose their own taxes and raise local militias. However, with the national debt having doubled to £130 million, George Grenville, the King's choice for first minister, began the series of measures that would lead to the cry of 'no taxation without representation'. It was never going to be easy for a government, 3,000 miles away, to exercise authority over free-minded colonials and expect it to be policed by 8,000 troops and a limited number of salaried officials; in Virginia, the largest colony, apart from the Customs service, 'only seventeen men held office from the king'.[4]

From the viewpoint of the government in London, requiring the Americans to pay a contribution towards the cost of their own defence did not seem unreasonable. British troops would prevent French expeditions into territories held by the colonists; they would hold the Indian tribes at bay in the west (provided the colonists did not provoke them by expanding westwards beyond the 1763 Proclamation Line); and the British Navy would protect trade routes between America, the Caribbean, and Britain. Having experienced a revolution against the tyranny of absolute monarchy, and less than enamoured of the civilian government of Cromwell, the English saw the right of Parliament to raise taxes as a bulwark against 'the only real threat to their liberty [which] came from the power of the crown'. By disputing Parliament's right to raise taxes in America (by the nature of their colonial status Parliament was sovereign), the colonists 'attacked the citadel of English liberty'.[5] In 1765, the government introduced the Stamp Tax, the first direct tax levied by London on the colonists. This revenue-raising measure required all legal documents and newspapers to be printed on special paper incorporating a stamp to show that the tax had been paid. The wide-ranging nature of the tax meant that it affected almost everybody, especially those with commercial dealings and the consequent reaction might have been expected

3   N.A.M. Rodger, *The Command of the Ocean: A Naval History of Britain, 1649–1815* (London: Allen Lane, 2004), p.330.
4   N. Bunker, *An Empire on the Edge: How Britain Came to Fight America* (London: Bodley Head, 2015), p.19.
5   Rodger, *Command of the Ocean*, p.330.

if those imposing it had not lived 3,000 miles away with little understanding of the independent nature of the colonists. Following a storm of opposition in America the incoming Rockingham government abolished the tax. However, to reinforce Parliament's sovereignty over the colonies and therefore its right to impose taxes, the Declaratory Act was passed in 1766. Over the next 10 years, both sides in the argument took steps that led to the military confrontation of 1775.

With the repeal of the Stamp Act, the British government still needed to find ways by which it could raise revenue from the colonists towards their own defence. In 1767, Charles Townshend (Chancellor of the Exchequer) introduced a series of duties that bore his name. The Townshend Duties were imposed on a variety of items – paper, lead, paint, glass, and, most notably, tea. With yearly running costs for the army, navy, Customs, and other officials in America estimated in the order of £400,000,[6] the duties raised (£47,000 in the best year) were never likely to cover expenditure. Had ministers in London not been preoccupied with events in Ireland, the increasing militarism of Russia and Prussia and the ever-present threat of future war with France and Spain, they might have recognised that the situation in the American colonies was worsening. The British troops stationed in the west were progressively drawn into New York and Boston causing the newspapers to sound the tocsin against a standing army, 'the time-tested cudgel of would-be tyrants'.[7] The red coats of the British soldiers ('lobsters' to the radicals) were always likely to act as a focal point for radical opposition. On 5 March 1770, the tensions boiled over and resulted in the 'Boston Massacre'. British troops guarding the city's Customs House fired on the crowd, killing five. One consequence of the unfortunate incident was the repeal of the Townshend Duties – except for that on tea.

If modern audiences know anything of the American War of Independence, they know that 'it started with the Boston Tea Party', but there was more to it than that. As important as the tipping of the tea into Boston harbour was, it was not the first violent act of the revolution. On 9 June 1772, the *Gaspee* (commanded by Lieutenant William Dudingston) was enforcing the Customs laws off the American coast when the crew spotted an American sloop, *Hannah*, which set off up Narragansett Bay. There are differing accounts as to exactly what happened during the chase – did the *Hannah* lure Dudingston onto the shoals? – before the *Gaspee* grounded off Namquit Point, Rhode Island. During the night of 10 June, the Rhode Islanders took advantage of Dudingston's predicament; a number of boats (the number varies by account) rowed out to the grounded

---

6   Bunker, *Empire on the Edge*, p.52
7   J. Ferling, *Almost a Miracle: The American Victory in the War of Independence* (Oxford: Oxford University Press, 2009), p.23.

ship, boarded her, took the crew prisoner, and set fire to the vessel. This was a particular embarrassment to the British as it 'was more than a maritime event, it was a *naval* event'[8] and 'the first act of war perpetrated against the British Crown by the American revolutionaries'.[9] Willis goes on to state that the burning of the British ship was especially symbolic as it created an 'enduring spectacle' that was 'intensely and consciously provocative'[10] and would have done much to stoke revolutionary fervour. Dudingston, who had a bad reputation with the colonists for his 'foul mouth and his freedom with his fists',[11] was injured in the fight, sent home to Portsmouth in England and court martialled – standard procedure after losing a ship. He was honourably acquitted and later became a 'superannuated rear-admiral' and died in 1816.[12]

Dudingston attracted the ire of the locals by the way in which he approached his anti-smuggling role. Captains of His Majesty's ships may well have been 'officers and gentlemen' but they were not always above taking the opportunity to profit from their position of authority, especially when a long way from home. The smuggling of molasses, an essential ingredient for the production of rum, was a regular, clandestine trade along the Rhode Island coast. The captains of the British ships enforcing the blockade could supplement their salary with their share of prize money from the capture of the smuggling vessels; it was in their financial interest to take as many smugglers as possible. The boarding of American vessels to enforce the smuggling laws damaged the trade of the local merchants; their voices reinforced those of the radicals speaking out against Britain's treatment of the colonists. Without the clamour from the tradesmen, the arguments of the radicals might have remained 'the stuff of academic debate'.[13] Dudingston was at fault with the local authorities in that he had not presented his commission from the King to the local governor, as he was required to do, and consequently was considered by the locals to be no more than a pirate. Since 1965, the village of Pawtuxet, Rhode Island has celebrated the burning of Dudingston's ship with their annual Gaspee Day parade; their Gaspee Day Committee has even got a trademark for their event strap-line: 'America's First Blow for Freedom'.[14]

8   Willis, S., *The Struggle For Sea Power: A Naval History of American Independence* (London: Atlantic Books, 2015), p.27.
9   F. Armstrong, 'An act of war on the eve of revolution', *Naval History Magazine*, Vol.30, No.1 (Feb. 2016), available at http://www.usni.org/magazines/navalhistory/2016-02/act-war-eve-revolution (accessed 16 March 2018).
10   Willis, *Sea Power*, p.20.
11   Bunker, *Empire on the Edge*, p.54.
12   W.E. May, 'The Gaspee Affair', *Mariner's Mirror*, Vol.63, No.2 (1977), pp.132–134.
13   Padfield, *Maritime Supremacy*, p.226.
14   *Gaspee Committee*, www.gaspee.com (accessed 20 March 2018).

Despite Pawtuxet's claim to the 'first blow', it is the events of the night of 29 November 1773 in Boston that receive the most column-inches in the history books. The British East India Company had a surfeit of tea, which presented the Crown-chartered company with a financial headache. To ease the problem the government proposed that this tea should be shipped direct to America. By this means the price could be reduced to two shillings a pound (a big saving to the colonists, and undercutting the price of smuggled tea), but included in the price was a small tax of three pence per pound. Although the proposal was good for the American merchants, the tax on the product revived the radical calls against 'taxation without representation'. Their act of rebellion was to take the tea from the holds of the transport ships (*Dartmouth*, *Eleanor*, and *Beaver*), and throw it into the waters of Boston Harbour. The government in London could not ignore this deliberate act of provocation by the colonial radicals; their response came in the form of the Coercive Acts (the Administration of Justice, the Quartering, and the Quebec Act), as well as the proposal to blockade Boston Harbour (the Port Act). Events were moving inexorably towards some sort of conflict. George III was determined that 'the colonies must either submit or triumph [...] we must not retreat'.[15] Each side was digging in with the result that the situation escalated. At the first Continental Congress, in September 1774, the representatives resolved to implement a boycott of trade with Britain and the local militia were put on a more formal footing. In Massachusetts it was proposed that one in three men between the age of 16 and 60 should be 'ready to act at a minute's warning' – the 'minutemen'.[16]

The two men given the job of returning the allegiance of the 'unhappy and deluded multitude'[17] to their rightful sovereign were Lieutenant-General Thomas Gage and Vice-Admiral Samuel Graves. Gage had been the army commander in America for some 10 years before the trouble started, and was married to an American. In June of 1773, he and his family returned to London for his first visit in 17 years. During the summer of that year, his wife gave birth to their sixth child at Highmeadow, one of his family's two ancestral estates. Gage was no doubt getting used to being back in England and enjoying the life of a country gentleman, but events intervened. In January 1774, London heard the details of the Boston Tea Party. Gage's years as Commander-in-Chief in America, together with his family and social ties to that country through his marriage to Margaret Kemble of New Jersey, meant that he was a useful person to brief the King and

15   C. Hibbert, *Redcoats and Rebels: The War for America, 1770–1781* (London: HarperCollins, 1992), p.25.
16   Ferling, *Miracle*, p.27.
17   NDAR, Vol.2, pp.777–778, King's speech to Parliament, 26 October 1775.

his ministers on the deteriorating situation in the thirteen colonies. Gage was aware that George III was intent on bringing the colonies back into line and that may have influenced his advice to the King: 'they will be lyons [sic], while we are lambs; but, if we take the resolute part, they will undoubtedly prove very meek'.[18] Rather rashly, Gage had told the King that it would only require four regiments to prevent further disturbance. The general may well have preferred to remain in England but his unfortunate boasts meant that he had made himself the natural choice to retrieve the situation and he sailed, with his wife, on the 20-gun sloop *Lively*, arriving in Boston on 13 May 1774 after a 24 day voyage. After landing, Gage resumed his duties as Commander-in-Chief as well as those of the royal governor of Massachusetts,[19] whose charter had been declared void after the dumping of the tea. Shortly after his arrival, Gage implemented the Port Act, closing the port of Boston. By 15 June 1774, no ships were to be allowed to leave. An entire community were effectively punished for the actions of the few who, on that night in November, had disguised themselves as non-tea-drinking 'Mohawks' and dumped the East India Company's merchandise into the cold waters of the harbour. On 1 July 1774, the 5th and 38th Regiments arrived in Boston aboard naval transports. The town was now the garrison home of five British regiments, the force that Gage had boasted would enable him to control the situation. By October 1774, he was rowing back on his optimism and writing to Lord Dartmouth (Secretary of State for the Colonies) that 20,000 troops would be needed to do the job.[20] On 13 May, local Boston representatives in the Faneuil Hall moved a motion to request that all thirteen colonies boycott British goods (later agreed by the Continental Congress); the stage was set for a confrontation.

On 1 July 1774, Vice-Admiral Graves sailed into Boston on the *Preston* to take over command of the North American station from Rear-Admiral John Montagu. Gage and Graves took on an enormous challenge for which they, the services they led, and the administrative systems that supported them, were not prepared. Back home in London, the government did not appreciate quickly enough the scale of the problem they were trying to control, a problem made worse in 1778 with the entry into the conflict of the old enemy, France, followed in 1779 by Spain. When Graves assumed his new command, he had only 26 ships at his disposal with which to assist army operations, as well as blockade the whole of the eastern seaboard of North America – he was on a hiding to nothing. In April 1775, Graves wrote to Philip Stephens (First Secretary at the Admiralty – we

18   A. O'Shaughnessy, *The Men Who Lost America: British Command during the Revolutionary War and the Preservation of the Empire* (London: Oneworld, 2014), p.22.
19   Ferling, *Miracle*, p.24.
20   Philbrick, *Bunker Hill*, p.126.

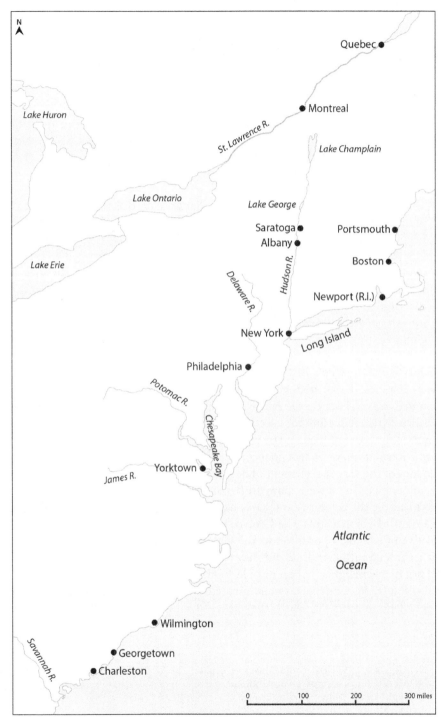

Map 1: East coast of America

will meet him frequently in this account) to state the problem he faced from American sea captains: 'smuggling is carried to such a height, and so systematically followed, that without the utmost Vigilance and care, there is no detecting them to Condemnation'.[21] However, the blockade was making life difficult for some Americans, mainly those merchants who relied on free traffic through the ports to support their businesses. The Provincial Congress in Cambridge (close to Boston) distributed copies of a resolution from its meeting of 6 December 1774, in which they complained about the restriction to trade and requested assistance for the citizens of Boston and Charlestown.

> The Operation of the cruel and iniquitous *Boston*-Port-Bill, that Instrument of ministerial Vengeance, having reduced our once happy Capital and the neighbouring Town of *Charlestown*, from Affluence and Ease, to extreme Distress; [...] It is therefore Resolved, That it be recommended to our Constituents the Inhabitants of the other Towns, Districts and Parishes within this Province, that they further contribute liberally to alleviate the Burden of those Persons who are the more immediate Objects of ministerial Resentment, and are suffering in the common Cause of their Country.[22]

The insurrection, which had started in Boston, was spreading throughout the coastal colonies. The British government realised that it was in fact facing what amounted to a civil war on the American continent and that it had to reassert royal authority or risk reduction to 'a second rate European power'.[23]

In the shorthand of history, the conflict between Britain and the colonies is the War of Revolution, or Independence, and while both terms are correct they give little hint of the very real element of civil war that made up much of the character of that conflict. There were many in Britain who disagreed with the need to use arms to coerce the colonists, and there was by no means unanimity in America on the aim of rebellion against the Crown. In 1775, the uncertainty surrounding the objective of colonial opposition to the Crown was summed up to Congress by a speaker from South Carolina: did they want independence 'or do We only ask for a Restoration of Rights [...] on our old footing'.[24] The answer was not made clear until 4 July 1776. Congress was dominated by those who wanted no part of the independence movement, which they believed would only disturb their profitable

21   NDAR, Vol.1, p.178, letter from Graves to Stephens, 11 April 1775.
22   NDAR, Vol.1, p.5, copy of the declaration.
23   Syrett, *American Waters*, p.28.
24   Ferling, *Miracle*, p.70.

trade. The merchants of the commercial ports of New York, Pennsylvania, and the Delaware saw the very real advantages to the security of trade that came from the protection of the British Navy. In December 1775, 82 inhabitants of the town-port of Yarmouth wrote to the governor, George Legge:

> We do all of us profess to be true Friends & Loyal Subjects to George our King, We were almost all of us born in New England, we have Fathers, Brothers & Sisters in that Country, divided betwixt natural affection to our nearest relations, and good Faith and Friendship to our King and Country, we want to know, if we may be permitted at this time to live in a peaceable State, as we look on that to be the only situation in which we with our Wives and Children, can be in any tolerable degree safe, your Excellency cannot be unacquainted how easy a thing it is for those people, if they once suppose us their Enemies, to burn and destroy all before them in this Quarter: We are in no Capac[it]y to defend ourselves. […] We beg of your Excellency not to conclude, as we desire to be Neuter, that we are in any measure disaffected to our King or his Government, For we do assure your Excellency we never have done, neither have we any disposition to do any thing [sic] whatever, by way of Aiding or Assisting the Americans in their Opposition to Great Britain. It is self preservation and that only, which drives us at this time to make our Request.[25]

Here we have one group of inhabitants appealing to the British governor against the possible action that might be taken against them by their fellow Americans. Port towns felt particularly vulnerable, as it was their merchants, wishing to continue their trade, who were at risk from the rebels (or patriots, depending on your standpoint) who were enforcing the boycott of trade with Britain. Eighteen of the inhabitants of the port of Falmouth – 10 of whom classed themselves as 'merchants' – appealed directly to the captain of a British ship, stationed in their port, for the continuance of the protection that a King's ship afforded them against their fellow Americans.

> That since the Arrival of His Majesty's Ship under your Command, we have been relieved by your Spirited Conduct from those Anxieties natural to Persons who are abnoxious [sic] to the Enemies of our happy Constitution; and by your courteous and kind behavior to all the Friends of Government, flattered Ourselves with the pleasing Prospect of a continuance of your Protection; but those agreeable Sensations are

25   NDAR, Vol.3, pp.3–4, letter from inhabitants of Yarmouth to Legge, 8 December 1775.

entirely vanished, and we are reduced to the last degree of despair, by your information, that when Captain Coulsin's Ship will be ready for Sea, You are immediately to leave this Place – and consequently Us, a prey to the Sons of rapine and lawless Violence. We therefore intreat that in your goodness You will remain with us till we can make known our deplorable Situation to General [Thomas] Gage, which we shall do without delay.

We further intreat You will be so obliging to represent our dangerous Situation to Admiral [Samuel] Graves – and as we are now deprived of sending a Petition to his Excellency by Land and having no effectual Method of conveyance by Water, we beg You will suffer an Officer, and a few Men from your Ship to proceed for that purpose.[26]

While there are many examples of protestations of loyalty by sections of the American communities, they should also be seen in context; frightened townspeople will frequently appeal to those they believe will be most likely to deliver them a quiet time, as in the following example. In September 1776, after the Declaration of Independence, the British were putting troops ashore around New York. After the bombardments and the landings, Henry Duncan (captain of the *Eagle*) prepared to go ashore.

A flag of truce was hoisted in the town when I put off from the ship, but was hauled down soon after I put off. On approaching the town there appeared to be a rabble on the walls. [I] Ordered the boat to push on shore. At the landing-place I was met by the mob, who gave me three cheers, took me on their shoulders, carried me to the Governor's Fort, put me under the English colours now hoisted, and again gave me three cheers, which they frequently repeated, men, women, and children shaking me by the hand, and giving me their blessing, and crying out 'God save the King!' They carried me to my boat, and we parted with cheering and my promising to send them some troops. The *Fowey* and *Mercury* went close to the town.[27]

That morning the guns of the town had been shelling the British ships. Welcoming the 'victors' is not an uncommon occurrence in war, but the motive may well be one of survival rather than genuine friendship. It is fair to say that British commanders were usually sceptical of American declarations of loyalty; too often, those making

26   NDAR, Vol.1, pp.261–262, letter from inhabitants of Falmouth to Lieutenant Mowat, 2 May 1775.
27   NDAR, Vol.6, p.846, journal of Captain Henry Duncan.

them were seeking protection rather than demonstrating any wish to take up arms to back up their stated position.

The examples cited above are all from New England colonies. The uprising, and military confrontation, began in the Boston area and led the British government to see the rebellion as a 'northern' aberration; the southern states were considered to be more loyal and some of their governors were to make the case that if British troops were sent to the south then they would be met by thousands of Loyalists ready to take up arms in support of the King. Some of the governors' protestations of good faith were met by shipments of arms, even though they were not given full credence, as in the case of Governor Martin of North Carolina.

> His Majesty's Governor of North Carolina having represented that there are very favorable [sic] Appearances in that Province of a disposition in a large body of His Majesty's well disposed Subjects to deliver themselves (by taking up Arms in Support of Government) from the Tyranny and Oppression exercised by those who have formed themselves into Committees & Congresses for the avowed purpose of Rebellion – I am commanded by The King to signify to your Lordship His Majesty's pleasure that Ten thousand Stand of Arms and Six light Field pieces together with 200 Rounds of powder and Ball for each Musket and Field piece.[28]

These were to be sent to the Commander-in-Chief to 'enable him to afford such Aid and Assistance to the Governor of North Carolina as the Situation and Circumstances of that Province may from time to time require'. In his response to Governor Martin, Dartmouth was less than convinced of the likelihood of such an uprising.

> In such a situation I must confess to you, that I think you are too Sanguine in your expectations of being able, if properly supported, in the manner you suggest to induce a large part of the Inhabitants of North Carolina to take up Arms in support of Government.[29]

In July 1775 the Admiralty in London was still unsure of the extent of the rebellion but recognised that they needed to make preparations 'in case the other colonies should become in the same state of rebellion as New England is'.[30]

---

28   NDAR, Vol.2, pp.713–715, letter from Lord Dartmouth to Master General of the Ordnance, 12 September 1775.
29   NDAR, Vol.2, p.718, letter from Lord Dartmouth to Josiah Martin, 15 September 1775.
30   SP, Vol.1, p.65.

The government in London believed that they were dealing with a 'little local difficulty' (apologies to Macmillan) which they could control from 3,000 miles away. As part of the plan, ships should be stationed off the coast of America to 'annoy the rebellious provinces, to awe those that are refractory, to enforce the Acts for restraining their trade, and to countenance and protect the friends to Government'.[31] A large number of the Americans who lived in the southern colonies either were plantation owners, or associated with them and their produce. As was to become apparent in the 1861–1865 Civil War, their values and way of life was different from those of their northern neighbours; if there was going to be any significant Loyalist support in the colonies, then it was more likely to be in the south than the north. We will see in a later chapter that this possibility was to affect British strategy in the war. One example of the north/south divide is given by a doctor who was attending to prisoners of war held by the British in old 'hulks' in New York harbour in 1776: 'Great Division prevails [...] among the Southern and Northern Rebels. The Southward officers now prisoners have petitiond [sic] Lord Howe to be separated from the N. England Rebels and they are now kept in Different vessells [sic] in consequence of that application'.[32]

As well as disagreements between Americans over the need for rebellion and its consequences, not all of those defending the Crown's position were fully convinced of the need for hostilities with the colonies. The Howe brothers, who commanded both the British army and navy for a large part of the war, as well as being peace commissioners, were less than wholeheartedly behind the roles they were asked to fulfil. The admiral's less than fulsome support for the war was obvious in March 1775 when he voted in Parliament for the restraining of New England's trade: he declared that it was 'the only moderate means of bringing the disobedient provinces to a sense of their duty, without involving the empire in the horrors of civil war'.[33] Lieutenant-General Gage, in spite of having lived for years in America and being married to a local beauty, did not understand the country and its people. Although he was in favour of aggressive action to restore the status quo, he was hostage to his earlier statements to the King regarding the capabilities of the colonists and the number of troops needed to subdue them. In October 1774, he believed that 20,000 troops would be required and by November, he was urging caution and the suspension of the Coercive Acts. He was replaced after Bunker Hill. After hostilities got under way, some began questioning the advisability of burning fishing towns, destroying farms and taking provisions without payment; might these actions not further inflame the locals against

31   SP, Vol.1, p.64.
32   NDAR, Vol.6, p.656, diary of Dr Moffat at Sandy Hook.
33   O'Shaughnessy, *Men Who Lost America*, p.90.

British rule? Even ordinary soldiers sometimes had qualms. One Irish deserter from the British 40th Regiment wrote home to explain his action: 'finding they were striving to throw off the yoke under which my native country – sunk for many years – induced me to share the same freedom that America strive [*sic*] for'.[34] As the war progressed, despite George III's determination to retain the colonies, the threat from France and Spain, together with the wish to hold Gibraltar, caused America to be relegated to a 'secondary consideration'.[35] The changing focus of the war away from the northern colonies to those in the south, and the need to reinforce the Caribbean against the Bourbon threat post-1778, would create headaches for those services delivering support to the army.

As well as misjudging the scale of the rebellion, the British also exhibited little respect for the Americans as worthy opponents for the redcoats. We have already noted Gage's comment that only four regiments would be needed to put down the rebellion; after all, an 'American army' did not exist. Until George Washington moulded a Continental Army out of the troops provided by the individual states, the British were facing local militias; states were jealous of their independence from each other and had yet to take on a true federal structure. When Fort Ticonderoga was taken in May 1775 by a mixed force of men from Connecticut, Massachusetts, and New York, they found provisions and 'near two hundred pieces of ordnances, of all sizes, from eighteen pounders downward'.[36] The need to recover these weapons for use by the colonists was addressed by the Provincial Congress of New York on 24 May 1775. The meeting recognised that this would mean men from one state operating in another (a prerequisite for a truly Continental Army), but hoped this would not cause problems.

> There is no doubt but that our brethren in Connecticut will feel great reluctance at the idea of ordering any of their troops to march within the bounds of this Colony, for the purpose of defending the Fort of Ticonderoga and the Cannon and Stores above mentioned at Fort George; but we pray you to cast away all fears of offending us on this occasion. We shall be happy to hear that you have placed a part of your forces in these posts, with intent to defend them until they shall be relieved by troops from this Colony.[37]

---

34 M. Urban, *Fusiliers: How the British Army Lost America but Learned to Fight* (Croydon: Faber and Faber, 2007), p.17.
35 NDAR, Vol.11, p.1111, letter from Admiralty to Vice-Admiral Howe, 22 March 1778.
36 NDAR, Vol.1, p.506.
37 NDAR, Vol.1, p.520, Provincial Congress of New York, 24 May 1775.

The American colonists (before Washington had whipped them into shape) were not trained, disciplined soldiers. They were farmers and woodsmen, individuals with their own weapons who shot at their targets from behind cover. The British saw this as 'not playing the game;' redcoats fought in line, delivering fire in unison before going in with the bayonet. Major Pitcairn (Marines) gave his opinion of the enemy to Lord Sandwich: 'The deluded people are made believe that they are invincible. [...] When this army is ordered to act against them, they will soon be convinced that they are very insignificant when opposed to regular troops'.[38] Pitcairn died at Bunker Hill a few weeks later, shot by one of those 'deluded people'. Pitcairn's view accorded with that of Lieutenant-General James Murray, who had succeeded Wolfe at Quebec: 'the native American is an effeminate thing, very unfair for and very impatient of war'.[39] The colonists, not unnaturally, had a different opinion of their capabilities.

> This one County of Fincastle can furnish 1000 Rifle Men that for their number make the most formidable light Infantry in the world. The six frontier Counties can produce 6,000 of these Men who from their amazing hardihood, their method of living so long in the woods without carrying provisions with them, the exceeding quickness with which they can march to distant parts, and above all the dexterity to which they have arrived in the use of the rifle Gun. Their [sic] is not one of these Men who with a distance less than 200 yards or a larger object than an Orange – Every shot is fatal.[40]

While Pitcairn's may have been the more commonly held opinion of the colonists prior to Bunker Hill, it started to change immediately after that battle. During this first, major engagement they had shown themselves to be other than 'the despicable rabble too many had supposed them to be' and they had shown 'a conduct and spirit against us they never showed against the French'.[41] One British officer, wounded at Bunker Hill, considered that the Americans, if well commanded, were 'full as good soldiers as ours, and, as it is, are very little inferior to us even in discipline and countenance'.[42] As is often the way, soldiers on their way to a conflict have not learned the hard knocks of their comrades in theatre, and so start their war with the cockiness of ignorance. In July 1776, Ambrose Serle (General Howe's private secretary) had just completed a 'most tedious

---

38   NDAR, Vol.1, p.89, Pitcairn to Sandwich, 14 February 1775.
39   Syrett, *American Waters*, p.33.
40   NDAR, Vol.1, p.106, letter, 24 February 1775.
41   Hibbert, *Redcoats and Rebels*, p.55.
42   Urban, *Fusiliers*, p.45.

passage' of nine weeks, from England to New York. On his arrival, Serle wrote a long letter to Lord Dartmouth with news of his journey and the army, which he said was in 'high Spirits' and good health; only nine out of 1,000 men were 'indisposed'. However, he was concerned that while the troops were keen to get at the 'Rebels' he was afraid that they 'hold them too cheap. A certain Degree of Disdain it may be right to indulge; but an Excess of it, in the case of an obstinate Resistance (which, from the Numbers of the Rebels, amounting to near 30,000, is not improbable), would occasion a Disappointment, that might end in Despair'.[43] Later events would show that Serle had demonstrated unknowing foresight.

Misunderstandings and arrogance on the part of British ministers had come up against a minority of fiercely independent minded radicals in the American colonies. Had London not been at such a distance, it might have been possible to discuss the issues and settle them more amicably. But that was not to be. British arrogance required the colonials to accept London's authority with little or no discussion. The mistake was compounded by the belief that the Americans could not come together to offer a credible opposition to the British Army. Once hostilities started, the problems really began for the authorities in London. The impasse between the British and the more radical of the colonists was summed up in a statement made by the King to his first minister, Lord North: 'The New England governments are in a state of rebellion. *Blows must decide* whether they are to be subject to this country or independent' [my emphasis].[44] How could the army and navy, both of which had been allowed to atrophy after the Seven Years War, be augmented, transported to America and then supplied and supported from 3,000 miles away, for an indefinite period of time? The problem was hard enough, but made no easier with the need to be vigilant against the possibility of France and Spain taking advantage of Britain's predicament, and entering the war on America's side.

43   NDAR, Vol.5, pp.1214–1215, letter from Serle to Dartmouth, 25 July 1776.
44   Philbrick, *Bunker Hill*, p.168.

2

'Blows must decide'

In 1763, Britain exited the Seven Years War with her navy triumphant and France humiliated. During the following decade, as the American rebellion progressed from hostility to the Stamp Act, through the burning of the *Gaspee* and the tipping of the tea into the harbour, the French kept a watchful eye on Britain's growing problem. The French foreign minister, Vergennes, did not believe that the colonists could be cowed militarily and so he steered French foreign policy 'secretly and slowly'[1] towards confrontation with London. From their side, British ministers – ever wary of the enemy over the water – realised that they needed to conclude their differences with America as quickly as possible if they were to avoid a possible war with France.

Before the 'shooting war' broke out in 1775, the army in America was small. Its role was to guard against French activities in Canada and to protect the western frontier of the colonies against attacks by Indians. The small size of the British force, and the fact that it was not put there to take an aggressive stance towards the Americans, meant that it could draw (and pay for) its supplies from the local farmers and traders. Obviously, the transport of the troops to and from those shores had to be done by sea but as the army was small and there was no military emergency, this was a task that could be handled by existing arrangements. The outbreak of hostilities and the consequent need to greatly increase the size, scope and support of the army in America required the British authorities to make major changes to those services that would have to provide the troops with everything they would need to eat, move, and fight. In an age of the internet, mobile phones, and almost instantaneous, updated newsfeeds, it is worth remembering that this war was run by small groups of officials wielding quill pens and their letters taking at least six weeks to travel each way.

---

1   Syrett, *American Waters*, p.28.

In Britain it is the government that makes the decision to go to war, not the army, and it is the responsibility of the ministers in London to give direction to the senior commanders and make the necessary arrangements for the forces deployed to be raised, transported, supplied, and paid for. In the context of the American War, the Cabinet planned and the Secretaries of State executed. The Cabinet consisted of the First Lord of the Treasury, the three Secretaries of State (Northern, Southern, and Colonies), the Lord Chancellor, the Lord President, the Lord Privy Seal, the First Lord of the Admiralty, and (after 1778) the Commander-in-Chief of the army.[2] The fact that the First Lord of the Admiralty was in the Cabinet from the start reflects the greater importance of the navy to Britain, an island nation, over that of the army. Since the time of Cromwell, the British had had an aversion to a standing army, preferring to augment a small cadre with hired troops from continental nations in time of war. Cabinet decisions were put before the King for his agreement before being passed on to the appropriate Secretary of State for implementation. Cabinets of the eighteenth century, like those of today, were made up of individuals, not all of whom could get along well, even when conducting a war.[3] Unlike today, the Cabinet frequently met over dinner and after one such meeting (following the fall of Yorktown) the King remarked to Sandwich: 'I perceive the Cabinet dinner yesterday rather had the appearance of a meeting of persons cautious not to state their opinions to each other, instead of ministers assembled to forward the business of the nation'.[4]

Chairing the Cabinet was the First Lord of the Treasury. Lord North recognised his lack of suitability to lead a war cabinet – 'Upon military matters I speak ignorantly, and therefore without effect'[5] – and his frequent requests to the King to be allowed to retire from his position were rejected. At this challenging point in its history, Britain's government was led by a man described by Edmund Burke as 'of admirable parts, of general knowledge, of a versatile understanding, fitted for every sort of business, of infinite wit and pleasantry' but who 'wanted something of the vigilance and spirit of command that the time required'.[6]

The two figures in the Cabinet who will feature most often in this account of the war are the First Lord of the Admiralty, Lord Sandwich, and the Secretary of State for America, Lord George Germain. America had been merely a department

2   D. Syrett, *Shipping and the American War 1775–83: A Study of British Transport Organization* (London: Athlone, 1970), p.2.

3   A useful summary of some of those conflicts is given in N.A.M. Rodger, *The Insatiable Earl. A Life of John Montagu, 4th Earl of Sandwich* (London: Norton, 1993), pp.220–225.

4   SP, Vol.4, p.206.

5   P. Mackesy, *The War for America, 1775–1783* (Lincoln, NE: University of Nebraska Press, 1993), p.21.

6   Hibbert, *Redcoats and Rebels*, pp.17–18.

within the previous Colonial Secretary's remit but, as the situation deteriorated, it became the primary focus of the new Secretary. Both Sandwich and Germain would come in for criticism for the way in which they carried out their roles in the war: Sandwich for slow mobilisation of the navy and Germain for his strategic ideas, which 'were based on false assumptions',[7] especially his overestimation of the extent of Loyalist support and the popularity of the revolution as expressed by some of the colonial governors. For those wishing to read more on these two principal characters, Rodger's *The Insatiable Earl* and O'Shaughnessy's *The Men Who Lost America* can be highly recommended.

Whatever the criticism of Sandwich, and we can come to some of that later, it was his department – the Admiralty – which conveyed the army to America and supported it while it was there; without it, the war could not have been fought. When the war began, some of the functions that were later to be taken on by the Admiralty were carried out by other departments, especially the Treasury. However, the scale of the operation required to support up to 100,000 men, 3,000 miles from their supply bases, dictated that the Admiralty (with processes and procedures developed during the Seven Years War) should assume the lead role in all aspects of supplying the army. In principle, the First Lord of the Admiralty was subordinate to the Southern Secretary but, as Rodger states, 'only an inexperienced or supine First Lord, which Sandwich was not, would have expected to be under any real control by a Secretary of State;[8] this was his third time in the role. As stated earlier, plans agreed in Cabinet were sent to the appropriate Secretary of State for action, and in the case of the navy these went to the Admiralty and then to the Navy Board. A reading of the files in Kew shows what a tremendous breadth of issues passed over the desks of Sandwich and his staff – anything from the promotion of a ship's lieutenant in some remote station, to the loading of six months' supplies for a whole army: and all of this had to be done by an incredibly small staff. In 1760 the Admiralty office had only 'about forty staff [...] including nineteen clerks, rising to about fifty-nine in 1810, including thirty-two clerks';[9] somewhat different from today's Ministry of Defence.

Throughout the war, the Admiralty ('one of the most complex machines on earth')[10] played a major role, not only in its more obvious guise as the controlling arm of the navy's ships and commanders, but also for its critical part in the support of the army. 'Without sea power the American War of Independence simply could

---

7   O'Shaughnessy, *Men Who Lost America*, p.186.
8   Rodger, *Sandwich*, p.221.
9   R. Morriss, *The Foundations of British Maritime Ascendency: Resources, Logistics and the State, 1755–1815* (Cambridge: Cambridge University Press, 2011), p.140.
10   Mackesy, *America*, p.15.

not have been fought at all'.[11] The Admiralty Board was responsible for controlling operations, the staffing of the fleet, and the promotion of its officers. To assist Lord Sandwich in the running of the Admiralty, described by one historian as the largest bureaucracy in the world,[12] two men will occur frequently in this account: Philip Stephens and Charles Middleton. Stephens was the department's First Secretary and many of the letters written by the various admirals in North American and Caribbean waters were addressed to him. Middleton had succeeded Maurice Suckling – Nelson's uncle who died in July 1778 – as Comptroller. Rodger, one of our foremost historians of the British Navy (and biographer of Sandwich), described Middleton's appointment as 'the single most important decision Sandwich took in his entire career', as Middleton went on to do 'more than any other man to reform the civil administration of the Navy'.[13]

Subordinate to the Admiralty were three additional boards: the Navy Board, the Victualling Board, and the Sick and Hurt Board. In simple terms, the Navy Board looked after the 'hardware', the purchase of the materials for the building and maintenance of the ships, and the dockyards in which the work was carried out. The Victualling Board controlled the contract process for the provisioning of the fleet. The contracts let by the Board detailed the quantity, quality, and delivery times for the victuals, which would then be loaded onto warships before they sailed from England, or dispatched to warehouses around the world for later use by the fleet. As the name implies, the Sick and Hurt Board provided hospital facilities to the sailors. At the outbreak of the war, the Admiralty and its subordinate boards had little to do with the army, but that would change as the conflict progressed, the size of the army increased, and the difficulties of supplying the troops became more apparent. Outside the authority of the Admiralty was the Ordnance Board, which supplied guns, ammunition, and powder to the navy and the army. Once hostilities had broken out, and the troops were confined within the bounds of Boston, they lost the facility to feed themselves from local resources. From that point on, everything that the army ate, wore, and fought with had to be transported to them – a point that is frequently glossed over in general histories of the war. Too often, there is little in these accounts to suggest how much planning (or how large an effort) was required to maintain this supply chain.

At this point, it is appropriate to give a brief overview of the way in which naval expenses were raised by the government. Every year, Parliament received a request for naval funding, the Estimate, a figure arrived at by a formula, which

11   R. Holmes, *Redcoat: The British Soldier In The Age Of Horse And Musket* (London: HarperCollins, 2001), p.18.
12   Syrett, *Shipping and the American War*, p.35.
13   Rodger, *Sandwich*, p.160.

had 'long ceased to bear any relation to reality'.[14] The Estimates had three parts: Ordinary costs (the fixed costs of the naval establishment), Extraordinary costs (new building, ship repairs, etc.), and Sea Service costs (those required to fund the number of men in the navy over the period of the Estimate). The latter was based on a formula that allowed for £4 per man per lunar month (a figure that had not changed since 1650); in 1797, this figure was raised to £7. The sum voted on then went into one 'pot' from which money was drawn as needed. The £4, or 80 shillings (80/-) was made up of:

Wages 30/-
Wear and tear 27/-
Victualling 19/-
Ordnance 4/-

As an example, in 1756, when 40,000 men were needed, the required vote was for £2,080,000.[15] The Estimate was the means by which the money to be spent by the navy was determined, the actual spending was done via bills of exchange, which were a marketable commodity.

The Navy and Victualling Boards, and their agents around the world, paid for the supplies they purchased with these bills of exchange but instead of being payable in the usual 90 days, Navy Bills were paid 'in course'. At the time of issue, the bills were numbered so that they could be paid sequentially ('in course'). The payment period for the numbered bills, and the interest the government would pay on them, was published regularly in the financial press. By this means, the navy had created a market in its own bills. Because the interest was backed by the government, and they had a sound track-record for paying up, there was confidence in a system that allowed the navy to consistently spend at a level above its revenue. These bills earned interest of between four percent and five percent over the period of their 'course' after the first six months. Either the bills issued in payment for the provisions could be held for the period of their course, which effectively meant holding a short-term investment that paid interest, or they could be sold on. Because the bills had their course promulgated in the financial press, they had a discount value on the financial market. The bills could be sold on to traders who specialised in holding these investments. These bills allowed the Navy and Victualling Boards to run their own 'public debt system, outside Treasury control'.[16]

---

14   Rodger, *Sandwich*, p.134. For those wishing to know more about the financial system, see Rodger, *Sandwich*, and Rodger, *Command of the Ocean*.
15   Morriss, *British Maritime Ascendancy*, p.114.
16   Rodger, *Command of the Ocean*, p.293.

At the end of the Seven Years War, the British Navy was supreme at sea, at least in the eyes of the British nation. However, not all was as well as its last success might suggest. As invariably happened, the advent of peace heralded a period of financial restraint, while the government returned to policies of 'sound money'. Any tightening of the government purse meant cut backs for the navy; ships were taken out of commission and put in 'Ordinary;' many naval officers found themselves shore-bound and on half-pay; ordinary sailors (especially those who had been 'pressed' into service) returned to their normal sea-going jobs. The economies forced on the navy also affected the dockyards. Ships were built, repaired, and maintained at these facilities, but they were also the main warehousing sites for ships' provisions and supplies. These yards, with their warehouses, dry-dock, mast towers, and rope houses were expensive and they had not been expanded sufficiently during and after the recent war with France. There was a further problem with British dockyards and supply facilities with regard to the American War – their location. Most of the sites in Britain were on the south coast and the Thames; all of them were east of Plymouth. The prevailing wind in the English Channel was westerly, which was significant in an age of sail. For ships to get out into the Western Approaches, to the west of Ushant or the Scillies, and for their voyages to North America, they had to beat their way down the Channel against the prevailing wind, and that could take weeks. For an army dependent on its food supplies coming from England, that had a significant impact. On 23 July 1776, Philip Stephens wrote to Vice-Admiral Howe (in America) to inform him that three ships detailed to escort a convoy of troop reinforcements had 'put to Sea from Spithead on the 28th of last Month; but were not able to get out of the Channel, the Wind coming strong to the Westward, which obliged them to put into Plymouth where they remain with their Convoy',[17] which included 12 victualling ships. The distance between these two moorings is approximately 150 miles, yet that was as far as they had travelled in one month. This gives some indication of the delays that were an everyday problem for those planning the resupply of the troops in America.

Wars wear out ships as much as exchequers, and the situation faced by Sandwich when he took over as First Lord in 1771 was one of a navy in serious need of some attention; the fleet 'had been exceedingly neglected for some years past, was greatly out of repair, that there was scarcely any timber in any of the dockyards, and a total despondency at the Navy Office as to the means of procuring it'.[18] In 1771, there were nominally 86 ships of the line, listed as in good condition, available to Sandwich. However, this was not a true picture. Many of the ships that had been

17   NDAR, Vol.6, p.492, letter from Stephens to Howe, 23 July 1776.
18   SP, Vol.4, p.282.

built during the Seven Years War were constructed in a hurry from unseasoned wood; they may have lasted that war, but by Sandwich's time, they were in dire need of repair. By 1778, when the French entered the American War, only 43 of these ships were on the serviceable list and only 17 had not required major repairs.[19] The Admiralty had some serious work ahead of it if it was to rebuild the fleet, implement copper bottoms, fix the issues in the dockyards that would be needed to build the vessels, and procure the necessary stocks of seasoned wood – but this topic is outside the scope of this book. Suffice to say that Sandwich did much of this and the changes made during the American War stood Britain in good stead for the later French Revolutionary Wars.

After the ravages of war, people look forward to a period of peace and prosperity; their thoughts do not turn naturally to rearming for the next conflict. Britain was unprepared when it entered the two world wars of the twentieth century, and was similarly ill-prepared for the hostilities in America in 1775. If a British army were to be transported to the colonies and supported with all the supplies and provisions that it required, while at the same time protecting the East and the West Indies and guarding home waters against the possibility of an aggressive move by the French, then the government would have to declare full mobilisation of the navy. Those ships that had been taken out of commission and placed in 'Ordinary' – effectively mothballed with a skeleton crew, no masts, ropes, rigging, or guns – would typically require at least two months to be returned to service. Ships in ordinary were in the water, though not at sea, and so any deterioration in the condition of their hulls below the waterline was not likely to be noticed. Frequently it was only the survey done prior to recommissioning that brought the true condition of the vessel to official notice. The effective strength of the navy was always approximate: 'sometimes even a majority of the ships nominally on the list were not in practice capable of being sent to sea, or not in any reasonable time'.[20] Throughout the coming war with America, and its subsequent escalation to include France and Spain, the Admiralty struggled with the scope of the operations it was required to cover. Before the first shots had been fired at Lexington and Concord, George III (in a message to both Houses of Parliament) was concerned that to bring a speedy end to the events in America 'some addition to his forces by sea and land [would] be necessary'.

On 14 February 1775, '2,000 Men (including 490 Marines) were voted for the Year 1775, in addition to the 16,000 voted on the 13th December 1774'.[21] The mobilisation of the navy, necessary for any expeditions in America, would

19 SP, Vol.4, p.305.
20 Rodger, *Sandwich*, p.133.
21 NDAR, Vol.1, pp.398, 400.

be expensive and consequently would have to pass through Parliament. In the November 1775 debate on the Navy Estimates for 1776 it was moved that 28,000 seamen should be voted for 1776, and that the fleet off America, commanded by Rear-Admiral Shuldham, should 'consist of 78 sail'.[22] The proposal was opposed by Admiral Keppel on the grounds that the number of men was 'inadequate to a war, and too large for a peace establishment'. Keppel was right; there was no point voting for a number that could do little more than give a false sense of security. The point was reinforced during the debate by Captain Luttrell who objected to the numbers put forward on the grounds that they would result in an 'insufficiency of the number of seamen applied for to man the ships already in commission, and those fitting for foreign service'.[23] Luttrell pointed out that of the 28,000 they were being asked to raise, if the marines and others who were 'under the command of our general at Boston' were removed, then 'the number of foremast men will not exceed 14,000', a number totally inadequate for a fleet of 78 sail.

Ships of the line were 'rated' according to the number of guns they carried; most 3rd rates carried 74 or 64 guns, a 4th rate carried 50-60 guns, a 5th rate 32–44 guns, and a 6th rate averaged 24.[24] The majority of the ships on the North America station were either 4th, 5th, or 6th rate. The average ship's complement for these rates is given in the following table, which confirms the argument of both Keppel and Luttrell that the number of men requested in the Estimate was insufficient.

Table 1: Examples of British men of war by rating

Rate	Guns	Complement	Tonnage
1st	100	880	1,800–2,090
2nd	84	750	1,920
3rd	74	600–700	1,550–1,830
4th	60	400–435	1,060–1,300
5th	38	250	940
6th	28	200	580–610

Britain did not fully wake up to the need for mobilisation until it was almost too late. Ships take time to build and crews need to be recruited and trained; the sheer scale of the job needed meant that it would not happen in a hurry. A

22 NDAR, Vol.3, p.335.
23 NDAR, Vol.3, p.336.
24 N.A.M. Rodger, *The Wooden World: An Anatomy of the Georgian Navy* (London: Norton, 1986), p.348.

74-gun ship of the line required an average of 2,000 oak trees for its construction: the navy's annual consumption of trees was around 40,000, each of which took 100 years to grow to the required size.[25] In June 1776, alarmed by signs that the French were taking steps to increase their navy, the government called for a limited mobilisation. In his turn Sandwich wrote to North in October of that year that 'The French are certainly greatly ahead in their preparation, and I dread the consequences of their being at sea before us'.[26] Sandwich, faced with the reluctance of the government to mobilise, had to limit the size of ships available to Howe's American squadron to 44-gun and 50-gun two-deckers – he had to save the larger ships for the protection of the English coast against any possibility of a French invasion. The failure of Sandwich to impress on his colleagues the urgency of the situation in the face of a growing French threat 'ensured that the Royal Navy would go to war at a crippling disadvantage'.[27] Figures for the number of ships available to the navy are difficult to reconcile, especially with the time it took for communications between London and the far-flung stations of the British navy. However, a snap-shot was given to the Cabinet in June 1776, which will serve as a start point. In British ports there were 29 ships of the line 'compleatly [sic] fitted as guardships, which, with the aid of a Press, might be all at sea in a Fortnight'.[28] Guardships were 'battleships in commission in port'[29] ready for mobilisation to a full war footing; hence the two weeks necessary to victual and fit them for sea. At the time of the report, 'All our Frigates (that do not want considerable repair) including Ships of 50 Guns, and Two of 64, are in America, or appropriated for the American Service;' this left very few for home waters. Of the approximately 30,000 men employed by the navy there were 'about 15,000 on the American Service' and some 8,000 at home. As the report indicates, for the war that Britain was fighting in America in 1776, the navy had only smaller vessels while the larger ships were held at home against the threat of French involvement. It should be remembered that the whole war was fought against the background of the Bourbon threat. A hint of the extent to which the Admiralty was looking over its shoulder at the French, while supposedly supporting the army in America, is indicated by a paragraph in the report to the Cabinet.

> In case of a War 20 Ships of the Line may be depended upon as ready for Sea (if there is no difficulty about getting Men) within a Year from the

25   N. Mostert, *The Line Upon The Wind: An Intimate History of the Last and Greatest War Fought at Sea Under Sail, 1793–1815* (London: Jonathan Cape, 2007), p.64.
26   SP, Vol.1, p.216.
27   Rodger, *Command of the Ocean*, p.334.
28   NDAR, Vol.6, pp.425–427.
29   Rodger, *Sandwich*, p.197.

time of their receiving Orders to fit out; but it must be observed that it will usually require a Month to prepare each Ship for receiving Men, and at least two Months more before she will be manned and ready for Sea.[30]

No wonder Sandwich was frustrated at his lack of success in persuading his ministerial colleagues to implement full mobilisation earlier than they did. However, as the comment above indicated, the ships needed men and that, in the eighteenth century, meant press gangs.

The ability of the navy to support the army in America was indirectly dependent on the success or otherwise of the press gangs. The size of the manning problem is demonstrated in the following table.

Table 2: Men in the Royal Navy, by year[31]

Year	Men
1763	75,988
1764	17,424
1775	15,230
1776	23,914
1777	46,231
1778	62,719
1779	80,275
1780	91,566
1781	98,269

As the table shows, as soon as peace was declared in 1763, the number of men in the navy dropped dramatically, and continued to fall until 1775, when shooting began at Lexington. Then, over the period of the American War, the same navy had to increase by 650 percent. An increase on this scale, which would have to include a large number of experienced seamen, could only be achieved by coercion – the press gang. There were strong disincentives for anyone thinking of joining the navy, not least of which was the low pay, which was received only infrequently. The rates of pay had remained unchanged between 1653 and 1797; an able seaman received 24 shillings for a lunar month and an ordinary seaman 19 shillings.[32]

---

30   NDAR, Vol.6, p.426.
31   Morriss, *British Maritime Ascendancy*, Table 6.1, p.226.
32   Morriss, *British Maritime Ascendancy*, pp.231–232.

Pay days were often a year apart, and deductions were made for slops (clothing), breakages, and tobacco. The severe punishments available to ships' captains, often for quite minor offences, did not help with recruitment. How, then, did the navy encourage 'volunteers'?

The need for a 'press' could be declared in a Royal Proclamation, such as that of 22 March 1776: 'Whereas it is Our Royal Intention to give all due Encouragement to all such Seamen, who shall voluntarily enter themselves in Our Service; We have thought fit, by and with the Advice of Our Privy Council, to publish this Our Royal Proclamation'. Here, and in the instructions to the officers in command of the press gangs, the authorities were careful to use the word 'volunteer' for those who joined, usually after having been plied with drink. To encourage men to take up his offer, George III was offering Royal Bounties of £3 for Able seamen and £2 for those rated as Ordinary.[33] Orders for raising men were sent by the Admiralty to individual officers, such as those to Captain Collingwood[34] and Captain Kearney,[35] both in 1776. The officer and those in his 'gang' would often arrive with 'fife and drum' to help to encourage patriotic feelings in the local populace. A piece of advice was given to the captain to help him with the recruitment:

> And, the better to enable you to carry on this Service, you are to keep the eight first good Seamen who may enter constantly in Town with you, in order that they may be employed in assisting you & the Petty Officers in raising other Voluntiers [sic]; allowing them one Shilling and three Pence a day each for their subsistence which is to be in full of all charges and claims for Refreshments.

However, it was normally free drink, the 'King's shilling', and the Royal Bounty (rather than patriotism) that caused men to wake up the next morning to the reality that they had joined the navy. Having enlisted, many soon decided that it was not the career for them and as many as 42,000 deserted during the war.[36]

Those volunteers who were already seamen were supposed to be no less than 20 and no more than 50 years old, while those who were landsmen could fall into the 18–50 year age bracket. While individual press gangs may have only recruited a few men, the cumulative effect could be quite large. On 30 October 1776, the *Public Advertiser* in London reported a recent visit by the recruiters.

33   NDAR, Vol.4, p.985.
34   NDAR, Vol.4, pp.1008–1010.
35   NDAR, Vol.4, pp.905–906.
36   Mackesy, *America*, p.176.

Monday Night upon the Flood Tide, about twenty Boats properly mann'd [*sic*] and officer'd [*sic*] came up the River from Deptford and Woolwich, when a General Press began, and every Man was taken on board the several Ships they boarded, except the Master, Mate and Boys. The Number of Men impressed as above is variously reported: some say 1,500, others 2,000, but it is generally thought that it did not exceed 8 or 900. Monday Night Press Warrants were sent down to all the Western Ports to impress as many Seamen as possible for the Service of the Navy, and it is supposed the Press will be general through all England.[37]

The following day in Parliament, some voices spoke out against the impressment. The Earl of Shelburne wanted to know why 'bands of ruffians' could drag 'the unhappy master of a numerous family from them' and he refused to back Press Warrants for the present 'barbarous war'.[38] The *Public Advertiser*, following up on its article of the previous day, declared that the 'Press for Sailors was as hot on Monday in all the Sea-ports in the Kingdom, as in the Thames; and by Accounts received of the Number already got and entered, they amount to about 5000, which is *Half the Number that is wanted*'[39] [my italics]. These recruitment activities were mentioned in a puckish comment by the French ambassador in London to Vergennes: 'the impressment is at the point where it is beginning to snatch away servants from behind their masters' carriages'.[40] The removal of men to crew the King's ships caused concern to many businessmen who saw their workers whisked away to sea, while still wanting the navy to have the strength to protect their trade. In August 1777 the *London Chronicle* reported that while plans were drawn up for armed merchant ships to escort vessels 'against the depredations of American privateers' operating on the British side of the Atlantic, the merchants wanted assurance that 'the men raised for the purpose of manning these ships would be allowed to remain on board them so long as the contract existed, without being liable to be turned over to any other of his Majesty's ships'.[41] In other words, they did not want them removed by press gangs. Farmers were also fearful for their workforce, especially at harvest time: 'A petition will be presented in a few days, to the Admiralty from the counties in general for protections for the harvestmen, as it is to be feared that there will not be hands enough to get it in without; as poor men are afraid to go to their daily labour'. The navy's need for men, and the use of impressment to plug the gaps, was not confined to British ports. In November

37   NDAR, Vol.7, p.718.
38   NDAR, Vol.7, p.719.
39   NDAR, Vol.7, p.721.
40   NDAR, Vol.7, p.755.
41   NDAR, Vol.9, p.591.

1775, the master of a ship arriving in Boston wrote to the ship's owner that 'the Admiral [Graves] pressed all our hands: they served all the transports in the same manner'[42] – in other words, all the crews of the transports which had brought provisions were now pressed into the navy. This practice caused obvious problems for those trying to organise supply convoys for the troops in America.

The conduct of war, especially one taking place thousands of miles from home shores, requires some continuity of command. Between the time of the *Gaspee* incident in 1772 and the surrender at Yorktown in 1781, the navy on the American station had seven different leaders, not to mention those who commanded in the Caribbean. Additionally, those commanders were not always chosen strictly on merit, or for their ability to get along with the army commander, with whom they would need to work closely.

On 1 July 1774, Vice-Admiral Samuel Graves arrived in Boston on his flagship HMS *Preston* to relieve Rear-Admiral John Montagu. Together with Graves were the remaining troops to make up Gage's four regiments (there were now five in Boston), with which he had optimistically claimed he could quell the rebellion. Graves had left England on 29 April, taking two months for the voyage and demonstrating how even changes of personnel could take months after the effective decision had been taken in London. Graves's orders were to enforce the Navigation Acts and the blockade of Boston, which had been implemented by Montagu before his arrival, as well as patrolling the coast from the St Lawrence to Florida. When hostilities started, following the events at Lexington and Concord, Graves had only 30 ships available to him. The Admiralty had a 'scheme' for a force 'to be employed on the Coast of North America', which amounted to 50 ships, but as the table below shows, 20 of them were not there in August 1775.

Table 3: Ships for the North American station, August 1775[43]

Ships	Guns	On station	Outbound to station	Additional requested
5	Each with 50	1	4	
2	Each with 44		2	
21 frigates		7	7	7
14 sloops		14		
8 schooners		8		
Total of 50		30	13	7

42   NDAR, Vol.2, p.1200.
43   NDAR, Vol.1, pp.1350–1351.

The table also reinforces the point that the Admiralty was limiting the size of ships available to Graves, as only one of those on station was of 50 guns. In their outline of the 'scheme', the Admiralty intended that (of the 50 ships proposed) 22 were to be around Boston; three at Rhode Island; eight at New York; two in the Delaware; eight off Virginia; four off the Carolinas and Georgia; two in the St Lawrence River; and one off Florida. However, Graves was allowed to station the ships as he thought best: 'their Lordships do not mean that you should therefore confine yourself to the disposing of your Force precisely in that manner, but leave it intirely [sic] to you to make such other disposition of it as you shall judge most likely to answer the important Objects to which it is to be directed'. Graves was to be in command at an unfortunate time, the battle of Bunker Hill; the corralling of Gage's army in Boston and the subsequent evacuation of that town would all take place on his watch.

The operations did not go well for the Admiral, and he came in for a lot of criticism, not all of it warranted. In the view of David Syrett, Graves was 'not very inspiring' but he had been 'much maligned'. In the early months of the war, 'without instructions, hampered by poor communications and lacking co-ordination, Graves's small and ill-constituted squadron confronted a continent in rebellion'.[44] Major-General John Burgoyne, who arrived in Boston in May 1775, was less willing to find excuses for Graves, as he demonstrated in a letter to Germain.

> It may perhaps be asked in England – what [is] the Admiral doing? I wish I was able to answer that question satisfactorily. But I can only say what he is not doing. That He is not supplying the troops with sheep & oxen the dinners of the best of us bear [me]ager testimony – the want of broth in the Hospitals bears a more melancholy one. He is not defending his own flocks & herds, for the enemy has repeatedly and in the most insulting manner, plundered his own appropriated islands. He is not defending the other islands in the harbour; for the enemy landed in force, burned the lighthouse at noon day, & killed & took a party of marines almost under the guns of two or three men of war. He is not employing his ships to keep up communication & intelligence with the servants & friends of Government at different parts of the Continent, for I do not beleive [sic] Genl [Thomas] Gage has received a letter from any correspondent out of Boston these six weeks. He is surely intent upon greater objects you will think – supporting in material points the dignity & terror of the British flag – & where a number of boats have been built for the rebels, privateers

44   Syrett, *American Waters*, p.2.

fitted out, prices carried in, the King's armed vessels sunk, the crews made prisoners, the officers killed – He is doubtless enforcing instant restitution & reparation by the voice of his Cannon, and laying the towns in ashes which refuse his terms – Alass! He is not – The British thunder [is] diverted or controlled by pitiful attentions & quaker-like scruples; & under such influence Insult [and] Impunity, like Righteousness & peace, have kissed each other.[45]

Burgoyne, who would later surrender Saratoga to the rebels, wanted a fire and brimstone approach from an admiral who had decided 'on a basically passive role for the North American Squadron'.[46] In orders issued by Graves to some of his captains in May 1775 (after the events of Bunker Hill), he stated that they were 'not to act offensively except for the immediate preservation of his Majesty's Ships under their Command, or except upon the special Requisition of the civil Magistrates in cases of the utmost Danger'.[47] It was his hope that an accommodation could be reached between Britain and the colonists, but that was not to be. What made matters worse was that the differences between the army and navy commanders was obvious to others, including civilians. The former Massachusetts Attorney-General, Jonathan Sewall, had no good word for Graves when writing from London in January 1776.

What Excuse can be found for a British Admiral, who, with 30 or 40 Ships under his Command, suffers a Garrison to starve tho' surrounded with plenty of every Necessary, within the reach of his Ships! who tamely & supinely looks on & sees Fishing Schooners, Whale-boats and Canoes riding triumphant under the Muzzles of his Guns, & carrying off every Supply destin'd for your relief! Heaven grant you patience, & reward every one according to the Deeds done in the Body. – I can tell you, for your Comfort, that he is cursed as hard upon this Side [of] the Water, as he can be on yours – he has now no Advocate here, & I believe will scarcely find a Friend in England upon his return.[48]

While the criticism against Graves was growing, there were those who recognised that the situation in America was also due to the policies pursued in London; mobilisation had started late and the admiral had insufficient ships for the role he

---

45   NDAR, Vol.1, p.1190, letter from Burgoyne to Germani, Boston, 20 August 1775.
46   D.A. Yerxa, 'Vice-Admiral Samuel Graves and the North American squadron, 1774–1776', *Mariner's Mirror*, 62: 4 (Nov. 1976), p.375.
47   NDAR, Vol.1, p.500.
48   NDAR, Vol.3. p.496, letter from Sewall to Edward Winslow.

was given. In a debate in Parliament on the Navy Estimates, James Luttrell spoke out against those who would lay the blame on Graves for the situation in America, rather than recognise that the orders issued to him had been so worded as to avoid blame falling on ministers in London.

> Sir, talking of America, a right hon. member said, there had been a fault in the navy. Will the noble lord declare that admiral Graves has ever received positive orders that he did not execute; or have they been, as I have reason to believe them, from the operations of the fleet, so *artfully discretional*, [my emphasis] that if your ships should be wrecked upon that frozen coast, or any misfortune attend them, the blame may be laid on the admiral, and his reputation as an officer be sacrificed to shelter the wicked proceedings of these ministers.[49]

Whatever the rights and wrongs, the impression gained in London was that Graves had lost the confidence of those he commanded and a change at the top was necessary, as Lord Rochford spelled out in a letter to Sandwich.

> I should not act with that confidence I have in you, if I concealed from you the bitter complaints that have come home against Admiral Graves. Officers of distinction have written a state of facts that cannot be contradicted [...] The King, who is apprised of all this, has authorized me to tell you that he does not see, after every letter laying such blame on him (the Admiral), how the command can any longer be left in such improper hands.[50]

Sandwich had written to Graves in August 1775 to warn him of the voices speaking out against him, and urging more action from 'the very great naval force' that the country believed was stationed off the American coast. As the First Lord advised him, he left himself open to censure 'for doing too little, though I should be greatly surprised if you incurred any blame by rather overdoing your part in the other extreme'.[51] The warning did not produce the desired result and, as Sandwich explained to Graves, he had to be recalled: 'the world [had] expected something essential to be done both by the fleet and army'. As General Gage had been sent home, this made Sandwich's 'resistance to your being recalled utterly ineffectual'.[52] David Syrett commented that 'had Graves been an abler commander, there could

---

49   NDAR, Vol.3, p.337, debate on Navy Estimates.
50   NDAR, Vol.2, pp.708–709, letter from Rochford to Sandwich, 8 September 1775.
51   NDAR, Vol.2, pp.688–689, letter from Sandwich to Graves, 25 August 1775.
52   SP, Vol.1, p.74, letter from Sandwich to Graves, 17 September 1775.

have been little difference in the effectiveness of the Royal Navy during the first year of the war;[53] put simply, there were insufficient ships. Graves's dismissal demonstrates the effect that slow communications had on decisions that needed taking and the passing of information on which those decisions depended. It took four months from the King's decision to replace him before Graves received official notification. In his narrative of events, written in the third person, Graves wrote bitterly of the way he had been replaced by an officer of junior rank.

> In this way (as if a matter of course) by a junior Officer, who had not a Flag when the Vice Admiral was appointed to the American Command, came his first and only notice or intimation, either from the Admiralty or any part of Government, of having given dissatisfaction. Nothing could be more unexpected or extraordinary than this Recall: for it bore date the 29th of September, and he had Letters from the Board of the entire Approbation of his Conduct down to the 6th of the same Month.[54]

Even the French minister, Vergennes, thought that Graves and Gage had been wrongly blamed for events: 'the entire Council of the King of England does not seem to be favourably disposed towards them. [...] they will lose their commands because *they have been made responsible for all the defeats*' [my emphasis].[55]

At the end of December 1775, Graves was replaced by Rear-Admiral Molyneux Shuldham who arrived in Boston on 30 December 1775 after a journey of 61 days. Shuldham brought with him the official notification of the change of command, which took effect on 15 January 1776. Eighteenth century commanders, naval and army, were not always chosen for their abilities; they were incredibly sensitive regarding their perquisites, and quick to take offence at anything they deemed to be a slight on their honour or which did not accord with the grand position they believed they held. In July 1775, Shuldham was informed that he was to be second-in-command to Graves in America.[56] He would have been aware that he was being raised to the position of Commander-in-Chief because Graves had been recalled for his performance. In those circumstances, one might assume that his uppermost thoughts would be concentrated on how to perform better than his predecessor but that would be to overlook the importance of the visible symbols of status. At anchor at Spithead, waiting for a favourable wind, Shuldham complained to the Admiralty about 'the Careless and unfinished manner in which

53   Syrett, *American Waters*, p.10.
54   NDAR, Vol.3, p.300, Graves' narrative.
55   NDAR, Vol.2, p.679, Vergennes, 18 August 1775.
56   NDAR, Vol.1, p.1331, Admiralty to Shuldham, 19 July 1775.

I found my Appartment' in his flagship, which was 'so very unfit for an Officer of my Rank'.[57] A few days later, and still at Spithead, he suggested that he should have another ship as his flagship.

> I must take the liberty of representing to you, that the *Chatham* [his flagship] is the worst and Oldest of any of the Fifty Gunships upon that Service [America], as well as extremely unfit and inconvenient for a Flag-Officer Commanding in Chief on a Service where his Ship is to be his constant residence, without the probability of lying a Night out of her during the course of his Command.[58]

Shuldham suggested that he should be given the *Vigilant* in place of the *Chatham* but their Lordships at the Admiralty thought otherwise, as Philip Stephens explained in a letter to the admiral.

> I am commanded by their Lordships to acquaint you that as Fifty Gun Ships are judged to be of a sufficient size for the Service on which you are going, they cannot consent to the *Vigilant* being fitted out for that purpose; and that as the *Chatham* has lately had a Vice Admiral on board of her, Their Lordships cannot conceive but that she is very fit for what she is now going to be employed in.[59]

Only a month into his appointment, the Admiralty must have been wondering if their new commander had his priorities in the right order. Finally, on 18 October 1775, Shuldham informed the Admiralty that 'I am now getting under sail with a fresh Wind at WSW to try, tho' without much Expectation of Success, to make some progress to the Westward'.[60] While the Admiral may have had a high opinion of himself and the size of ship that his position required, others were dubious as to his abilities. William Eden, Under-Secretary at the Northern Department, wrote critically of him (and Graves) to Germain: 'I am very sorry to say, however, that I find the Idea entertain'd of Shuldham by some who know Him well, is by no Means better than that of the wretched Commander whom He supersedes'.[61]

On his arrival in America Shuldham appeared to get his defence in early for any setbacks that might happen on his watch or any criticism from those who had previously been under Graves's command. He informed Sandwich that the

57   NDAR, Vol.2, p.752, letter to Stephens, 6 October 1775.
58   NDAR, Vol.2, p.754, letter to Stephens, 10 October 1775.
59   NDAR, Vol.2, p.764, letter from Stephens, 18 October 1775.
60   NDAR, Vol.2, p.764, letter from Shuldham, 18 October 1775.
61   NDAR, Vol.2, p.769, Eden to Germain, 21 October 1775.

armed vessels of the rebels had multiplied quickly, that 'many of our storeships and victuallers' had been taken and 'how successfully they [the rebels] have defeated all our force, vigilance, and attention, by their artifice, but more by their being too early in possession of all the harbours, creeks, and rivers, on this coast, most of which they have fortified'.[62] The new commander was letting it be known that his predecessor had dropped the ball but he hoped that Sandwich would give him his support and defend his conduct 'in the arduous task I am engaged in, against the many malevolent attacks I must expect will be made up on it, particularly by the friends and dependants of my predecessor, who it is natural to suppose will not be very warm in their good offices towards me'. He did not demonstrate the confidence of a Rodney or a Nelson. Unfortunately, for Shuldham, his appointment would be a short one and Graves's comment on the injustice he felt at being replaced by a junior officer would be one of the factors in Shuldham's removal. On 13 February 1776, only six weeks after his arrival in Boston, Sandwich was writing to him on a 'disagreeable subject [...] in consequence of a general opinion, it has been thought proper that Lord Howe should come out to take the command of the fleet in America'.[63] To soften the blow, he was awarded an Irish peerage and promoted to Vice-Admiral. Shuldham did not receive this message until 22 May. The *London Chronicle*, 6 February 1776, referred to the seniority of Shuldham in its coverage of the issue.

> We are assured, that Admiral Shuldham is not to have the command of the fleet destined to serve against the Americans, and that Lord [Richard] Howe is certainly appointed, and has accepted the command. This change is in consequence of a representation made to his Majesty shortly after Admiral Shuldham's nomination, by the senior flag officers, of the impropriety of placing a junior to command older officers, and that in short it would be looked upon as an affront offered them, and they would certainly lay down their commissions, rather than serve on such terms, which the naval arrangements made in this kingdom have heretofore been unacquainted with. This had such weight with his Majesty, that Lord Howe, as the senior Admiral, was appointed, and is now preparing to take the command.[64]

Vice-Admiral Lord Howe was in a unique position; not only was he the naval commander but he was also the brother of General William Howe, the

62   SP, Vol.1, pp.104–105, Shuldham to Sandwich, 13 January 1776.
63   SP, Vol.1, p.119, Sandwich to Shuldham, 13 February 1776.
64   NDAR, Vol.4, p.889.

commander of the British army in America, and both of the Howes were peace commissioners. Their dual role as military commanders while also serving on the peace commission led one historian to state that the brothers 'implemented a doomed policy of limited warfare to encourage reconciliation'.[65] The admiral was close to his younger brother, and gave priority 'to supporting the army, rather than blockading the coast and launching raids'.[66] Lord Howe was in command at the same time as ministers in London were becoming aware of the growing potential threat from France. The dilemma faced by the Admiralty – to cover the war in America while being capable of resisting an invasion fleet in home waters – had implications for naval strategy, as summed up by David Syrett.

> The Admiralty would not give up the two-power standard in Europe and Germain and the Howes would not tailor military operations in America to fit the requirements of the naval war. Therefore, the blockade of America in 1777 was doomed to be ineffective, and the Royal Navy would be incapable of suppressing the raiding of commerce by the Americans.[67]

The complaints against Lord Howe's performance led to his request to return to London in 1778 to defend his conduct 'in a public circus of recrimination'.[68]

The year following Howe's return to England was a sorry period of change at the top of the navy in America. The replacement commander was Rear-Admiral James Gambier, an officer of 'no real talents'.[69] Gambier's elevation to fleet command had never been on the books and demonstrates how influence and patronage could damage the war effort: 'The Admiralty never intended that Gambier should command anything'.[70] He had been sent out to America as second-in-command to Lord Howe as a way to get him to resign as commissioner of Portsmouth dockyard, so allowing someone better to command that important facility in the event of war with France. The removal of Gambier was further complicated by his relationship to the Pitt family, as well as his being the brother-in-law of Charles Middleton, Comptroller of the Navy. There were few precedents for removing a dockyard commissioner, 'and this position had almost the status of property',[71] so Gambier was sent as second-in-command to Howe. It is difficult to like Gambier from reading his letters to Sandwich; the sycophantic style is reminiscent of Dickens'

65   Bicheno, *Rebels & Redcoats*, p.30.
66   O'Shaughnessy, *Men Who Lost America*, p.119.
67   Syrett, *American Waters*, p.70.
68   Willis, *Sea Power*, p.247.
69   Willis, *Sea Power*, p.234.
70   Syrett, *American Waters*, p.119.
71   Syrett, *American Waters*, p.119.

'ever so 'umble' Uriah Heap. Extracts from a letter of his to Sandwich demonstrate why he was not the man for the job. On 6 July 1778, he addressed Sandwich as 'My honoured Lord […] my revered patron'.[72] His letter continued:

> They [the letters from Sandwich] are my only balm, and on them will I rely […] in the comfortable hope that your continued friendship will not let me be kept abroad a second in command at any rate, nor permit the promises that I was considerately honoured with be annihilated and unperformed to the distress and hurt of a devoted servant, honoured with your friendship, who wishes to deserve it, and who has quitted a certain subsistence [Portsmouth dockyard] for an amiable wife and five helpless children to endeavour under your auspices and protection to better support and educate them at the cheerful risk of his life and health on a remote service of unequalled fatigue, difficulty, and unremitting attention.[73]

There was much in this letter to suggest that Gambier did not have the makings of a Commander-in-Chief. Gambier's deficiencies were recognised by Howe who had told Vice-Admiral John Byron, at Rhode Island, that Gambier had a commission 'as commander in chief *during the absence of a superior officer*' [emphasis in the original].[74] The process by which Gambier was selected for the position was flawed, and the man was not up to the job. His wish to be returned home to his family was recognised by the King – 'he will not be sorry at receiving permission to return home'[75] – and by Sandwich, 'your most favourite object is that of returning home'.[76] To one observer, the admiral's return in the spring of 1779 was to the 'universal joy of all ranks and conditions. I believe no person was ever more generally detested by the navy, army, and citizens than this penurious old reptile'.[77] The decision had been taken by the Admiralty, 23 January 1779, to replace him with Rear-Admiral Marriot Arbuthnot.

In the eighteenth century, distance equated to time, and that meant that a decision taken in the January could take months to be implemented. Gambier was to step down, Arbuthnot was to take his place, but in the meantime Captain Sir George Collier (who emitted energy 'like sparks off a grindstone')[78] would take temporary command on 4 April 1779. Collier brought to the role the fire and

72   SP, Vol.2, p.295.
73   SP, Vol.2, p.298.
74   SP, Vol.2, p.317, letter from Gambier to Sandwich, 11 October 1778.
75   SP, Vol.2, p.325, letter from King to Sandwich, 26 October 1778.
76   SP, Vol.2, p.326, letter from Sandwich to Gambier, 1 November 1778.
77   Syrett, *American Waters*, p.120.
78   Willis, *Sea Power*, p.328.

enthusiasm of the younger naval officer. In May and June of 1779, Collier, with 28 ships and a force of redcoats, wreaked destruction on coastal towns in Virginia. The King took note of the comparison with his earlier commanders-in-chief: 'It is rather remarkable that Sir G. Collier, with so scanty a force, should have been during five months able to effect more against the rebels than the admirals that commanded such large fleets'.[79] However, Sir George was only place-filling until Arbuthnot arrived at New York on 25 August 1779, seven months after his appointment by the Admiralty. The time taken for Arbuthnot to get his fleet and troop transports on their way to America highlights the issues facing those who were planning operations from 3,000 miles away. It had been intended that the admiral should be ready for sailing on 20 February 1779, but the weather, the need to embark 3,000 troops and load 1,500 tons of camp equipment, as well as wait for additional escort vessels from Vice-Admiral Darby's Channel Fleet, delayed his eventual departure until 24 May 1779.[80] Arbuthnot was not the man to command the navy at this critical period: 'If the lords of the Admiralty had gone through the navy list looking for a flag officer who should not be sent to New York, they could not have come up with a better choice than Arbuthnot'.[81] However, we get ahead of ourselves; these command changes were all in the future. Of more pressing concern in 1775 was the maintenance of the garrison at Boston, while surrounded by the increasingly rebellious population of New England.

The problems facing those in command in America and in the ministries in London were how to transport reinforcements to the colonies and how to feed and supply the troops and ships' crews. The task was enormous, while the organisation – at least initially – lacked the processes and procedures needed to administer a supply chain across thousands of miles of Atlantic Ocean. However, by hard work and application, the army was supplied, if not always as timely and in the quantities it would have liked. Food was a major issue. It was required in enormous quantities, in a state fit for consumption (if not by modern standards) in a period when refrigeration technology only went as far as blocks of ice, and storage was the responsibility of the cooper and his iron-bound barrels. Soldiers had to be transported by sea, though most had probably never stepped on a boat, let alone lived within its confines for two to three months. As well as men, the army needed horses and, as the colonists refused to sell them to the troops, these also had to be transported from Britain. The journey must have been horrific for these poor animals tied up below decks with no opportunity for exercise and unused to the movement of a man-of-war at sea. For those that did make it, they would need

79   SP, Vol.3, p.135, letter from the King to Sandwich, 23 September 1779.
80   Mackesy, *America*, pp.260–261.
81   Syrett, *American Waters*, p.121.

forage and oats, which again had to be transported by sea. The next few chapters explain how these logistics challenges were faced and (largely) overcome by the clerks at the Boards in London and a wooden navy in the age of sail.

3

'Good, wholesome, and sound'

In April 1775, as the British troops marched out of Boston to destroy the rebel arsenal at Concord, the British had a reasonable expectation that their soldiers could be supplied with food, horses, fodder, and other necessaries from local merchants. This supply chain had worked during the Seven Years War, and in the succeeding years up to Concord. However, the situation in America had changed: Britain was now at war with the colonists and 'fresh food, forage, fuel and transport had to be obtained in America and therein lay the basis of a whole neglected phase of the war'.[1] In his introduction to his book on logistics in the American War, Bowler stated that 'In the study of warfare, logistics and military administration have been neglected stepchildren'. Without the support of the bureaucracy at home, the army in America simply could not have operated; everything the army required to operate in America had to come to them by sea. Logistics, a term that had not been coined at that time, had come into its own: 'the planning and implementation of the production, procurement, storage, transportation, distribution and movement of personnel, supplies and equipment'.[2] The tendency for military histories to be written from the viewpoint of generals and commanders (while paying little attention to logistics) was pointed out by Bowler:

> The military histories of the American Revolution have by and large concentrated on the great set-piece battles such as Bunker Hill, Long Island, White Plains, and Brandywine Creek. They have neglected, or failed to see as a whole, a deadly and vitally important battle that went on continuously as a result of the British logistical dependence on North America. [...] As he [George Washington] could deny them [the British]

---

1   Bowler, *Logistics*, p.66.
2   Bowler, *Logistics*, p.vii.

forage and horses, so he could paralyze their land operations; as he could deny them fresh food, so he could increase discontent and sickness.[3]

An army's supply needs are not limited to food. In September 1944 as he pushed his tanks inland after D-Day, General Patton gave a typically colourful description of his main priority: 'I'll shoot the next man who brings me food. Give us gasoline; we can eat our belts'.[4]

The main contracting firm for supplying the army in America was Nesbitt, Drummond, and Franks, and they warned the Treasury that the current arrangement around Boston was about to break down as the local suppliers would be forced, by the more radical elements in the colonies, to choke off provisions for the British troops. The result of the engagements at Lexington and Concord was an increase in the number of British soldiers, initially to around 10,000 men, and their virtual confinement to the environs of the port of Boston. For troops to 'live off the land' they need to be in military control of the territory that would supply them. In the case of the British in America in 1775, that was not the situation on the ground and any move out of the base area required the carriage of all supplies needed for the period of the expedition. Once these were consumed, the troops had to either find more or retire on their supply base. Unable to hold territory, the British army was bound to its ports: Boston and New York. The availability of supplies became a large factor in a general's decision on whether or not he could begin a campaign. Looking back on his taking of Fort Ticonderoga in 1777, Burgoyne remarked that for every hour that he contemplated the strategy of the army, he had to spend another twenty wondering how to feed it.[5] Given the time that it took for supply convoys to be assembled and loaded in Britain, and then to make the Atlantic crossing, commanders frequently required six months' of supplies before undertaking expeditions away from their base. However, there were only 23 of the 79 months (between Lexington and the surrender at Yorktown in 1781) when the army had supplies at this level.[6] Even when the army was static, a minimum of two months was deemed necessary because of the time taken to resupply across the Atlantic; falling below that reserve might mean the need to evacuate before the troops ran out of food. With only four months of provisions available to him in mid-1779, Clinton complained to London that his force was being neglected and consequently he could not carry out his plans for that year. When the situation improved at the end of the year, he mounted his attack against

---

3   Bowler, *Logistics*, pp.66–67.
4   C. D'Este, *A Genius for War: A Life of General George S. Patton* (London: HarperCollins, 1996), p.648.
5   O'Shaughnessy, *Men Who Lost America*, p.150.
6   Bowler, *Logistics*, pp.94–95.

Charleston, his most successful as Commander-in-Chief,[7] but when supplies fell away again, he felt unable to capitalise on this success. Shortages did not only affect the army. In March 1777, Lord Howe wrote to Stephens at the Admiralty that he had no knowledge of the storeship *Elephant* and Ordnance ship *Unity*, which had sailed from Spithead on 5 December 1776, and that 'The want of those Stores, but of Cordage most especially, becomes now so considerable, that it will greatly affect the Employment of the Cruizing [*sic*] Ships'.[8] The *Elephant* had put into Halifax with storm damage and did not make it to New York until 13 May 1777.[9] Like it or not, British ministers had got themselves into a war where the forces deployed were totally dependent on a supply line that was 3,000 miles and three months long. An idea of the quantities involved is given in the following table.[10]

Table 4: Provisions shipped, 27 May 1777–11 November 1781

Type	Quantity
Bread, flour, and rice	79,465,184 lb
Salt beef	10,711,820 lb
Salt pork	38,202,081 lb
Fresh meat	3,093,952 lb
Butter	3,997,043 lb
Oatmeal	7,282,071 lb
Pease	427,452 bushels
Molasses	176,672 gallons
Vinegar	134,378 gallons
Rum	2,865,782 gallons

These enormous quantities exclude the annual requirement for 14,000 tons of hay and 6,000 of oats for every 4,000 horses, as well as the clothing, tents and camp equipage, ammunitions and naval stores.

At the outbreak of the war, it was the responsibility of the Treasury to procure provisions for the army, but they also had to take on the task of arranging for the transportation of the supplies from Britain to Boston. Having no specialised knowledge of maritime affairs, the running of dockyards and the chartering of transport vessels, the Treasury suggested to the Admiralty that it should take over

7   Bowler, *Logistics*, pp.130–136.
8   NDAR, Vol.8, pp.230–231.
9   NDAR, Vol.8, p.989.
10   Bowler, *Logistics*, p.9.

this role. The suggestion was rebuffed on the grounds that this was 'no part of the Duty of that Office [the Admiralty] and that they could not under take [*sic*] the Service'.[11] The Treasury was stuck with the responsibility, and that led to a number of problems. As the war developed, so the Americans became adept at capturing British supply ships with the consequence that insurance rates escalated and there was a need for transports to be armed. Those shipping firms who had been willing to take on contracts for the shipment of supplies to America now baulked at the additional costs involved. However, shipping was only one part of the problem; the Treasury also had to develop a receiving and shipping depot at Cork as well as an agency for receiving, storing, and issuing supplies in America. To that end, Robert Gordon was hired to take on the management of Cork, while Daniel Chamier took on the role of Commissary General in America. It was the job of the Commissary to inform London of the number of mouths to be fed and then to distribute the provisions sent from Britain. Where he could, he would try to buy locally but the British army never occupied enough territory to feed the average of 35,000 men and 4,000 horses with the 37 tons of food and 38 of forage that were required daily. The job was further complicated by the need to move the provisions from the receiving port to the troops in the field and to do this the Commissary Department had on hire an average of 50 ships of between 16 and 160 tons.[12] For the years from the start of the war until the Navy Board relented and took over the responsibility from the Treasury, the supply system for the army was inefficient, not least because there were too many departments competing against each other for the same resources, ostensibly to help fight the same war. In this 'sellers' market' the civilian contractors were the winners. When the victualling of the army was moved from the Treasury to the Victualling Board, 'the result was a marked improvement in both efficiency and economy'.[13] That is to get ahead of ourselves. Before getting into the mechanics of how the army was supplied, both before and after 1779, it is worth reviewing how the mature processes operated by the navy, were then expanded to include the needs of the troops.

Navy ships tended to be at sea for months at a time and would normally be victualled sufficient for a period of three to six months, depending on the theatre to which they were sailing. Fresh food had to be procured on an opportunistic basis but the staples (salt meat, butter, cheese, and beer) had to last for months in wooden barrels in the ship's hold. David Syrett made the statement that 'The Victualling Board issued bad provisions with such regularity during the eighteenth century

11   Syrett, *Shipping and the American War*, p.129.
12   Bowler, *Logistics*, pp.29–32.
13   Rodger, *Command of the Ocean*, p.377.

that rotten food was an integral part of life on board the King's ships'.[14] There is no doubt that bad provisions were received, but not all the time, and not without the Board taking what measures it could to try to prevent it happening. The navy recognised that poor and inadequate food would result in crews that could not work their ships. Daniel Wier (who replaced Chamier as Commissary General), after a particularly bad supply situation, wrote to the Treasury in February 1779 to say that he had the pleasure to inform them that 'the provisions of every kind lately sent out are very good and sound'.[15] Numerous instances can be found in the records to support the comments of both Syrett and Wier. The processes in place to check the condition of provisions at the time the contract was let, on their delivery, transportation and receipt at the unloading dock in America, were extensive and were improved during the war to take account of problems arising. The *intent* was to deliver supplies on time and which were 'good and sound', but the lack of refrigeration, the use of wooden barrels before canning technology was invented, and the vagaries of winds and tides worked against the efforts of the clerks at the Board. The diet of the soldiers and sailors was unvarying and repetitive, but it must be judged against that which they and their civilian labourer counterparts were used to, not twentieth century supermarkets.

> The diet supplied by the establishment was plain and very restricted in its range, but it provided more than sufficient calories for hard physical work. [...] By the standards of the poor [in Britain] naval food was good and plentiful. To eat meat four days a week was itself a privilege denied a large part of the population, if only because in many parts of the country firing was too expensive for the poor to cook every day. [...] The seaman who had a hot dinner daily, with beef and beer, bread and cheese, and sometimes vegetables and fruit, was eating well by his standards, and it seems he knew it, for in an age when seamen could and did complain freely, it is remarkably difficult to find them grumbling about the food (cheese perhaps excepted).[16]

The point has already been made that it had originally been intended that the troops in America would source their provisions locally – clothing, camp equipage, and ordnance would still come from Britain – and the ships of the navy would receive their fresh meat and vegetables from the ports controlled by the troops. While local supplies were not totally cut off (some merchants will always find

14   Syrett, *Shipping and the American War*, p.190.
15   TNA, T 64/114, f.138.
16   Rodger, *Wooden World*, pp.85–86.

a way to make a profit), they could no longer be relied upon, as was recognised by the Admiralty in March 1775: 'Their Lordships being apprehensive that the Contractors for Victualling His Majesty's Ships in North America may meet with difficulties in furnishing them with Provisions in some of the Colonies on account of the present Disturbances, have directed the Victualling Board to send out to you upon Freight 4 Months Provisions of all species for 4275 Men'.[17] Because local supplies had not been completely cut off, navy ships could still find suppliers who were willing to provide stores on the proviso that they were not to be taken to the troops in Boston. Additionally, naval raids on seaports and local islands provided some forage and livestock for the troops. In July 1775, the New York committee of safety addressed themselves to a demand from the captain of HMS *Nautilus*, at Sandy Hook, for '4,000 pounds of bread, 300 pounds of beef, 500 pounds of pork, 12 bushels of peas, 200 pounds of butter, 200 pounds of cheese [and] 200 galls of rum'. The agent (who was contracted by the British) asked the committee 'whether or no I shall supply the provisions' and stated that he was authorised by the captain to assure the committee that 'the *Nautilus* is not going to Boston, but to the southward'.[18] The request was allowed. The following extract from the journal of the New York Provisional Congress demonstrates that the provisioning of naval ships, for their own use, was regularised, although it would later be stopped.

> Mr Lott [Royal Navy Victualling Agent in New York] having received an order from the purser of His Majesty's ship *Asia* to supply the said ship with sundry provisions, takes the liberty herewith to hand the same, and to request the favour that the Honourable Congress will be pleased to signify their opinion whether the order shall be complied with, and whether he shall be at liberty to supply the said ship with such other provisions as she may from time to time have occasion for, *for her own use*, during her stay in this Colony. City of New York, May 27th, 1775 [my emphasis].[19]

The Congress ordered:

> That Abraham Lott, Esqr., be at liberty to comply with the order for provisions now laid before the Congress, and the Congress declare that Mr Lott shall be at liberty to furnish such other provisions as above mentioned, to the said Ship *Asia*, for her own use, while in this port, he

---

17   NDAR, Vol.1, p.419, letter from Stephens to Graves, 3 March 1775.
18   NDAR, Vol.1, p.866.
19   NDAR, Vol.1, p.549.

laying before the Congress (or the General Committee of New-York if this board should not be sitting) a list of the Supplies so made from time to time.

In the early months of the war, New York was a possible victualling port for individual ships, provided they did not take more than was required for the feeding of the crew. Some navy captains recognised the advantage of this arrangement. In December 1775, Captain Hyde Parker wrote to Graves regarding one of the admiral's instructions. Graves wanted ships carrying provisions to the inhabitants of New York to be stopped and diverted to the troops at Boston. Hyde Parker pointed out that as the port was on an island the civilians were dependent on these small ships for their everyday needs and to stop them would cause starvation. Additionally, Hyde Parker suggested that this order should not be enforced at New York, as the port 'at present furnishes every necessary we ask for' and he believed that, if the British supplied transports and convoys then the local merchants would 'supply Boston with Cattle and other necessaries'.[20] Hyde Parker was backed up by a letter from Captain Vandeput to Graves:

> We have for a considerable time past had every Supply that we have demanded sent on board to Us, without any Molestation to the Boats which have brought it; nor do I expect there will be any unless some of the Rebel Troops from Connecticut, or New Jersey, should come into the Town, and prevent the Towns People from acting as they seem at present inclined.[21]

However, this cosy relationship was to come to an end early in 1776. Although there were a large number of Americans who were not in favour of the activities of the radicals, and wanted to remain loyal to the Crown, the state of affairs whereby New York furnished supplies to the ships of the enemy could not continue. On 8 April 1776, George Washington issued a General Order:

> The General, informs the inhabitants, that it is become absolutely necessary, that all communication, between the ministerial fleet and shore, should be immediately stopped, for that purpose, has given positive orders, that the ships should no longer be furnished with provisions: Any inhabitant, or others, who shall be taken, that have been on board, or near

20   NDAR, Vol.3, p.154, letter from Hyde Parker to Graves, 18 December 1775.
21   NDAR, Vol.3, p.158.

any of the ships, or going on board, will be considered as enemies, and treated accordingly.[22]

The New York Committee of Safety took Washington's order to heart, and in their minutes of their 18 April 1776 meeting did resolve that

No Inhabitant of this Colony upon any pretence or for any purpose whatsoever either in Person or in writing directly or indirectly do presume to have or maintain any Intercourse whatsoever with any Ship or Vessel belonging to or employed in the service of the King of great Britain or any of his Officers or Ministers, or with any Person or Persons on board of the same upon pain of being dealt with in the severest Manner as Enemies to the Rights and Liberties of the united North American Colonies.[23]

With Washington's order, and the arrival of his troops in the port city, 'the *modus vivendi* with the Royal Navy collapsed'[24] and by the end of April British warships had had to withdraw from the port and narrows of New York.

The coastline of New England was dotted with small ports and islands, all of which were potential sources of provisions, although the locals might not be willing providers. In a direction to Graves, the King demonstrated his involvement in the minutiae of the conflict, as well as a lack of appreciation for how much the Rebels resented British authority.

I am commanded by The King to signify to your Lordships His Majesty's Pleasure that Vice-Admiral Graves be instructed, that he do from time to time, send such of the Transports as can be spared from other Service, to the several ports in those Colonies in North America which are in Arms against The King, under Convoy of one or more of His Majesty's ships as the Case shall require, with Directions to the Commanders of such Ships to demand of the Inhabitants of the Maritime Towns, that they do furnish, at a reasonable price, such Supplies of Provision and other Necessaries as may be procured there, for the Use of His Majesty's Fleet [&] Army and that the said Commanders do, in Case of refusal to comply

22   NDAR, Vol.4, p.722.
23   NDAR, Vol.4, p.1150.
24   J. Black, *War for America: The Fight For Independence, 1775–1783* (Stroud: Alan Sutton, 1991), p.94.

with so just and reasonable a Demand proceed hostily [*sic*] against such Towns as in open Rebellion.[25]

There were colonists who were willing to accept payment for the fresh meat and hay that the soldiers and horses needed, and they preferred British coin to Continental paper money. One captain, accused in a local newspaper of having set his own price for provisions, wrote to the agent to make a rebuttal:

> Will you do me the favour to contradict a paragraph in Mr Holt's paper, in which he says that the man of war had stopped several vessels with provisions, and that we had set our *own price* upon whatsoever we chose *to take*? The truth is, that we have not *taken* or *bought* any sort of provisions from any vessel, except three hundred oysters which I bought yesterday, and for which I gave the owner two shillings more than what he told me was the market price[26] [italics in original].

The writer went on to state that there were even receipts taken for the items in question. Graves believed that paying the locals for their produce would lessen the chances of antagonising them, and might assist with the peace process. An example of his 'gently, gently' approach is contained in his instructions to the commander of HMS *Falcon*. The cattle on an island near the town of Falmouth had to be prevented from reaching the town, and so onward to the rebels. No injury should be done to the locals and if possible, the cattle should be sold to the British.

> Whereas in the present Rebellious State of this Country it is extremely difficult to procure fresh Meat even for the sick of his Majs [*sic*] Squadron under my Command, and whereas I am informed there is a great quantity of Cattle upon Elizabeth Islands near Falmouth in this Province, which it is absolutely necessary to prevent being carried to the Main; You are hereby required and directed with all possible Dispatch to proceed to Tarpawlin Cove in his Majs Sloop under your Command and there endeavour to hinder any Cattle live Stock or Hay upon the Islands being taken off, but you are upon no Account to suffer any Injury to be done to the Property or the Persons of the Inhabitants by any persons whatsoever, *so long as they shall demean themselves like dutiful and peaceable Subjects to his Majesty*; and if by any means you can prevail upon the Owners of the

25   NDAR, Vol.2, p.713, letter from Lord Dartmouth to the Admiralty, 12 September 1775.
26   NDAR, Vol.2, p.59, letter from Vandeput to Lott, 9 September 1775.

Cattle to dispose of them for his Majesty's Use, you are to acquaint me thereof as soon as possible with the Terms upon which they are inclined to sell [my emphasis].[27]

However, Graves does make the point that civility is only to be extended to those colonists who are inclined to recognise the authority of King George. Where the locals refused to assist the demands of the British captains, then force was to be used, or at least threatened as in the following example. When his small squadron was off Wilmington, North Carolina, Captain Parry wrote in no uncertain terms to the local magistrates requiring them to assist with the victualling of his ships:

His Majesties Ships not having received provision agreeable to their regular Demands. I Shall as soon as possible be off Wilmington with his Majesties Sloop *Cruizer* and other armed vessels under my Command to know the reason of their not being supplied. I expect to be supplied by six this Evening with the provisions I have now demanded of the Contractor. If his Majesties ships or Boats are in the least annoyed it will be my duty to oppose it.[28]

In their defence, the magistrates claimed that even under normal circumstances it would 'have been impossible to procure such a Quantity in this Town in so short a time as your Excellency mentions'. It was even more difficult now that 'The Trade of this Colony hath been distressed by the Kings Ships even contrary to the acts of the British Parliament'. As the war progressed, it became less likely that the British could buy provisions from merchants who were either ready for a quick profit, or had a real allegiance to the monarchy. The colonial governments were making it illegal for trade to take place between the warring parties. In these circumstances, troops had to be used to take the needed supplies, as the Master's log of the brig *Halifax*, which was 'wooding and watering', recorded on 5 September 1776:

At 8 Landed the Marines on Hewlets Island to Guard the Boats in takeing [*sic*] the Cattle from thence. At Noon the Rebels came down of[f] West farm point and Fir[e]d several small shot. Fird [fired] 4 four Pounder [with] Round and Grape and drove them off got on B[oard] Bullock from Hewlets [Island]. PM the *Brune* Made our Signal for a Petty Officer – Fird several shot at the Rebels on West Farm point.[29]

27   NDAR, Vol.1, p.252, letter from Graves to Linzee, 30 April 1775.
28   NDAR, Vol.4, p.102.
29   NDAR, Vol.6, p.709.

Although the navy continued to take supplies from coastal towns when the opportunity arose, they were totally inadequate to the needs of the troops and sailors. Every year a third of a ton of food and supplies had to be shipped for every man in America, and that did not include the weight of the barrels and casks in which they were stored. By 1782, 29,000 tons (excluding packaging) was shipped to soldiers around the world.[30] When Lieutenant-General Clinton's troops left Philadelphia in 1778, his baggage train extended for 12 miles. Logistics had become a major factor in overseas warfare.

The responsibility for procuring and dispatching the provisions lay with the Victualling Board, but they relied on the commanders of the army and the navy to supply them with accurate returns of the number of mouths to feed. To be fair to the Admiralty, they did try to stay ahead of the perceived problem and wrote to Graves in July 1775 that 'as they [the Admiralty] do not think it safe to rely wholly upon the Contracts that have been made for supplying your Squadron with Provisions they will direct the Victualling Board to send out to you in due time a further supply of Provisions than those mentioned in my Letter of the 24th *Ultimo*'.[31] By 1781, the challenge facing the supply line had grown from 4,275 men to approximately 86,000 troops and 98,000 sailors. The records are replete with letters from army and navy commanders in America advising that they were running short of provisions and urgently required to be resupplied. However, these same officers were partly responsible for their situation; the details they sent to London were late and inaccurate so that the Victualling Board and Treasury were unsure how many mouths they were meant to feed. One example is a letter from John Robinson (at the Treasury) to General Howe, 1 May 1776:

> Much of the Distress and most of the Difficulties which you have experienced at Boston from a scantiness of provisions have been occasioned by contrary winds and the tempestuous season [but] *very great inconveniences have arose* [sic] *from the want of constant and regular Returns of the Numbers of persons victualled and the number of the Rations actually drawn* [my emphasis].[32]

In 1779, the Secretary at War (Charles Jenkinson) had to point out to General Clinton that the inaccurate returns from America meant that he could not give to Parliament 'that accurate information [...] which is from time to time expected

---

30   Mackesy, *America*, p.66.
31   NDAR, Vol.1, p.1318, letter from Stephens to Graves, 6 July 1775.
32   TNA, T 64/106.

and required of me'.[33] How hard can it be, one might ask, to know how many troops and sailors are under the Commander-in-Chief? Would that it were that simple. The nature of the war in America was one of civil war, and that meant that among the colonists were those who were still loyal to the Crown, and so sought the protection of the army. Additionally, the British enlisted the help of some of the native Indian tribes, but the mouths to be fed also included the women and children who were attached to the British regiments, as well as American prisoners of war. Much of the confusion between America and London arose from the number of 'additional' mouths to feed. The army at that time allowed a percentage of the men to take wives with them when they travelled abroad; in July 1777, General Howe's army was accompanied by 652 women and children. The women were 'wives, common-law partners, and camp followers who acted as nurses, seamstresses, launderers, cooks and vendors'.[34] In January 1777, Wier detailed the number he was victualling at Philadelphia as 22,715 men, 2,394 women, 1,211 children, and 350 wagoners. The discrepancy grew as the war progressed and more and more women, Indians, Loyalists, refugees, and prisoners of war required feeding. In July 1778, Wier wrote from New York to say that he was expecting provisions to arrive for 36,000, but he was actually distributing 'at least 46,000 rations per day',[35] and by 1782, the army was feeding 28,169 mouths above its strength.[36]

Fundamental to the eighteenth century processes for victualling the army and the navy was the 'ration', the food to be provided each day to deliver the number of calories the men would require for hard physical labour. Janet Macdonald has calculated that the ration issued to the sailors provided 5,000 calories a day,[37] which was necessary for working and staying warm in the cold, wet conditions of a man-of-war. The 'menu' may have catered for the men's energy needs, but variety was not high on the list of priorities, and it remained the same as that issued during the Seven Years War, and then on through the conflict with Napoleon. Given the limitations of long-term storage, the primary focus was on foodstuffs that could be packaged and transported and would still be edible after a period of months. All of these points were conditions of the contracts drawn up between the Treasury, the Victualling Board, and the various contractors who would be supplying the provisions. The seven-day ration, listed in the table

33   Bowler, *Logistics*, p.247.
34   O'Shaughnessy, *Men Who Lost America*, p.107.
35   TNA, T 64/114, f.65.
36   Syrett, *Shipping and the American War*, p.172.
37   J. Macdonald, *Feeding Nelson's Navy: The True Story of Food at Sea in the Georgian era* (London: Chatham, 2004), p.10.

below, was for one man, and was the basis of the tenders on which contractors were asked to bid.

Table 5: One man's rations for seven days[38]

Sailor	Biscuit (lb)	Beer (gallon)	Beef (lb)	Pork (lb)	Pease (pint)	Oatmeal (pint)	Butter (ounces)	Cheese (ounces)
Sun	1	1		1	1/2			
Mon	1	1				1	2	4
Tues	1	1	2					
Wed	1	1			1/2	1	2	4
Thurs	1	1		1	1/2			
Fri	1	1			1/2	1	2	4
Sat	1	1	2					
Total	7	7	4	2	2	3	6	12
Soldier								
Weekly total	7		7 of beef or 4 of pork		3	Half pound	6 oz butter or 8 oz cheese	

Note: the soldier's ration is from Morriss.[39]

Although the ration was unvarying, there were times when certain items were unavailable and something else had to be substituted, or the men were due a payment in lieu, but that is beyond the scope of this account – those interested can find details in Macdonald. Soldiers were victualled according to a slightly different scale (see Table 5), but if they were 'living off the land' while on operations, then the food available would depend on that taken with them, and whatever they could source by foraging. However, when troops were transported on naval vessels their ration was reduced. Those in transit (soldiers, women, and children) were deemed not to require the same food intake as the sailors because they were not called on to do the same physical work. Soldiers were to be fed at two-thirds the rate of a sailor (the Victualling Board defined this as 'six soldiers are to have the same as four sailors'),[40] while women and children were rationed at one-half and

38 Macdonald, *Feeding Nelson's Navy*, p.10.
39 Morriss, *British Maritime Ascendancy*, Table 7.2, p.295.
40 Syrett, *Shipping and the American War*, p.188.

one-quarter, respectively.[41] The clerks at the Victualling Board were punctilious about not issuing full rations to soldiers in transit and refused to pass the accounts of those ships that did supply soldiers with the full ration.[42] However, there were exceptions to this rule. Where troops had had to fill in for sailors in working the ship – the vessel might not be fully manned, or there was sickness on board – then they might claim the full sailor's ration. In May 1775, the purser of the *Chatham* claimed that he should have his account credited as he had had to feed soldiers at full allowance as sickness had reduced the crew to the level where they could not man the ship; the credit was allowed.[43] Exceptions were also made where troops were about to go on operations and were expected to be fit and healthy to meet the enemy, or where the rest of the army was ashore, and to continue to keep those still on board on two-thirds ration would cause discontent.[44] The rules laid down by the Victualling Board were sufficiently strict that Lord Howe had to explain to Philip Stephens why he had deviated 'from the general Method of victualling the Troops in Transports' while they were off New York in 1777.[45]

Missing from the regular ration are any kind of vegetables, fruit, or fresh meat, all of which were essential to prevent the onset of scurvy. Individual ships' captains could take opportunities when near coastal towns to purchase, or take by force, supplies for their own needs, but army units needed much larger quantities. During the periods that the troops were confined to Boston or New York, they had to try to get the vegetables as best they could from local resources. Getting live animals for fresh meat was a big problem. Storeships were sent from England with live animals on board, but six weeks at sea took a heavy toll. In December 1775 'one ship that Sailed with 1400 Sheep has landed only 18',[46] while in January 1776 the captain of a transport wrote to the owners that 'but fourteen hogs [were] alive'[47] from his shipment. Another ship in the same convoy had started out with 130 sheep on board but only managed to bring in five, 'and all as thin as you could expect, and, as the sailors say, only fit for lanterns'. For fresh meat, the army had to rely on local purchase, or foraging.

To supply the army – and the navy – with the vast quantities of food, provisions, camp equipage, clothing, and ordnance needed for the war, the Treasury and the Navy Board needed processes and procedures for buying the items and conveying

41   O'Shaughnessy, *Men Who Lost America*, p.12.
42   Syrett, *Shipping and the American War*, p.188.
43   TNA, ADM 111/72.
44   TNA, ADM 1/487, ff.421–422.
45   NDAR, Vol.9, p.188, letter from Howe to Stephens, 29 June 1777.
46   NDAR, Vol.3, pp.212–213.
47   NDAR, Vol.3, pp.834–835.

them to the end user. The first step was to make the suppliers aware of the items needed and in what quantity, bids could then be considered and a supplier chosen.

By the time of the American War, there was a well-established network of agents and contractors who were used to doing business with the government agencies. Tenders needed to be promulgated a long time before the goods were needed, as the full procurement process was a long one. Once the tenders had been issued, contracts had to be let and, after checking the bought goods for quality, the provisions had to be transported to the port of departure for America. Frequently the items had to be loaded into a different transport ship before the convoy was assembled and then sent off on the six-week trip across the Atlantic.

The initial step in the supply line was the tender, which would be published in the newspapers read by the contracting community. Those wishing to bid were invited to send sealed bids to the department raising the tender and the lowest bid was normally the one accepted. On 31 March 1775, tenders were requested for the supply of '600 Quarters of English Wheat to be delivered in Three Weeks by Weekly Proportions'. Four merchants submitted bids, the most expensive was for 55 shillings and sixpence a quarter, the lowest – from John Milward – was 52 shillings and 10 pence (Milward's was accepted).[48] As well as tenders for specific commodities, as in the example above, tenders were also put out for quantities of rations, using the scale outlined in Table 5. These large contracts were often the subject of a number of meetings, rather than closed bids. On 31 January 1776, the Treasury met with one of the largest contractors (Nesbitt, Drummond, and Franks) to request a tender to supply the rations for 12,000 troops in America. In the meeting, the contractor proposed a price of 'five pence three farthings per ration, delivered in England or at Corke (sic) at such times as the Lords of the Treasury shall appoint'.[49] The price proposed, 5 3/4d, was to feed a man for one day, including delivery to the port from which it would leave for America. The contractor, conscious that the goods were going to a war zone, requested that the Treasury should take on 'all Risque and Charges after the Delivery'. At this point the contractors withdrew and the Treasury considered the offer with the result that they proposed carrying the provisions in armed ships, but the price would be only 'five pence farthing [5 1/4d]' for one ration. A second meeting was convened on 2 February 1776 at which the contractors agreed to deliver beef, pork, butter, and oatmeal to ships provided by the government, at Cork; flour, bread, pease, and rice would be delivered at London, Bristol, and Portsmouth at 5 1/4d. All provisions were to be 'good, wholesome and sound' and would be examined at these ports by 'such Person or Persons as this Board shall please to appoint' for the

---

48   TNA, ADM 111/72.
49   TNA, T 29/45, ff.27–31.

purpose of ensuring that they met the agreed quality. On 8 February, the terms were agreed. However, more than 12,000 troops had to be provided for and the Treasury used the contract with Nesbitt, Drummond, and Franks as the template for a number of smaller contractors who were called in on 9 February. All of them agreed to similar terms, which provided for the provisioning of a further 24,000 men in America, and 12,000 in Canada – a total of 48,000 men. The various boards that contracted for the provisions were aware that the condition of them on arrival in America depended on their original quality and the way they were packed. To take account of this, conditions were stipulated in the tenders:

> The beef to be of the first quality [...] and cut in pieces of seven pounds each. The pork of the first quality and cut in pieces of 4 lb each. The flour to be made from wholly kiln dried wheat of the first quality; the butter, cheese, rice and pease to be also of the first quality – the whole to be put up in strong sufficient and good packages and the beef and pork, in barrels and half barrels with four good iron hoops on each.[50]

Quality control of the food delivered to the troops and sailors was an ongoing bone of contention between the contractors and the end users, and will be covered in more detail later in the chapter.

Government contracts have always been open to exploitation by wily contractors, who were often more 'business aware' than the civil servants and clerks who had the job of administering them. There was corruption, but there was also a cat-and-mouse game of profiting by 'trying to get away with it', as exemplified by a survey carried out in July 1779 at New York. As well as some of the barrels of pease being found to be 'musty, mouldy & unfit for use', there were problems with the beef and pork, many of the barrels were 'old, rotten & stinking', and 'the best appears to have been often repacked in some apparent Frauds, having a mixture of very bad meat in the middle & covered over with that which was somewhat better & most of it thrown in without being regularly packed'.[51]

The long lead times on these contracts, as well as the physical distance between the receiving commissariat and the supplier, together with poor (or non-existent) headcount returns, led to obfuscation. Contractors often billed for more than the original contract. By December 1777, the Treasury had been overbilled the sum of £21,451 9s 7d by Nesbitt, Drummond, and Franks,[52] and the Treasury wanted this sum deducted from future contracts. In their defence, the contractor claimed

50   TNA, T 29/46, f.421.
51   TNA, T 64/114, f.194.
52   TNA, T 29/46, ff.403–405.

that 'since the month of October 1776' they had been subsisting prisoners of war in various parts of America, and that this accounted for £9,000 of the overbilling. The Treasury rebuttal was that as this was an arrangement between the contractors and General Howe, they would not authorise payment until they received a certificate from the general to confirm the arrangement. A letter from the Treasury to Howe and his Commissary General, Wier, instructed them that in future they must stick to formal contracts. Exchange rates also provided an opportunity for a little profit taking. The Treasury attempted to stop this by requiring certificates to be attached to invoices, counter-signed by 'two or three Emminent [sic] Merchants' that the goods were 'charged at the Market prices', that expenses were 'at the usual and Customary Rates', and that the exchange rate was the 'Current Exchange at the time'.[53] While the Navy Board had become accustomed to the complications and detail involved in these contracts from their experience in the Seven Years War, the Treasury quickly became overwhelmed by the issues, and desperately wanted the navy to take over the responsibilities involved in supplying the army in America. Once this was done, in 1779, the Navy Board 'succeeded in imposing a higher standard of contract performance and great efficiency in the reception and inspection of provisions'.[54]

For the troops in America, and the sailors at sea, the important points about the victualling chain were that the food was available in the amounts to which they were entitled, and that it should be fit to eat; the proof of the pudding was, quite literally, in the eating. There is no doubt that, judged against modern standards, the food was of a lower quality than we would consider putting before our soldiers and sailors. Without refrigeration and canning, the exporters had to rely on salting and pickling. Much of the meat was boiled before serving, butter was difficult to keep in hot climates, water was bad after long periods in wooden barrels and fresh food (vegetables as well as meat) was difficult to come by. With all those provisos, the authorities did try to ensure that the contractors supplied good quality products, on time, and with guarantees of 'shelf-life'. Quality control was taken seriously.

The agents who received the items from the contractors had the responsibility for assuring their quality before onward shipment to America. The problem for the Board's agents was that the produce was packed, either in barrels, boxes or sacks, and checks required these to be opened and examined. One consequence of detailed checking was the delay it caused in the onward shipment to the troops, which itself would cause problems in America. In 1780, the Navy Board agent in

53   TNA, ADM 111/73.
54   N. Baker, *Government and Contractors: The British Treasury and War Supplies, 1775–1783* (London: Athlone Press, 1971), p.241.

Cork, John Marsh, felt that it was necessary to open every barrel passing through his hands, resulting in his rejection of 2,928 barrels of pork. The knock-on effect was a delay in the shipment, as the contractors now had to source, package and deliver replacements for the rejected items.[55] While the agents had opportunities to take financial rewards from their positions – it was almost expected that they would do so – their 'middle man' role was a difficult one. Contractors, businessmen to the core, were not above trying to cheat the system, and one way was to include bones in the sealed barrels of beef and pork. In 1781 the Navy Board attempted to stop this practice by including in contracts the stipulation that 'the Pork be free from Heads and Feet and the Beef from Legs, shins and Marrow Bones'.[56]

In the same way that the Board's agent had to protect himself from inferior items delivered by the contractor, so the Commissary at the receiving end in America (Daniel Chamier) needed to ensure that he did not receive and pass on poor quality goods. In late 1776, Chamier complained of the 'badness of the bread' recently received in 13 victuallers from England. Gordon, as the agent in Cork, was instructed by the Treasury to get a grip and to acquaint the Treasury 'how he came to receive Bread of an inferior quality' and to take measures to mark the packaging 'in order to distinguish and show from whence each package was received; that the defects may be ascertained and that it may be known under whose contracts such defects arose'.[57] However, the ball could bounce both ways. Following the marking of the contractors' packaging, agents in America were reprimanded for complaining about the quality of any provisions they received, while failing to make reference to the marks on the packaging, as required by the 'survey' procedures. The survey had been a standard naval procedure from at least the Seven Years War: if casks were opened aboard ship, and the contents found to be short measure or of poor quality, then a survey was held. This was conducted by a panel of ship's officers and if products were condemned, a report was sent back to the Admiralty and the ship's purser would have his account credited for those goods.[58] It was this process that was used by the commissary agents in America for quality control of the food delivered to the army. The survey was also relevant to troops in transit, as their mess food came from the same barrels as those which fed the ship's crew; they may have been on 2/3 allowance, but they expected to receive what they were entitled to. There are numerous examples in the ships' logs of these surveys.

55   Bowler, *Logistics*, p.105.
56   Baker, *Contractors*, p.109.
57   TNA, T 29/46, f.66.
58   Rodger, *Wooden World*, p.84.

HMS *Otter*, 20 April 1776, they had bought pork from a local agent: 'Opened a Cask of Pork, contents 110 pieces, short 6 pieces'.[59]

HMS *Glasgow*, 31 October 1775, 'Condemn'd and hove overboard, Bread Fifteen hundred and twenty three pounds'.[60]

Although the Commissary General in America was admonished for failing to indicate the contractor's mark on defective goods, the navy pursers – who were closer to the crews than the army agent was to the troops – made sure they included it: 'Ship's log, HMS *Richmond*, 5 January 1778: 'Opend [*sic*] a Cask of Beef *No. 2269* Con[tain]s, 180 Sh[or]t.6 [my italics on cask number]'.[61]

While shortages in casks aboard ship might look relatively small, poor quality victuals in the quantities shipped to feed an army could be very significant. In an attempt to cut the amount of bread that was considered bad on arrival in America, the Treasury tried sending ship's biscuit (as used by the navy). In the first delivery of 379,512 pounds, 285,984 were condemned by Chamier as 'Indifferent in quality' and 'mouldy in the heart'.[62] In April 1777, General Howe commented that 'The bad quality of the Bread and Flour is too generally complained of'.[63] There is no doubt that there were many complaints regarding the quality of the food delivered to the army in America, but it should also be borne in mind that the agents receiving the goods had a vested interest in complaining, if only to ensure that they were not held to blame for the quality. Daniel Chamier was court martialled for 'groundless complaints' regarding bread and flour, but was acquitted; the fault was deemed not to be his but was 'owing to a very great neglect on the other side of the water'.[64]

The food provided to the navy has received a good deal of criticism from historians and novelists, but was it really that bad, or was Rodger closer to the truth with his comment that in comparison to that eaten by the poor in Britain the sailor's diet was 'good and plentiful?' The quantities condemned by survey indicate that the majority was fit for purpose and, as Rodger points out, 'The officers had no interest in concealing any deficiency, and the purser had some interest in exaggerating it'.[65] Because the items in the weekly diet – and the means by which they were sourced, packed, and transported – were the same in the American War

---

59   NDAR, Vol.4, p.1209.
60   NDAR, Vol.2, p.860.
61   NDAR, Vol.11, p.43.
62   Bowler, *Logistics*, p.100.
63   TNA, T 64/108, f. 104.
64   TNA, T 64/108.
65   Rodger, *Wooden World*, p.84.

as in the Seven Years War, comparisons of the quality of the food between those two periods are valid.

For the years 1778–1780, the Victualling Board produced a report for the House of Commons on the condemnation rate of bread; condemnation was classified as 'thrown overboard, returned into store, or condemned in the stores and storeships'.[66] The average for those years was 1.7%, somewhat higher than the 0.3% of 1749– 1757. Morriss suggested that this higher rate may have been a result of food being kept for longer – the time to collect and ship the provisions to America – or was subject to more damaging conditions of storage and transportation. Morriss's point has merit. In the case of beer, the difference between the two periods was larger, but Morris's comment on storage and transportation may well be equally valid. In the period 1749–1757, the condemnation rate was 1% (one tun in 103), while between 1777 and 1781, the beer brewed in Portsmouth (twice the volume of that from London) averaged around three percent, or one tun in 37. The long period of storage and transportation would appear to have had a detrimental effect on the victuals, which, given the packaging technology, is not really surprising. One of the unintended consequences of the war was a drying up of the supply of wooden staves from America. It is difficult to overemphasise the importance of wooden barrels for the transportation and storage of food. For storage barrels, the coopers needed staves, particularly the high quality oak and beech products from Virginia. The significance of the staves to the British was recognised by the colonists. At the Continental Congress in April 1776, the inhabitants of the 'thirteen United Colonies' were to be allowed to export goods, wares and merchandise 'except staves and empty casks'.[67] The trade (before it was stopped) was huge, with most vessels travelling between America and Britain carry thousands of staves. On 5 May 1775, notice was given for contractors to tender for 260,000 to be delivered to London, Portsmouth and Plymouth; 170,000[68] of them were for London and the victualling wharfs on the Thames. Without well-made barrels, the provisions stored in them would deteriorate and leak. The Baltic was a possible alternative source, but their importation was subject to import duties. The contractors petitioned the Treasury for a reduction in the duty, but this was refused by the Commissioners of Customs.[69] Not all government departments placed the same priority on winning the American War. The Customs officials would be equally unbending over duty on imported rum for the army and navy.

---

66   Morriss, *British Maritime Ascendancy*, p.307.
67   NDAR, Vol.4, p.683.
68   TNA, ADM 111/72.
69   Baker, *Contractors*, p.118.

When the provisions finally arrived in America, frequently some months after the original tenders were promulgated, the Commissary General then had to receive, store, and distribute them to the troops. The following table gives some idea of the quantities involved for the provisioning of 40,000 men for 12 months.

Table 6: Provisions for 40,000 men for 12 months[70]

Item	Quantity
Flour	14,560,000 lb
Pork	7,280,000 lb
Beef	1,820,000 lb
Butter	780,000 lb
Oatmeal	1,040,000 lb
Pease	97,500 bushels

Before the war started, the army in America was only a few regiments strong and there was no infrastructure in place for handling provisions on this scale – and that excluded clothing, camp equipment, and ordnance. Once the provisions arrived from Britain, where could they be stored? At New York, by the latter stages of the war, the army was using up to 40 warehouses, as well as storeships in the harbour. This lack of adequate storage was particularly acute in 1778 when Wier stated that they had to pile provisions 'in the open fields without cover', and where the fidelity of the sentries placed to guard them 'might be often times called in question'.[71] The issue of the use of ships as warehouses was a thorny one between London and the agents in America. The storeships were often the transport vessels in which the provisions had arrived from Britain. To maintain the supply chain, the Boards in London relied on commanders in America sending these ships back after they had been unloaded. However, because of the shortage of warehousing, and a natural inclination to hold on to what they had, many of these ships remained in America, to the exasperation of London. In 1780, the Navy Board informed the Treasury that none of the victuallers that had gone to America the previous year had returned to Britain.[72]

For an army to operate effectively, especially a long way from its home bases and on land where it has only limited control, it needs more than just food. One item was money, hard cash – or 'specie', as it was termed. The soldiers, many of whom

70   Baker, *Contractors*, p.23.
71   TNA, T 64/114, f.3.
72   Syrett, *Shipping and the American War*, p.163.

were foreign troops in British employ, needed paying, as did any contractors in America who could be persuaded to supply the army. In Loyalist areas, many did, and they preferred to have British coin to Continental paper money. The request for money to cover the army's needs came from the office of the Commander-in-Chief and was handled by Harley and Drummond, agents on behalf of the Treasury. The requests were submitted to the agents in America, who issued the cash and then submitted the requisition to Harley and Drummond who, for a commission of 1.5%, were then reimbursed by the Treasury. The cash was sent to America in naval vessels 'made available by the Admiralty on specific request from the Treasury'.[73] The captains of these ships could also receive a small allowance for carrying the specie. On 12 August 1777 the Treasury issued instructions for £100,000 to be sent to America – £50,000 on the *Fowey*, and £25,000 each on the *Grampus* and *Tortoise*. British ships carrying cash were a valuable prize for American privateers, so cargoes of specie needed insurance. In the case of the *Tortoise*, it was inadequately covered and Harley and Drummond suggested that its share should be carried in the *Grampus*, keeping the insurance rate to one percent.[74] From 1770–1783 more than £17 million was moved to America.

While food and drink are the obvious items needed by an army abroad, they also needed tents when on operations (or where there were no suitable barracks), clothing, and all the paraphernalia of soldiers in the field. Every unit in the army needed a new issue of clothing every year – 20 tons for an average regiment. In 1779, the War Office calculated that the troops in America needed 443 tons of clothing, with an extra 223 tons for those in Canada.[75] As well as tents to sleep in, the soldiers needed blankets to keep warm; 52,000 were ordered in 1776 with an ongoing requirement for 10,000 a year after that.[76] Because of a shortage of barrack accommodation, many soldiers lived on the transports that had been held back in America, and they needed beds; 20,000 were ordered in June 1777 and were 'much wanted for the use of the Soldiers on board the Transports'.[77] Before the outbreak of hostilities, many of the following items might have been sourced locally in the thirteen colonies, and no doubt many American traders rued the loss of trade. In December 1778, orders were placed for '12,000 tents, each to accommodate five private soldiers, 30,500 pairs of mittens, 61,000 pairs of shoes, 61,000 pairs of shoe soles, 30,500 pairs of leggings, linen and thread for 61,000 shirts, 12,000

73   Baker, *Contractors*, p.177.
74   TNA, T 29/46, f..323.
75   Syrett, *Shipping and the American War*, p.215.
76   Bowler, *Logistics*, p.16.
77   NDAR, Vol.9, p.397.

haversacks, 12,000 canteens, 3,000 camp kettles, 3,000 hand hatchets and 1,200 wood axes'.[78]

In April 1780, the transport ship *William and Elizabeth* carried 463 tons of equipment for General Clinton's army. A breakdown of the cargo is given in the following table.

Table 7: Cargo of the *William and Elizabeth*[79]

Item	Quantity
Private tents with poles, pins, etc.	4,875
Bell tents with poles, pins, etc.	392
Drum cases	520
Powder bags	266
Hatchets	4,922
Kettles and bags	4,892
Canteens	22,588
Haversacks	22,420

Washington's army needed supplies as much as the British but they did not have an established supply chain behind them. For the Continental troops, one solution was for their 'navy' – largely privateers like the renowned John Paul Jones – to capture British storeships on their way to America. Many ships were taken and two of the most significant were the *Nancy* (carrying ordnance) in 1775 and the *Mellish* in late 1776. Jones was a Scot 'with good maritime experience'[80] who had settled in Virginia. When the war started he secured a commission in the fledgling Continental Navy and became one of their 'most aggressive and single-minded' officers. On 13 November 1776,[81] Jones was captain of the American frigate *Alfred*, when he fell in with the *Mellish*, *en route* for Quebec with 12,000 uniforms for Burgoyne's army. Present at the capture of the *Mellish* was Lieutenant Trevet, of the Continental sloop *Providence*:

> She was [un]loaded, and all the clothing taken out and waggons prepared to send them on to Gen. Washington['s] army, at that time his army being in a distressed situation for clothing, and in this Ship was every article complete for a Soldier from the hat, to the shoes, and at that time

78   Baker, *Contractors,* p.210.
79   Morriss, *British Maritime Ascendancy,* p.517.
80   Willis, *Sea Power,* p.324.
81   NDAR, Vol.8, p.743.

I can say with pleasure I had rather taken her, than a Spanish Galleon with hard money, although we took Continental money for our parts of all the prizes.[82]

We should not ignore the morale effect that losses of this kind would have had on the British troops who had to persevere through a New York winter with tattered uniforms, knowing that the equipment they were waiting for was now benefiting their opponents.

The loss of the *Mellish* and her cargo was a wake-up call to those responsible for organising shipments to the troops. The ship had 20 soldiers on board, and was armed with six three-pounders and six swivel guns to protect her cargo, which was valued at 'upwards of £80,000 sterling'.[83] Although the *Mellish* had sailed with an escort, HMS *Richmond*, her loss demonstrated that similar shipments needed better protection in future. In May 1777, clothing was to be sent to eight regiments in Canada and the Admiralty were asked to provide a vessel of 'about one hundred sixty tons' and 'of sufficient force to defend herself against any Rebel Cruizer [*sic*] she may be expected to meet with in her voyage'.[84] The ship that was proposed was of 234 tons, had 12 4-pounders and two 6-pounders, with a crew of 16, but was considered 'insufficient for the security of so valuable freight'. The weight of the clothing alone was 160 tons and it was decided to use a ship armed with 16 6-pounders and 4 4-pounders, crewed by 40 seamen, but with an additional 50 troops on board as well as a naval officer 'to fight the ship in case of her being attacked'.[85] Britain may well have had the world's mightiest navy, but considerable resources had to be diverted to protect the army's supply line from the exploits of the Rebel privateers.

By 1778, the army's supply situation was becoming acute; the inaccurate returns from army commanders, the long and slow supply line, the inexperience of the Treasury in supplying an army so far from home, together with the entry of the French into the war and the activities of American privateers, all came together to cause severe problems for the troops. While the army never completely ran out of food, the stocks did run dangerously low (by December 1778 New York was down to two weeks' supply of flour) and were insufficient to build up the reserves necessary to allow the army to go on campaign. The commanders in America were not blameless for the situation as their poor returns and the holding back of transports in America only exacerbated the problem. At New York in October

---

82   NDAR, Vol.7, pp.329–330.
83   NDAR, Vol.7, p.807.
84   TNA, ADM 1/4133, f.134.
85   TNA, ADM 1/4133, f.156.

1778, there were 146 transports – 32 earmarked for an expedition to St Lucia, 42 unfit for work and to be sent home, and 72 in a state to be used.[86] As a result of this 'hoarding', the Treasury had to hire a complete cargo fleet of 22 ships. In mitigation, the army commanders needed to have some ships available to them for transporting any supplies they could take by local raiding and foraging expeditions, as well as for moving troops around such a large area of operations as Canada, America, and the West Indies.

The supply situation worsened during 1778. By October of that year, the letters of the Commissary General were sounding more and more desperate. Wier was pleading with the Treasury for a more rapid dispatch of the supply convoys as the victualling ships had 'lately arrived so long after one another, that the provisions of one fleet are expended before the arrival of the next and by that means we are never before hand'.[87] His letter of 21 December 1778 stated that he was distressed 'exceedingly' as they had only seven days' bread and flour and had had to give rice to the men on two days in lieu of the flour to eke out the supply – the troops did not like rice. The Treasury could have improved matters had they not adopted the position of assuming that any supplies sent were adequate for the number of mouths, that they were in a condition to be consumed, and that they had arrived safely, in spite of knowing about the activities of the American privateers. Bowler summed it up well: 'While the Treasury basked in a pedantic sense of righteousness fostered by 3,000 insulating miles of ocean, the army slid to the brink of disaster'.[88] It was not as though the Treasury was not trying; by January 1778, it had 72 victuallers and storeships in service (20,030 tons), besides 43 small oat ships (6,972 tons). The cost of shipping for the previous two years had been the enormous sum of £438,460. In spite of the efforts of the department, the army was inadequately supplied and something had to be done if the war was to be successfully prosecuted. Recognising their ineptitude, the Treasury appealed again to the Navy Board to take over the provisioning of the army, and this time the request was successful. However, the Navy Board started from a less than ideal position and General Clinton's supply situation through 1779 was never at the level that he would have liked. Even though six victualling convoys had arrived by September, he never had more than five months' supplies on hand – he wanted six to allow campaigning from a secure supply base. The first of the Navy Board fleets (29 ships) allowed him to amass provisions for seven months but,[89] even with the Navy Board in control, the situation deteriorated again during 1780.

86 Mackesy, *America*, p.234.
87 TNA, T 64/114, f.87.
88 Bowler, *Logistics*, p.121.
89 Bowler, *Logistics*, pp.124–125.

In an attempt to regularise the resupply of the army a system was introduced whereby transport vessels would make two voyages a year from Britain in two main convoys, the first to leave in late spring of each year, the second in late summer. For this to work, ships had to be sent back from America rather than being retained by local commanders, and therein lay the seeds of a problem that lasted through 1780. Effectively, the army – having its own transport requirements – was largely responsible for its shortages. However, it was not helped by the slowness with which ships in Britain were loaded, assembled, and dispatched. The second convoy of 1779 demonstrates the issue. The convoy was assembled in Cork in September 1779, but did not sail until 24 December, a bad time for the Atlantic. Severe weather caused the convoy to sail to the south and arrived in Charleston in early March 1780. Then 13 of the 28 ships remained in Charleston with only the remainder proceeding to Clinton in New York.[90] Against this background, it was impossible for the army to plan operations based on supplies from home. By November of 1780, the supply problems had been overcome and the army had nine months' worth of supplies on hand.

If the army was to suppress the rebellion and regain the colonies for the Crown, then it needed to be able to operate away from the seaports through which its supplies arrived, and here the navy could not help. Once the troops moved inland they required horse-drawn vehicles to provide supply transport, and these would not be easily sourced. In 1776, General Howe, in Halifax after the evacuation of Boston, requested London to send out forage by sea 'as no supplies can be depended upon to be gotten in America'.[91] Between 1776 and 1780, the army employed an average of 739 wagons, 1,958 horses, and 760 drivers. These convoys of wagons were vulnerable to attack by rebels – one in August 1780 lost 50 wagons and 250 prisoners[92] – and could extend over a number of miles. When Clinton marched his army overland from Philadelphia to New York in 1778 his baggage train 'extended near 12 miles' and he later described it as 'wantonly enormous' but they had to carry their own provisions 'as our march lay through a devoured country inimical almost to a man'.[93] Mention has already been made of the ways in which victualling contractors might 'bend the rules' to their own profit, and those who supplied horse transport were no less sharp on the uptake; unfortunately, some of them were army officers. The Quartermaster's Department needed to keep on hire an average of close to 700 four-horse wagons, complete with drivers who were paid for by the owners, at a daily rate of 12 shillings. However, a problem lay

90   Bowler, *Logistics*, p.132.
91   TNA, T 29/45, f.185.
92   Ferling, *Miracle*, p.457.
93   Black, *War for America*, p.157.

in the contract provisions which required the Quartermaster to have responsibility for 'the outfits, feeding the drivers and horses, keeping the horses shod and the wagons maintained, and replacing horses and wagons lost in service'. This contract was very profitable for the owners, and the Commissioners of Public Accounts calculated that an owner of 50 four-horse wagons would recoup his investment after five months 'and thereafter receive a clear income of £9,855 8s 4d *per annum*'. Quick to see the possibility to make money 'the wagons on hire were owned by army officers and three-quarters of them by the Quartermaster General himself and his two deputies'.[94] The practice was stopped in 1782.

This chapter has outlined some of the problems faced by the Navy Board, the Treasury and the army in America in trying to keep the troops supplied with food. Many of the issues also affected the sailors, but not to the same extent; they could always sail into a small seaport and indulge in a little local raiding to supplement their rations. The supply stemmed from the rapid increase in the size of the army stationed in America, the length of the supply chain, the poor administrative systems that meant that London was never sure how many men it was feeding and, most importantly, the lack of transport vessels because of their retention in America by the very troops they were trying to provide for. These problems did have an operational impact, and were one of the causes of the need to evacuate Boston in 1776. However, while soldiers and sailors did sometimes have to go on short rations, the army in America never reached the point where troops were starving.

---

94   R.A. Bowler, 'The American Revolution and British Army administration reform', *Journal of the Society for Army Historical Research*, 58:1980, p.71.

4

'On which the subsistence of the army immediately and entirely depends'

Once the British government had made the decision to send an army to quell the rebellion in the American colonies, it became dependent on the availability of transport ships, contracted from civilian merchants, for the supply of all the troops' requirements. The enormous tonnage of stores to be moved, in ships that – on average – could only carry between 100 and 300 tons each meant that large numbers were required; in July 1776, the Navy Board had 416 transports (amounting to 128,427 tons) under charter[1] and in 1778, the Treasury had 115.[2] One of the consequences of the Navy Board's refusal to take the responsibility for supplying the army from the Treasury, before 1779, was that these two boards competed against each other for the same ships, so driving up the rate paid. As the war progressed, the issue of the provision of transport ships became more critical to the success of the troops in America.

It is a truism to state that the role of the storeships and transports was to convey stores and men to the army, they were not warships in the same was as a British navy 'ship of the line', although they frequently carried a small number of guns in case they were attacked by American privateers. Although they did not have the charisma of a warship like the *Victory* and find little place in the histories of the war, their role was vital. The *Elephant* serves as a typical example of these workhorse vessels, many of them built at Whitby and Hull. She was similar to the Whitby collier that was converted to become Captain Cook's ship, *Endeavour*. In June 1776, the Admiralty directed the Navy Board to hire two ships of 300 tons each to carry stores to America. Failing to find any of that size for charter

---

1   D. Syrett, 'The fitting out of H.M. Storeship *Elephant*, July 1776', *Mariner's Mirror*, 74:1 (1988), p.67.
2   Morriss, *British Maritime Ascendancy*, p.366.

the Board did find a ship for sale, the *Union*; her name was changed to *Elephant* after she was bought. While ships were chartered at a rate per ton of cargo, so the *Union* was for sale at a price per ton. The owners wanted £9 per ton 'of the hull, masts, and yards. Stores and the like would be an additional cost'.[3] The Admiralty valued these items at only £6 7s 6d per ton but, such was the shortage of available ships, they paid the asking price. The original request had been for ships of 300 tons, but the *Elephant* was rated at 382 tons 'burthen'. Transport ships were rated, and charged for, according to the weight they were expected to carry, rather than the volume of the ship in cubic feet. However, the formula used by the navy's dockyard officers differed from that employed by the merchants and ship owners. The *Elephant* was only a shade over 102 feet long, 29 feet at the beam, and with only two decks and a hold, the latter being nearly 12 feet deep. Because of the risk posed to British transport vessels by Rebel privateers – John Paul Jones sailed as far as the British coast – the ship was armed with 10 4-pounder cannon and eight swivel guns, and manned by a crew of 40. The following table lists the crew roles and is probably typical of most of the small transports of that time.

Table 8: Crew of the storeship *Elephant*[4]

1 lieutenant (the commander)	1 carpenter
1 master	1 surgeon
1 midshipman	1 servant to the lieutenant
1 clerk and steward	1 servant to the master
1 boatswain	30 able seamen
1 gunner	

It should be no surprise that French and British diplomats spent a lot of their time trying to gauge the intentions of the other, and one way of doing that was to take note of the requests for agents and contractors to charter ships for the other's navy. The Admiralty's attempts to buy ships like the *Elephant* would have been transparent to any spies working for the French because the requirement to hire was promulgated in the local press. In March 1775, before the British had started to reinforce General Gage in America, Monsieur Garnier (a French diplomat in London) sent a report to the Count de Vergennes (the French foreign minister), of which the following is an extract.

---

3   Syrett, 'Storeship *Elephant*', p.67.
4   Syrett, 'Storeship *Elephant*', p.68.

If no changes occur between now and that time [May 1775], the entire forces bound for America will consist of 14,635 infantry men and 1200 marines under the orders of General Gage; also, 7 ships-of-the-line, 16 frigates, 18 corvettes, 7 schooners, with crews totalling 7,600 men. All these ships are assigned to the waters of Northern America as well as the waters of the West Indies. *The transport ships chartered by the Navy Department for the passage of 7 infantry regiments, 1 light Cavalry regiment and 700 marines under orders to go to America, form a total of 17,345 tons*[5] [my italics].

The previous chapter has pointed out the problem that the authorities in London had when trying to contract victualling and other supplies; in a similar way, the hiring of transport vessels had its own difficulties. Contracts for ships needed in the spring to transport troops had to be placed by the preceding December, but the results of recent operations were frequently unknown in London until after the contracts were let. If more troops were needed than the contracted ships could carry, there would be a delay in sending them, with consequences for planned operations. In 1776 Sandwich tried to make provision for these situations by keeping transport vessels on hand: 'The Navy Board have now 4000 tons of Transports unappropriated, and they are directed allways [*sic*] to keep that stock in hand to answer occasional demands'.[6]

The scale of the contracting was huge and ongoing. Every time a regiment had to be sent to America, ships needed hiring to move the men and their equipment. In March 1776, the British needed to move 8,200 men and 30 horses of the Hessian and Brunswick division; requiring 16 transports of 5,416 tons.[7] In April of that year, the *Juno* and *Blonde* escorted 20 transports and eight Ordnance storeships from Plymouth to Quebec with troops of the 21st Regiment.[8] In the same month, the *Carysfort* and *Pearl* escorted 40 transports from Cork to Quebec. The need was constant. Ever watchful of British shipping activity, Garnier sent a report to Vergennes in Paris, 8 May 1776, informing him that a fleet, which had left Portsmouth two days earlier with more reinforcements, was very large:

The fleet which transports them consists of 135 transport ships. It is convoyed by a ship of 50 guns called *Preston*, a hospital ship also of 50

---

5   NDAR, Vol.1, p.424.
6   NDAR, Vol.4, p.1137, letter from Sandwich to the King, 23 May 1776.
7   NDAR, Vol.4, p.1004.
8   NDAR, Vol.4, p.1050.

guns called *Jersey*, the Frigate *Rainbow* of 44 guns and the *Emerald* of 32, and two fire-ships.[9]

To the modern reader, the sizes of the fleets crossing the Atlantic seem almost unbelievable, our current navy being so small. Writing in August 1776 Ambrose Serle, who had just completed a 14 week crossing from England to Sandy Hook with Admiral Hotham's fleet 'to the number of 107 sail', stated that these and their 92 transports made a sight to gladden British eyes but not so for the rebels who 'flocked out of their lurking Holes to see a Picture, by no means agreeable to them'.[10] The safe arrival of large convoys would have been the occasion for a celebration. On 14 August 1776, following the arrival of the ships carrying Serle, there was a 'great formal dinner' on board the flagship, *Eagle*. All the senior officers (and Serle) were in attendance, 'to the number of 34 Persons'. They all expressed great Satisfaction at their Entertainment, which indeed was worthy of the truly noble Personage who gave it'.[11] At anchor in New York, while the worthies were at their dinner, were 20 warships – from the *Eagle* at 64 guns, to the *Syren* with 28: 'The whole Fleet consists of about 350 Sail. Such a Fleet was never seen together in America before'. The naval support of the British army in America was on an enormous scale.

The supply of transport ships was not inexhaustible, and this was causing big problems. For the Navy and Treasury Boards, competing against each other, the problem was sourcing sufficient ships at a reasonable price. For the army in America, the problem was that provisions were not arriving in the quantities and timescales that the commanders required – on top of which they needed vessels to move troops from one operational area to another. In spite of the frequent reminders from London that transports must be returned after unloading, the army had to retain some flexibility of movement, as well as providing makeshift warehouse facilities for the volume of stores they needed to have on hand. The simple solution for the army was to retain transport ships in local ports but to counter this Rear-Admiral Shuldham, in February 1776, was directed by the Admiralty to have command of all transports in America. This control by the navy commander was contested by Generals Howe and Clinton, but it remained with the navy throughout the war.

The availability of transports was a constant problem for the army commanders, and it is difficult not to have sympathy for them. Provisions were essential if the army was to be capable of fighting, but six months' supply requires a large volume

9   NDAR, Vol.4, p.1109.
10   NDAR, Vol.6, pp.155–156.
11   NDAR, Vol.6, p.214.

of storage space. New York, a principal port for the British after they had left Boston, had lost many of its warehouses to arson and ships had to be used in their place: 'the want of storehouses well situated for security from the Treachery of Villains in the Town' had made this necessary.[12] Admiral Howe, who saw his role as one of supporting his brother, General William Howe, reported in October 1776 that there were 72 transports (with a tonnage of 20,335) 'at New York in good condition in every Respect to remain in North America'.[13] Their retention would have given flexibility of movement to his brother's troops, but would have caused a headache in London among those responsible for sending army victuals. By 1780, the problem had become so acute that it could not be fixed by simply offering the contractors more money. The victualling transports sent to New York and Georgia in 1779 had not returned by June 1780, although they were needed for the 'second embarkation for New York' – London was trying to send two large convoys a year. As a result of 'transports amounting to above 9000 tons' being retained in New York the Boards could not hire more vessels and no premiums were sufficient 'to induce the Owners of Ships to make up the Deficiency'.[14] By October 1780, the Navy Board, their exasperation obvious, resolved to

Represent to the Admiralty the necessity of their Lordships interfering [with] their authority with the officers commanding abroad not to detain more transports for the use of the army than are absolutely necessary, nor to direct storeships or victuallers to any other purposes than those for which they are sent out, and to furnish convoys with them to Europe as soon as they are cleared, and request their Lordships to procure instructions of a similar nature to be given to the Commanders in Chief of the Army. Send a copy to the Treasury and desire their Lordships assistance in procuring & giving such directions as may be requisite to produce the speedy return of the ships from abroad that we may thereby be furnished with a proper succession to carry on the service, without which we cannot be answerable for the consequences. Acq[aint] the several agents [for transports] abroad herewith and direct them to be particularly attentive to apply in time for convoy for transports under orders to return to Europe [and] to keep no more than are absolutely necessary, but to return them by every opportunity.[15]

12   TNA, T 64/108, f.104.
13   TNA, ADM 1/488, ff.481–482.
14   TNA, T 64/200, f.113.
15   Syrett, *Shipping and the American War*, p.163.

The transport situation had reached such a pass that the surrender at Yorktown was almost fortuitous; to quote David Syrett, 'it was only the end of the war early in 1783 that saved the British forces abroad from a major provision crisis'.[16] The Navy Board, at the end of 1782, told the Treasury that 'If all the shipping in Europe was employ'd in the service of the Army they would not prove sufficient, under this kind of management'.[17] The Navy Board may have been exasperated by the critical situation and an ever diminishing fleet of transport vessels, but they could not afford to stop trying as the army depended upon them.

The contracting process typically began with a request to move troops, often in the King's name, as in the following example from Sandwich to Germain:

> Your Lordship having, in your Letter of the 21st August last, acquainted us that as the Issue of the present Campaign in North America cannot be known here in time to prepare for the Operations of another, if another shall become necessary, His Majesty had come to the Resolution of making every preparation for the further Prosecution of the War that depends upon this Country, so early that in case the Rebellion is not subdued this Campaign, the next may open the Moment the Season will admit, and Your Lordship having, in your aforesaid Letter, signified His Majesty's Pleasure, that we do give the necessary Orders for providing Ships of sufficient Strength to defend themselves against any of the Rebel Cruizers, for the Conveyance of 3,000 Tons of Tents, Camp Equipage & other Stores to North America, to be in readiness to receive the same by the End of December, it being His Majesty's express Commands that the whole should be assembled at Spithead in readiness to sail from thence, under the Convoy of such of His Majesty's Ships as we shall think proper to appoint, on the 1st Day of Febry [sic];We are to desire you will be pleased to acquaint His Majesty, that the Navy Board have, in Obedience to Directions we gave them, in pursuance of His Majesty's Commands aforementioned, acquainted us that they have purchased six Ships whose Names are in the Margin, to perform this Service, which Ships are Armed with 26 Guns and will be provided with a Complement of 160 Men each. We are further to inform His Majesty that the *Nabob* one of the aforementioned Ships is arrived at Longreach and ready to receive such part of the aforementioned Camp Equipage & Stores as may be thought fit to be sent on board; that the rest are equipping with all possible Expedition in order to proceed thither also, and that so soon as

16   Syrett, *Shipping and the American War*, p.165.
17   Syrett, *Shipping and the American War*, p.180.

they are arrived there, we shall not fail to give Your Lordship immediate notice thereof.[18]

The opening sentence of the order reinforces a point made previously: that London was making decisions on requirements while in ignorance of the success (or otherwise) of recent military operations in America.

In the early months of the rebellion, when it was assumed that it would be a short war, contractors took on the risks involved in transporting goods and troops, but as it became obvious that the period of hostilities would be protracted, so the government found that they had to assume the risk involved. Transports had to be armed or escorted, contractors wanted compensation for loss or damage to their ships and even for 'wear and tear'. Following the surrender at Yorktown, 32 victuallers were lost to the Americans, the owners received immediate partial compensation, and the balance to be paid after the ships' accounts had been certified.[19] For their part, owners had to prove that any loss was not as a consequence of actions by the ship's master, such as leaving the convoy to sail on his own, a common occurrence. In November 1775, Captain Talbot of the *Niger* complained of ships, which had left his convoy 'intentionally'. The Navy Board ordered that the freight bills for these ships were not to be made out 'till the matter of leaving their Convoy is cleared up'.[20] Storeships were hired on the basis of 'tons burthen' (as in the case of the *Elephant*), but those to carry troops were contracted on a formula of tons per person. In addition, as the 'freight' was human, provision had to be made for accommodation and food. The usual formula for the hire of vessels was two tons for a soldier, with one and a half ton for each woman carried.[21] Allocating a tonnage per person might seem strange, but it could be related directly to the size of the vessel and the space available per person. The figure could be decreased for shorter journeys as in the case of the transport of the 6th Regiment from St Vincent in the West Indies to North America; on this occasion the rate for each soldier was one and a half tons.[22] Baggage was accounted for separately and in the case of the 6th Regiment, 90 tons was allocated.

In December 1776, a contract was raised in the West Indies for the transport of parts of the 8th and 47th Regiments from Montserrat to North America, which serves as an example of the many that were raised during the war and demonstrates that the accommodation and victualling of the troops was part of the contract. The contractors (Dover, Taylor, and Bell of St John, Antigua) were asked to supply

18   NDAR, Vol.10, p.1046, letter from Sandwich to Germain, 29 November 1777.
19   Syrett, *Shipping and the American War*, p.84.
20   TNA, ADM 111/73.
21   TNA, ADM 111/73.
22   NDAR, Vol.4, p.978.

a vessel of 200 tons, 'mounting Fourteen Carriage Guns, & Twelve Swivels: Navigated by Twenty five Men'. The ship, the *Lord North*, was to be loaded with 'all such Soldiers, Women Arms Ammunition, Provisions and Stores' as necessary. The contract went on to detail arrangements for accommodation and victualling:

> During the Continuance of the Troops on board the ship *Lord North*, It is declared and Agreed that the Officers shall be accomodated [*sic*] with the Great Cabbin [*sic*] and other Cabbins of the Ship except a Proper Cabbin for the Master and A small one for the Mate, and that the Gunroom Forecastle and Steerage or Such part thereof as shall be necessary be reserved for Lodging the Seamen. The Troops are to be provided at the Cost and Charge of the Owners with Coppers or Furnaces Sufficient and Necessary for the Boiling and dressing their Provisions, and also with Cans and Pumps for serving them with Water &ca, in their Voyage as well as with, Platters Spoons Candles and Lanthorns [*sic*]. They are to be Victualled at Navy Two Thirds Allowance, from the Kings Provisions put on board with them from the *King George* Transport; and to be Provided with Water Casks and Hammacoes [hammocks], at the Expence of His Majesty; For which Provisions, Water Casks and Hammacoes, the Master of the Ship *Lord North* is to give Proper Receipts, and duly to Account for the Expenditure of the Same at the end of His Voyage, and he is to return into his Majesty's Stores at New York all the Kings Provisions that are remaining on board at the Time he shall Land the Said Troops at New York; and also the Water Casks and Hammacoes, for all which he is to take proper Receipts, and also a Certificate from the Commanding Officer of the Kings Forces of His Having Performed the Conditions of this Contract.[23]

Provided that they carried out their end of the bargain, and against a penalty of £500 for noncompliance, the contractors 'shall be allowed and Paid, the Sum of Four Pounds Sterling for each Person, belonging to the Kings Troops taken on board the Said Ship *Lord North*'; the money would be paid after the contractors had produced the 'Accounts Receipts & Certificates'. As was normal, the payment would be 'in Course of the Navy, and if not paid in Six Months then to be allowed Interest as usual'. As detailed in Chapter 2, the payment of the Navy Bills 'in course' meant at a future date, but the Bills were a tradable commodity, which the contractor could either keep or sell on at a discount.

23   NDAR, Vol.7, pp.391–392.

Although the market for transport ships was tightening as the various boards took up the available vessels, the Navy Board wanted to ensure that those it took on contract were fit for purpose. When a price was agreed with the owner, it was 'subject to survey;' a process of inspection that took place at the naval dockyard at Deptford. When the vessel arrived at the dock, it was 'surveyed by the master attendant, master shipwright and clerk of the survey at Deptford yard, and [...] hired and freighted on their report'.[24] The Deptford team carried out extensive inspections of the timbers, planking, masts, yards and rigging. In one example from 1775, the *Liberty* had several pieces cut out of her side to examine the timbers, which were found to be 'very much decayed, and the ship in general, in those parts damp and defective'.[25] The Treasury, which until 1779 was doing its own hiring of ships through its agents, had no expertise in surveying and so chartered vessels 'without inspection or supervision',[26] and at a higher price than the more competent Navy Board. The third board in the market for ships, the Ordnance Board, rarely had trouble hiring vessels as it 'paid top money for ships'. They were able to do this because their need was much smaller than the Navy Board's. In the period from 1776 to 1782 the Navy Board had an average of 322.5 ships per year under charter, while the Ordnance had an average of only 25, and chartered only a total of 110 during the entire war.[27]

As vital as the transport ships were to the supply and maintenance of the army in America, the Navy and Treasury Boards in London were conscious of the costs involved, and the need to control them. The competition between the Boards was unhelpful, but a definite advantage to the ship owners. The rate at which ships were chartered was expressed in pounds sterling per ton per calendar month, and during 1775, when the war started, this had stood at 10 shillings. During 1776, with the increasing competition between the Boards, the rate moved up to 11 shillings and then 12 shillings and sixpence by the middle of 1776 – the Ordnance Board regularly paid one shilling per ton more than the others did. In 1777 the Treasury instructed their agents (Mure, Son, & Atkinson) to reduce the rate they were paying to 11 shillings, only to be told that 'a reduction of the freight cannot at present be made to 11 Shillings per ton without great hazard and perhaps disappointment to the service'.[28] One of the concerns for the Treasury was that the increase in freight rates caused by the war would draw ships away from the commercial trade, so affecting the British economy. As well as paying a higher rate

24   Syrett, *Shipping and the American War*, p.108.
25   Syrett, *Shipping and the American War*, p.109.
26   Mackesy, *America*, p.67.
27   D. Syrett, 'The procurement of shipping by the Board of Ordnance during the American War, 1775–1782', *Mariner's Mirror*, 81:4 (1995), p.411.
28   TNA, T 29/46, f.231.

per ton than the other boards, the Ordnance paid for its charters in cash for two months of every four it had on contract, with the balance settled in Navy bills to be paid 'in course'. This 'cash in hand' was a real inducement to the ship owners and a definite trading advantage over the other two boards who paid only with Navy Bills. An alternative to hiring ships from British owners was to go abroad, and this did have one advantage, as Sandwich pointed out to the King in February 1776:

> The Navy board are directed to send an Agent to Holland as well as to Hamburgh, as we have reason to believe that many transports may be got there; and we flatter ourselves that as soon as it is known that we are determined to deal with foreigners, we shall get the better of the combinations among the owners of Ships at home.[29]

The First Lord hoped that foreign competition would put a dampener on the rates charged by British shipowners.

Freight rates might not stir the blood of the military historian, but they were important. Between October 1775 and July 1777, the cost of contracting transports amounted to £1,132,034, of which £409,600 was still outstanding on Navy Bills.[30] By 1 February 1780, the value of navy bills in circulation had risen to £4,051,268 of which £950,571 was spent on transport.[31] In other words, transport costs totalled 23% of the navy bills in circulation. The increase in the value of the bills was a concern for the Navy Board as it risked affecting the credit of their 'public debt system'. With transport accounting for such a large percentage of the outstanding bills, any increase in freight rates from 10 to 11 and then 12 shillings per ton would result in a large increase in that debt.

> If the freight rate of ships in the transport service was increased too much, the number of navy bills in circulation would rise steeply There would then be a corresponding increase in the rate of discount, and the credit of the Navy would as a result be jeopardized. Thus, the Board could not go into the open market when it needed shipping and offer any freight rate necessary to procure the tonnage required.[32]

The delays in providing the required supplies to the army, and the consequent impact on land operations in America, were partially caused by the seemingly inconsequential price rise of a shilling per ton on freight rates. Some ship brokers

---

29   NDAR, Vol.4, p.923, letter from Sandwich to the King, 20 February 1776.
30   NDAR, Vol.9, p.679.
31   Syrett, *Shipping and the American War*, p.89.
32   Syrett, *Shipping and the American War*, p.90.

attempted to drive up the cost by playing the Navy Board off against the Treasury. In the early months of the war, at Liverpool, only two ships were available because the freight rate could not compete with the profits available from the Greenland fishery and the slave trade.[33] The King's wish to see the American colonies back under British control was not given the same priority by those who made their profits from the hiring out of ships.

Once the ships had been contracted and loaded, they had to be sailed safely to their destination in North America or the West Indies. In the age of sail, privateers, weather and limited navigation presented enormous problems for the masters of the transport vessels, and the financial risks fell largely on the government; risks that had to be mitigated. American privateers were a threat to British ships throughout the war and the loss of the *Nancy* Ordnance ship, together with the stores and equipment on the *Mellish* (mentioned in Chapter 3) had shown that not only were they blows to the British, but a great boon to Washington's soldiers. The protection of supplies in transit was made more difficult by three boards being involved in the contracting of transport vessels with the result that 'there were at least three different and uncoordinated policies for protecting ships carrying military supplies to America'.[34] As a result, different approaches were tried.

Convoys were to be an essential part of the supply chain, but arguments went to and fro over other proposals, some of which were adopted. On 21 August 1778 Lord Townshend (Master General of Ordnance) wrote to Germain to give it as his opinion that 'the best method of transporting the most essential & interesting Stores to the Army & Navy upon the American Station, is by conveying them in 40 Gun-Ships' but if it 'shall *not* be judged expedient that these Ordnance Stores should be conveyed by Men of War' [my emphasis], then he wanted 'the Ordnance to hire or build Ships of greater force, than seems at present to be understood to be within this Department'.[35] The Admiralty's response to Germain regarding Townshend's proposal to use 40-gun ships was not favourable:

> We are to acquaint Your Lordship, for His Majesty's Information, that all His Majesty's Ships of forty Guns are now employed in America, except the *Launceston* which is condemned & can never go to Sea. That if His Majesty had more Forty Gun Ships, or other Frigates, than what are now employed, they would all be wanted for the Protection of the various Branches of Trade, and for carrying on the American War; which, by

33   Syrett, *Shipping and the American War*, p.91.
34   D. Syrett, 'Lord George Germain and the protection of military storeships 1775–1778', *Mariner's Mirror*, 60:4 (1974), p.396.
35   NDAR, Vol.6, p.558, letter from Townshend to Germain, 21 August 1778.

what now appears to us, requires as many Frigates as the late War with France & Spain. That if Men of War were fit to carry out Stores of any kind, they would of course be employed in our own Department for that Purpose, for Provisions & Stores; but as this Method is not practiced by us, from our Knowledge that it would be perverting them from their proper use as Ships of War; we must, in the strongest manner, represent to His Majesty against their being employed in any other Department.[36]

Two of the main strategies employed to protect the supply vessels were to arm them, or to send them in convoys or sometimes to do both. Ships could be armed with 4 or 6 pounder guns, as well as a number of swivel guns, but they could also carry a number of troops to deter privateers. Carrying the troops on board would also ensure a steady stream of recruits to America and it became 'common practice throughout the war'.[37] Throughout the conflict, the different boards tried different methods of protection; was it better to have armed transports sailing alone, or should they be protected by warships; should ordnance be carried on ships of the line, or were convoys the answer? All were tried, with varying degrees of success. At the start of the war, the Treasury had the least understanding of the problems involved in transporting supplies to America. They had a simple answer, use their agents on a normal peacetime, commercial basis. In the autumn of 1775, they contracted the agents (Mure, Son, & Atkinson) to send provisions for the garrison in Boston. Thirty-five ships were assembled and were to be escorted by HMS *Flora*, 36 guns. The convoy was a disaster. Only eight of the ships reached Boston: 'the remaining twenty-seven vessels were either captured or driven by the weather to the West Indies'.[38]

By far the greater number of victualling transports travelled in convoy, usually escorted by one or more naval warship. Frequently convoys were held up in the departure port waiting for an escort to be assigned to them. Alternatively naval ships about to depart were instructed to take with them any transports waiting to leave. Assembling a convoy was a complicated task and was frequently subject to very long delays. In June 1779, the Admiralty were given notice of the need to provide escorts for a victualling convoy due to leave Cork, but it did not get away until 24 December 1779; on board were six months' rations, which should have been consumed in 1779. Even when they did get away, they faced some six weeks of Atlantic storms and eighteenth century navigation. As the problem of determining longitude had not yet been solved, the determination of position at

36   NDAR, Vol.6, p.574.
37   Syrett, 'Protection of military storeships', p.398.
38   Syrett, 'Protection of military storeships', p.397.

sea still had an element of uncertainty, as Captain Henry Duncan's entry in his journal for 7 July 1776 indicates. He had spoken with a whaling brig while at sea and

> She informed us of our being much farther to the eastward than we reckoned. We judged ourselves to be within a few leagues of Sandy Hook, but found by her that we were to the eastward of Nantucket Shoals [...] We came much nearer to the Nantucket Shoal than ships in general do, or than we intended.[39]

It is easy when reading of ships losing their way to forget how basic the navigation tools were. Captains of vessels were often having to use 'signs of nature' to bring their precious cargoes to port. Duncan gives us another example from his time with the *Medea*, 22 November 1780 and *en route* to America:

> This day we found ourselves considerably to the north-west, which makes me believe that we were in the Gulf Stream; saw some small white birds which made me believe that we were not far from soundings [able to 'sound' the bottom with a lead weight on a line]; in the evening sounded with 140 fathom of line; no ground. [On the following day] Saw some small straws and bits of broken bulrushes amongst the gulf-weed, which the master (an American) said was an indication of our being near soundings; but by my reckoning we are still 111 leagues from Sandy Hook.[40]

Three days later Duncan 'saw a gannet; they are said not to go far from soundings'. It was not until the afternoon of the 30th that they saw Sandy Hook – nine days after they believed they were 'not far from soundings'.

Duncan's two examples demonstrate the problems of accurate navigation in the years before accurate timepieces overcame the problem of determining a ship's longitude, but sea captains and masters also had to deal with the vagaries of the Atlantic weather systems. Convoys might leave port together, the storeships and transports escorted by British men of war, but that was no guarantee that they would remain in convoy for the voyage. In Sir Peter Parker's letter to the Admiralty, he outlines how many ships had already separated from his convoy. He stopped a passing brig and asked them to take his despatch to Stephens; the 38 vessels that left Cork some four weeks earlier had been reduced to only 15.

---

39 NRS, *Journals of Henry Duncan, 1776–1782* (London: Navy Records Society, 1901), p.117.
40 NRS, *Duncan*, pp.170–71.

I take this opportunity by the *Cleveland* Brig to inform their Lordships, that I sailed from Cork the 12th past [February 1776], with His Majesty's Ships *Bristol, Active, Actaeon, Solebay & Carcass* Bomb, her Tender, *Sibella* Storeship, seven Army victuallers, Three Ordnance Vessels & Twenty seven Transports – The *Sphynx* join'd us that Morning off the Harbour, and I sent her in to wait for the *Thunder* Bomb [...] That Night it blew fresh from the So[outh] W[es]t and the next Morning we missed Nine Sail, which I suppose put back to Cork; from that time 'til within these few Days, we have had Storms of Wind & contrary, and we are now only thirteen Sail in Company besides the *Bristol* & *Solebay*. The Frigates that have parted Company will no doubt make the best of their way to the Rendezvous off Cape Fear, and be ready to protect the Transports as they arrive, tho' I have not any apprehensions for them from the Rebels, so far to the Southward. All that are with us are in good health & no accident of any consequence has happened, excepting to the *Thetis* Victualler, who sprung a Leak & is gone into the nearest Port in Spain to stop it & to follow us as soon as possible.[41]

One of the passengers sailing with Commodore Parker in the *Bristol* was Major-General Charles Cornwallis, on his way to Boston with a reinforcement of troops. He took the opportunity of the meeting with the brig to send a letter to Germain, acquainting him with their progress, or lack thereof.

We have now but fourteen sail in Company with us, notwithstanding the utmost care & attention of Sr Peter Parker, & of the fourteen there are but six or seven transports with troops. I fear there is no chance of our arrival on the American coast before the end of next month at soonest, & the assembling the fleet off Cape Fear where there is no port may be a work of some time.[42]

Parker's letter to Stephens does not give the impression that the delays and separation of the convoy are other than normal for an Atlantic crossing. Both letters give some indication of the problems inherent in the eighteenth century sea journeys. Supplies and reinforcements might be requested and then agreed by London, but the weather and navigation (not to mention Rebel privateers) would determine if and when they got there. These were not the easiest conditions under which an army commander might make his operational plans.

41 NDAR, Vo.4, p.951, letter from Commodore Parker to Stephens, 7 March 1776.
42 NDAR, Vo.4, pp.951–952, letter from Cornwallis to Germain, 7 March 1776.

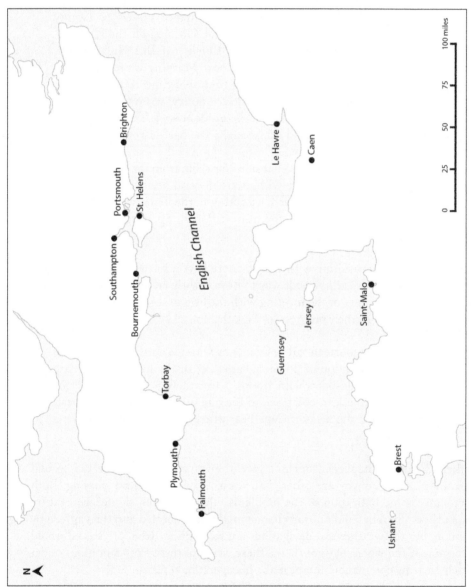

Map 2: The English Channel

While the majority of ships carrying troops and supplies to America did so as part of a 'convoy', that term had a specific connotation under British insurance law: the merchant ships had to be sailing under the escort of a naval force whose commanding officer had been given specific instructions from his superiors to undertake that convoy. When sailing from Britain that authority came from the Admiralty but when sailing from America they were authorised by the senior naval officer in that area, 'usually based upon instructions from the Admiralty'.[43] In November 1776 Captain Tyringham Howe, commanding HMS *Thames*, was given the following instructions by the Admiralty, before sailing from Spithead.

You are hereby required and directed to take under your command His Majesty's Storeship the *Elephant* (Lieut Bechinoe who commands her being directed to obey your Orders) & under your Convoy the several Store Ships & Victuallers mentioned on the otherside [sic] hereof & also any Navy Transports with Recruits for the Army under the Command of General Sir Wm Howe which may be ready to accompany you & then put to Sea with the very first opportunity of Wind & Weather and make the best of your way with them to New York; taking all possible care to keep the said Store Ships Victuallers and Transports together during the Voyage & to dispose of the *Elephant* Store Ship & also of the Ordnance Store Ships (which are Arm'd) in such manner as will best contribute to the protection of the others; And upon your Arrival at New York You are to put yourself & the *Elephant* Store Ship under the command of Vice Adml Lord Howe commander in chief of His Majesty's Ships & Vessel[s] in North America and follow his orders for your further proceedings And at the same time You are to deliver to his Lordship the Packets you will receive herewith directed for him. In case any of the abovementioned [sic] Store Ships shou'd not be arrived at Spithead when this reaches you, You are to wait their [sic] til their arrival and then use the utmost dispatch in proceeding as above directed; And in case there shou'd be any other Ships or Vessels at Spithead than those abovementioned which are bound to New York with Provisions Stores or Necessarys [sic] for the Use of His Majesty's Navy and Army there you are to take them, or such of them as may be ready under your Convoy also, & see them in safety to that place. Given &c 23rd Novr 1776[44]

---

43   D. Syrett, 'The organization of British trade convoys during the American War, 1775–1783', *Mariner's Mirror*, 62:2 (1976), p.172.
44   NDAR, Vol.7, p.757.

The 14 ships detailed to join Howe's convoy were two Ordnance storeships, 11 'Treasury Store Ships with Camp Equipage Clothing and Stores for the Army', and the last one was a 'Navy Victualler with Sour Krout Marine Clothing and Medicines for the Hospitals'.

Although convoys provided a measure of protection for the chartered ships (the example of the *Mellish* shows that it was not perfect) they had commercial limitations for the ships' owners, and, it must be said, British warship captains were very 'sniffy' about merchant captains and masters. For the charter companies, the motivation was not patriotism but profit; delays in assembling the convoys, and the prescriptive rules put on the masters of their ships when in a convoy, could work against maximising that profit. Victualling convoys had to assemble their cargoes from different parts of Britain, meeting up at a departure port (Deptford, Plymouth, etc.) and joining their naval escort. Wet provisions (beef, pork, and butter) came from Cork, while dry provisions (flour, pease, and oatmeal) came from England. Given the slow loading process, inspection, and sailing between ports, the formation of a convoy could take weeks. Any delay could impact the cash-flow and profit of the merchants, apart from the operational impact on the soldiers in the colonies. In April 1777 'a great Number of Merchant Ships with valuable Cargoes [were] waiting for Convoy impatient to proceed on their Voyage' but were delayed by the late arrival of the *Proteus*, loaded with 'camp equipage', but 'wind bound' at Deptford. It was suggested that the convoy sail without her and when the *Proteus* did arrive at Spithead, 'another Frigate may be in readiness to sail with the *Proteus* from Spithead by the time she arrives there'.[45] As well as delays causing a potential loss of profits to the owners, they could increase expenses for the Admiralty as they were holding the ships on contract for longer than had been intended. In May 1775, the Commissioners of the Excise were withholding permission for the trans-shipment of 30,000 gallons of brandy to the troops in Boston – import taxes were due, even if the goods were only in transit, and needed as part of the war effort. The victualling ships that were held up by this late delivery were to sail without the *Proteus,* to prevent paying extra expenses on the ships lying idle.[46] There are numerous similar examples in the records. Ships' owners could increase their profits by sailing independently of convoys, but they risked losing all to privateers, in which case there would be no compensation from the government. To get the best of both worlds, masters of merchant ships might start under the protection of a convoy and then leave in an attempt to be the first to land the cargo. Big profits might be made this way. Ships from the West Indies carrying sugar could influence the market if they arrived before the rest of

45   NDAR, Vol.8, p.752, letter from Admiralty to Germain.
46   TNA, ADM 111/72.

the convoy; the first to unload could demand a higher price, so increasing their profit. The market price dropped when the rest of the convoy arrived and flooded the market.

Sailing discipline was something that the navy stressed when a convoy was first assembled. One of the most important topics was that of signals, and the obedience of ships' masters to those displayed by the naval captain responsible for the convoy's safety. Signalling by flag was the navy way, there was no alternative, but it was 'hit and miss' as to whether the target ship would see the signal, and it required that the convoy commander had fully explained his signal system to the masters of the ships in the convoy. Claiming not to have seen a signal was a frequent excuse, while navy captains were sure that the act was deliberate. Captain Smith, HMS *Lark* (escorting 24 victuallers), complained to the Admiralty in August 1776 about the conduct of the masters in his convoy:

> I am sorry to acquaint You that several of the Ships under my Convoy are exceedingly refractory and inattentive to the Signals made for His Majesty's Service, which gives me reason to believe that some of those who sail best incline to make the best of their way, which may occasion detriment to the Service.[47]

When ships left a convoy, the risks to the vessel and its cargo were no longer carried by the Admiralty, which required reports from the convoy commander of the circumstances so that they could rebuff any claims by the ships' owners. In December 1776, Captain Williams gave his report to the Admiralty regarding a recent convoy for which he had been responsible:

> I have Inclos'd herein as I am desired to be very particular when, and the reasons why, that Part of the Convoy left us, I therefore judge it Most Adviseable to send up my Journal for their Lordships Inspection, which will point Out to them the reason of Many Of Our Convoy leaving us, and by Which their Lordships Plainly will See *was Occasion'd by their Paying so little or no Attention to Any Signals Made by me*, and I hope their Lordships will allow its not in the power of two of His Maj[esty's] ships to keep so large a Convoy together against their Inclinations [my emphasis].[48]

47 NDAR, Vol.6, p.149.
48 NDAR, Vol.7, p.810, letter from Williams to Stephens, 27 December 1776.

Many of the procedures adopted for the sending of victuals, provisions, stores and ordnance to the troops in America were put in place following the loss of the *Mellish*; some details of that voyage will demonstrate the problems faced by transport vessels at that time. The *Mellish*, carrying uniforms and clothing for the troops, was to sail under the escort of HMS *Richmond*. The importance of the cargo, with the approach of winter in North America, was recognised by the Admiralty:

> It being of the utmost consequence to the King's Service that the said Ships should arrive in safety at the places of their respective destinations, My Lords have ordered them to be manned and armed that they may defend themselves in case they should by accident lose their Convoy and be attacked by any of the Rebel Cruizers And for their greater security an Officer and 20 Soldiers are embarked on board each of them.[49]

Atlantic crossings were not the easiest voyages on which to try to maintain station in a convoy as the weather could well cause ships to lose sight of each other and separate. The transport vessel would then have to continue the journey under its own navigation, a situation that made the Admiralty uncomfortable in this instance, given the importance of the cargo. To mitigate the chances of the freight being lost if the *Mellish* should become separated from the *Richmond*, Midshipman Horsenail was assigned to the transport. The role of Mr Horsenail was spelt out by the Admiralty in their instructions to the captain of the *Richmond*, John Gidoin:

> And whereas we have directed the Navy Board to appoint Mr Horsenail a Midshipman of the Navy to go on board the *Mellish* with Instructions to superintend the navigating her to explain to her Master the Convoy Instructions & Signals, and in case of separation to Direct the Ships proceedings agreable [*sic*] to the Rendezvous & Orders you may give him & in conjunction with the Officer commanding the Troops put on board her, to assist in defending her against the Cruizers of the Rebels in case she should be attacked, You are farther required & directed to give Mr Horsenail such additional Instructions as you shall judge proper for the purposes aforementioned & to lend to the *Mellish* from the Ship you command a careful diligent Petty Officer to assist Mr Horsenail in executing the duty with which he is charged.[50]

49   NDAR, Vol.6, p.594, letter from Stephens to Lord Howe, 7 September 1776.
50   NDAR, Vol.6, p.575, letter from Admiralty to Captain John Gidoin, 28 August 1776.

We tend to stereotype the midshipman as a very young boy under the training and supervision of his ship's captain. Here, he is given a great deal of responsibility and considered better qualified than the merchant vessel's captain and master in the art of navigation. This was an early instance of a midshipman being given this role (which was adopted on many later convoys), but it also failed to prevent the ship being taken.[51] As well as the soldiers on board, it was assumed that if the *Mellish* were armed, then it would be able to protect itself. To that end the ship's owners, 'have undertaken to provide them with the Guns & Swivels expressed against their Names, with ten rounds of Powder to each'.[52] The *Mellish* carried six 3-pounders and six swivels and was due to sail from Deptford on 12 August 1776 to join up with the *Richmond*. A Navy Board comment on the crewing of the *Mellish* demonstrates that not all Englishmen saw a need for the war or were prepared to fight the American colonists: 'Write to Mr [John] Wilkinson to provide another Master & Mate for the *Mellish* Transport, the present ones having declared that in case of her being attacked on her passage to America, they would not defend her'.[53] In spite of the precautions, the *Mellish* became separated from the *Richmond* and was taken by the American ship *Alfred*, captained by John Paul Jones. According to Jones, the British ship, 'made some defence but it was triffling'.[54] The *Alfred* was not alone but part of a small squadron, which included the continental sloop *Providence*, commanded by Lieutenant John Trevet. In his account of the action Trevet claimed that the *Mellish*, 'haled [hauled] down her colours to the Sloop Providence'[55] – most accounts cite Jones's claim that she was taken by the *Alfred*, presumably basing his claim on his seniority as commander of the American squadron.

The efforts of the clerks and bureaucrats in London who spent their working days trying to hire transport vessels to convoy supplies to the army in America do not get much mention in the histories of the war, and yet their work was vital. The troops could not eat, clothe themselves, or fight without the contents of the holds of those ships. It was doubly galling to see them fall into the hands of the Americans, whose need was at least as great as that of the British, as Trevet's journal points out:

> As soon as they [the captured ships] arrived, […] she was [un]loaded, and all the clothing taken out and waggons prepared to send them on to Gen.

51   NDAR, Vol.6, p.576, fn.2.
52   NDAR, Vol.6, p.537.
53   NDAR, Vol.6, p.557, Navy Board minutes, 21 August 1776.
54   NDAR, Vol.7, p.111, letter from Jones to Continental Marine Committee, 12 November 1776.
55   NDAR, Vol.7, p.329, Trevet's journal,

Washington's army, at that time his army being in a distressed situation for clothing, and in this Ship was every article complete for a Soldier from the hat, to the shoes, and at that time I can say with pleasure I had rather taken her, than a Spanish Galleon with hard money.

The *Mellish* was only one of many ships that fell to American privateers. In February 1778, Alderman Wooldridge, in the House of Lords, stated that

[T]he number of ships lost by capture, or destroyed by American privateers, since the commencement of the war, to be 733, of which, after deducting for those retaken and restored, there remained 559; the value of which, including the ships, cargoes, &c. amounted, upon a very moderate calculation, to £1,800,633 18s.[56]

The damage done by the privateers was not just to the supply of ships, but also to the expenses incurred in their charter. Wooldridge went on to tell their Lordships that insurance, which before the war had been between 2% and 2.5% on ships to America and North Carolina, 'was now more than double, even with the convoy, and without convoy, unless the ship was a ship of force, 15 per cent'. Additionally, 'seamen's wages were now raised from 25 and 28, to 55, and in some instances up as high as 65 shillings, per month'. However, trade was the life-blood of Britain and in spite of the conflict, 'there was [only] a slight decrease during the war in total exports and imports'.[57] The relatively small impact on British trade, and the fact that the army in America was supplied throughout the conflict, can be attributed to the implementation of an extensive convoy system to protect British shipping against enemy attack. However, the success was won in the face of criticism of that system from all sides, Navy officers, government officials, merchants and shipowners. Syrett has an admirable summation:

[D]espite heavy losses of shipping, economic dislocations, and strategic embarrassments the convoy system enabled the British to continue their overseas commerce during the American War to a far greater extent than any of the other belligerents. Because of her ability to maintain seaborne trade, Britain was the only one of the warring nations involved in [the] American War to emerge from the conflict without serious financial problems and with her economy intact.[58]

---

56   NDAR, Vol.11, p.967.
57   Syrett, 'British trade convoys', p.169.
58   Syrett, 'British trade convoys', p.178.

5

'Hell is in the forecastle, the devil at the helm'

Ships of Britain's eighteenth century navy were not a place for the fainthearted; cramped, cold and wet, the wooden world in which the sailors – and troops in transit – lived was one of hard work and strict discipline. Sailors, whether volunteers or pressed men, became used to it but for the troops who went aboard it would have been a whole new experience. For the majority, it was likely to be their first time afloat. Soldiers were used to exercise and drill, but ships allowed little space for these activities, so keeping fit was a problem. Used to sleeping in tents, they had to become accustomed to hammocks and while discipline in the army was not 'relaxed', it could be draconian aboard ship. Troops often had to spend weeks on their transport ship waiting for a favourable wind, before facing a voyage of more than six weeks of Atlantic weather. In his 1920 article, Major Evan Fyers stated, 'Of the accommodation provided for troops and their experiences on board ship there is very little to be gleaned from naval history'.[1] In most of the general histories, their movements by sea have little detail of how or under what conditions the troops were transported. One of the best windows into that wooden world is the Naval Documents of the American Revolution, a source that this author has found invaluable. Although they were not sailors, and so unable to assist in handling the ship (except in exceptional circumstances), many of the conditions under which they lived while at sea were similar to those of their *matelot* colleagues. The cold and wet must have been hard for the troops to come to terms with; they would have had little exercise to warm them up, and inadequate clothing for keeping dry. According to Rodger, 'the life of the seaman was always arduous, but it is unusual to find either officers or men making much of the weather as a hardship'. While the conditions may have been something that

1   E. Fyers, 'The transport of troops by sea', *Mariner's Mirror*, 6:11 (1920), p.322.

the sailors were used to, being at sea off the Canadian coast in winter would have drawn some complaints from the soldiers.

> The running ropes freeze in the blocks, the sails are stiff like sheets of tin, and the men cannot expose their hands long enough to the cold to do their duty aloft, so that topsails are not easily handled.[2]

Before setting foot in the New World the soldiers sent to bring the rebellious Americans to heel had to become accustomed to life in the confined space of a ship. The transports and men of war were usually too large to moor alongside a dock, requiring them to anchor in the deeper water of the harbour. The first challenge for the troops, most of whom were unlikely to be able to swim, was to be ferried out in lighters to their ship, where they would then make their way up a narrow ladder, or scramble up a net hung over the side of the vessel. On reaching the deck, those who were travelling in a man-of-war would have been struck by the fact that, as large as the ship was, space was at a premium. A 74-gun ship of the line was approximately 175 feet long and 45 feet in the beam, but most of those on the American station were a little smaller as they were 64-gunners and below. Into this small space was crammed the crew and the troops. In July 1777 HMS *Eagle*, 64 guns, was in harbour in New York waiting to sail for Chesapeake Bay; in its 175 foot length the ship mustered 995 men. Of these, 497 were seamen, officers and marines while another 498 were listed as 'supernumeraries', or troops.[3] If there had been a ship's cat, there would not have been room enough to swing it. Previous chapters have made reference to the fact that small numbers of women were allowed to accompany regiments when travelling aboard, but a ship in port could become an extension of the gin shops and brothels on shore:

> boat loads of defiled and defiling women are permitted to come alongside; the men, looking over the side, select whoever best pleases his lustful fancy, and by paying her fare, he is allowed to take her and keep her on board as his paramour, until the ship is once more ordered to sea'.[4]

When the *Royal George* sank at Spithead in August 1782 there were reported to be upwards of 400 women on board: 'Of these the bulk were the lowest order of

2   Rodger, *Wooden World*, p.62.
3   NDAR, Vol.9, pp.262–265.
4   Mostert, *Line Upon The Wind*, p.86.

prostitutes'.[5] As troops could be on board for some weeks before sailing, they no doubt also partook of the services on offer.

Life on board was hard for the sailors and must have been especially so for the soldiers. A Guards officer described it colourfully as, 'continued destruction in the foretops, the pox above-board, the plague between decks, hell in the forecastle, the devil at the helm'.[6] While the ship's crew was organised into two 'watches', meaning that only half of them would be trying to use the sleeping area at any one time, the soldiers did not 'work ship' and so would all have been eating and sleeping at the same time and would have been constantly disturbed by the sailors' watch changes. One historian has given an account of the likely shipboard routine for troops in transit to America.

> Each morning the cabins and berths were cleaned and probably disinfected with vinegar. If the weather permitted, all the bedding was brought up on deck and aired. Some army officers made their men wash themselves every day. During the hours of daylight as many men as possible were kept on deck. No smoking between decks was allowed. Troops were forbidden to gamble and to drink spirits over and above the daily ration of rum. All lights and fires were put out in the early evening and on some ships army officers kept watches throughout the night. If the ship entered port no officer or soldier was permitted to go ashore without consent of the commanding officer.[7]

The routine was regimented and proscriptive, for discipline and health reasons, but there were occasional variations and additions. The log of HMS *Boreas* noted that on 1 September 1776, at 7:00 a.m., they 'Perform'd divine service;'[8] no doubt where troops were carried they would also attend. On the *Asia*, at 1:00 p.m. on 5 November 1777, they 'Fir'd 15 Guns it being the Anny [*sic*, anniversary] of the Gunpowder Plot'.[9] A relatively frequent event, on naval ships and transports, would have been the burial at sea of those who died on the journey. The entries in the ships' logs were brief and to the point: 'Departd [*sic*] this Life Edwd [*sic*] Gulliver Seaman', 11 March 1776, HMS *Chatham*.[10] Death from sickness and

5   R. and L. Adkins, *Gibraltar: The Greatest Siege in British History* (London: Little, Brown, 2017), p.xxiv.
6   Syrett, *Shipping and the American War*, pp.182–183.
7   D. Syrett, 'Living conditions on the Navy Board's transports during the American War, 1775–1783', *Mariner's Mirror*, 55:1 (1969), p.93.
8   NDAR, Vol.6, p.659.
9   NDAR, Vol.2, p.896.
10   NDAR, Vol.4, p.383.

disease is covered a little later in this chapter, but it could also happen from the most bizarre of circumstances. On 18 January 1777, HMS *Diamond* fired 21 guns in honour of the Queen's birthday but the 'Most unluckey [*sic*] Accident' happened: due to mishandling of the guns two balls went through the side of the transport (*Grand Duke of Russia*), which was lying alongside. In the transport, five men were killed and two more were injured 'as they wer [*sic*] all Sitting in the Fore Castle at their Dinner'. Lord Howe ordered that a court martial should be held to try Lieutenant Duckworth – First Lieutenant of the *Diamond* – as well as the gunners involved in the mishap.[11]

The confined space left little room for privacy, recreation, or sleeping. Sailors slept in hammocks; slung fore and aft, the regulations allowed only 14 inches width for each hammock but, with one watch always on deck, each sailor had 28 inches to himself.[12] Soldiers who were carried in warships were likely to have also had to use hammocks, but the arrangement was different for those in transport vessels. These ships were normally converted merchantmen with their holds divided up into cabins with two-tier berths, each tier holding six soldiers.

> The men were packed like herring. A tall man could not stand upright between decks, nor sit up straight in his berth. To every such berth six men were allotted, but as there were room for only four, the last two had to squeeze in as best they might. Thus the men lay in what boys call 'spoon fashion', and when they tired on one side, the man on the right would call 'about face', and the whole file would turn over at once; then when they were tired again, the man on the left would give the same order, and they would turn back to the first side.[13]

While the soldiers' living conditions were cramped and uncomfortable, they must have seemed even worse for the women and children who travelled with the regiments: 'Regimental histories seldom, if ever, refer to this particular aspect of internal economy'.[14] The women were likely to have had a screened-off area in the hold, among the troops, but 'each ship was left to make the best arrangements possible in the circumstances'. The number of women and children carried, though not large, was significant; on 3 April 1777 there were 13 transport ships in New York harbour with 1,942 'passengers' among which were 91 women

---

11   NDAR, Vol.8, p.362.
12   Rodger, *Wooden World*, p.61.
13   Syrett, *Shipping and the American War*, p.185.
14   W.B. Rowbotham, 'Soldiers' and seamen's wives and children in H.M. Ships', *Mariner's Mirror*, 47: 1 (Feb. 1961), p.43.

and 12 children.[15] Even when regiments moved within America to take part in landings and operations, women and children might go with them, as in the case of Cornwallis' 33rd Regiment leaving New York for Charleston in 1779 with 76 women and 42 children.[16]

Bedding for the troops was very scanty; 'a sack of straw to serve as a mattress, a blanket, a pillow and a coverlet'. The bedding was provided by the contractors, which afforded them another opportunity to take a profit at the expense of the soldier. In June 1776 a complaint was made that the bedding provided was 'infamously scanty; the pillows in particular not being above 7 inches by 5 at the most, resembling rather pincushions, but not so well stuffed'.[17] The common soldier may have suffered great inconvenience on these journeys, but conditions were a little less harsh for their 'betters'. In 1778, three members of the peace commission were to travel to America on the *Trident*. One of those members, Mr Eden, insisted on taking his wife and child and 'four female attendants' with him.[18] He also complained that having Lord Cornwallis (returning to his command in America) aboard the same ship would be 'impossible', presumably on the grounds of space. Cornwallis did travel with them, but Eden's presumption of his own importance is quite staggering. However, even officers considerably lower down the pecking order than Eden and Cornwallis could situate themselves much better than the troops. In 1773, before the conflict, the 23rd Regiment was moved to America and an account of the voyage was sent in a letter by Lieutenant Frederick Mackenzie (adjutant) to his parents: the officers 'rose at 7, breakfasted always at 8, had what we called a Meridian at 12, consisting of Cold Meat and Punch. Dined at 2, tea at 6, and supped at 8, and were generally in bed at 10 o'clock'.[19]

Army officers, and ship's captains, often bought their own provisions to take with them; Mackenzie and the others of his regimental mess were no exception and had paid between £10 and £15 a head not to eat the ship's victuals. Amongst a great deal of meat, butter, bread, and other essentials were 63 fowl and ducks, six pounds of Souchong tea, 50 dozen eggs, six bottles of mustard, 20 dozen bottles of porter, six dozen bottles of port, and 10 pickled tongues.[20] They were not going to let a sea voyage get in the way of eating and drinking well. Mackenzie's grocery

15 NDAR, Vol.8, p.740.
16 F. and M. Wickwire, *Cornwallis and the War of Independence* (Northampton: History Book Club, 1970), p.59.
17 Syrett, 'Living conditions', p.90.
18 SP, Vol.1, p.371.
19 G. Jones, 'The voyage of the 23rd Foot to New York In 1773', *Journal of the Society for Army Historical Research*, 38:1960, p.50.
20 Jones, 'Voyage of the 23rd', p.56.

list is unlikely to have been the norm for all army officers travelling to America, but neither is it likely to have been unique.

Once on board, the soldiers (and any women who accompanied them) ate the same food as the sailors, but less of it. The Victualling Board had decreed that 'six soldiers are to have the same [ration] as four seamen',[21] with women receiving the same as the troops; children were on half-rations. The sailors were divided up, six men to a 'mess;' one of the six would fetch the food from the ship's cook, and they would all eat together. The soldiers are likely to have had a similar regime, although they sometimes had to cook the food in their own groups, as a comment by Brigadier-General Heath makes clear. Heath's men were to be transported around part of the American coast in March 1776 but there were no facilities aboard for cooking their food: 'as there will not be accommodations on Board the Transports for Cooking a Sufficiency of Provisions, the Commanding Officer of Each Regiment will Direct that Six Days Provision be Cooked, This Day if the Fresh Provisions be ready'.[22] The navy supplied the food to the troops, but was reimbursed by the Victualling Board after a laborious and time-consuming process. When provisions were issued to a transport ship, an account was sent to the Victualling Board. At the end of the voyage, the commanding officer of the troops had to make out three receipts stating the number of men victualled, at what allowance, and for how many days. Only after the accounts were reconciled with the original provisioning report could the account be audited and settled.[23] The Victualling Board did not look kindly on any situations where troops in transit were provisioned above the two-thirds allowance. In these situations, the ship's accounts would not be settled until the ship's owner had paid for the one-third allowance that had been overprovided by the ship's master. However, there were circumstances where it was necessary to victual the troops at the full allowance. When the men were to take part in an amphibious assault then their officers naturally wanted them fit and ready to go; the ship's master was not in a position to refuse when a senior army commander ordered him to provide full rations. In June 1777, Lord Howe had to go into writing to explain to the Admiralty why he had found it necessary to provision some troops (who were waiting to take part in a landing near New York) at full allowance.

> It was intended that the Movement of the Army which afterwards took place from Staten Island to Long Island, should have been executed very soon after the Arrival of the said Reinforcement. In which View it was

21 Syrett, 'Living conditions', p.92.
22 NDAR, Vol.4, p.492, Heath's order, 24 March 1776.
23 Syrett, *Shipping and the American War*, pp.187–188.

proposed not to disembark those Corps, until the Descent was made on Long Island. But as those Troops would then continue (which actually happened for some time) upon the Sea-Victualling, which the Rest of the Army, besides other local Gratificat[ions,] were at whole Allowance, which caused some Discontent amongst the Foreign Troops, the Change in the Sea Victualling was made at the General's Desire. The Duration of the Extra Victualling being expressed 'until further Order', had Reference to the uncertain Time those Troops (daily expected to be sent on Service) would remain embarked.[24]

Here Howe is pointing out the unreasonableness of provisioning those troops already landed at whole allowance, while those who would fight with them – but not yet landed – would only receive two-thirds. He draws attention to the fact that this would naturally cause 'Discontent' among those affected. Daniel Wier, Commissary General in America, tried to dissuade army commanders from ordering the masters of transports to give the additional rations, but the masters were outranked by those holding the King's Commission. As a result of this practice, 'the owners of transports were forced to subsidize amphibious landings in America by paying one-third of the provisions consumed by the troops for several days before the beginning of the operation'.[25]

Within the confined space of a transport ship or man-of-war, discipline would have been essential, for troops as well as the sailors. Much has been written and mythologised about the use of the 'lash' on British warships. While there is little doubt that discipline was harsh and punishments severe, they were hard times; in England children could be hanged for offences which the modern reader would judge no worse than petty larceny. The captain of a warship, even more than his counterpart on a merchant vessel, was very much king of his domain. The Articles of War gave great authority to the captain, but also allowed him wide discretion over their interpretation, and some captains were much harsher than others in the sentences they awarded. To ensure that the crew were in no doubt where the power lay, the Articles were read to the whole crew on a regular basis when at sea, as in the case of Captain Furneaux of the *Syren*: ship's log, 8 February 1776, 'At 10 the Articles of War were read to the Ship[']s Comp[an]y'.[26] The captain of a transport ship would not have had authority over the King's troops, they would have been subject to the discipline of their own officers, but those on a warship are likely to have witnessed naval discipline, and been subject to it. The records

24   NDAR, Vol.9, p.188, letter from Howe to Stephens, 29 June 1777.
25   Syrett, *Shipping and the American War*, p.92.
26   NDAR, Vol.3, p.1189.

are full of examples of how savagely it could be applied, and how variable it was for the same offence. It all came down to the individual captain. This variability in the severity of the sentences was not unique to that time, a reading of the World War One battalion war diaries at The National Archives will quickly demonstrate the lack of consistency with which drunkenness and insubordination were treated by the different army units in that war. The *Regulations and Instructions relating to His Majesty's Service at Sea* stated explicitly that 'no captain could on his own authority punish a man with more than twelve lashes'.[27] However, the crimes covered in the Articles of War included many that were of a severity that required a court martial, something that was difficult to hold at sea. As a result, in the absence of a court martial, captains awarded more than the allowed dozen strokes. On 29 January 1778, Captain Fanshawe (HMS *Carysfort*) punished a sailor with two dozen lashes for drunkenness.[28] A soldier on a naval ship would have been a witness to the flogging, which was carried out on deck with the man tied to a grating and all hands 'summoned to witness punishment'. In some circumstances, the audience was much larger than just the ship's company, as happened on 15 November 1777 in Rhode Island harbour:

> Ship's log, HMS *Chatham*; at 9 AM the *Diamond* made the Signal for all Boats to Attend the Punishement [*sic*] of a Deserter belong[ing] to the said ship [...] At 10 a Seaman belonging to the *Diamond* received along Side 50 Lashes According to the Sentence of a Court Martial.[29]

In this case, all the ships' crews in harbour had to witness the sentence as a deterrent to further cases of desertion. The example demonstrates that courts martial could award many more than a dozen strokes. Again, on 6 February of that year, also at Rhode Island, the *Chatham* had called for all ships at anchor to send boats with witnesses to the flogging of seaman Roberts; he received 150 lashes.[30] Sentences of this severity were brutal and in one case at Plymouth, the surgeon in attendance had to call a halt to the punishment.

> With respect to John Evans who has received 165 Lashes in part of the punishment inflicted on him by Sentence of a Court Martial, and who in the Opinion of the Surgeon will not be in a condition to undergo the remainder of his Punishment for a considerable time, I am to acquaint

27   Rodger, *Wooden World*, p.218.
28   NDAR, Vol.11, p.233.
29   NDAR, Vol.10, p.499.
30   NDAR, Vol.7, p.1136.

you that, upon your intercession therein, their Lordships are pleased to remit the remainder of the Punishment.[31]

The note does not say how many lashes would have been delivered if the full punishment had continued; even their Lordships could see that 'enough was enough'.

Just as in today's armed forces, an officer's behaviour was judged differently from that of a common soldier or sailor (he was expected to behave as a 'gentleman'), so the way in which his misdemeanours were viewed and punished might be different from those of a 'ranker'. On 19 January 1776, the day after a seaman from HMS *Syren* was given 24 lashes for drunkenness, Lieutenant Pennington of the same ship died of wounds 'supposed to be received by a Pistol Ball in a duel with Lieut Cuming of the Marines'. For this offence (murder?) the captain of the ship informed the Admiralty that 'Mr Cumming [his name is spelt variously] is now under Confinement on board'.[32] In May that year, Sir Peter Parker asked the Admiralty to convene a court martial[33] to try Cumming for the death of Lieutenant Pennington. Cumming's honour, rather than his back, would suffer if the decision of the Board went against him. In a similar vein, in September 1777, Captain Tollemache (HMS *Zebra*) fought and lost a duel with Captain Pennington of the Guards, a passenger on the ship. Tollemache received 'a Wound under the left Breast of which he expired immediately; the latter [Pennington] was wounded in 7 different Parts, but is like to do well'.[34] It is difficult not to believe that had an ordinary seaman killed a marine in a sword fight, he would have received a severe flogging, or worse. In this case, when Lord Howe sent his periodic report to the Admiralty in October 1777 he made no mention of the duel: 'The Captain of the *Zebra* dying the Night of his Arrival at New York, Lieutenant Orde of the *Eagle* has been nominated to that Vacancy'.[35]

Desertion caused real problems for sea captains, whether in the King's navy or commanding merchant vessels. British seamen on warships were not only subjected to harsh discipline; they were also poorly paid. Most of the sailors and soldiers who were sent to America had no grievance with the colonists and, given the right incentive (money or a new wife), would readily desert. Conscious of the attractions in America, the colonists openly advertised for British servicemen to leave their current jobs and join the revolution. At Salem, 15 June 1775, a broadsheet was produced for distribution among the British forces in Boston:

31   NDAR, Vol.8, p.549.
32   NDAR, Vol.3, pp. 867, 932.
33   NDAR, Vol.5, p.110.
34   NDAR, Vol.9, p.980.
35   NDAR, Vol.10, p.76.

'TO THE SOLDIERS AND SEAMEN SERVING IN THE BRITISH FLEET AND ARMY IN AMERICA'

Your situation is very unhappy, being dishonoured by the most infamous service, and under the command of the most vile and miserable wretches that ever disgraced the name of Briton. General [Thomas] Gage, to his eternal infamy, has commenced a thief, robber, murderer, and common butcher of his fellowmen; he has violated the most solemn compacts, and become an apostate to every thing that is honourable or virtuous . . . Admiral [Samuel] Graves has added to the crimes of a common pirate, that of forcing Americans, whom he hath impressed, to act against their own countrymen. Turks and Indians would scorn such rascally conduct, and surely every British soldier and seamen must detest such an odious scoundrel. Gentlemen, the Americans will entertain a respect for you, consider you as their brethren, and wish to live in harmony with you, and to make you free citizens of America. May you soon be freed from the service of tyrants, become the glorious defenders of freedom, and join the victorious Americans.[36]

The problem of desertion was significant enough for the men of the Royal Irish Regiment at New York to be moved back on board navy ships, rather than leave them ashore, as Major Hamilton spelled out to the Governor of that city.

The Loss of our Men by Desertion is so great, and the Apprehension of losing more, I therefore think it necessary for the good of the Service to retreat on Board his Majesty's Ship the *Asia*, and have applyed to Captain [George] Vandeput, who has been pleased to offer all the Services and Protection in his Power, and tomorrow (if you have no Objection) shall embark the five Companys [*sic*] under my Command.[37]

The movement of the men from shore to ship took several days, 'in which time several soldiers deserted'.[38] In June 1777, Lord Howe issued an instruction to the officers under his command, restricting shore access for the sailors on the American station.

36   NDAR, Vol.1, p.685.
37   NDAR, Vol.1, p.616.
38   NDAR, Vol.1, p.625.

The Captains and Commanders of the Ships and Vessels of War are desired not to give leave for any of their Seamen or Marines to be absent from their Duty on Shore at any time without a Certificate under their hands respectively specifying the time and occasion for which such Leave of absence has been granted: Those who are found wandering on Shore without such Certificate will be deemed Stragglers: and if absent more than twenty four Hours taken up as Deserters.[39]

Rewards were to be posted for the apprehension of these men, and this was to be taken from the wages of the deserter when he was caught – a double punishment. In the case of a British sailor deserting to an American privateer, which was subsequently captured by a British warship, the man could expect especially severe treatment, as a letter in the *London Chronicle* spelled out: 'This morning the boatswain of the *Rising State[s]* American privateer was flogged from ship to ship [at Portsmouth] for deserting from the *Worcester* man of war, and afterwards serving on board the said privateer'.[40] Thomas Cummings (the said boatswain) might not have thought it at the time, but he was 'lucky;' on 5 December 1777 Lord Howe ordered that the death sentence on William Domineer – who had served on the *Fox* before it was captured by an American privateer – should be 'carried into immediate execution'. The man had been found 'in arms' on the *Fox* when it was retaken from the rebels by the *Flora*.[41]

The grass on the American side of the hill may have appeared greener to the British soldier or sailor, but desertion was not a one-sided traffic. Probably the most famous American deserter was Benedict Arnold, but there were many others whose names do not carry Arnold's notoriety. The Americans often put up reward notices for the return of named individuals who had deserted from one of their ships or army units. One such example was for five men, promulgated in the *Providence Gazette* in January 1776.

DESERTED from the Continental Navy, the following Persons, viz, Daniel Collier, a short thick Fellow, about 23 or 24 Years of Age, has a red Face, Pockbroken stutters very much, supposed to be gone to the Eastward. – An Indian Fellow named Ben Hazard, about 23 or 24 years of Age, about 5 Feet, 5 or 6 Inches high, supposed to be gone to Hoosack. – John Young, about 5 Feet 3 Inches high, about 35 Years of Age, been in Newport, had on a light coloured Jacket and Breeches – Elijah Simmons,

39   NDAR, Vol.9, p.75.
40   NDAR, Vol.8, p.840, *London Chronicle*, 15 May 1777.
41   TNA, ADM 1/488, f.93.

48 Years of Age, 5 Feet 10 Inches high, pitted with the Small-Pox, stoops when he walks, wears his Hair, which is somewhat grey – Richard Springer, a middle sized Man, of a middle Age, supposed to be gone to the Westward. – Whoever will take up and secure either of the said Deserters, and bring them, or give Information to the Subscriber, shall receive Thirty Shillings Lawful Money Reward for either of them, and all necessary Charge.[42]

Some of the rebels even deserted to British warships, which no doubt surprised the British sailors; ship's log HMS *Hunter*, 1 January 1776, 'came in some deserters from the Rebels'.[43] America may have seemed to British sailors and soldiers as a 'land of the free', but when the thirteen colonies set out to create a navy, they adopted many of the disciplinary measures used by their British enemy; one of these was flogging for desertion. In January 1777, John Thomson was tried for having deserted from the *Warren* to the British, but he had obviously been recaptured and was to be flogged before the 'fleet' in the same manner as a British sailor.

The Opinion of this Court is that John Thomson, have a pun[ishment] of Sixty four Lashes upon his bare back with a Cat of nine tails – to [be] inflicted along Side the Several Vessels in the Fleet – *vizt* 19 Lashes [along] Side the Ship *Warren* – 15 Lashes along Side Ship *Providence* – 15 Lashes alo[ng] Side the *Columbus* – and 15 Lashes along Side the Sloop *Providence*.[44]

Desertion from the navy was on a sufficiently large scale to have an impact on the army in America. Captains of British warships were under pressure to maintain their crews as close to full complement as possible. When a ship was short-handed the temptation was to press gang men from the transport vessels that were supplying the army, this in turn meant that supplies for the troops were delayed because of the manning problems. According to Rodger 'the total number [of men] recruited during the American War was more than double the maximum number serving at any one time. There was roughly one case of desertion for every three men recruited'[45] with the rate peaking at over 16 percent in 1776. In a ship's log, deserters were recoded as having 'Run' and between January 1776 and

42   NDAR, Vol.3, pp.633–634.
43   NDAR, Vol.3, p.625.
44   NDAR, Vol.7, pp.944–945.
45   Rodger, *Command of the Ocean*, p.398.

September 1780, 42,069 were so recorded.[46] The loss of sailors through desertion had to be made good by 'pressing' men where they could be found, and that usually meant taking them from American sailing vessels or from the transports sent from England. The governor of Nova Scotia made the point to Admiral Graves that Britain was keen for Loyalists who left the rebellious thirteen states to be given asylum in his province. However, the taking of local seamen to man British ships was hurting Nova Scotian trade, which would deprive the West Indies of lumber and would have a 'Tendency to prevent many well Affected persons from coming into the Province from the other Colonies which the Government at home seem desirous to encourage'. The governor hoped that Graves could use his influence so that 'the Seamen belonging to Vessels owned in Nova Scotia may not be impress'd'.[47] But the navy needed men, as Graves explained to Commodore Arbuthnot (in command at Halifax): 'It is far from my intention to distress the Inhabitants of Nova Scotia, but it is my Duty and the Duty of every Officer under my Command to endeavour to man the Squadron on this Station'. Where possible he would avoid taking the local Nova Scotia men – 'these I am content to exempt from being impressed' – but men who had recently emigrated from Britain were to be 'fair game': 'I insist upon every old Countryman being taken under the above restrictions'.[48] It had been illegal to impress men in America but the Admiralty informed Graves that this was no longer the case: 'The Clause of the Act of the 6th of Queen Ann which forbid[s] the impressing of Seamen in America being repealed by an Act passed in the last Session of Parliament'.[49]

Whatever the effect of impressment on local colonial trade, the practice that most affected the British army in America was the taking of men from the supply ships they depended on, to serve in the King's warships. In June 1775, General Gage had to write to Graves to tell him that the transport ship *Pallas* could not sail from Boston to New York 'for want of men'. The army needed transport vessels for the movement of troops and supplies around the American coast, as well as from Britain. In this case, Gage was asking for the navy to supply men to crew the *Pallas* and to desist from pressing transport crews:

> I am to beg you would Order Men from your Ships to Man her, & I shall likewise be Obliged to you to give Orders to the Ships under your Command not to inlist or impress the Seamen belonging to the transports, as his Majesty's Service is much retarded for the want of them,

46   Morriss, *British Maritime Ascendancy*, p.259.
47   NDAR, Vol.2, p.657.
48   NDAR, Vol.3, p.7.
49   NDAR, Vol.1, p.492, letter from Stephens to Graves, 24 June 1775.

and cannot be properly carried on, and as they are the *only means left me to Supply his Majesty's Troops under my Command with every Necessary of Life* [my emphasis].[50]

Gage was conscious of the importance of the transports to his supply but Graves's reply contained something of the 'if we don't do it, someone else will' justification.

The Fact is that from ill usage they will not stay in the Transports tho' the Wages is 12/6 [12 shillings and six pence] More than the Kings Pay p[er] Month And if they are not allowed to Enter on board the Men of War, so many Men as are determined to leave the Transports will be lost to the Service. We never impress the Transports people but in Cases of very bad behavior and at the Masters Request nor Inlist them till they have first declared they will not serve in the Transport.[51]

Gage did not accept the Admiral's assertion that his captains 'never' pressed transport crews, and pointed out to him the effect that the practice had on army operations.

I have the Honor to inclose you Copies of two Letters I have received, respecting the impossibility of the Transports going to Sea for want of Men, which at this time is of Infinite Consequence to His Majesty's Forces here; I have before wrote to you on this Subject, and beg to have an Answer, that I may know what I have to depend on. My being obliged to trouble you frequently on this Subject, is owing to the Men belonging to the Transports, being impressed and suffered to enter on Board the Men of War.[52]

When General Howe took over command of the army in America from Gage he took up the issue with Lord Dartmouth in London, but he recognised that navy warships were also not leaving Britain fully manned, and that this exacerbated the problem.

I beg leave to Remark the great want of Seamen experienced this Summer, for the navigating of Transports, for manning armed Vessels, and Boats on particular Services, and on many other occasions, which induces me to

50   NDAR, Vol.1, p.656, letter from Gage to Graves, 11 June 1775.
51   NDAR, Vol.1, p.656, letter from Graves to Gage, 11 June 1775.
52   NDAR, Vol.1, p.1141, letter from Gage to Graves, 14 August 1775.

urge the Necessity of sending out Seamen to complete the Transports to their proper Number, a Return whereof is inclosed. It is also to be wished that the King['s] Ships had their War Establishment, as they would then be able to spare Men for extra Services, and not have the same Reason for Pressing out of the Vessels from Europe, and other Parts coming with Supplies for the Navy and Army, a Practice which may greatly affect us in future, unless your Lordship shall be pleased to direct that Protections be given to Vessels sailing from Britain, and Exemptions to others who may bring such Supplies.[53]

For the captains of the King's ships it was often a case of deciding which order carried the greater reprimand if it were disobeyed; ignore the order to refrain from pressing men from transports and victuallers, or ignore the requirement to keep his ship at full complement. In 1779, the Lords Commissioners of the Treasury warned the Admiralty that unless it disciplined its officers for pressing these men 'it will be utterly impossible for the [Treasury] Board to supply H.M. Troops [...]'[54]

Army commanders in America were in constant need of troop reinforcements, and they wanted them to be fit to fight. Unfortunately, the environment on board an eighteenth century warship or troop transport made sickness a constant problem. The long passage, overcrowding, poor ventilation below decks, lack of exercise, bad water, and poor diet were all likely to lead to illness. Scurvy, usually associated with the navy, was an illness caused by diet not occupation, and was as prone to break out among soldiers at sea and on land as it was among sailors afloat. The preventative and curative properties of lemons, limes, sauerkraut, and fresh vegetables were well known, following the work of Gilbert Blane and James Lind. However, these antiscorbutics were not always available and large numbers of sailors and troops died of this preventable disease. During the American War, 1,243 sailors were killed in naval actions while 18,541 died of disease.[55] During the siege of Gibraltar in 1780, one of the junior officers in the garrison noted the immediate effect of lemons on the sick soldiers of the garrison: 'The salutary effects were almost instantaneous: in a few days, men who had been considered as irrecoverable, left their beds to congratulate their comrades on the prospect of once more becoming useful to their country'.[56]

53   NDAR, Vol.2, p.1155.
54   Bowler, *Logistics*, p.244.
55   Mostert, *Line Upon The Wind*, p.89.
56   Adkins, *Gibraltar*, p.161.

Similarly, in America, where the local farmers and merchants refused to trade with the British, the army frequently relied on the navy to provide them with the fresh produce to ward off disease. In January 1776 an army captain wrote home that 'Several Vessels have Arrived with porter, potatoes and sour crout for the Army which is of infinite Service as many of the soldiers are much Afflicted with the Scurvy'.[57] Cut off from the supply of fresh vegetables and fruit, and effectively confined to ports and towns such as New York, Boston, and Philadelphia, the British troops were as at risk of scurvy as their counterparts in Gibraltar. In August 1776 General Harvey had attended a meeting at the Treasury Board to advise them that General Howe's army should receive a quarter of a pound of sauerkraut per day, per man, for the next six months to help fight an outbreak of scurvy.[58] The agents (Mure, Son, & Atkinson) were directed to dispatch the sauerkraut along with an unspecified number of tons of 'carrot, turnip and cabbage seed'. The fact that the fresh provisions for the alleviation of scurvy among the troops had to come from Britain indicates the extent to which the army relied on the navy for absolutely every item they needed to subsist and fight on the American continent. However, there was one item that could be sourced in the colonies and was believed to have antiscorbutic qualities: spruce beer. Water was needed by troops and ships' crews, in large quantities, but could go bad in prolonged or poor storage. The navy could take porter and rum on board for their voyages, but for the soldiers in America it was more problematic; porter could also turn bad, and rum could make them drunk. During the winter of 1775–1776, some 468,750 gallons of porter were provided for the 12,000 men at Boston. The transport of this item alone would have required a large proportion of the available victualling and supply fleet. An elegant solution was spruce beer. The needles of this easily available tree were boiled and the spruce essence was then fermented with molasses and water and the resulting beer was issued at the rate of three to four quarts per man per day.[59] However, as the army grew in size the production could not meet the demand and it deteriorated in transit when the army was on the move.

Unsurprisingly, large numbers of troops became ill or died, not only on the Atlantic crossing, but also on transports during amphibious operations off the American coast: when the 23rd Regiment made the journey in 1773 the ship's motion made them all 'very sick throughout April'.[60] Expeditions from New York to the Carolinas and the Delaware in the summer turned out to be longer than anticipated, and unbearably hot. In August 1776, Captain Snape Hamond (HMS

57   Hibbert, *Redcoats and Rebels*, p.61.
58   TNA, T 29/45, f.300.
59   Bowler, *Logistics*, p.8.
60   Jones, 'Voyage of the 23rd', p.50.

Roebuck) was off the Virginia Capes with a number of British troops on board under the command of Lord Dunmore. Sickness broke out among the ship's crew and the troops to the extent that the intended landing had to be abandoned and the ship returned to New York: 'to prevent the disgrace His Majestys Troops might suffer when their extream [*sic*] weakness became known to the Enemy'.

> A violent bilious intermitting fever, together with a most inveterate scurvy had for these two months past raged with g[reat] violence both in the men of war & Transports, and was so mortal that the *Roebuck* had lost 30 of her best seamen, and had 76 on the Surgeons sick list. The *Fowey* had 35 Men sick, and Lord Dunmore's Army was reduced to about 150 Rank & File, one third of which was incapable of duty. I therefore thought it necessary to consult with his Lordship on the measure the most proper to pursue in our weak situation, the result of which was that we should make the best of our way to New York'.[61]

As bad as conditions could be for the troops, it was even worse for the horses that travelled with an eighteenth century army. The animals were 'stabled' below decks, with no facilities for exercise, standing in their own filth while being thrown around as the ship made way through Atlantic gales. In June 1776, 845 horses embarked in England as part of a wagon train to be sent to America; only 478 made it to New York (almost four months later); a further 165 of these were dead by February of the following year.[62]

As the only means of transport between Britain and America, the navy was fundamental to the operations of the British army in the thirteen colonies. For the troops who were sent out to fight, many of whom would never have been to sea before, the experience of life on board these ships must have been traumatic, and especially for those who found themselves subject to naval discipline. Although food was carried on board for the soldiers, it was rationed at two-thirds that of a sailor, which would have been less than they were used to on land. While ships' captains did what they could to prevent sickness on board (antiscorbutics, fumigation, and the scrubbing of decks with vinegar), illness and a lack of exercise would have made it difficult for the men to go straight from the ship to action against the enemy.

61   NDAR, Vol.6, p.174, Snape Hamond's narrative, 13 August 1776.
62   Bowler, *Logistics*, p.24.

6

'Few people dare to supply us'

By 1775, the government in London was coming to the conclusion that something had to be done about the recalcitrant colonists in America; they were not paying their taxes, they had thrown tea into Boston harbour, and they had burned the *Gaspee*. The Colonial Secretary, Lord Dartmouth, directed Gage to use 'a vigorous Exertion of [...] Force' against the rebels whose resistance 'cannot be very formidable'.[1] The morning of 19 April 1775 was 'crisp, windy [and] chilly'[2] as General Gage's troops left Boston for Concord, Massachusetts. Gage's intelligence led him to believe that two of the principal provocateurs, Samuel Adams and John Hancock were in Lexington, about a dozen miles north-west of Boston, while a cache of arms was believed to be held at Concord, a small town a further five or six miles along the road. Lieutenant-Colonel Francis Smith was to take a force of light infantry and grenadiers – variously reported as being between 600 and 900 men strong – to arrest the two rebel leaders and destroy the Concord arsenal. Gage expected little opposition from the locals as British officers had a low opinion of American fighting ability against trained, regular soldiers. Gage's plan called for the British troops to be on the march early in the morning, so giving them the advantage of surprise. However, in the words of one historian, 'Gage's best-laid plans were bollixed'.[3]

In previous chapters we have detailed some of the administrative challenges and problems that faced those who had to send troops, provisions, supplies, and armaments to the British Army in America, but how well and in what ways did the navy support the army in military operations on that continent? From the point of view of this narrative, the story starts on the night of 18/19 April 1775,

---

1 Ferling, *Miracle*, p.28.
2 P.C. Hoffer, *Prelude to Revolution: The Salem Gunpowder Raid of 1775* (Baltimore, MD: Johns Hopkins University Press, 2013), p.94.
3 Ferling, *Miracle*, p.29.

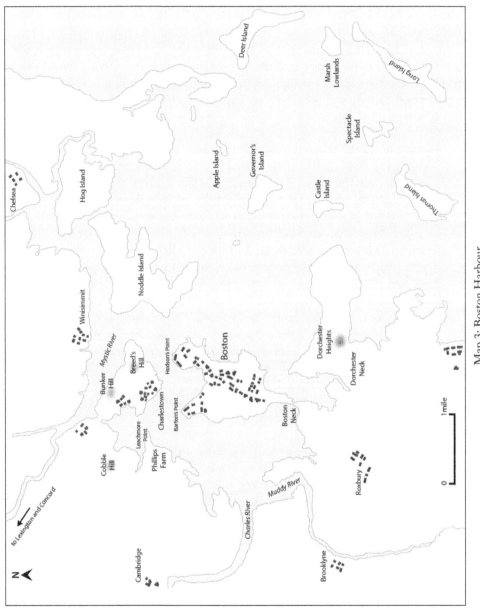

Map 3: Boston Harbour

and the final preparations for the march to Lexington. Boston town was on a peninsula, connected to the mainland by Boston Neck, but if the troops had used this route it would have added miles to their march. The plan was for the navy to transport the men from Boston to Charlestown, from where they had a shorter, direct march to Lexington. Unfortunately, the navy had too few boats available and the transfer of the troops took much longer than expected, giving time for the rebels to raise the alarm – the folk legend of Paul Revere and his cry 'The British are coming!' One lieutenant who took part in the operation was scathing of the way it was planned and executed:

> [F]ew but the Command[in]g Officers knew what expedition we were going upon. After getting over the Marsh where we were wet up to the knees, we were halted in a dirty road and stood there 'till two o-clock in the morning waiting for provisions to be brought from the boats and to be divided, and which most of the Men threw away. [...] Thus ended this Expedition, which from beginning to end was as ill plan'd and ill executed as it was possible to be; had we not idled away three hours on Cambridge Marsh waiting for provisions that were not wanted, we shou'd have had no interruption at Lexington, but by our stay the Country People had got intelligence and time to assemble. We shou'd have reached Concord soon after day break, before they cou'd have heard of us, by which we shou'd have destroyed more Cannon and Stores, which they had had time enough to convey away before our arrival; we might also have got easier back and not been so much harrassed [sic], as they wou'd not have had time to assemble so many People; even the People of Salem and Marblehead above 20 miles off had intelligence and time enough to march and meet us on our return.[4]

The expedition had been something of a fiasco in which Adams and Hancock had escaped Colonel Smith's clutches. The British troops were given a taste of 'backwoods' warfare in which the 'Rebels followed the Indian manner of fighting, concealing themselves behind Hedges and Trees, and skulking in Woods and Houses, where they galled the Soldiers exceedingly'.[5] Casualty figures are notoriously difficult to compile but Ferling records the British as suffering 65 dead and 207 wounded while the rebels lost 94 'dead wounded or missing;' as

---

4   NDAR, Vol.1, pp.199–201, diary of Lieutenant John Barker, 19 April 1775.
5   NDAR, Vol.1, p.206, letter from Graves to Stephens, 22 April 1775.

Brigadier-General Percy remarked later, anyone expecting a New England army to be 'an irregular mob [...] will find himself much mistaken'.[6]

Throughout the war the navy was called on to play an essential role in amphibious operations; these did not always go well, and there were frequent occasions on which the army and navy commanders did not see eye to eye, or where each, in his report to London, tried to 'big up' the contribution of his own command while denigrating that of the other. Graves, whose lack of boats had caused the delay in landing Smith's men at Charlestown, emphasised the navy's role in his narrative and his report to the Admiralty. When troops were put ashore 'to cover the retreat of our harrassed [sic] Soldiers' on their return from Concord he made great claims for the role of the *Somerset* which he had had placed 'exactly in the Ferry way' between Boston and Charlestown.[7] According to Graves:

> [I]t was the *Somerset* alone that preserved the detachment from Ruin. The vicinity of that formidable Ship to Charles Town so intimidated its Inhabitants that they (tho' reluctantly) suffered the Kings Troops to come in and pass over to Boston, who would otherwise have been undoubtedly attacked, and in their defenceless conditions such a proceeding must have been fatal to all the Land Forces on that side, exhausted as they were with Fatigue and without Ammunition; & the consequence of their destruction might have been that of the rest of the army in Boston, for, had the Charles town people massacred those poor harrassed [sic] Soldiers just returned from Lexington, there can be no doubt but they would have immediately crossed to Boston, where they were certain to find 19 out of 20 willing and ready to assist them in finishing their work.[8]

To ensure that the Admiralty were also aware that the troops were indebted to the Navy, he informed Stephens that:

> I can with great truth inform you that the *Somerset* being within a Quarter of a mile of Charles Town Kept its Inhabitants in awe and thereby secured to the Troops an unmolested retreat into that Town, and a peaceable Embarkation for Boston.[9]

However, as a team player Graves wanted to reassure London that 'Their Lordships may depend on my heartily co-operating with the General and on my giving him

6   Ferling, *Miracle*, pp.32–33.
7   NDAR, Vol.1, p.179, narrative of Vice-Admiral Graves, 11 April 1775.
8   NDAR, Vol.1, p.193, narrative of Vice-Admiral Graves, 19 April 1775
9   NDAR, Vol.1, p.206, letter from Graves to Stephens, 22 April 1775.

every assistance in my power in support of such measures as shall be thought best for his Majesty's Service'.

The military action at Lexington and Concord demonstrated to Gage and Graves that they were in a real fight, it was not merely an insurrection by a few armed farmers, and if the British were to succeed in recovering the colonies to the Crown (a highly unlikely event), then they would need to cooperate more fully. The expedition also demonstrated the problems of communication between America and London. On 27 July 1775, Graves (expecting a reaction from London to the recent events) wrote to one of his captains to say that 'We are in hourly expectation of Letters from England in answer to our Account *of April 19*',[10] two and a half months after the event [my emphasis]. Not everyone in Britain was in favour of the war so it was important that British commanders got their version of events into the London press before the colonists; in the case of Lexington and Concord, the colonists won the race. On 30 May 1775, the *London Gazette* stated that:

> A report having been spread, and an Account having been printed and published, of a Skirmish between some of the People in the Province of Massachusets Bay [*sic*] and a Detachment of his Majesty's Troops; it is proper to inform the Publick, that no Advices have as yet been received in the American Department of any such Event.
>
> There is reason to believe that there are Dispatches from General [Thomas] Gage on board The *Sukey*, Captain Brown, which, *though she sailed Four Days before the Vessel that brought the printed Account [from the colonists] is not yet arrived* [my emphasis].[11]

Not unnaturally, the arrival of the Americans' story, before that from General Gage, caused some irritation in London but it would take another six weeks before the army commander would get a sense of this from Lord Dartmouth:

> [I]t is very much to be lamented that We have not some Account from you of this Transaction, which I do not mention from any Supposition that you did not send the earliest Intelligence of it, for we know from Darby that a Vessel with Dispatches from you sailed four days before him. We expect the Arrival of that Vessel with great Impatience, but till she arrives I can form no decisive Judgment of what has happened, and therefore can have nothing more to add.[12]

10   NDAR, Vol.1, p.987, Graves to Captain Wallace, 27 July 1775.
11   NDAR, Vol.1, p.477, *London Gazette*, 30 May 1775.
12   TNA, CO 5/92, f.130.

There was also a difference in emphasis between those in America and the ministers in London, regarding the significance of the event. To Admiral Graves the incident 'had the worst consequences to the King's Authority [...] In fact the Rebellion is general;' in his view 'the Governments of Rhode Island and Connecticut and the Committees of New York, Pensilvania [*sic*], Jerseys and Philadelphia [...] are actually making the most vigorous preparations for War'.[13] On the other hand, Dartmouth considered that the account carried by the *London Gazette* was 'chiefly taken from a Salem Newspaper [and] plainly made up for the purpose of conveying every possible Prejudice and misrepresentation of the Truth'. Based on the questioning of the captain of the ship that had brought the account to Britain, it was Dartmouth's view – expressed in a letter to Gage – that:

> [T]he whole amounts to no more than that a Detachment sent by you to destroy Cannon and Stores, collected at Concord for the purpose of aiding Rebellion were fired upon at different times by the People of the Country in small Bodies from behind Trees and Houses, but that the Party effected the Service they went upon, & returned to Boston, and I have the Satisfaction to tell you that the Affair being considered in that light by all discerning Men, it has had no other effect here than to raise that just Indignation which every honest Man must feel at the rebellious Conduct of the New England Colonies.[14]

Today we might say that Dartmouth was applying a certain amount of 'spin' to the story, but he was not alone in wanting to believe that the American rebels could not put up a decent fight when faced with the might of Britain's disciplined soldiers and a navy which had exited victorious from the Seven Years War. However, as Graves noted to Dunmore, 'The Town of Boston is shut up by the Rebel Troops'[15] and the garrison's problems were only just beginning.

A foreign army can only command supplies from the geographic area that it controls, and therein lay Gage's problem. His army was garrisoned within the bounds of Boston, effectively an island with a narrow neck of land connecting to the mainland. Map 3 shows that Boston Neck could be dominated by any American artillery on the Dorchester Heights, and with Washington's army holding a defensive arc from Dorchester to Charlestown, Gage and his men were effectively holed up in Boston. All their supply needs would have to come by sea. This point was made by Graves to Stephens in August in response to information

---

13   NDAR, Vol.1, p.372, Graves to Lord Dunmore, 20 May 1775.
14   TNA, T 64/108, f.131.
15   NDAR, Vol.1, p.372.

that the contractors responsible for supplying his ships in American ports could no longer source the needed provisions; 'our entire dependence for Supplies in future must be on Great Britain'.[16] Local suppliers were afraid to trade with the British in defiance of proclamations and orders from rebel assemblies and by May 1775 'The Confederate Colonies' were showing open rebellion and 'all shipments were stopped by them'.[17] As 1775 progressed, so the British position was to worsen; local supplies dried up, and the supply chain from Britain was experiencing the problems detailed in previous chapters.

When the rebel army started to fortify positions on the Charlestown Peninsula, so cutting off one of the routes from Boston to the mainland, the British needed to respond. Charlestown, and the area around it, were pretty well deserted in June as Gage had warned the townspeople that he would reduce the town by gunfire if the provincial army moved in, which they did on the night of 16 June. The British 'won' the ensuing action at Bunker Hill and Breed's Hill, but at great loss. The British lost 226 dead and about 900 wounded – a casualty rate of around 40%. As is often the case in a direct attack by infantry, the officers leading the assault suffered disproportionately; 19 were killed and 70 wounded. On the other side, the American losses were 'about half those of the redcoats'.[18] The fight was much harder than the British, with their disdain for the 'tatterdemalion farmers and workers',[19] had expected to face. General Gage, who had earlier told the King how easily the rebels could be brought to their senses, changed his view after the engagement: the Rebels had 'show[ed] a spirit and courage against us they never showed against the French' but as regards Boston, 'I wish this cursed place was burned. The only use is its harbour [...] but in all other respects it is the worst place either to act offensively from, or defensively'.[20]

Throughout the engagement, the naval involvement had been limited. The troops were rowed across the 800 yard wide Charles River by sailors from Graves's fleet, 30–40 regulars in each boat, for an unopposed landing on the peninsula. Once ashore, the navy's role was to provide covering fire from the heavy guns of the fleet, but Graves showed too much caution in this regard as a result of an earlier incident. In May the admiral's nephew, Lieutenant Thomas Graves, was ordered by him to take the schooner *Diana* and cut off the escape of some rebels who had been killing livestock on Noddle's Island [Map 3]. Unfortunately, it did not go well. With a narrow waterway, and an outgoing tide, he attempted to take the schooner out of the creek but the boat had to be abandoned. Early the

16   NDAR, Vol.1, p.1179, Graves to Stephens, 19 August 1775.
17   TNA, T 64/108, f.46.
18   Urban, *Fusiliers*, p.43.
19   Ferling, *Miracle*, p.52.
20   Bicheno, *Rebels and Redcoats*, p.36.

following morning, with the ship set on fire by the provincials, the flames reached the magazine and the *Diana* exploded.[21] The consequence of this for Gage's troops on 17 June was that Graves was reluctant to sail his ships in to the Mystic River, where they could have given covering fire to those troops on the beach approaches to the south-east of Bunker Hill. The majority of the fire support provided by the navy came from the 12-pounders mounted on two gunboats to the west of the peninsula, supported by 'The *Lively, Glasgow, Falcon*, with the *Symmetry* Transport and an Arm'd Sloop [which] kept a Constant fire upon the Rebels, to prevent their annoying the Troops on Landing'.[22] In his narrative report of the action, Graves stated that the shallowness of the water caused him to withhold his larger ships which, 'therefore could give no other assistance, than that of lending Boats, Men, Ammunition and other Stores to the small [boats], which was done'.[23] While the army had been sorely tried that day, Graves's ships had not done as much as they might, and he would later come in for criticism from London. In his report of the action, he was keen to appear to have given Gage all the help he needed:

> The Admiral not only offered and gave every assistance in his power, but went ashore in person to be near General Howe, for the sake of seeing whether any further aid could be given, and of ordering it immediately; & whilst he was there the General observing the mischief his left Wing sustained by the fire from Charles Town, the Admiral asked him if he wished to have the place burned, and being answered Yes, he immediately sent to the Ships to fire red hot Balls (which had been prepared with that in View).[24]

Following their withdrawal into Boston, the British forces found themselves in a poor situation. Their navy, in spite of successes by American privateers, was commanding at sea – Washington acknowledged that they had 'the entire command of the Water' – but the army had limited access to the mainland, no local source of food and was surrounded on three sides by a large provincial army. The British admiral had a tricky job in support of the army; on the one hand, he had to protect those supply convoys bringing provisions for the troops; on the other he had to enforce the Boston Port Act, which prohibited any trade with Boston. Not surprisingly, this could cause problems. In March 1775 Gage informed Graves that a ship from New York, loaded 'with Kings Provisions', had been turned away,

21   Philbrick, *Bunker Hill*, pp.266–268.
22   NDAR, Vol.1, p.701, ship's log, HMS *Preston*, 17 June 1775.
23   NDAR, Vol.1, p.704, narrative of Vice-Admiral Graves, 17 June 1775.
24   NDAR, Vol.1, p.704, narrative of Vice-Admiral Graves, 17 June 1775.

and he hoped that two more from that city (he named them for Graves) would be allowed to dock. The navy was effectively blockading the army. Something of the tension that existed between the army and navy commanders can be detected in Graves's tetchy reply:

> [I]n answer [to Gage's complaint], to represent to you that The Act of Parliament allowing no Supplies of Provisions or Fuel, to be brought for the Inhabitants of Boston but such as are cleared at Marblehead [the Customs office], and Stores for the Use of Government only in Vessels Commissioned by or in the immediate pay of the King; My orders to the Captains of the King's Ships under my Command are consonant to these Regulations, and nothing is permitted to pass in or out but as the Law directs; except by License under My hand and Seal which has always readily been granted when the King's Service would suffer by too strictly following the Letter of the Law; and I am greatly chagrined to find that in doing our Duty afloat We have occasioned any embarrassments in Your Excellency's Military Department. However I cannot help thinking this Might have been avoided by the Contractor's acquainting your Excellency, at an early period, that he expected this Vessel to arrive from New York; Your Excellency may be assured that I have great satisfaction in facilitating rather than impeding the Entrance of Supplies for the Army, where the Act is defective or not sufficiently explicit; And whenever Your Excellency is pleased to send Me the Names of Vessels bringing Provisions or Stores for the Army, I shall not only chearfully [sic] grant them permission to enter, but direct them to have any assistance the Squadron can afford. The Passes your Excellency has Now desired for the Sloops *Sunna* [*Susannah*] and *Speedwell* will be delivered upon Mr Loyd's application for them to My Secretary.[25]

In recognition of how a strict interpretation of the rules might impact Gage's army, Graves issued amended instructions to his captains in the hope that not all American merchants would cease their trade with the Boston garrison:

> I therefore desire that you will make it publick, that all Vessels who shall bring to Boston for sale live Cattle, Sheep, Hogs, Poultry, Pulse, Fruit, Grain, Flour, Oats, Hay, Vegetables, & other Necessaries of Life, shall

25   NDAR, Vol.1, p.130, Graves to Gage, 7 March 1775.

have my Protection and be at Liberty to depart with their Vessels and Crew, whenever they have disposed of their Cargoes.[26]

A month later, in May 1775, Graves extended the protection to those ships that were carrying naval stores and provisions, provided that they went direct to Boston:

> Whereas in the present Exigency of his Majesty's Service it is necessary to facilitate as much as possible the bringing to Boston, Provisions, Lumber and Firewood for the use of the Army and Navy, You are hereby required and directed notwithstanding any former Orders to allow all Ships and Vessels laden with Provisions, Grain, Hay, Straw, Lumber, Firewood, and Spars, and which shall be properly cleared at the Port of Lading, to come into this Harbour, although they may not have my pass or a Clearance from Salem, taking Care however that all such do *proceed straight up to Boston*, and to no other Place within this Harbour[27] [my italics].

Needless to say, the trade allowed by Graves's system of passes was very small and had little influence on the army's increasingly precarious supply situation.

The position into which the British had backed themselves by their withdrawal into the confines of Boston was obvious to Washington when he arrived to take over the American force after the events at Bunker Hill. His summation of the situation in a letter to his brother included a prescient comment on the later need for the British to leave Boston for New York.

> The Enemy are sickly, and scare [*sic*] of Fresh provisions, Beef, which is chiefly got by slaughtering their Milch Cows in Boston, sells from one shilling to 18d [18 pence] Sterling per lb.; and that it may not get cheaper, or more plenty, I have drove all the Stock within a considerable distance of this place, back into the Country, out of the Way of the Men of war's Boats; In short, I have, and shall continue to do, every thing in my power to distress them. The Transports are all arrived and their whole Reinforcement is Landed, so that I can see no reason why they should not if they ever attempt it, come boldly out and put the matter to Issue at once if they think themselves not strong enough to do this. [T]hey surely will carry their Arms (having Ships of War and Transports ready) to some other part of the Continent, or relinquish the dispute; the last of which the Ministry, unless compelled will never agree to do. Our Works, and

26   NDAR, Vol.1, p.230, Graves to Captain Bishop, 27 April 1775.
27   NDAR, Vol.1, pp.502–503, Graves to ships' captains at Boston, 22 May 1775.

those of the Enemy are so near and quite open between that we see every thing that each other is doing.[28]

From mid-June 1775 until March 1776, the British troops were effectively confined to the town of Boston and were completely dependent on the navy for their supplies and transport. As winter approached, the provisioning would become more difficult and, in the end, would be a major factor in the decision to evacuate the town for New York. The limited access to fresh food had consequences for the health of the men, sailors as well as soldiers. Even before the action at Bunker Hill, Gage was reporting to Lord Dartmouth that 'The Sudden Refusal of all the Colonies to Supply the Troops with Necessaries of any kind, has put us to Shifts to increase our Stock of Provisions'.[29] One such 'shift' was to try to circumvent the 'severe prohibition of the Rebel Generals' on the sale of provisions to British troops, which had even extended to owners dismantling their small vessels as 'few people dare to supply us'.[30] Another was suggested by Graves to the agent in New York: use subterfuge and give incorrect consignee information when hiring a transport ship to take supplies to Boston:

> As every stratagem must be used to procure provisions at this Juncture, the Contractor for the Navy at Boston has ordered his Correspondent Mr Wm McAdams at New York to charter a Vessel from 80 to 100 Tons, and to put on Board her Bread, Beef, Peas, Oatmeal, and Rice. These Provisions are to be consigned to John Grant Esqr Spanish Town Jamaica, and the Vessel of course will be cleared for that place. No person in New York can possibly know but she really is intended for Jamaica, not even Mr McAdams himself, who is ordered to write an Account of his Proceedings on this Business, And to draw upon London for the Amount. When this Vessel so laden goes down the River you must seize her, and putting a sufficient Strength on board send her to Boston; but I desire this may not be done till she is at the Hook [Sandy Hook, NY], that the knowledge of this transaction may not get to New York and prevent our future Success, for which Reason all the People and the Master must be sent hither.[31]

28   NDAR, Vol.1, p.983, letter from George Washington to his brother, 27 July 1775.
29   NDAR, Vol.1, p.663.
30   NDAR, Vol.1, p.326, Graves to Stephens, 13 May 1775.
31   NDAR, Vol.1, p.913, Graves to Captain Vandeput, 18 July 1775.

The stratagem was employed on a number of occasions, although the relief to the garrison would have been slight, but every little helps. In September 1775, Graves was again trying a similar ruse, but this time with a little twist.

> A Vessel will be freighted by [John Mansfield] of Newport with Fuel and Victual, and will purposely throw herself in the Way of some of your Ships to be seized. And it will be necessary, to preserve the Master from the Resentment of his Countrymen on his Return, to put on the Appearance of compelling him to come to Boston; but it will be proper also to take out some of the People and send yours instead, as the Crew may not be depended on.[32]

The rebels could only be fooled so often, maybe threats and promises of the release of pressed men would help to oil the wheels, as Graves proposed to the town of Salem in May 1775.

> If the Town of Salem mean to approve themselves good Subjects, quiet and peaceably disposed, they have now an Opportunity to shew it. Let Mr Brymer ship off his Provisions, and let me have assurances that my People may come as formerly to purchase and that they shall be supplied and allowed to carry away what they want for the Kings Service, paying for the same, and I will not only order every prest [*sic*] man to be discharged who is an inhabitant of Salem, and direct no more to be impressed but I will give the Town any Protection and Assistance they can desire to enable them to continue firm in a dutiful Conduct towards his Majesty which cannot in my Opinion fail of producing the happyest [*sic*] Consequences to themselves.[33]

Even the French Ambassador in London was aware of the supply situation in Boston: 'It is now necessary to send even the flour from England in order to support this army [...] England cannot depend at present on any source of supply in that part of the world'.[34] The lack of fresh provisions for the garrison, and their effective state of siege must have given heart to Washington:

> They suffer greatly for want of fresh Provisions, notwithstanding they have pillaged several Islands of a good many Sheep and Cattle. They are

---

32   NDAR, Vol.2, p.253, Graves to Captain Wallace, 30 September 1775.
33   NDAR, Vol.1, p.501, Graves to collector of taxes at Salem, 21 May 1775.
34   NDAR, Vol.1, p.491, De Guines to Vergennes, 23 June 1775.

also scarce of Fuel, unless, (according to the acct. of one of their Deserters) they mean to pull down Houses for Firing. In short, they are, from all accts. suffering all the Inconveniences of a Siege.[35]

The raids by individual ships from Graves's fleet, and the ruses employed to divert cargoes to Boston, may have eased the situation a little, but they were no solution to Gage's growing problem. The cutting off of local supplies had been anticipated by the Treasury's main contractor (Nesbitt, Drummond, and Franks) and additional supplies were ordered from Britain, hopefully sufficient for 10,000 men until July 1776. However, these victualling ships were not expected to sail until the first week of October 1775.[36] In Boston, Gage had a less optimistic view of his situation. The number of mouths was continually increasing, especially as more and more Loyalists took refuge in the town, expecting to be fed by the army. As we saw in Chapter 3, London was continually haranguing commanders in America to give accurate returns of the number of mouths to be fed. On 30 June 1775, the Treasury reminded Gage that they 'desire that you will in future give as early notice as possible to this Board of the Requisitions you may make for the supplies you may want'.[37] In January 1776 the Treasury wanted to know what supplies were held in Boston as they believed that the troop transports, recently sent to Boston, had been victualled for six months and so the army should have 'great quantities of provisions remaining on board' and they wanted to know if the commander-in-chief had made 'any returns of such provisions'.[38] There was obviously a large disconnect between those in London who were attempting to keep the army supplied and those on the ground in Boston, a problem made no easier by the slow communications and lack of adherence to administrative procedures by the army commanders. Gage wanted the contractors to hold sufficient food in hand for his troops for a six-month period; because of the increasing number of troops, the inflow of Loyalists and refugees, late shipments from Britain, losses at sea and the fact that London did not know how many they were victualling for, the supplies did not reach the six-month level. By early October 1775, his men had had two months during which they 'existed on the food stocks of troop transports and naval vessels and often had less than thirty days' supplies on hand'.[39] When five ships arrived in October 'most of the 5,200 barrels of flour on board proved to be rotten'. The longer that the army remained in Boston, the more difficult became the problem of provisioning them. The navy was not affected to the same degree;

35   NDAR, Vol.2, p.68, Washington to his brother, 10 September 1775.
36   Bowler, Logistics, p.42.
37   TNA, T 64/106.
38   TNA, T 29/45, f.15.
39   Bowler, Logistics, p.43.

ships could go into ports and demand supplies, on pain of retribution if the locals demurred, and they could resupply each other at sea if they were running short. Gage was overdependent on his supply convoys, on their arrival on time and with the victuals they carried being in good order. By December 1775, General Howe – who had replaced Gage – was of the opinion that if supply ships did not arrive by the end of the month 'I shall be obliged to put the troops upon short allowance'.[40]

In October and November 1775, the Treasury took determined action to get on top of the army's supply problems. The main contractor (Mure, Son, & Atkinson) put in a great deal of effort to assemble a fleet of 36 transport ships with all the provisions the army would need. Beef, pork, bread, and cheese were loaded, but so were additional items, which it was hoped would ease the winter months for the Boston garrison: 500 tons of potatoes, 60 tons of onions, 50 of parsnips, 40 of carrots, 20 of raisins, 4,000 sheep and hogs, and 468,750 gallons of porter.[41] Mure and Sons had gone to a great deal of trouble to try to ensure that the cargoes arrived in the best condition: the ships' masters were to be paid a bonus for each animal that was delivered alive – the voyage was a notorious killer of livestock. Unfortunately, the garrison was not to have it so easy. Winter in the Atlantic is a dangerous place for wooden sailing vessels and this was to be no exception. The convoy was hit by a tremendous storm; the ships were scattered, some returning to Ireland, others spending weeks attempting to put in to Boston, and still more gave up and sailed to Antigua in the West Indies. Howe's concern about the ships arriving before the end of December was about to become real. Admiral Shuldham, on board *Chatham* in Boston harbour, reported that:

> Of the Thirty five Vessels Freighted by Mure and company with Provisions and Supplys [sic] for the use of the Fleet and Army only Eight are Arrived, and on board those not above a Twentieth part of the Sheep were bought in Alive.[42]

Had the convoy arrived complete, then the garrison would not only have had sufficient food for the winter, but there would have been transport vessels to allow an earlier evacuation of Boston than actually happened. In January 1776 Vice-Admiral Young (commanding at Antigua) informed the Admiralty that he was making arrangements for those victuallers and transports that had been diverted to the West Indies, to be escorted to Boston 'or any other Port the Fleet may

40   TNA, T 64/108, f.2.
41   Bowler, *Logistics*, p.53.
42   NDAR, Vol.3, p.793, Shuldham to Stephens, 15 January 1776.

Rendezvous at'.[43] The garrison at Boston was in dire straits, as a result of the misfortunes of the convoy. Attempts were made to obtain provisions from the West Indies, but with little success. Vice-Admiral Young wrote to General Howe in February to say that 'I am Sorry to find there is very little to be purchased at this Island beside Flour [...] it gives me much concern to perceive by your Letter the Kings Army at Boston, are likely to encounter such Strong necessities, and I sincerely wish it lay in my power to remove all their difficulties, but this at present is a very bad place to get assistance at, of the kind you need'.[44] It was not until the end of March 1776 that Young was giving directions for the last of the ships of the convoy to be escorted to Boston;[45] many had required extensive repairs, but the 13 ships did not sail until April and by then the British had evacuated Boston.

The supply situation had been a big factor in General Howe's decision to evacuate Boston (more on this later). In March 1776, his stores held only three weeks' supply of beef and the 'army almost totally subsists on what Mr Shuldham has been able to spare from the Naval stock of provisions'.[46] Writing from Halifax after the evacuation was complete, Howe told John Robinson (the Treasury Secretary) that the supply situation on its own 'would soon have reduced me to the necessity of evacuating Boston and removing the Army to a Place that afforded some Resources'.[47] The garrison's position was further weakened when the rebels took post on the Dorchester Heights on the night of 4 March, giving them command of the Neck which connected Boston to the mainland; as Germain reported to the King, General Howe had 'been obliged to quit Boston for want of provisions, and from the position of the Enemy'.[48] The months between the events at Concord (April 1775) and the evacuation of Boston (March 1776) were difficult for General Gage and Admiral Graves. To some extent, Gage had made himself a hostage to fortune by telling the King that he could put down the rebellion with only four regiments. Lexington and Concord had been a humiliation for British arms and while Bunker Hill was a British 'victory', it was pyrrhic in that the army was effectively walled up in Boston, totally reliant on the navy for all its needs. Nick Bunker summed up Gage as 'preoccupied with Boston [and] allowed his political mission to dictate his thinking even when it had already proved to be incapable of fulfilment. [He] chose to make Boston an American Singapore, a fortress supplied by sea but surrounded by a hinterland that he could neither defend nor control'.[49]

43   NDAR, Vol.3, p.706, Young to Stephens, 9 January 1776.
44   NDAR, Vol.3, pp.1210–1211, Young to General Howe, 10 February 1776.
45   NDAR, Vol.4, p.561, Young to Captain Scott, 28 March 1776.
46   NDAR, Vol.4, p.1080, Sandwich to the King, 2 May 1776.
47   TNA, T 64/108, f.59, item 23.
48   NDAR, Vol.4, p.1081, Germain to the King, 2 May 1776.
49   Bunker, *Empire on the Edge*, p.309.

To put backbone into Gage's irresolute command London sent out three major-generals – William Howe (the senior of the three and brother of the Admiral), Henry Clinton, and John Burgoyne – but Gage had to be replaced. The General was called home for 'consultations' following the news of Bunker Hill. With the letters from London taking weeks to arrive in America, Gage did not hear of his recall until 26 September; on the 30th he wrote to Graves that 'I know the great use you have for His Majesty's Ships, I will not distress you by an Application for a Ship of War to carry me and have therefore ordered a transport to be got in readyness [sic] with all expedition'[50] and it was 11 October before he had handed over his command to General Howe and sailed for England on the *Pallas*.

The initial months of the war had not gone well, and its progress had not been helped by the poor relationship between Gage and his naval counterpart. The admiral came in for criticism from civilians as well as his own officers; he received notice of his recall on 30 December 1775 and was replaced by Rear-Admiral Shuldham, 15 January 1776, returning to England on the 27th of the month.[51] Hearing of the change in command one inhabitant of Boston was moved to write that:

> It must be a Change for the better, for so much Ignorance, Stupidity, Pride, Avarice & whatever You have a mind to add in the same Strain, never centered [sic] in one Commander of a Fleet in the British Navy since the Flag was' hoisted, as in one that is not unknown among us. We are told that the present Commanders in Chief of the Navy (I mean Mr Shuldham) and Army have a very good Understanding with each other, from which we hope to see good Effects.[52]

Opinions are personal and vary between individuals. A letter in the *Public Advertiser* in London defended Graves: 'On the Information I have procured, I do not scruple to assure you he has been cruelly used. [The fleet was] Ill manned, ill provided, ill supplied'.[53] Cruelly used or not, the voices raised against Gage and Graves, and the shirking of responsibility by ministers, did not go unnoticed by the French ambassador in London when he noted that 'they will lose their commands because they have been made responsible for all the defeats'.[54]

When Graves arrived on station, he had insufficient ships to impose the blockade of the American coast and close Boston harbour, as London had directed. Also,

---

50   NDAR, Vol.2, p.250, Gage to Graves, 30 September 1775.
51   NDAR, Vol.3, pp.794–795, 1078.
52   NDAR, Vol.3, p.811, letter from N. Taylor to Joseph Taylor, 16 January 1776.
53   NDAR, Vol.3, p.878, *Public Advertiser*, 27 February 1775.
54   NDAR, Vol.2, p.679, De Guines to Vergennes, 18 August 1775.

his less than fulsome support for the action at Bunker Hill – he had held his ships back from the Mystick River following the *Diana* incident – opened him to criticism at home. Sandwich warned Graves in July that 'you may be blamed for doing too little [the nation expected great results from its navy], but can never be censured for doing too much'.[55] However, Burgoyne's letter to Germain 'did for him' with the King who authorised Lord Rochford to tell Sandwich that the command in America could 'no longer be left in such improper hands'.[56] On 17 September 1775, Sandwich wrote to Graves telling him of his recall, but tried to sugar the pill: 'I shall in every place [...] do you the justice you deserve, and declare my opinion that it has been more owing to accident than to misconduct that the operations of the fleet during this summer have not carried that importance with them that the nation expected'.[57]

Had Graves been a more opportunistic and aggressive commander he would still have been handicapped by a lack of ships. This was compounded by London's fear that France would take advantage of Britain's involvement in America. In a debate in the House of Commons (see Chapter 2), Captain James Luttrell expressed the view that Graves was being made the scapegoat for the lack of ministerial decisiveness towards the colonies 'and his reputation as an officer [was to] be sacrificed to shelter the wicked proceedings of these ministers'.[58] As the war progressed, the poor working relationship between army and navy commanders would not be confined to Gage and Graves.

If the British were to recover the American colonies then they had to leave Boston. The army had limited operational flexibility while it was surrounded by Washington's forces and its supply situation was becoming dire. For all his limitations, Gage had correctly assessed the strategic importance of the Hudson Valley. It gave access to the interior and to Canada as well as forming a natural barrier between Connecticut, Rhode Island, and Massachusetts in the north from much of New York State, New Jersey, Pennsylvania, Virginia, and the Carolinas. Controlling the Hudson would 'open a virtually continuous communication between Britain's main bases in Canada and New York city, so splitting the United States asunder along a north-south axis, and likewise severing the lateral supply line across the river that was vital of the survival of the Patriots' Continental Army'.[59]

55 SP, Vol.1, p.67, Sandwich to Graves, 30 July 1775.
56 SP, Vol.1, p.73, Rochford to Sandwich, 8 September 1775.
57 SP, Vol.1, p.74, Sandwich to Graves, 17 September 1775.
58 NDAR, Vol.3, p.337, House of Commons debate, 1 November 1775.
59 S. Brumwell, *Turncoat: Benedict Arnold and the Crisis of American Liberty* (London: Yale University Press, 2018), p.1.

The government's plan for 1776, after an evacuation of Boston, was for a massive invasion of New York in the early spring. It was hoped that this strike would be sufficiently overwhelming as to bring the rebels to their senses in the one campaign. However, the best laid plans are always subject to 'events'. An American expedition into Canada ('which jarred with the rhetoric of a purely defensive struggle against imperial tyranny')[60] caused the loss of Quebec and a change of British priorities. The recovery of the Canadian city was prioritised over the invasion of New York and resources were further diluted by an abortive expedition to North Carolina in response to (incorrect) claims by the governor, Josiah Martin, that the Loyalists would rise up if the British Army landed on their shore. Before any of this could happen, the navy had to evacuate the troops from Boston.

60   Brumwell, *Turncoat*, p.47.

7

'In bad plight we go to Halifax'

The winter of 1775–1776 was a hard one for the British troops in Boston. There were insufficient barrack facilities for the men, food was short, and there was little wood or coal to be used for heating and cooking. The living conditions, together with food shortages, meant that outbreaks of sickness were almost inevitable and in September 1775, Gage was reporting dysentery among the troops and the local population. By November, 'the sickness of the army [had] rather increased'.[1] Staying warm and dry was a big problem for troops and civilians alike. There were no supplies of wood on the peninsula, other than that within the buildings, coal and wood had to be brought in by the navy and the transport ships from Britain. One example was the transport ship *Stakesby* which, in October 1775, left England with 85 *chaldrons* (or cauldrons) of coal, approximately 105–110 tons.[2] Sailing vessels at that time normally carried stones in the bottom of the ship as ballast to aid stability and sailing performance, and it was suggested that all ships sailing for America should carry coal instead of stones to alleviate the troops' situation.[3] The winter temperatures in Boston would have been quite alien to the British troops and a shortage of fuel was the last thing they needed on top of food shortages. Because of the unreliability of the sailing of transports from Britain, the coal they might carry could not be relied on and so other measures had to be taken to make up the supply; fences and abandoned houses were torn down for firewood and even the Boston Liberty Tree fell to the woodman's axe, yielding 14 cords for the fire.[4]

We have already seen that the 35-ship convoy, which should have resupplied Boston for the winter, had been dispersed to the four winds by a major Atlantic

---

1   TNA, CO 5/92, f.323.
2   NDAR, Vol.2, p.797.
3   NDAR, Vol.1, p.663, Gage to Dartmouth, 12 June 1775.
4   Ferling, *Miracle*, p.101.

storm. By December 1775, Howe's supply situation was becoming desperate. Although locally sourced provisions were almost unavailable, some did come on the market, though of poor quality and at exorbitant prices: 'mutton, which would be burned in any market in England, sells for two shillings a pound'.[5] Although the army was suffering from a shortage of provisions, navy ships were often in a better situation. Before sailing from Britain it was normal for them to be victualled for six months, which meant that they had four months' worth of food on board on arrival in Boston. This advantage over the soldiers was mentioned in a letter from a midshipman on board Shuldham's flagship, the *Chatham*:

> The army has been scarce of provisions by reason of many of their victualling ships being blown to the West Indies; however, that is not the case with the navy. I can assure you from good authority, that they have sufficient to serve them till October next, after having spared a good deal to the army. We have had a great deal of fresh provisions of all sorts from Halifax and the Bay of Fundy during the winter, though rather dear. Five or six vessels of one kind and another have arrived from the West Indies within this month, chiefly laden with rum, molasses and limes, and within these few days several victuallers for the use of the army, and other ships, have arrived, after very long passages, from England and Ireland.[6]

The writer refers to the navy having 'spared a good deal to the army', highlighting the point that naval ships could sometimes act as a 'supplier of last resort' to the troops. The same point was made by Shuldham to Sandwich when the army left Boston due to the 'necessitous state to which it is now reduced' whereby it 'almost totally subsists on what I have been able to spare from our naval stock of provisions'.[7] With the convoy bringing his winter supplies scattered between Ireland and the West Indies, and with less than three weeks' supply of meat on hand, General Howe knew that he had to get out of Boston; his problem was getting sufficient transport ships to carry the troops and the civilians who wanted to leave. Had the convoy arrived he would have had shipping enough for the intended move.

In September 1775, Howe had received orders from London that he should move his army from Boston to over-winter in New York, from where they could launch the campaigning season in spring of 1776; the plan was scuppered with the scattering of the provisions convoy and the loss those ships as potential troop

5   SP, Vol.1, p.107, Shuldham to Sandwich, 13 January 1776.
6   NDAR, Vol.4, p.473, letter 23 March 1776.
7   SP, Vol.1, p.123, Shuldham to Sandwich, 23 March 1776.

transports. On 26 November, Howe acknowledged the receipt of the orders but their late arrival meant that the proposed move could not go ahead due to the lack of ships. He had calculated that he needed 35,172 tons of transport capacity to move the army and even if the convoy had arrived as planned this would still have left a shortfall of 11,602 tons. Additionally, the winter weather would have been too bad for them to make two journeys.[8] The position of Howe and Shuldham was made still more difficult by the slow communications with London. In his 23 March 1776 letter to Sandwich, Shuldham pointed out that before leaving Boston 'I presume we shall receive some instructions from Government, which we have been and still continue in impatient expectation of. The latest we have had are those I brought as far back as the latter end of October'.[9]

With the conflict having a large element of a civil war, there were many Loyalists who wanted to leave Boston rather than stay and suffer the revenge of the returning Rebels. The British recognised that they needed to 'do the right thing' by the Loyalists, but this would put further strain on the available transport: 'One great Difficulty among the many of this Operation will be the Number of the inhabitants who, I [Howe] expect, will desire to be removed with their Effects and Merchandize [sic]'.[10] If the troops and Loyalists were to be got away safely then a truce would be necessary. On 8 March 1776 some of the 'Select men of Boston' wrote to the 'Continental Army Commanders' to let them know that General Howe was 'determined to leave the Town with the Troops under his command' and that 'he has no Intention of destroying the Town, unless the Troops under his Command are molested during their Embarkation;' however, 'If such an opposition should take Place, we [the Select Men] have the greatest Reason to expect the Town will be exposed to entire Destruction'.[11] In the event the British and the accompanying Loyalists were allowed to embark unmolested and sail out to an assembly area at Nantucket Roads, from where the whole fleet left for Halifax; 8,908 troops, together with 924 Loyalists,[12] were evacuated on 17 March.

> [On] the 17th instant [...] His Majesty's Troops being safely Embarked, and the Transports Anchored in King Road, from whence, as fast as they were Watered and ready for Sea they proceeded to this place [Nantucket Roads]; where they are all collected and will proceed by the

8   TNA, CO 5/92, ff.318, 324.
9   SP, Vol.1, p.124, Shuldham to Sandwich, 23 March 1776.
10   TNA, ADM 1/4132, f.4, letter from Howe to Dartmouth, 16 January 1776.
11   NDAR, Vol.4, p.229.
12   Syrett, *American Waters*, p.24.

first opportunity of Wind and Weather under Convoy of the Ships in the Margin, to Halifax.[13]

On 27 March the *Chatham* 'in Company with HM Ships *Centurion Lively Savage & Tryal* Schooner with Sixty Six Sail of Transports & other Vessels' left Nantucket for Halifax. The following extract is taken from a letter written by one of those on board the *Chatham*, the archive does not indicate if the author was a civilian or military man, but I suspect the latter from the content:

The retreat of the Troops from this garrison (Boston) cannot fail to be differently represented in England; for which reason I have found time from our great hurry to give you some account of it. In the first place, the General's not receiving any letters or despatches from Government since the middle of October, could not fail of making everybody uneasy; it looked as if we were left destitute to get out of a bad scrape as we liked best. Our provisions falling short, added to our discontent. The fleet afforded us no relief; little indeed was in their power their own ill equipment was enough to make them as dissatisfied as ourselves. The Provincials, who knew exactly the state of our garrison, harassed us from their batteries, with an intention of making our people more dissatisfied, in hopes of desertions. Finding no probability of supply, and dreading the consequence of further delay, it was thought prudent to retire to the ships, and to save what we could. Our not being burdened with provisions, permitted us to save some stores and ammunition, the light field-pieces, and such things as are most convenient of carriage. The rest, I am sorry to say, we were obliged to leave behind; such of the guns as, by dismounting, we could throw into the sea, were done so; the carriages were disabled, and every precaution taken that our circumstances would permit, for our retreat was by agreement. The people of the town who were friends to Government, took care of nothing but their merchandise, and found means to employ the men belonging to the transports in embarking their goods; by which means several of the vessels were entirely filled with private property instead of the King's stores. By some unavoidable accident, the medicines, surgeons' chests, instruments, and necessaries, were left in the Hospital. The confusion unavoidable on such a disaster, will make you conceive how much must be forgot where every man had a private concern. The necessary care and distress of the women, children, sick, and wounded, required every assistance that could be given. It was

13   NDAR, Vol.4, p.472, Shuldham to Stephens, 23 March 1776.

not like breaking up a camp, where every man knows his duty; it was like departing your country, with your wives, your servants, your household furniture, and all your encumbrances. The officers, who felt the disgrace of their retreat, did their utmost to keep up appearances. The men, who thought they were changing for the better, strove to take the advantage of the present times, and were kept from plunder and drink with difficulty. In bad plight we go to Halifax. What supply we are to expect there I do not know; our expectations are not very sanguine. The neglect shown us bears hard on us all; the soldiers think themselves betrayed, the officers all blame the Admiralty, and your friend, Lord S[andwich], is universally execrated. The sea officers complained they were hurried out of England in a most shameful condition, not half manned, and ill provided. Fleet and Army complain of each other, and both of the people at home. If we fare as ill at Halifax as we have done here lately, I fear we shall have great desertion, as the opportunity will be more convenient.[14]

The evacuation of Boston was only possible because of the support of the navy and its commanding superiority over the naval resources available to the Americans, but the leaving was an event to be trumpeted by the provincial forces, and the *Boston Gazette* was not slow in taking the lead. The paper reported that colonial troops had taken possession of the town, 'in the name of the Thirteen United Colonies of North America'. Here was an opportunity to indulge in a little hyperbole at the expense of the King and the Home Country; Boston had been occupied by 'the flower of the British army, headed by an experienced General, and supported by a formidable fleet of men of war, [who] had, but an hour before, evacuated in the most precipitous and cowardly manner [...]'[15] Britain had been humbled and their opponents had a right to some triumphalism: 'Our Quitting Boston has raised the Spirits of the Rebell [*sic*] Party beyond description[,] they look upon themselves [as] invincible'.[16] The hurried nature of the evacuation from Boston, together with the slow communications between that port and London and the failure to ensure that there were adequate patrols of the entrances to the harbour after they had left, led to further embarrassment. A large convoy of transports had left the Clyde in April 1776 with regiments of Highlanders on board for delivery to Boston. Unfortunately, the news of that town's evacuation had not reached Britain by the time of sailing. Admiral Shuldham had assured the

14   NDAR, Vol.4, p.490.
15   NDAR, Vol.4, pp.497–498, *Boston Gazette*, 25 March 1776.
16   NDAR, Vol.5, p.62, letter from Major Hutcheson to Major General Haldimand, 12 May 1776.

Admiralty in April that, following the evacuation, he had 'stationed a Squadron of His Majesty's Ships in Nantasket [*sic*] Road, under the command of Captain [Francis] Banks of the *Renown*, for the purpose as he expressed it, "of intercepting and sending to Halifax the Ships with the Supplies ordered to Boston, and which would consequently be Ignorant of the removal of the Fleet and Army."'[17] During the passage from the Clyde, the convoy was scattered and two transports (with troops on board) sailed into Boston harbour without being stopped by the navy, and the troops taken prisoner. The King was not amused, as Germain's letter went on to spell out:

> His Majesty remarked, with much Surprize, that in the account given by General Howe in his Letter to me of the 7th of July, of the Capture of two Transports with part of the Highland Regiments onboard, those Transports are said to have been carried into Boston, without having been intercepted by any of His Majesty's Ships [...] His Majesty was therefore pleased to command me to signify to your Lordships His Majesty's Pleasure, that you do direct Lord Howe to inquire into the Truth of these Facts, and into the conduct of the Officers commanding such of His Majesty's Ships as have been stationed in Nantasket Road, or appointed to Cruize in the Bay of Boston since the Evacuation of that Town by the Army, and to report the same to your Lordships for His Majesty's Information.

Unsurprisingly, troop transports were not the only vessels to be unaware that Boston had fallen. In May two supply ships made the same mistake, one of them carrying supplies that Howe's troops would have welcomed, but were probably no less appreciated by the Rebels: 'on board 50 tons of coal, 256 whole barrels and 130 half barrels of beef, 300 fi[r]kins of butter, 200 boxes of candles, 40 barrels of flour, 49 barrels of barley, a qu[a]ntity of hams, 100 boxes of soap'.[18]

If Boston was in the wrong position from which to launch the recovery of the colonies, Halifax – some 550 miles north-east of New York as the crow flies – was even further removed, and no better provisioned. Halifax was a dockyard, capable of careening and repairing ships, but not building them. As such, it provided limited facilities for fleet maintenance and would have been of more importance had a 1771 suggestion of Rear-Admiral James Gambier to build a dry-dock been

17   NDAR, Vol.6, p.548, Germain to the Admiralty, 16 August 1776.
18   NDAR, Vol.5, p.6, *New-England Chronicle*, 9 May 1776.

implemented.[19] As a repair facility, the yard did not have the accommodation required to give shelter to Howe's troops and those Loyalists who had travelled with them. By 2 April all the troops and civilians who had left Boston had arrived in Halifax after an uncomfortable journey: 'never was an Army so Crouded [*sic*] in transports, owing to the want of Shiping [*sic*]'.[20] Although the troops were not surrounded as they had been at Boston, they were as dependent on the supply ships coming north from the West Indies as they had been before the evacuation; as the governor of Nova Scotia (Francis Legge) explained to Germain, 'the Army and Fleet [was left] with not more than one Months Allowance for both'.[21] Even the horses that had accompanied the troops on the voyage from Boston had to be taken 38 miles outside Halifax to get any grass.[22] With only limited barrack facilities ashore, many of the men had to remain onboard the transports – further limiting the number of ships available to those back in London who were valiantly attempting to charter ships to carry provisions.

The fact that he had had to transport the Loyalists from Boston to Halifax was a big headache for General Howe; they were under the protection of the army, they needed feeding, and they wanted him to find them a passage to Europe. He had assured them that he would assign the first available vessel but wanted London to be aware that 'there is an absolute Necessity for issuing Provisions to the whole of them, about 1,100, from the Kings Stores',[23] and so rations for them would need to come from Britain. This was another example of the victualling service at home having to provide for more than just the troops, but being dependent on Howe to provide them with numbers. Although reliant on provisions from Britain, the British did try to source what they could in Nova Scotia, as well as by foraging further afield. Captain Barkley in the *Scarborough*, together with two transports and a number of marines, had been sent to Georgia 'to procure Rice and other Supplies for the use of the Army; and I have the pleasure to inform you that the Quantity which has been obtained by this measure is very considerable and is of the greatest Consequence in the present necessitous State of the Army'.[24] Ever watchful, the French were also aware of Howe's situation: 'From Halifax, we have reliable intelligence that General Howe's Army is in miserable condition. A number of the troops have to remain on board for lack of lodging ashore. The

19   J. Gwyn, *Ashore and Afloat: The British Navy and the Halifax Naval Yard before 1820* (Ottawa: University of Ottawa Press, 2004), p.23.
20   NDAR, Vol.4, p.1222, Hutcheson to Haldimand, 24 April 1776.
21   NDAR, Vol.4, p.745, letter from Legge to Germain, 10 April 1776.
22   Urban, *Fusiliers*, p.66.
23   NDAR, Vol.4, p.1284, Howe to Germain, 25 April 1776.
24   NDAR, Vol.4, p.1223, Shuldham to Stephens, 24 April 1776.

soldiers are suffering of dysentery and were on half-allowance until the arrival of the supply ships'.[25]

By May 1776, Howe was hoping to be able to move from Halifax: 'I hope my Design of removing with the Army from hence to New York, as soon as I am enabled by a Supply of Provisions, may not meet with the Kings disapprobation'. As so often during the war, the availability of supplies was a major factor in all operational decisions: 'I tremble when I think of our present State of Provisions, having now Meat for no more than thirteen Days in Store'.[26] And when he did get away he intended leaving the women and children at Halifax to be 'subsisted at the usual Allowance of half a Ration for each Woman, & one Quarter for a child, in which a Supply of Rice, lately arrived from Georgia, will be a principal Article'. One of the problems that Howe and Shuldham had had to overcome when evacuating Boston was the availability of sufficient transport but he now felt in a better situation for the planned move to New York: 'By the Addition of Vessels taken into the Service, & of Arrivals at this Port since leaving Boston, we shall have a sufficient Quantity of Tonnage for the Removal of the Army from hence, without the Inconvenience of the Officers & Soldiers being crowded, which was experienced on our Way to this Port'.[27]

The move of Howe's army from Halifax to New York was one part of a planned build-up of British forces for the spring campaign in 1776. It was hoped that if this force could deliver one overwhelming blow to the provincial army, then the rebels would come to their senses; but first the troops had to be assembled in America. Sandwich was told in February 1776 that 27,480 infantry were to be sent from Europe for the campaign, a massive task for the existing transport and logistics systems. An undertaking of this magnitude had to be done in stages and the forces involved were split over four groups. The original estimate was for a total of 77,200 tons of transport shipping,[28] and with most ships being of 250–400 tons burthen, this required the chartering of a substantial number of ships. Even then, it was an underestimate, as it did not allow for transporting recruits, camp equipage and clothing, all of which required a prodigious amount of cargo space.[29] Bold plans require a unity of purpose, clear aims and goals and the administrative ability to bring them to fruition; sadly, these were not all apparent during the operations of 1776. When the Commissioners of the Navy received the orders to provide transports for the 27,000 troops 'they were not informed of the places of

25   NDAR, Vol.6, p.415, letter to Vergennes, 11 June 1776.
26   NDAR, Vol.4, p.1436, Howe to Germain, 7 May 1776.
27   NDAR, Vol.4, p.1436, Howe to Germain, 7 May 1776.
28   Syrett, *Shipping and the American War*, p.197.
29   The transport requirements are covered in great detail in Syrett, *Shipping and the American War*, pp.196–208.

embarkation, destination, or the names of the units', these details – essential one might think – were to follow at a later date 'in a series of supplementary directives'. One result was that when the Board received orders to transport a unit, it 'did not know if the unit in question was part of the 27,000 men for whom ships had already been ordered or an addition to that number'.[30]

Some of the many problems the Boards encountered when hiring transport ships have been outlined in Chapter 4, but Sandwich reassured the King in January 1776 that 'we shall be ready in time with all the transports that are wanted'.[31] Hugh Palliser, one of the Lords of the Admiralty, was less sanguine: 'it must be remembered that we are now required to provide (as it were instantly) more transports than the greatest number employed in the last war, which were years growing to that number'.[32] Palliser's contrasting of the effort required in 1776 with that required during the Seven Years War, puts the scale of the effort into context. But it was not only men, provisions and tents that were being transported; when the 10,000 Hessians and Guards sailed in May 1776 they did so together with 1,500 sets of clothing for the marines in America, 82 flat-bottom boats (for amphibious landings), and 131 wagons.[33] Sandwich was rightly 'full of Comfort, & rather exulting'[34] when the last of the transports left Spithead in May. By then the Navy Board had taken up 146,189 tons of shipping (including victuallers and local ships chartered in America); this was '46,471 tons more than at the height of the last war'.[35] Those involved deserve credit for a remarkable achievement, carried out with administrative systems that were never designed for a task of that magnitude.

Although enormous efforts had gone into the movement of the 27,000 troops, the campaign season did not start on time and, while some of the delays are accounted for by the confusion over the details of the intended movement of the different army units, that was far from being the only cause. Howe's army was not helped by the lack of clear aims and goals that were needed for the prosecution of the operations against the colonists. Ministers had their attention distracted by the events in Canada and the Carolinas. The Americans had invaded Canada in the winter of 1775 and the British government had to direct shipping resources to the relief of Quebec. The arrival of HMS *Isis* and the attendant supply ships was a good example of 'power projection' but reduced the shipping available for America: 'Upon the arrival of the Men of War and the Transports from England,

---

30   Syrett, *Shipping and the American War*, p.198.
31   Syrett, *Shipping and the American War*, p.198.
32   SP, Vol.1, p.97, letter from Palliser to Sandwich, 6 January 1776.
33   Syrett, *Shipping and the American War*, p.204.
34   Rodger, *Sandwich*, p.228.
35   Rodger, *Sandwich*, p.228.

under the command of Capt Charles Douglas, since created a Baronet, the Rebels abandoned the seige [*sic*], the 6th of May 1776, and fled with great precipitancy'.[36]

While the intervention of the *Isis* had been successful, the government's decision to get involved in the Carolinas, at the same time as Howe was still trying to extricate his army from Boston, was a mistake. Ministers had the belief that the southern states had a high percentage of Loyalists who, if assisted by British troops, would fight the rebels and hold these states for the Crown. This perception was reinforced by statements from states' governors, like Josiah Martin of North Carolina, as Lord Dartmouth's letter to the Admiralty spelled out:

> Governor Martin having represented that there are in the Province of North Carolina, very favorable [*sic*] Appearances of a disposition in a large body of His Majesty's Subjects, to free themselves from the Tyranny and Oppression exercised by those who have formed themselves into Committees and Congresses for the avowed purpose of Rebellion, and to take up Arms in Support of The King's Government; It has been thought fit to order that Ten Thousand Stand of Arms and Six light Field Pieces should be immediately sent to the Commander in Chief of His Majesty's Forces in North America, to the end that he may as Occasion shall require give proper Aid and Assistance to Governor Martin for effecting the Services he recommends.[37]

The governor had wanted to give the British government the impression that there was a large body of men ready to fight with the British in North Carolina, but he had been forced to flee to the protection of the British and was writing from HMS *Cruizer*. In his response Dartmouth did not have Martin's optimism: 'I must confess to you, that I think you are too Sanguine in your expectations of being able, if properly supported, in the manner you suggest to induce a large part of the Inhabitants of North Carolina to take up Arms in support of Government'.[38] Whatever reservations some might have had, an expedition with seven regiments was to sail, under Sir Peter Parker, in early December – nearly three months after Martin's request. However quickly a convoy and troops might be assembled, it would always be subject to the vagaries of the weather and it was 29 December 1775 before Parker and his ships left Portsmouth. In his explanation to the King, Sandwich stated that the delays were 'occasioned by contrary winds and accidents'.[39]

36   NDAR, Vol.5, p.595, narrative of Lt. Starke, R.N.
37   NDAR, Vol.2, p.713, Dartmouth to the Admiralty, 12 September 1775.
38   NDAR, Vol.2, p.719, Dartmouth to Martin, 15 September 1775.
39   NDAR, Vol.3, pp.500–501, Sandwich to the King, 11 January 1776.

While Parker's ships were *en route* from Britain, Captain Barkley, who had sailed from Boston on 4 January 1776 to get rice from the Carolinas, arrived off Cape Fear on 21 March and reported that the province was 'in utmost Confusion and in open Rebellion'.[40] At the same time, Martin, aboard *Cruizer*, was complaining that those troops he had expected to see in early February had still not arrived in March. The omens were not looking good for a successful operation.

The expedition to North Carolina was a failure. General Clinton had been sent from Boston by General Howe in January with 3,300 troops to *rendezvous* off Cape Fear with the seven regiments in Parker's convoy. A *rendezvous* of this nature, with large fleets from New York and Britain meeting in the same area of sea (at an agreed time) in the age of sail, was always likely to be problematic. As we have seen, Parker did not leave until the end of 1775 and did not arrive off Cape Fear until 3 May, where Clinton had been waiting since March. While the two fleets were in transit, the whole point of the expedition had been nullified by the rebels defeating a Loyalist force at Moore's Bridge on 27 February 1776. There was now no Loyalist force to join together with the much-delayed British troops for a march through the Carolinas. Not only had the expedition come to naught but the two fleets, which had been at sea for some four months before coming together off the Carolina coast, were now short of provisions.

Before sailing north again to rejoin Howe's army, Clinton decided to launch an amphibious operation against Sullivan's Island in the approaches to Charleston (this is covered in Chapter 9). Once again, this proved abortive – Willis described it as 'the naval equivalent of Bunker Hill'[41] – and he 'requested Sir Peter Parker that he would lose no Time in conveying the Troops under my Command to Sir William Howe. But contrary Winds and various other Impediments prevented our Sailing from South Carolina before the 21st of July, and it was the 31st before we arrived at Sandy Hook'.[42] Amphibious operations, and the support delivered by sea, is covered in Chapter 9, but this outline of the southern adventure demonstrates how dependent the army was on the navy, and how its operations were consequential on any delays in that support, whether from slow loading and dispatch, or adverse weather in the Atlantic. Had the government not decided to send Clinton and Parker on their abortive trips to the south then more assistance could have been given to Howe in his evacuation of Boston; the 20 transport ships in Parker's convoy could have been sent to Boston in December 1775, allowing the army to leave months earlier.

---

40   NDAR, Vol.4, p.443, letter from Barkley, 21 March 1776.
41   Willis, *Sea Power*, p.110.
42   NDAR, Vol.5, p.1309, Clinton's narrative, 31 July 1776.

Keen as the King and his government were to recover the colonies (although there were voices against), they could not ignore the fact that France would grab any opportunity to take advantage of Britain's involvement in America. For their part, the colonists had high hopes of the French coming into the conflict on their side, while ignoring the irony of 'an absolute monarch being the ally of a people contending for freedom'.[43] They particularly looked forward to the opportunity of having the French Navy face the British ships, so nullifying their enemy's naval advantage. These pressures presented North's government, and especially the Admiralty, with a dilemma; how to blockade the American coast and support the army over there, while taking precautions against any possible French invasion threat in the Channel, at the same time protecting Gibraltar and also keeping a watchful eye on the Spanish. How would Sandwich prioritise his resources to cover the various eventualities, once America reverted to secondary importance following the entry of France into the conflict in 1778?

43   Brumwell, *Turncoat*, p.162.

8

'Our safety depends upon our having a powerful fleet at home'

The British had had to evacuate Boston. Their position there had become untenable, but Halifax was not the base from which to launch the recovery of the colonies; it was too far away and had inadequate facilities. Howe, with the large number of reinforcements being sent from Britain, needed to take New York and its harbour. Once this was done, he would have a base that allowed better control of the Atlantic seaboard, as well as access to the Hudson Valley. The general was in a hurry to leave Halifax, but this would have to be by sea. The long overland routes, the lack of horse-drawn wagons, and the reluctance of local farmers and merchants to sell him provisions hampered his army's freedom of movement and 'absolutely prevented us this whole war from going fifteen miles from a navigable river'.[1] Howe's troops eventually sailed for New York on 11 June 1776, courtesy of the navy and the hired transports, but this dependence on the sea was at the root of a dilemma for those back in London – which was to have the highest priority, defence of the Channel (and England) or the recovery of America?

The British Navy came out of the Seven Years War as the most powerful in the world, but peace was an opportunity for the government to make savings; navies are expensive, even if they are necessary for an island nation. In the interlude between the two wars (as we saw in Chapter 2) a large number of ships of the line were put in ordinary, sailors were released back to their normal employment, and many commissioned officers went onto half-pay. To return the navy to a full war footing would require money and time. While Sandwich was mindful of the need for early mobilisation once the war with America had started – and the French were likely to take advantage of Britain's entanglement – Lord North 'flinched

---

1   Mackesy, *America*, p.82.

from the cost of preparation'.[2] The process of mobilisation can be viewed as a deterrent, or as an act of war; the months prior to the First World War serve as an example of the latter. Lord North was concerned that British naval mobilisation would be considered provocative by France, and so it did not begin until after France had shown its hand and signed the Treaties of Commerce and Alliance with the colonies in February 1778. From this point on, Britain was on the back foot *vis-à-vis* naval parity with the Bourbon powers. As one historian comments, 'This was the only war of the eighteenth century in which England failed to win ascendancy at sea'.[3]

At the beginning of the twentieth century, Britain had a policy of maintaining its navy at a sufficient strength to equal the combined might of the next two most powerful naval powers, France and Russia. A similar philosophy was held by Sandwich during the American War: 'I lay down as a maxim that England ought for her own security to have a superior force in readiness at home to anything that France and Spain united have in readiness on their side'.[4] The laying up of the fleet in ordinary, the late mobilisation, and the time to return to a full war footing was apparent in the number of ships available. It must be said that ship numbers vary according to the sources used. Mackesy quotes 102 (in commission) of 50 guns or more in 1779; Rodger gives a figure of 145 in 1778, of which 94 were in commission and 51 in ordinary. In his 1777 letter to North, Sandwich stated that the home fleet consisted of '36 ships of the line in commission and fit for service'. However, crew shortages and a need for some ships to have their hulls cleaned meant that 'upon a sudden emergency we should not be able to get more than 30 of them at once to sea'. A ship of the line was one that was 'large enough to form part of the line of battle',[5] which meant 64 guns or more.[6] In 1776, Howe, off the American coast, had only nine ships of 50 guns or greater, of which only two qualified as ships of the line.[7] Sandwich was concerned that 'our antagonists' had 'at least 36 of the line' of which 30 were at sea. For Sandwich, the greatest threat for which the navy must be prepared was that at home and so any ships detached to America (or any other foreign station) should be replaced without delay, otherwise 'we shall be in a defenceless state at home'.[8] While defence of the Channel was the First Lord's main priority, he recognised a need to send 'considerable reinforcements to Lord

2   SP, Vol.1, p.201.
3   Mackesy, *America*, p.166.
4   SP, Vol.1, p.236, letter from Sandwich to North, 3 August 1777.
5   Rodger, *Command of the Ocean*, p.765.
6   N. Blake, *Steering To Glory: A Day in the Life of a Ship of the Line* (London: Chatham, 2005), table on p.23.
7   NDAR, Vol.6, pp.167–169.
8   SP, Vol.1, p.237.

Howe' and his dilemma should be borne in mind when considering the level of naval support delivered to the army throughout the war. The French should not be allowed to '[G]ive such a blow to the English fleet that it would be difficult ever to recover. *The loss of America would in such an event be by far the inferior consideration*' [my emphasis]. Indeed, according to Sir Hugh Palliser at the Admiralty, ships should not be dispersed to the other side of the Atlantic 'only to secure and support an army who it seems cannot support itself'.[9]

Although (as already stated) the army could only operate in America if it was supported by sea, that support would not be the navy's first priority. When the French did later join the conflict, the Admiralty had a number of roles to cover: watch the French squadrons at Brest and Toulon and, if they sailed, warn London of their possible destinations; defend convoys supplying relief to the siege of Gibraltar; protect the commercially important sugar islands of the West Indies; and guard India and the East Indies against any French intrusion on British trading interests in the important spice trade. Simply put, the navy had inadequate resources to do all that would be asked of it, and that could result in commanders at the different stations deciding their own priorities. It was probably natural that Admiral Lord Howe, as the brother of the army commander in the colonies, made his first consideration the support of the troops in America over blockade duties, as Sandwich pointed out to North in December 1777:

> The mode of carrying on the war in America has been such for the last two years that the fleet has not been employed in the purposes in which it can be most useful towards distressing the enemy, [with the number of ships available to Howe] it was natural to suppose that with such a force properly stationed he could have made it very difficult for the Americans to receive their supplies, carry on their trade, and fit our privateers to annoy the trade of Great Britain. The contrary however has been the case because the greatest part of Lord Howe's fleet has been employed in convoying, embarking and disembarking the troops, and attending the operations of the army, which his Lordship in his first letters after his arrival in America mentions as his principal object, to which all others must give place. I do not mean to say that this was wrong, but the consequence of it was that our trade suffered, and that the enemy got the supplies from Europe by which they have been enabled to resist us.[10]

9   SP, Vol.1, p.234, Palliser to Sandwich, 22 July 1777.
10   SP, Vol.1, pp.327–328, Sandwich to North, 8 December 1777.

Sandwich went on to make the point that no force would be 'sufficient entirely' to impose a blockade of such a coastline and put a total stop to trade and privateering. However, Howe should have been able to 'distress them infinitely more than has hitherto been done'. According to Sandwich, 'the idea of the Admiralty from the beginning of the war' was to have some ports on the American coast where the navy could careen and refit their ships. The army's role (according to Sandwich) should then have been to pull back and defend these facilities, as 'no such naval war as is now recommended can be maintained so as to answer the purposes expected'. In his preoccupation with helping his brother Lord Howe, who had been 'by his instructions directed to consider and propose to us what ports were in his opinion properest for these purposes [...] has as yet made no return thereupon', had failed to select the ports the navy needed for these maintenance facilities. The First Lord advised North that 'Lord Howe should be told that his principal object now should be to block up the American ports'.

The blockade of the American coast could not be the only concern for the Admiralty and the commanders in America. When the British left Halifax for New York in 1776, the French had not entered the conflict, but that possibility could not be discounted. In that event, France might decide to send a squadron to the West Indies, North America, the East Indies or the Mediterranean: 'We shall not know where the storm will fall'.[11] Even if they could predict where the blow would fall there was the problem of slow communications; forces in America would be reacting to news that was weeks old. In December 1775 a ship's captain sent a message home to the owners to say that it had taken 'ten weeks and three days' to make the passage from Liverpool to Boston, and a further 'three and twenty days beating off and on to get in'.[12] Troop operations that required reinforcements faced similar problems. A convoy of Hessians sent from Germany to Howe's army in 1776 took 125 days to make the crossing, by which time many were sick with diarrhoea and scurvy.[13]

Britain may have prided itself on the strength of its navy, but ministerial concern over the possibility of an invasion of Britain, should the French throw in their lot with the Rebels, meant that the ships on the American station were always going to be smaller than full-blown ships of the line. As we have already noted, Sandwich was against sending line of battle ships to America, preferring that they 'should be kept at home'. By the end of 1776, both of the Howes were writing to London to request more and larger ships; the general told Germain

11   SP, Vol.1, p.333, Sandwich to North, 8 December 1777.
12   NDAR, Vol.3, p.97, Captain Perry, 14 December 1775.
13   Ferling, *Miracle*, p.126.

that 'not less than 10 ships of the line' were necessary to support the army[14] – the ships were not forthcoming. The problem was not always the availability of ships; finding sufficient men to crew them was also a concern. In January 1777, Sandwich pointed out to Lord Howe that there were 'six King's vessels' in Canada – where they were 'of no use'.[15] The ships' crews were short of 350 sailors, and a further 13 transports were similarly idle for the want of 120 men. However, following the British defeat at Trenton, December 1776, the Cabinet overruled Sandwich – very much at Germain's urging – and ordered that six ships of the line be sent to America along with an additional 6,000 troops. Trenton had been a disaster. According to one account Colonel Rall ('a drunken fool') had been 'carried to bed' after Christmas festivities from which he was 'roused by the sound of cannon and drumbeats;' 918 of his 1,200 men were captured and a further 105 killed or wounded.[16]

Only a few weeks after the news of Rall's defeat reached London, Major-General Burgoyne was preparing to leave Britain to take over command in Quebec from Carleton. The general was to sail in the *Apollo* and his letters to the Admiralty give some insight into how easily a general's ego could be affronted while he expected the navy to accommodate his personal needs, never mind that there was a war on. The *Apollo*, together with Burgoyne and 'three or perhaps four servants', was to escort a convoy and so could not sail until that was assembled. Sandwich, knowing that the King hoped to get him away earlier, had the 20-gun, copper-bottomed *Ariadne* put on standby for the general. The change of vessel may have met the King's wish for Burgoyne to more speedily arrive in Canada, but it was not to that general's liking: 'I think myself ill treated [...] I really feel myself offended & shall make my complaint to the King – The first Lord of the Admiralty may get the better by dint of power but I shall have my triumph in the opinion of the world'.[17] By 23 March, he had 'succeeded in the contest', and would be sailing in the *Apollo* but, as his letter to the ship's captain shows, his main concern was his baggage:

> I am very sorry to encumber you with so much baggage as will be delivered with this letter, but it was indispensible [*sic*]– & the bedding which is the most bulky part will be for my use on board without taking up more room than our Cotts [*sic*]. I must request you will order it to be taken care of till a Servant of mine arrives. I will likewise request you to order preparation

---

14   SP, Vol.1, p.46.
15   SP, Vol.1, p.171, Sandwich to Howe, 6 January 1777.
16   Urban, *Fusiliers*, p.99.
17   NDAR, Vol.8, p.696, Burgoyne to Captain Pownoll, 20 March 1777.

to be made for me at the best Inn at Plymouth & should rather wish to
have a bed in a private house if such can be hired for my stay.[18]

Seven months after his concern over his comforts at sea, Burgoyne would be
surrendering to the Americans at Saratoga.

With one eye always on the French, the Admiralty had to be prepared to protect
trade convoys making their way in and out of the Channel. The dependence of
sailing ships on the strength and direction of the wind presented problems to
those deciding where and how to base and deploy ships of the line off the south
coast of Britain. Large fleets required anchorage, dry-dock, careening, repair, and
resupply facilities, and it was not sufficient that the location should merely have a
large and accessible harbour. The prevailing wind in the Channel is westerly, and
so assists ships entering from the west and sailing to the Thames, but harder to do
the reverse. A French fleet based at Brest can enter the Channel with ease but a
British fleet, based at Portsmouth, would have to beat against the wind to meet it.
In time of war, to protect the Channel and the trade convoys from a squadron at
Brest, it was necessary to have ships at sea – and this meant that they had to be to
westward of the Scilly Isles. This force, the Western Squadron, served the country
well in the Seven Years War but was somewhat neglected in that against America.
Lord Vernon had put the case for the strengthening of the Western Squadron
in 1745: 'I have always looked upon squadrons in port as neither a defence for
the kingdom, nor a security for our commerce, and that the surest means for
the prevention of both, was keeping a strong squadron in the Soundings, which
may answer both these purposes, as covering both Channels and Ireland, and at
the same time secures our commerce'.[19] For a maritime nation such as Britain,
the protection of the nation's trade while throttling that of the enemy 'was less
glamorous but equally crucial to the success of the British war effort',[20] but Britain
did not have that level of control of European waters during the American War.
The requirement to watch the navies of France and Spain, while supporting the
army in the American colonies, meant that the Admiralty was unable to set up a
Western Squadron of sufficient strength to dominate the Western Approaches.[21]
In an ideal world, a squadron of ships of the line would be permanently stationed
off the Scillies, but that required a large number of ships that could be rotated
between a dockyard and their sea-station, and be replenished with fresh food at

18   NDAR, Vol.8, p.703, Burgoyne to Captain Pownoll, 23 March 1777.
19   NRS, *The Vernon Papers* (London: Navy Records Society, 1958), pp.445–6.
20   M. Duffy, 'The establishment of the Western Squadron as the linchpin of British naval
     strategy', in M. Duffy (ed.), *Parameters of British Naval Power, 1650–1850* (Exeter:
     University of Exeter Press, 1998), p.76.
21   Duffy, 'Western Squadron', p.76.

sea by a fleet of victuallers. If the squadron spent time in port, only coming out when the enemy fleet had left its base, it would be too late to be effective, as the King stated in a letter to Sandwich: 'much time and perhaps the opportunity of effecting an action will be lost, if he [Darby, commander of the Channel Fleet, then in Torbay] is to receive orders for that purpose from hence not till we hear that the ships [of the French] have been detached'. George III was of a mind that military force should be used when necessary; any reluctance could be interpreted as weakness by our enemies as he made clear to the First Lord: 'This country, with such numerous enemies, must be ruined unless what we want of strength is made up in activity and resolution. Caution has certainly made this war less brilliant than the former; and if that is alone to direct our operations […] it is easy to foretell that we must be great losers'.[22] A strong Western Squadron would have enabled Britain to control the entrance to the Channel, hold the French fleet in Brest (and prevent its sailing to America), and protect inbound and outbound convoys, but slow mobilisation and the sending of ships overseas limited the opportunity and so prevented Britain gaining superiority at sea. Sending ships to blockade the coast of America, as well as transport fleets to support the army with food and other essentials, were necessary; not to have done so, and possibly lose the army and the colonies, was an option, but one that would have been difficult to sell to the people and the King. However, there were too many calls on too few ships, and supporting and controlling an army so far from home, with eighteenth century communications, 'abandoned the initiative to the enemy'.[23]

As early as December 1775, with access to local supplies all but denied to them, the army commanders began to recognise that they had a supply problem, and that this would present challenges for the navy.

> It seems the demands from the small army now in America are so great as to be thought impossible to be furnished. The wagons and draught cattle is [sic] prodigious. If this is the case, what will it be when we have another army there of above 20,000 men, if they can't make good their quarters, and command carriages and cattle, and subsist and defend themselves, without the aid and defence of the fleet, who whilst so employed can perform no other service? I think some people begin to be astonished and staggered at the unexpected difficulties we are in.[24]

22   SP, Vol.4, p.55, the King to Sandwich, 3 September 1781.
23   Rodger, *Sandwich*, p.274.
24   SP, Vol.1, p.88, Palliser to Sandwich, 29 December 1775.

General Howe had recognised that his army could not operate at any distance from a navigable river and that meant employing the navy's ships and men in a variety of roles as one navy officer commented:

> You have no idea of the number of men it takes to attend upon such an army as this; with all the ships we have (which is two thirds of those employed in America) when all the flat boats, galleys, gondolas, horse stages etc, etc, are mann'd there is scarce men enough left on board many of the ships to move them so that we really want six or eight lines of battle ships; not so much perhaps for the use of the ships, as for their large complements of men for the purposes before mentioned.[25]

It would be wrong to see naval support during the war as being limited to ships at sea protecting convoys and blockading the coast. Naval ships took part in amphibious landings, sailors hauled ships' guns ashore and operated them during combined assaults, ships had to protect harbours and ports used by the British on the American coast, and ships' crews foraged ashore for fresh meat and hay to augment the shipments from Britain. With all the calls on these vessels, the naval commanders could probably have done without some of the requests from local dignitaries and state governors who believed that their position entitled them to additional protection from British officers. Within a few months of the outbreak of hostilities Admiral Graves was making the Admiralty aware of the number of letters he was receiving 'from the Governors of South and North Carolina to shew their Lordships how pressing they are for an additional number of ships and small Vessels to be stationed within their Governments',[26] requests he felt unable to comply with. In August 1776 Captain Snape Hamond, HMS *Roebuck*, wrote of

> [T]he support & protection that I have been under the absolute necessity of giving to Lord Dunmore [royal governor of Virginia] & his floating Town, consisting of a Fleet of upwards of 90 Sail, destitute of allmost [sic] every material to Navigate them, as well as seamen, has given full employment for three Ships, for these three month past, to prevent them from falling into the hands of the Enemy.[27]

A military officer would see the supplying of help to a royal governor as assisting the King's legally appointed representative, but doing similarly for a plantation

---

25 D. Syrett, *Admiral Lord Howe: A Biography* (Stroud: Spellmount, 2006), p.62.
26 NDAR, Vol.1, p.1002, Graves to Stephens, 29 July 1775.
27 NDAR, Vol.6, p.66, Snape Hamond to the governor of the Isle of Wight, 5 August 1776.

owner (with slaves) probably did not fall into the same category: ship's log, HM Sloop *Otter*, 13 January 1777: 'Sailed hence the *Rebecca* Sloop in order [to] protect a Planter on the River St Marys with his Negros to get his Stock of Corn'.[28]

When the navy had to move large bodies of troops, such as for the expedition to the Carolinas in 1776, senior army officers obviously had to be found accommodation on board one of the larger ships, and this could involve the ship's captain and crew having to take special measures. In this case, Admiral Graves directed one of his ship's captains to comply with the request from General Howe:

> Whereas his Excellency Major General [William] Howe has applied to me to appoint a Ship of his Majs Squadron to receive on Board Major General [Henry] Clinton and other Officers of the Army to proceed on a particular Service; and having his Majesty's Ship under your Command for that purpose. You are hereby required and directed to receive Major General Clinton, his Retinue and Servants and such Officers as the General may desire, and you are to cause Cots to be made for them and Births built with Old Canvas and Deals, and to accommodate them in the best manner you can without prejudice to the Kings Service.[29]

The individual requests were not large when taken in isolation, but over the years of the war, they did put an additional strain on the navy's resources that they could have done without.

As we noted earlier, Sandwich had told North that Lord Howe's 'principal object now should be to block up the American ports;' he should blockade the coast from Nova Scotia to the Floridas. However, he was not told how the army was to be supported if he withdrew his ships and concentrated solely on a blockade strategy. His brother, the general commanding, had acknowledged that his army could not operate at any distance from a navigable river because of that reliance on naval support in all forms. One historian has stated that 'strategy is a luxury available to the side with the initiative',[30] but as soon as the French became involved, Britain, due to the late mobilisation, was on the defensive: 'Wherever we are attacked, there we must defend'.[31] Lord Howe, with his limited supply of ships, had two choices: impose a blockade at the expense of support for the army or assign support for the army a higher priority than the imposition of a blockade. Given that the government's policy was to land a massive blow against the Americans

---

28   NDAR, Vol.7, p.948.
29   NDAR, Vol.3, p.649, Graves to Captain Graeme, 6 January 1776.
30   Rodger, *Sandwich*, p.268.
31   Rodger, *Sandwich*, p.268.

at New York (that was the reasoning behind the 27,000 reinforcements they were sending), he had to prioritise the army over the blockade – the fact that it was his brother who commanded the army may also have been a consideration. At the end of the day, the blockade was always going to fail; the coast was too long, the ships were too few, and the calls on them were too many.

In 1776, the army was involved in three land operations: Canada and the relief of Quebec, the landings at New York, and Clinton's expedition to the Carolinas. The following table gives an indication of how the ships available were allocated. The reader must bear in mind the caveat that, as ships went into and out of repair and sailed home or arrived from Britain, total numbers would vary during the year.

Table 9: Ships available to support the army and maintain a blockade of the 3,000 miles of coastline[32]

Date	On Army support	On blockade
13 August 1776	39; 27 for New York; 12 for Canada	24
18 September 1776	42; 33 at New York; 9 in Canada	42
24 November 1776	54	20
	It is worth noting that Howe's 74 ships and 12,000 men compared with a total in the navy of 170 ships and 29,000 men.[33]	
5 January 1777	24 at New York (3 to leave for West Indies); 11 *en route* or about to depart for UK; 6 in St Lawrence; 24 based at Rhode Island & Halifax to blockade New England as well as protect Newport and Nova Scotia.	15 (of which 5 were for refit and one was unfit for use) to blockade from New York to Florida.
1 March 1777	23 (6 of them refitting) at New York; 2 *en route* to England; 7 in St Lawrence; 24 blockading New England and protecting Newport and Halifax.	16 (11 of which were about to depart for, or proceeding to, the West Indies) to blockade from New York to South Florida.

32   Figures compiled from data in Syrett, *American Waters,* pp.58–59.
33   SP, Vol.1, p.45.

It was all but impossible for the navy to blockade the whole American coast with this small number of sailing vessels. For the Americans (with no real arms industry of their own), the avoidance of any British naval vessels was especially important for their importation of arms, ammunition, and particularly gunpowder, of which 90% was coming to them by sea by the end of 1777.[34] There was also another vital part of a rifleman's kit that the Americans imported but which do not feature highly in the history books: flints. The muskets of the day used flints to create the spark that ignited the gunpowder, so in 1775 the Admiralty included them in its list of contraband for Admiral Graves. The order sent to the Admiral was not limited to 'finished' flints but also included those stones carried as ballast in ships sent from Britain to America.

> You are hereby required & directed to instruct the Commanders of all His Majesty's Ships and Vessels under your Command to examine all such Ships & Vessels as shall arrive in the different Ports in North America from Great Britain or Ireland, and in case they find the Ballast, or any part of it, to consist of Flint Stones, to cause such Flint Stones to be taken out & thrown into deep Water; and also to seize any Flints manufactured for the use of Fire Arms, which they may find on board such Ships.[35]

As Table 9 shows, the blockade was too porous to be effective and numerous vessels avoided the Navy's efforts. In January 1776 a citizen of Philadelphia wrote that 'We have recd [sic] 57 tons of salt petre & 30 tons of powder, & have intelligence of a vessell [sic] with 15 tons & 2000 stand of arms which is every day expected'.[36] The Americans were successful at evading the blockade for a number of reasons; they used privateers who captured British transport ships and took them into American ports, they received assistance from the French when in French ports, and they employed subterfuge – sailing with French papers and employing French masters. Prior to France joining the war, the British would have been reluctant to stop neutral, French ships. In May 1777 Lord Stormont, the British Ambassador in France, wrote to Lord Weymouth that:

> I have received the following secret Information, with regard to the two French Ships, now fitting out at Marseilles, which are to be laden with Stores, and various other Articles, for the use of the Rebels. In order to prevent these ships being Stopt [sic], or visited, by us, before they come

34   Mackesy, *America*, p.99.
35   NDAR, Vol.2, p.723, Admiralty to Graves, 19 September 1775.
36   NDAR, Vol.3, p.683, letter from Francis Lee to Richard Lee, 8 January 1776.

upon the Coast of America, there are to be Naval officers on board, bearing the french [sic] Kings Commission, and in case they are hailed by us, they will Pass for french [sic] Ships of War. I cannot absolutely answer, for the truth of this Information, but am much inclined to give it Credit. How insidious this Project is, and how contrary to all Friendship, all Good Faith, It is needless to say. Whether we should wink at the Execution, and trust entirely to the Vigilance of our Cruizers, on the Coast of America, (which Vigilance, so many french [sic] Vessels have escaped,) or declare to the Court of france [sic], in very polite, but very explicit Terms, that we have reason to suspect such a Project, and cannot permit the Execution of it, be the Consequences what they may, His Majesty's Wisdom must alone determine.[37]

In early June, these two ships had not yet sailed, but the Admiralty sent more information to Admiral Howe along with orders that they were to be stopped.

[T]he largest is about 400 Tons, the other about 340, that they will be mann'd with French Sailors, carry French Colours, and clear out for some of the West India Islands, but that their real destination was new England, with a liberty however, to make any safe Port in No America; that they will carry double Commissions, an ostensible and a secret one, that there will be on board each Ship a French Captain and one with a Commission from the Congress, that one [Joseph] Hynson is to have the direction of the expedition, that the other it is believ'd will be a Frenchman by birth, but in the Service of the Congress & bearing their Commission. [...] I am commanded by my Lords to communicate the above Intelligence to your Lordship, in order that you may order your Cruizers to keep a good look out for the said Ships and to seize them in case they should appear upon the Coast of No[rth] America.[38]

One of the American privateers who carried French sailors among his crew was Gustavus Conyngham (sometimes spelt Cunningham), who captured 60 British ships in 18 months[39] and became something of a bogeyman for the British. One of the captured vessels was the brig *Northampton*, on which he put a prize crew of 21 men. When the brig was recaptured by Lieutenant John Moore, in July 1777, he discovered that 16 of the prize crew were French.[40]

---

37   NDAR, Vol.8, pp.874–875, Stormont to Weymouth, 28 May 1777.
38   NDAR, Vol.9, p.380, Stephens to Howe, 6 June 1777.
39   Willis, *Sea Power*, p.191.
40   NDAR, Vol.9, pp.535–536, John Moore to Stephens, 26 July 1777.

The porosity of the blockade was highlighted in May 1777. Captain John Manley of the Continental (American) Navy sailed (unmolested by the British) from Boston harbour with a squadron of two frigates and nine privateers.[41] Lord Howe's 29 warships in the New York area were assigned to assist the army in pending operations in New Jersey, leaving him in an uncomfortable position: 'I am not able, in this case, to make any detachments from the number to proceed in pursuit of the enemy, which under the circumstances would be proper'.[42] As a result, the Navy suffered the extreme embarrassment of having a warship, the 28-gun *Fox*, captured by Manley's squadron on 7 June off the Grand Banks of Newfoundland.[43] The humiliation was expressed by Palliser to Sandwich: 'The escape of so many privateers of force from so great a fleet as we have in America to watch them, and the taking of the *Fox*, is very mortifying and disgraceful'.[44] There was some satisfaction for Howe's sailors when the *Fox* was retaken 'without any great Resistance on the Part of the Rebels', and Manley himself was taken in an action on 7 July 1777. Captain Collier commented on the importance of their prisoner to the Admiralty: 'His Capture will be extremely despiriting [*sic*] to the Rebels, as they plac'd the entire Direction of their Navy, in Him'.[45]

The involvement of the French in the American privateer trade (prior to them formally entering the war), while known to the British, had to be handled carefully. Although the French made 'positive assurances' that their sea captains were given orders that they should not assist the American privateers, and the French Court had an 'earnest Desire of maintaining the present Peace',[46] the British treated the comments from Paris with due caution. The French were considered to be acting as close to the wire as they could – 'They have taken the utmost line that can be allowed them'[47] – and any crossing of that line risked a war between the two countries which, while not wanted, was 'preferable to a state that must injure materially the commerce of this Country, and disgrace it in the eyes of all Europe': Britain could not be seen to be having its nose tweaked by the French. However, on the other side of the Atlantic, the Americans were quite openly trumpeting the arrangement, as an article in the *Independent Chronicle* demonstrates.

Boston, April 24, 1777.

41   Syrett, *Lord Howe*, p.65.
42   TNA, ADM 1/487, ff.401–402.
43   NDAR, Vol.9, p.47, journal of Captain McNeill, Continental Frigate *Boston*, 7 June 1777.
44   NDAR, Vol.9, p.520.
45   NDAR, Vol.9, p.272, Captain Collier to Stephens, 12 July 1777.
46   NDAR, Vol.9, p.531, Weymouth to Lord Grantham, 25 July 1777.
47   NDAR, Vol.9, p.531, Weymouth to Lord Stormont, 25 July 1777.

Last Monday arrived at a safe Port, a large Ship, from France, with the following Cargo, viz. 58 Pieces of Brass Cannon, Cloathing [*sic*] for 10,000 Men, Tents for ditto; 10 Tons Powder, Lead, Brass, and a Quantity of Blankets. A Colonel, and 24 Officers of Artillery came Passengers in the above Ship [*l'Amphitrite*]. […] Last Sunday arrived at a safe Port, from Bourdeaux [*sic*], in France, a large Ship, of 20 Carriage Guns, after a Passage of 54 Days, fitted out by private Merchants from that Port: Her Cargo consists of ready made Cloaths, Linnens and Woollens of all Kinds, Powder, and a great Number of Arms, &c &c. She has on board a Commission from the French King, empowering her, that in Case she was attacked by any British pirate Ships, to repel Force by Force, and capture them. Several French Officers came Passengers in the above Ship.[48]

The article included another two ships that had brought in a total of 6,900 'Stands of Arms' and 13,000 pounds of gunpowder. The examples showed that the British Navy could not close the coast of America to trade and contraband, but two newspaper accounts give slightly comic accounts of the steps taken by ships' captains (American and British) to avoid capture by the other side. The *New York Gazette* reported that 'Several of the Rebel Privateers, in order to intimidate the Merchant Ships, have placed Wooden Guns of a considerable Size upon their Decks. One of these lately taken had but four real Guns, and those very indifferent, with 12 or 14 of the other kind, which, all together gave the Vessel a very formidable Appearance'.[49] Meanwhile, a month previously, a British captain had a novel ruse for avoiding action with a Rebel privateer:

[He] hawl'd [hauled] up the ports, and let the people put their heads through, having first fixed pieces of white paper on their hats, to represent the muzzles of guns, and by this scheme the *Clayton* appeared like a 20 gun ship, and had the desired effect; the brig came within a mile and a half, and then bore away to the northward, with all the sail she could carry.[50]

Imaginative as some of the captains were, the captures at sea were large and would have had an impact on supplies for the army. In the Seven Years War, privateers (not American) took 1,855 merchant ships[51] but in the American war 3,386 were captured, 495 were retaken, 507 were ransomed, while 2,384 remained

48   NDAR, Vol.8, p.418.
49   NDAR, Vol.7, p.627.
50   NDAR, Vol.7, p.732, *The General Advertiser,* 8 November 1776.
51   Morriss, *British Maritime Ascendancy*, p.86.

in American hands: 'Thus a large percentage of the total tonnage of the British merchant marine was lost through enemy action during the American War'.[52] Lord Howe, with his commitment to supporting the operations of his brother's land army could not stop this attrition.

Although there were insufficient ships for an effective blockade, Germain believed there was an additional reason for the Rebels receiving supplies: Lord Howe was too lenient in his treatment of the American colonists. In his orders to Commodore Hotham, who was to command the station from the Chesapeake to Florida, Howe outlined how his subordinate should interpret the government's orders regarding the blockade. These instructions were a factor in London's criticism of his prosecution of the war.

> Whereas a Chief Object in the appointment of the large naval Force destined to be employed in North America, has been for carrying into Execution the Provisions of an Act passed in the last Session of Parliament for preventing all Trade and Intercourse with the several Colonies and Provinces therein mentioned; [Hotham was to] prevent the King's rebellious Subjects from succeeding in their endeavors [sic] to procure Supplies of Ammunition and other military Stores, And to take or destroy their Armed Vessels, by every Means in your power. [However, the following order was considered too lenient by Germain, they are my italics] *You are nevertheless at liberty in respect to these Instructions to grant, and it is advisable to take all suitable opportunities to allow, the Inhabitants dwelling upon the Coasts adjacent to the Stations of the Ships under your Orders, the use of their ordinary Fishing-Craft, or other means of providing for their daily subsistence and support; where the same does not seem liable to any material abuse.* And in your Signification thereof to the several Captains [in Hotham's squadron] You are to recommend to them to encourage and cultivate all amicable Correspondence with the said Inhabitants to gain their good will and confidence, whilst they demean themselves in a peaceable and orderly manner; And to grant them every other Indulgence which the necessary Restrictions from their Trade conformable to the Tenor of the before recited Act, will admit: In order to conciliate their friendly Dispositions, and to detach them from the Prejudices they have imbibed, to the subversion of all legal authority in the different Provinces concerned.[53]

---

52   Syrett, *Shipping and the American War*, p.77.
53   NDAR, Vol.7, p.569, Howe to Hotham, 23 December 1776.

It was this leniency that Germain, as American Secretary, could not condone. He wanted the Howe brothers to prosecute the war in a more ruthless manner and he had a supporter in the King who felt that the brothers should 'act with a little less lenity (which I really think cruelty, as it keeps up the contest) [...] the regaining of their affection is an idle idea, it must be the convincing them that it is their interest to submit, and then they will dread further broils'.[54] The King and Germain still believed that military force would bring the Americans to their 'senses'. Where Germain and the King saw Howe's actions as excessively lenient, Sandwich (possibly trying to sugar the pill) wrote to Howe to explain that while those at home might consider he was acting too softly towards the American, the Admiral was the man on the spot and so best placed to make an assessment:

> I conclude that the indulgence you have shown in allowing the inhabitants of the coast to have the use of their fishing boats is founded upon local reasoning, and for the good of the general plan which you are conducting with so much wisdom and propriety. But, uninformed as we are here of the reasons for the lenity when so little has been shown on the other side, most persons that I have conversed with seem to think that these kind of indulgences are more likely to protract than hasten the conclusion of this unnatural contest; for unless those who persist in rebellion severely feel the distress they have brought on themselves, I should much doubt whether anything but compulsion will bring them back to their duty. However, your Lordship, who is on the spot, is a much better judge than I can be of the propriety of this reasoning, and I have no other cause of throwing out this hint than because I would conceal nothing from you that I think you ought to know.[55]

Between 1775 and 1778, the British Admiralty had faced a dilemma: how to blockade the American east coast, support the army in America, protect British interests worldwide, and be in a position to defend the south of England against the possible threat of a French invasion – and all that with too few ships. When the French entered the conflict in 1778, the whole nature of the war changed; America became less of a priority than the West Indian Islands and the ships were moved from coastal blockade duty to the defence of New York, Newport, and Halifax. The French fleet (as we shall see) sailed from Toulon for America under the command of *Lieutenant-Général* d'Estaing and became the focus of attention for the naval commander in America – Lord Howe was in the process of

---

54   Mackesy, *America*, p.150.
55   SP, Vol.1, p.288, Sandwich to Howe, 20 March 1777.

handing over to Admiral Gambier in 1778. By September of that year, of the 78 warships available to Howe, 'Not one ship of the Royal Navy was stationed along the American coast between New York and St Augustine [Florida], Delaware Bay, Chesapeake Bay and the coasts of the Carolinas were unguarded: the blockade had ceased to exist'.[56]

56   Syrett, *American Waters*, p.112.

9

'His Majesty's Troops being landed without opposition'

If the British were to win back the colonies, then this would not be achieved by sitting back in sea-ports and being supplied by the navy; the troops would have to take the fight to the enemy. The distances between New York, Philadelphia, and Charleston (Georgia) would necessitate very long marches, but that was not their only problem; the army was too small to have substantial garrisons in the towns it wanted to occupy, it had insufficient troops to defend its line of march and carry out foraging expeditions, and General Howe believed that it was 'logistically impossible for the army to operate far from a navigable waterway in America'.[1] Mobility was necessary if the British were to return the 'unhappy and deluded' colonials to their true allegiance, and that meant transporting and landing the troops by ship: amphibious operations – an American term for 'operations involving an actual waterborne landing'.[2] In the modern age such operations, using specifically designed ships and landing craft, as well as diesel engines rather than the wind, are fraught with difficulty (Normandy in 1944 and the Falklands in 1982 are two good examples); how much more so with wooden sailing ships. But the British, before the entry of France into the war, had one big advantage – their navy was far superior to anything the Americans could float in opposition. This superiority gave them the advantage of keeping Washington in the dark as to where the British might strike once their ships left port, as the American commander made clear in a letter to the Continental Congress in July 1777: 'The amazing advantage the Enemy derive from their Ships and the Command of the water, keeps us in a State of constant perplexity and the most anxious conjecture'.[3] This

---

1   Syrett, *Lord Howe*, p.61.
2   R. Reed, *Combined Operations in the Civil War* (Annapolis, MD: Naval Institute Press, 1978), p.x.
3   Syrett, *Shipping and the American War*, p.230.

advantage allowed General Howe to mount a number of amphibious operations against strategic points along the American seaboard.

The landing of troops from ships at sea is a particularly hazardous operation, especially if it is an opposed landing, and would have been approached by the troops (many of whom probably could not swim) with some trepidation. Once at the disembarkation point the men would have had to go over the ship's side, encumbered by their kit and firearms, to clamber down to the row-boats allocated to take them to shore. The landing craft were usually flat-bottomed boats carried on the decks of the warships and transports. At the time of the American War these came in two sizes: one was 36 feet long and manned by 20 oarsmen, and the other was a little smaller at 30 feet long and with 16 oarsmen. Depending on their size, they could take between 40 and 60 soldiers as well as the sailors who did the rowing.[4] For some operations, such as that on Staten Island in 1776, boats might be specially built; on that occasion, they had ramps in the bow for unloading cannon and could carry up to 100 soldiers. Once the troops were in the boats, the oarsmen pulled for the shore; at Bunker Hill, the initial landings were from 28 boats in two lines of 14 each.[5]

In these combined operations, the army and navy commanders needed to work together, but each with his own responsibilities. It was the responsibility of the navy to transport the troops safely to the disembarkation point, but once the troops were ashore, command reverted to the army commander. Although the naval Commander-in-Chief was in charge of all the ships in the operation, he would normally appoint a senior subordinate to command the landing phase; in 1776, Lord Howe appointed Commodore Hotham to conduct the landing on Long Island, while at Charleston in 1780 Arbuthnot gave the job to Captain Elphinstone.[6] It was then the job of this officer to plan and coordinate the order in which they would 'disembark the troops from transports into small craft, to form these craft into assault waves, and then to convey the force to shore in combat formation'. Organisation was critical; units, stores and armaments needed to be loaded in a set order to ensure that troops had the right equipment when they landed. To help commanders identify what and who was being carried by the various ships in the assault convoy, different flags were flown from the ships' foremasts. Flags were also flown by ships with troops on board until such time as they had all disembarked; by this means the landing craft could see which of the transports still had men to be landed on the beaches.

4   D. Syrett, 'The methodology of British amphibious operations during the Seven Years' and American Wars', *Mariner's Mirror*, 58:3 (1972), p.273. Syrett has excellent detail on these operations in this article.
5   Philbrick, *Bunker Hill*, p.295.
6   Syrett, 'Amphibious operations', p.272.

During and after the landing of the troops the navy provided close support to the army commander – defence of the landing area from enemy shipping, fire support, assistance with guns on shore, and the provision of supplies, whether food or ammunition. Where the landing site took the enemy by surprise it could go ahead unopposed, as at Head of Elk in 1777, but when the operation was contested, as at Kips Bay in 1776, the ships' guns gave covering fire. In this case, five heavy frigates were stationed close to the American shore defences during the night before the landing and, as the first wave of flat-bottomed boats approached the shore, the guns were brought into action: '[T]hese warships opened a rapid and heavy fire on the American beach defences. In fifty-five minutes of firing, HMS *Orpheus* expended 5,376 pounds of gunpowder. The violent bombardment levelled the enemy field fortifications and drove the American defenders from the landing area in confusion'.[7] Once the initial landings were complete, the naval vessels and small boats were able to ferry men and provisions to shore as required as well as provide tactical mobility to the land commander if he needed to move small bodies of troops along the shore: 'the complex troop movements executed during the campaign around New York City in 1776 would have been impossible without water-borne transport'.[8] As we will see with the two landings at Charleston and New York in 1776, where an operation relied on the *rendezvous* of two forces, both conveyed by ships, the delay in the sailing of either of them could seriously impact the plans of the land commander. While the Charleston operation would leave much to be desired, that at New York went well with good cooperation between the sea and land forces.

The gun teams on a man-of-war were very capable of hauling heavy guns, and the army took some advantage of this. Willis claimed that the British sailors were 'world leaders in the art of heavy haulage over testing terrain' and in November 1776, at the New Jersey Palisades, they pulled 'eight field guns – four three-pounders, two six-pounders, two howitzers – and all of their ammunition boxes up 300 feet of sheer cliff'.[9] This was no mean feat and serves as an example of naval cooperation that rarely makes it into the general histories of the war. However, in comparison to the guns aboard ship, those hauled up the New Jersey cliffs might be considered small, whereas in November 1777, during the assault on Fort Mifflin, the navy provided some of its own heavy guns for the army siege:

> The Officers and Seamen of the Ships of War and Transports, were employed in the mean time with unremitting Fatigue and Perseverance,

7   Syrett, 'Amphibious operations', p.276.
8   Syrett, 'Amphibious operations', p.276.
9   Willis, *Sea Power*, p.136.

to convey Provisions, Artillery and Stores, to the Schylkill, between Fort Island and the Pensylvania [*sic*] Shore. Six 24 Pounders from the *Eagle*, and Four 32 Pounders from the *Somerset*, transported in the same manner, & the requisite proportions of Ammunition.[10]

Although these guns were not hauled up a 300-foot cliff, moving them from a ship to a flat boat and then getting them ashore would have been a major operation; a 32-pounder weighed upwards of three tons.[11] The assistance that the sailors gave towards the 'heavy lifting' was acknowledged by General Howe, and not just because they were commanded by his brother:

I cannot too highly acknowledge the signal Services the Army has received from the Perseverance and Activity of the Officers and Seamen under your Lordship's Command, since the King's Troops entered Philadelphia. And I shall be happy, by your Lordships Assistance, to have my Sentiments of them made as acceptable and generally known as possible.[12]

Lord Howe then had the General's appreciation 'made public' to the various ships that had taken part in the operation. We are so used to reading about the harsh treatment meted out to sailors that it is refreshing to see the occasional words of praise being passed on to them.

In April 1777, Captain Henry Duncan was commanding a small squadron during a landing to the north-east of New York, near Norwalk, and his journal gives a good account of how he and his ships assisted the army in this small operation: '25th [April] weighed and came to sail [...] At 1 pm made the signal for hoisting out the flat boats. [...] At 6 pm the landing was made good without opposition. The landing-place was exceedingly unfavourable'. For the next couple of days the ships were at anchor while the army went about its business, but on the 28th the troops moved back to the beach, under fire from the Rebels; we take up the story from Duncan's journal.

At 1pm saw the advanced guard of the army coming down the hills at a distance, the rebels harassing their rear with one gun and musketry from every stone fence. At two they drew near the beach; made the signal and sent the flat boats; at three began to embark the wounded and some prisoners; by half after three the most of our troops had got on the

10   TNA, ADM, 1/488, f.79, Howe to Stephens, 23 November 1777.
11   Padfield, *Maritime Supremacy,* p.250, gives 65 hundredweight; Blake, *Steering To Glory,* p.65, states 2 3/4 tons.
12   NDAR, Vol.10, p.519, General Howe to Lord Howe, 17 November 1777.

hill nearest the beach, and the rebels close to them. As I heard that our people's ammunition was mostly expended, despatched two boats to the men of war sloops and soon got a supply up to the army, which the general informed me afterwards was very seasonable, and gave the troops fresh spirits. [...] I now conceived it probable that the rebels might attempt to harass the rear-guard on the beach at coming off; [at this point Duncan appears to do more than one might expect of a naval officer] I therefore took the waggons and formed a traverse of them across the neck, leaving room for about 1,000 or 1,500 men to the westward of the *Senegal* [...] I sent and informed the general of the disposition for re-embarking the troops. [...] Soon after he came down. All the boats, by his arrival, were collected at the point, and with the assistance of transport boats, I suppose 1,000 of the troops were carried off in ten minutes; the whole were got off in a very short time. At six got under way with the fleet, after giving them time to remove the troops to their respective ships [...] Made the signal to hoist in the flat boats and steered to the westward under an easy sail.[13]

Although this was a minor operation Duncan's journal gives an appreciation of the extent to which a naval captain might be intimately involved in assisting the troops he has put ashore.

In the instances above, the Howe brothers worked well together, but this was not always the case and there are a number of other examples where the personal animosity of the commanders led to operational problems. The British expedition to Charleston, North Carolina (referred to in Chapter 7) in 1776, 'the first major British naval operation of the war' was an 'unmitigated disaster',[14] largely because of the failure of the two commanders to communicate and work together. Although the strategy for 1776 was to land a large army at New York and to operate against the Americans from this base, London was swayed by the voices of southern governors (and their wild dreams of Loyalist uprisings) to send an expedition to North Carolina. British ministers in London had a fundamental misunderstanding of their colonial opponents: they misunderstood the anti-taxation views that led to the events in Boston in 1775; the King refused to grant independence, which was the only concession the Americans would accept; and they believed that the rebellion was limited to the states of New England and that an accommodation could be arrived at in the Carolinas. The preconceptions of ministers were reinforced by governors in the south, such as Josiah Martin in South Carolina, who claimed that Royalist support was only waiting for British

13   NRS, *Duncan*, pp.143–144.
14   Willis, *Sea Power*, p.111.

troops to land on their shores. The result was the adoption of a 'southern strategy' and the involvement in those southern states of naval and military forces in America that might have been better used closer to home, and possibly preventing France from entering the war. The idea of a southern campaign 'germinated in London in the last weeks of 1775'.[15] We have already seen that Josiah Martin was among the most vociferous, although he was forced to leave his home and take up residence in one of His Majesty's ships off the coast of South Carolina. In March 1775, he wrote to General Gage that:

> [T]he people in some parts of this Country begin to open their eyes and see through the artifices and delusions by which they have been misled, and they discover good dispositions to renounce the power and authority of the committees that have been appointed by the recommendation of the Congress which have proceeded in some instances to arbitrary and intolerable exertions of power, and they appear inclined to disengage themselves entirely from the bondage which those little combinations seem to be preparing for them. Many of the Inhabitants in several Counties of this Province have already by their addresses to me disclaimed all obedience to those illegal tribunals and expressed in the strongest terms the most loyal and dutiful attachment to his Majesty and the firmest resolution to maintain and defend the Constitution and Laws of their country.[16]

Encouraging words, but events would prove them to be spoken in hope, rather than a realistic assessment of the mood of the people. Martin was so out of touch with the popular mood that he assured Gage that 'I can safely confide if your Excellency shall assist me with two or three Stand of arms and good store of ammunition, of which last we are totally destitute, I will be answerable to maintain the Soverignty [sic] of this Country to his Majesty'. In his reply Gage stated that he was unable 'to supply you with the number of Arms you Request' but can send some powder. However, Gage also indirectly acknowledged that his freedom of movement was limited by the Bostonians as he could 'get no safe Opportunity from this to send it to you I shall order you a supply by way of New York'[17] – he was effectively bottled up in Boston. However, as we saw in Chapter 7, the British did conclude an agreement with the Americans that allowed General Howe (who had replaced Gage) to evacuate Boston and move his army to Halifax.

15   Ferling, *Miracle*, p.126.
16   NDAR, Vol.1, p.150, Josiah Martin to Gage, 16 March 1775.
17   NDAR, Vol.1, p.180, Gage to Martin, 12 April 1775.

The British plans for 1776 were based on the hope that the rebellion in America could be stamped out with one big military campaign by a regular, trained army supported by the might of British sea power. For the campaign to be successful, the forces involved would require sufficient transports to supply the victuals and stores that the troops and sailors would need while operating away from their support bases. An operation on this scale would have provided logistical problems on an unprecedented scale. Syrett's assessment of the vision of those who planned it is worth quoting.

> It was an undertaking without precedent and, in many respects, beyond the physical and administrative capacity of an eighteenth century government. But when considering the elusiveness of the objective, the unique nature of the conflict, the necessity of conveying thousands of troops across the Atlantic and the vast size of America, and the physical, administrative and strategic problems of the undertaking, the astonishing fact about the British effort in 1776 is not that the campaign failed, but rather that it came so close to succeeding.[18]

Major-General Clinton received orders in January 1776 to lead a force from Boston to North Carolina and join up with Sir Peter Parker at Cape Fear. Based on earlier assurances, it was hoped that this expedition would encourage Loyalists to join the fight. However, it was all too late; by the time that Clinton had arrived at Cape Fear (Parker was some weeks away in the Atlantic) the Loyalists had already been defeated at Moore's Creek Bridge (near Wilmington) on 27 February 1776. In October 1775, with Clinton's army still in Boston, Sandwich wrote to Admiral Shuldham (who was still in England and would take naval command from Graves in January 1776) that five regiments in Ireland had been ordered to embark and would probably sail in December for North Carolina 'in order to take possession of that province and to make a powerful diversion by that means to the attacks of the rebels in the north'.[19] The landings did not happen until June of the following year, eight months later. Sandwich expected Admiral Parker, still in Britain, to be ready to sail 'in about a month' and to be the naval commander of the expedition. In spite of the October orders stating a sailing date in December, it was not until 8 January 1776 that all of the assigned troops were embarked[20] as the Admiralty and Ordnance Departments had been 'met with a variety of unexpected difficulties &

18   Syrett, *American Waters*, p.60.
19   NDAR, Vol.2, pp.775–776, Sandwich to Shuldham, 24 October 1775.
20   Syrett, *Shipping and the American War*, p.36.

delays';[21] such difficulties were becoming the norm for the sailing of large convoys. The operation against Charleston could only go ahead after Parker's force had joined up with that of Clinton, who was kicking his heels off Cape Fear awaiting the admiral's arrival.

The whole episode had been 'ill-conceived and mismanaged;'[22] those who had planned the expedition had failed to factor in the problems inherent in eighteenth century sea transport. Not only was Parker's convoy late in sailing from Ireland but the 36 vessels[23] (five ships of war and 31 transports of various kinds) were dispersed by an Atlantic storm: some two weeks after arriving Parker was still missing five transports, one Ordnance ship, and two victuallers.[24] Clinton's frustration at the delay in Parker's arrival is obvious in his later narrative of the war, although he managed to overlook the problem caused by the storm, an event completely beyond Parker's ability to control.

> On the 18th of April the first Transport of the Irish Fleet joined me; and *they continued to drop in every day after this by single Ships* to the 3d of May, when Commodore Sir Peter Parker with the Bulk of his Fleet at last made his appearance. It seems he did not leave Cork before the 13th of february [*sic*] – and the Reasons for this extraordinary delay he can best explain; but Sir Wm Howe was assured by the Minister the Armament should sail from thence by the first of December. There were however several Ships still missing, nor did the last of them join us before the 31st of May [my emphasis].[25]

When the two fleets did join off Cape Fear on 3 May 1776, where Clinton's men had already spent six weeks waiting at sea, the troops in both convoys had had a torrid time and were short of provisions, as Parker detailed in his report to the Admiralty.

> As I have found all the Ships and Vessels Here, and to the Southward in great want of Provisions, and as the *Levant* Victualler is ordered to Boston, and no Contractors in any of the Rebellious Colonies, and not knowing as Yet, how the Ships to the Southward are to be supplied, I have put the Squadron to Two Thirds Allowance of Bread, Beef, and

21 NDAR, Vol.3, p.467, *précis* prepared for the King regarding the expedition.
22 Syrett, *Shipping and the American War*, p.36.
23 NDAR, Vol.5, p.112. Various sources have differing numbers.
24 NDAR, Vol.5, p.110, Parker to Stephens, 15 May 1776.
25 NDAR, Vol.5, p.325, Clinton's narrative of the war.

Pork, [and] have taken about a Weeks Provisions from the Transports (which had near Twelve Weeks on Board).[26]

Although the fleets had joined, the men were not in a fit state to consider an opposed landing after 'being so long cooped up in transports', particularly the 46th Regiment, which 'was very sickly'.[27] Clinton's men, waiting for Parker's arrival, lacked beef and salt and 'subsisted mostly on a meagre allowance of fish, oysters, and cabbage, all cadged or pilfered from the surrounding country'.[28]

The operations in the vicinity of Charleston in 1776 are an object lesson in how things can go wrong without the guiding hand of one overall commander. In this case, Clinton and Parker were nominally working towards a common military goal, but they allowed their personal egos to get in the way of achieving it. The *Sandwich Papers* (Volume 1) contain the letters that passed between Admiral Parker (in the *Bristol*) and General Clinton (in the *Sovereign*) prior to the landings while both of their ships were at anchor off Charleston Bar. One might have thought it sensible that both commanders should be in the same ship while they planned and commanded the operation. Instead, this was all done by letter, sent between ships by row-boat. At one point Parker did suggest that Clinton should temporarily relocate to the *Bristol* as 'Plans might have been formed and carried into execution with more ease than they can be at present'. Unfortunately, Clinton did not feel able to take up the offer: 'I have much to lament that my exceeding bad state of health at Sea would make it very inconvenient for me at this time to remove on board the *Bristol*, which Obliges me to decline the Honor of Your polite invitation'.[29] However, he did suggest that 'in the mean time I will give directions that the *Sovereign* may be Anchored as near as the *Bristol* as possible'.

Further reading of the messages that passed between the two senior officers show that it was not just sea-sickness that held Clinton back; the two men did not get on with each other. When Parker laid out his suggestions for the use of his ships in support of the army, Clinton was dismissive of the level of the navy's participation, which he expected to be on a more significant scale than Parker proposed:

When we agreed to make our attempt on Sullivan's Island, it seemed to be our intentions first to consider the object and probability of Success on the Spot; [...] in this Attack I ever understood the Navy were to bear a

26 NDAR, Vol.5, p.111, Parker to Stephens, 15 May 1776.
27 NDAR, Vol.5, p.325, Clinton's narrative, 18 April to 31 May 1776.
28 Wickwire, *Cornwallis*, p.82.
29 SP, Vol.1, pp.134–135, Clinton to Parker, 5 June 1776.

considerable part, but by your late arrangement you have marked out for them *little more than reducing any insignificant Batteries that may be found on Light house or Cummins's Point* – I have ever been of the same opinion with regard to the Consequence of Sullivans Island, and if it is taken the Fleet must give their great assistance – I cannot think of landing on the North side of that Island as you propose without in the first place being assured their [*sic*] is no Surff [*sic*], that armed Vessels can approach near enough to cover my landing and retreat, and that such Naval force as can be brought into action may be ready at their Stations to co-operate, without which I am free to own any attempt I should make might justly be called rash and absurd [my emphasis].[30]

Parker, his ship moored close to Clinton's, was quick to gainsay Clinton's allegations of a lack of involvement:

I thought myself Sir sufficiently explicit in my Letter, and if You will be so good, as to consider my Arrangement, You will find that the Ships are to bear a very considerable Part; *that it is not confined to reducing any insignificant Batteries*, but to be ready shou'd there be Occasion to make a joint Attack with His Majesty's Troops, on the Batteries on Sulivans Island; according to my Ideas, these Words convey the very Wish you express 'that such Naval Force as can be brought into action may be ready at Their Stations to Co-operate' however to avoid all possibility of being misunderstood in Future, I do now assure You, that His Majesty's Ships under my Command, shall during the Course of the whole Expedition, give every Assistance in Their Power, and that I hope You will find considerable [my emphasis].[31]

The troops had not yet landed, nor had a plan been agreed on, but Parker felt the need to reassure Clinton that they were both pursuing the same end: 'I must now Sir beg the Fav[or] that shou'd I hereafter express myself in Terms that may appear to You Ambiguous, that You will put the best construction on Them, and believe me to be equally zealous with Yourself for the Success of His Majesty's Arms'. The British may have had an army and a navy off Charleston, but they did not have a 'combined' operation.

Naval operations such as this one were very dependent on winds and tides and Parker's messages to Clinton had constant references to their importance: 'In my

---

30   NDAR, Vol.5, p.352, Clinton to Parker, 2 June 1776.
31   NDAR, Vol.5, p.354, Parker to Clinton, 2 June 1776.

signals, I mentioned the first of the flood as the most proper time for placing the ships against the batteries; [...] I am now of opinion, in which all the masters concur, that the pitch of high water will be the best time'.[32] Poor reconnaissance and a lack of local knowledge meant that the landings did not go well[33] and Clinton's letter (he was ashore on Long Island) to Parker on 29 June indicates that he had no idea how the naval ships had fared: 'As I am anxious to hear from you since your attack of yesterday, and supposing you must be busily employed after the engagement by seeing no boat from you on her way to this island [...] [I] wait upon you for such information as you shall think proper to give'. In his narrative Clinton leaves little doubt that he held the navy responsible for the fiasco for which both commanders should shoulder blame; the 'long menaced Attack took place at last on the 28th of June', but without giving the signal 'as agreed on to prepare the troops'.[34] From the start the assault went wrong; three frigates went aground and 'the Troops remained all the Time on the Sands anxiously looking out for some Signal to let them know what the Squadron was doing'. As Clinton recorded it: 'Nothing therefore was now left for us to do but to lament that the Blood of brave & gallant Men had been so fruitlessly Spilt, and prepare for reembarking [sic] as soon as possible'. As an example of naval support for the army in America, this operation demonstrates little more than how it can all go wrong; Syrett described it as 'hastily organized and badly executed'.[35] Willis went a little further: 'the British couldn't even retreat with dignity' as a transport packed with Scottish soldiers ran aground and the troops were captured: 'This was the first major British naval operation of the war and it had been an unmitigated disaster'.[36] By the next day, the naval bombardment of the rebels had broken off and on the morning of 29 June:

[A]t day brake [sic] to our great Concern we found the fleet had retired, leaving a Frigate aground, which was afterwards burned; In this situation any feeble effort of ours would answer no good purpose, and finding that the Fleet had suffered a good deal, and that the Commodore had no intention of renewing the attack, I proposed to him that as soon as possible I might proceed with the troops Under my Command to the Northward, they are Now in great health, but I fear would not remain long so in this Climate. We shall sail in a few days for N. York.[37]

---

32   SP, Vol.1, p.138, Parker to Clinton, 16 June 1776.
33   Syrett, *American Waters*, pp.38–39.
34   NDAR, Vol.5, p.801, Clinton's narrative.
35   Syrett, *American Waters*, p.38.
36   Willis, *Sea Power*, p.111.
37   NDAR, Vol.5, p.984, Clinton to Germain, 8 July 1776.

The expedition was a failure, but that was hardly surprising given the manner in which it was conducted, with no single commander having overall control of the forces – naval and land – on the American continent, ministers in London making strategic decisions across communication lines that took weeks for messages to arrive, and friction between generals Clinton and Howe and between Clinton and Commodore Parker. General Clinton had been sent out to America as a subordinate of General Howe, a position that he first accepted, but later came to resent; he would later find himself in a similar situation with Cornwallis as his subordinate. Senior officers of this time were not averse to bypassing the chain of command in order to cast doubt on their seniors in the eyes of ministers in London. In a letter to Germain, following the abortive operation, Clinton took the opportunity to paint General Howe as exercising little control over events, although Clinton was the army commander on the spot. Clinton made the point that there had been little communication between himself and Howe, 'from whom I had not heard for four months', and Clinton complained that those orders he did receive had lacked precision. According to Clinton, Howe seemed 'to *intimate his wishes* [my emphasis] that some operations might take place in some of the Southern Colonies, and pointed out Charles Town [*sic*] in the province of South Carolina as an object of importance to his Majtys. [*sic*] Service'.[38] Clinton's letters and report indicate his lack of conviction in the whole escapade; he did not believe Governor Martin's claims that 'I own myself much inclined to think that a body of Troops once landed even in this neighbourhood would draw numbers of the people of the Country to your Standard, and that the facilities to enable an army to penetrate into the Country would grow upon you continually'.[39] In the general's opinion, 'there does not exist in any one [province] in America a number of friends of Government sufficient to defend themselves when the troops are withdrawn'.[40] In May, before the landings, he had written that 'The advanced Season of the Year and the depressed State of the Kings Friends in the two Carolinas, forbad our looking to the Southward;[41] indeed, he 'was expecting every moment to receive the Commander in Chiefs Summons to join him' (General Howe was evacuating Boston for Halifax at that time) and he would 'proceed to Virginia, and there wait Sir Wm Howes ultimate Directions'. In spite of Clinton's reservations about the Loyalists, the operation went ahead.

Although he was the army commander and might have been expected to authorise or at least approve any military moves that took place ashore, Clinton

38   NDAR, Vol.5, p.982, Clinton to Germain, 8 July 1776.
39   NDAR, Vol.4, p.430, Martin to Clinton, 20 March 1776.
40   Hibbert, *Redcoats and Rebels*, p.104.
41   NDAR, Vol.5, p.325, Clinton's narrative, 31 May 1776.

laid the blame squarely on Parker for the abortive attempt by the marines to take Fort Sullivan.

> For any further particulars relative to this affair and for the motives which determin'd the Commodore to make the attack in which he knew he could receive no assistance from the army, I must refer you to accounts from other hands.
>
> From this account it appears – that it would have been highly imprudent in the Land Forces to have attempted the passage; – That Sr P. Parker knew at the time of his making the attack that they did not intend it, and yet had made no preparations to possess himself of the Fort, which otherwise he might have done during the time that the Fire was silenced, and the enemy had abandon'd it'.[42]

Not surprisingly, Parker's account reads a little differently, and at one point he stated that 'Their Lordships will see plainly by this Account, that if the Troops cou'd [sic] have co-operated on this Attack, that His Majesty wou'd have been in Possession of Sulivan's Island'. However, he did not want to be seen to be pointing the finger at the army

> But I must beg Here to be fully understood, least [sic] it shou'd be imagined, that I mean to throw even the most distant Reflection on our Army; I shou'd not discharge my Conscience were I not to acknowledge, that such was my Opinion of His Majestys Troops from the General down to the private Soldiers, that after I had been engaged some Hours, and perceived that the Troops had not got a Footing on the North End of Sulivan's Island, I was perfectly satisfied that the Landing was impracticable; and that the Attempt wou'd have been the Destruction of many brave Men without the least probability of Success; and This I am certain will appear to be the Case, when General Clinton represents His Situation.[43]

One of the officers on board the *Bristol*, Parker's flagship, believed the operation would have been successful but for the nonappearance of Clinton's troops: 'Had the army, which was but four miles from us, and was to have joined us, come in due time to our assistance, we might have taken Charlestown, as we silenced the fort for an hour and half'.[44] The fort on Sullivan's Island, which had withstood

42 NDAR, Vol.5, p.802, 28 June 1776.
43 NDAR, Vol.5, pp.999–1001, Parker to Stephens, 9 July 1776.
44 NDAR, Vol.5, p.966, letter from an officer on HMS *Bristol*, 7 July 1776.

the naval bombardment, was later renamed Fort Moultrie in honour of the American officer who had commanded its defence. In their reports to London, both commanders were at pains to state that they had done all they could, but also to intimate that the other had failed to do likewise. Clinton stated that his *coup de main* was not put in place because of naval delays due to weather:

> Unfortunately, delays of various kinds have intervened, some occasioned by Contrary Winds and Storms, and other Circumstances, so as to protract the Movements of the Fleet, to a much more distant period than was at first expected, and to forebode that the operations of the army would be Converted from a Coup de main, to something too much like a formal seige [*sic*].[45]

In their attempts to put their actions in the best light while blaming the other for any failures, the two commanders, in their post-action reports, paint a sorry picture of a lack of preparation. The navy, in the form of Sir Peter Parker's convoy, had sailed to assist General Clinton's troops in a landing in the Carolinas, but the army commander claimed not to know what he was supposed to be doing. In his journal and his report to Germain, Clinton laid the responsibility for the decision to make a landing on Sullivan's Island on Commodore Parker. Based on intelligence Parker had received regarding the rebel defences, Clinton alleged that he 'was induced to acquiesce in a proposal made to me by the Commodore'.[46] No thought appeared to have been given to how Sullivan's Island or Charleston would be defended or supplied if their capture was successful and so, 'without a meaningful strategic objective',[47] the combined force had sailed from Cape Fear for Charleston on 31 May 1776.

For the navy to support the army in its endeavour to bring the Rebels to heel, it was not enough to simply deliver the troops; there had to be close and frequent communication between the two commanders. Clinton and Parker failed this basic test of leadership at Charleston and as a result, they made 'the British throughout America look ridiculous'.[48] There was nothing left to them but to sail to join General Howe's army, which had left Halifax for New York. The expedition to Charleston had been a 'sideshow' from the start; built on the wishful thinking of southern governors that Loyalists would rally to the flag if the British arrived in force. They came too late, unprepared and uncoordinated. The plan for 1776 had

45 NDAR, Vol.5, p.983, Clinton to Germain, 8 July 1776.
46 NDAR, Vol.5, p.982, Clinton to Germain, 8 July 1776.
47 Syrett, *American Waters*, p.37.
48 Syrett, *American Waters*, p.39.

been for a British landing in force at New York, but the distraction of the 'southern strategy' had diverted attention from that aim. With the failure of Charleston, focus could return again to General Howe and his troops and their plans to attack the city on the Hudson It was to be hoped that these combined operations would be more successful than the last.

While Clinton and Parker were pursuing their expedition off Charleston in the first five months of the year, Howe had evacuated Boston for Halifax with a view to moving on from there to New York after a short stay in the Nova Scotian port. We should also remember that during this time Rear-Admiral Shuldham had replaced Graves as commander on the North American station, and was himself superseded by Vice-Admiral Howe. While all these moves (Halifax and Charleston) were going on, the navy was also carrying out the essential role of being the eyes of the army on the American coast.

Captain Hyde Parker in the *Phoenix*, together with the *Asia*, had been stationed off New York while Howe's army was in Boston. From his moorings, he was able to command shipping access to the city and observe the American preparations (under General Lee) to defend it. Hyde Parker's report to Shuldham gives an insight into some of the problems faced by naval captains when they were required to hold a station for an extended period of time. One of these was the area he had to cover, as shown by the map of the New York area [Map 4]. He had only two ships with which to watch the Hudson River, Long Island Sound, and the entry to the harbour from Sandy Hook, all the while taking note of Rebel movements on Staten Island and Manhattan. The task was made harder by his reliance on the wind – a northerly would limit his movements up the Hudson – and the prevalence of ice during the winter months: 'very large fields of floating Ice that would have Subjected the Ships to the most extreme danger of being carried Adrift'. Winter was particularly hard on ships that had been at sea for an extended period of time, as Hyde Parker pointed out: 'We have had a most severe Winter during which it has been with the greatest difficulty we have maintained our Stations, this has not been done without the Ships Sustaining some damage, the *Asia* making Sixteen or Twenty Inches of Water in Twelve Hours, the *Phoenix* does not make Water but her Bottom is a good deal cut with Ice'.[49]

Hyde Parker, like many British officers (especially in the early months of the war), was conflicted in his attitude to the Americans and did not want to take unnecessarily aggressive action against them if this would mean driving them into the rebel camp. While he could see General Lee's men fortifying their positions in the town, he was reluctant to take decisive action. In his opinion, and he felt this was also held by the governor and General Clinton, 'the Majority of the Citizens,

49   NDAR, Vol.4, p.75-76, Hyde Parker to Shuldham, 26 February 1776.

particularly those of Property are faithful to the King' and if he fired on the town in response to Lee's movements it would be 'too Severe a Measure'. Although he regarded Lee's placing of his men where the British could see them as 'audacious', he did not use his ships' guns against them as he was 'persuaded that my firing upon them would involve the City in ruins, which I must confess I cautiously Avoid, being determined if possible to make the Act of committing Hostilities theirs and not Mine'. Independent command carried responsibility and risk; one of those risks, recognised by Hyde Parker, was how his actions might be construed by those higher up the command chain: 'I should hope I am doing right, and that this lenity on my side, may not be Misconstrued, as a want of Zeal in carrying on the King's Service'.[50]

One reason for naval captains to want to exercise some leniency towards the locals was that there were still some merchants and traders who saw a business in continuing to supply provisions to the King's ships. The merchants of New York had continued this service into 1776, in spite of Rebel pressure to prevent it. Usually the trade took place on the basis that the provisions were for the ship's crew and not to be taken to supply the army in Boston. In December 1775 Captain Vandeput of the *Asia* – part of Hyde Parker's small detachment – wrote that:

> We have for a considerable time past had every Supply that we have demanded sent on board to Us, without any Molestation to the Boats which have brought it; nor do I expect there will be any unless some of the Rebel Troops from Connecticut, or New Jersey, should come into the Town, and prevent the Towns People from acting as they seem at present inclined.[51]

From his watching station off the town Hyde Parker could see that Lee intended to do just that: 'Mr Lee much against the Inclination of the City, has cut off all supplies of Fresh Provisions'. In April, a General Order was issued by General Putnam (now Commander-in-Chief of the American forces in New York) to the citizens of that town:

> [I]t is become absolutely necessary, that all communication, between the ministerial fleet and shore, should be immediately stopped, for that purpose, has given positive orders, that the ships should no longer be furnished with provisions: Any inhabitant, or others, who shall be taken,

---

50   NDAR, Vol.4, p.75-76, Hyde Parker to Shuldham, 26 February 1776.
51   NDAR, Vol.3, pp.158–159, Vandeput to Graves, 18 December 1775.

that have been on board, or near any of the ships, or going on board, will be considered as enemies, and treated accordingly.[52]

The need for Putnam's declaration demonstrated that, just as there were British officers and men who were not wholly behind the war, so Americans were split between Rebels and Loyalists. One of the latter was Andrew Elliot, who passed information regarding rebel troops to the governor, William Tryon. Having read Putnam's notice, Elliot wrote, 'God help us in our distress – But still such Friends to Government as are left in Town keeps us [in] good Spirits'.[53] The extent to which the British did receive help is shown by the entry in the *Phoenix* log for 20 December 1775: 'Recd [*sic*] 1510 Lbs of Beef'.[54] In this case, even the British 44-gun warship that was blockading the town was able to take on provisions from New York while the British Army was 'holed up' in Boston. However, this limited facility for provisioning the ships at New York was coming to a close, and they were also about to lose their access to water, normally drawn from Governors Island, a little south of New York. The *Phoenix* log records that:

[In the morning] the *Savage* Sloop Weigh'd & Run up to the Watering Place at Straten [*sic*] Island, & Sent our Boats Watering under cover of her Guns, at 10 a Body of Rebels suddenly came down [and] Fired upon the People empd [employed] filling water, which obliged them to desist, their approach was so Sudden, that three of our People, could not make their Escape; [n]or was there possibility of getting off 27 Water Casks, which were ashore. Joseph Mitchell Seaman of the *Phoenix* & a Man belonging to the *Savage* were wounded in coming off.[55]

Towards the end of April Hyde Parker was advising Shuldham that the opportunity to receive supplies from New York really was coming to a close.

I do not imagine any Quantity of Provisions is to be expected in this Province, until the Continental Army has received a severe Blow, and the King's Troops get possession of the Country, for however well inclined the greatest part of the Inhabitants of this Province are to give every Assistance, it is not in their power; As the Rebel Committee are in

52   NDAR, Vol.4, p.722, General Orders New York, 8 April 1776.
53   NDAR, Vol.4, pp.724–725, Elliot to Tryon, 8 April 1776.
54   NDAR, Vol.3, p.196.
55   NDAR, Vol.4, p.698, *Phoenix* log, 7 April 1776.

possession of all the Landing Places, which totally prevents the Shipping of Provisions &ca [*sic*] unless by their Permission.[56]

With the American occupation of the watering place, and their firing on the British sailors, Hyde Parker withdrew the *Phoenix* to Gravesend Bay, nearly 10 miles south of New York and east of Staten Island to await reinforcements. 'By the end of April the maritime approaches to New York City had been surrendered to the Americans, who immediately began to fortify them in anticipation of a British invasion'.[57]

When General Howe's army left Boston for Halifax in early 1776, it was intended that it should be only for a short period. However, because of supply problems, the stay in Nova Scotia lasted 10 weeks. By May of that year the meat for the army was down to only two weeks' supply as only one of the Treasury victuallers sent out between August and November 1775 had arrived. On 11 June 1776, Howe's 9,000 troops sailed for New York in a fleet of 130 ships, arriving at Sandy Hook on 29 June.[58] This impressive show of strength was not lost on General Henry Knox of the Continental Army who, together with his wife, saw the fleet's arrival from their New York residence and he was moved to comment: 'My God, may I never experience the like feeling again'.[59] New York was considered the ideal base from which to operate against the Americans. Before he gave up the American command, General Gage had written that the prosecution of the war required the army to hold an area 'from whence [it might] draw supplies of provisions and forage, and that New York seems to be the most proper to answer these purposes'[60] – that was before Putnam's declaration to the townspeople. Additionally, the port commanded the Hudson River 'and thus split the rebellious colonies in two'. The strategic importance of New York to the British was recognised by General Washington and caused him to send General Charles Lee to defend the city. Lee was trusted by Washington and his position in the Rebel army demonstrated how close many from Britain were to the Americans; Lee had had a distinguished career as an officer in the British Army but, after retiring on half-pay after the Peace of Paris, he settled in America in 1773. He would now be fighting the army in which he had previously served. Washington and Lee were convinced that if the British gained New York then the consequences would be 'so terrible' as to be unimaginable; the control of the city and the Hudson – a line 'upon which

56   NDAR, Vol.4, p.1312, Hyde Parker to Shuldham, 29 April 1776.
57   Syrett, *American Waters*, p.16.
58   Mackesy, *America*, p.83.
59   O'Shaughnessy, *Men Who Lost America*, p.92.
60   Bowler, *Logistics*, p.63.

depends the Safety of America'[61] – would split New England from the southern states.

Unfortunately the campaign that the brothers were about to embark on was not to run to the original time-plan. It had been hoped that the operations could begin in spring, but as with Charleston, the plans were subject to delays that could not be controlled from America. General Howe and Admiral Shuldham (in command until Lord Howe arrived from England) left Halifax with insufficient men and ships for the expedition, but were to be reinforced from Britain. As with Charleston, the troops available in America for the New York landings would *rendezvous* at sea with the regiments to be sent from home and, as with the Carolina expedition, the joining of forces would be slower than originally anticipated. Once again, naval support was dependent on eighteenth century administrative systems and the weather. In Chapter 4, we saw that a convoy was being assembled in the Clyde to transport the 42nd and 71st Regiments to America. At the last minute, a critical supply issue caused the commanding officer of the 71st to request a delay in the sailing.

> Knowing well that your sailing Orders are of too positive a nature to admit of any delay in the execution of them, it would be highly improper to solicit an Extraordinary extension at this Juncture, did not an absolute necessity require it. By contrary Winds above one half of our Battalion Accoutrements all our Swords & Officers Fuzees [a type of rifle carried by officers], part of our Camp Equipage & the whole Ammunition of the Regiment did not arrive at the Carron from England before the 24th of this Month – An Officer with a Detachment is now employed in forwarding these Articles with the utmost Expedition to Greenock, and from the Accounts receiv'd from him late last Night, we have reason to believe the whole will arrive at Greenock upon the 28th at farthest. This being the Case we hope you will join in opinion that it is absolutely necessary for His Majesty's Service that the Fleet should remain for that time at Greenock than that the Troops who are destined for immediate Service, should proceed to North America without their Accoutrements & Ammunition.[62]

This convoy, escorted by only one warship – the 36-gun *Flora* – was critical to British plans. The Highland regiments awaiting 'accoutrements' were 3,500 strong, but there were also 9,100 Hessians expected at Spithead who would also

61   Ferling, *Miracle*, p.120.
62   NDAR, Vol.4, p.1062, Erskine and Campbell to Captain Brisbane, 26 April 1776.

be sailing, under Commodore Hotham, to join Howe – further complicating the *rendezvous* off the American coast. In his letter to Shuldham acquainting him of the preparations, Philip Stephens at the Admiralty alludes to the possibility of delays due to 'the arrangements which always attends upon so great a number of Troops'.[63] Along with the Hessians, Hotham's convoy would also contain 'several Navy Victuallers [...] loaded with four months Provisions for 10,000 Seamen'.

On 27 April, the *Flora* convoy of 33 transports sailed from the Clyde. Nine days later, '36 leagues west of the Scilly Isles', the convoy was scattered by a storm. According to the *Flora's* log, 'at 5 [a.m.] saw 5 sail of convoy it blowing excessive hard with hail sleet and very high sea at noon 5 sail in sight'.[64] Over the next two days, four more transports joined the *Flora*, making only nine of the 33 that had started the journey. The remaining 24 made their own way as best they could but two of them, carrying troops, were unfortunate enough to end up at Boston (now in the hands of the Americans) with the humiliating capture of 571 soldiers. The fate of the *Flora* convoy demonstrated yet again the difficulties inherent in eighteenth century transport by sea. While General Howe's 130 ships had arrived off Long Island on 29 June, providing General Knox with his breakfast surprise that we have noted above, he could not proceed until he had joined forces with those coming from England. After a 'most tedious Passage of nine Weeks' during which they had 'had contrary Winds for the much greater Part of the Way',[65] the general's brother arrived on 12 July with 'nearly 150 ships [...] including 10 large warships [...] 10,000 seamen and 11,000 troops'.[66] Communications being what they were, this fleet was unaware, when it left England, that General Howe and his troops had left Halifax for New York, so their journey included a detour to Nova Scotia *en route* to the *rendezvous* off Sandy Hook. The meeting of the two fleets was described by an enthusiastic Ambrose Serle (secretary to Lord Howe): 'A finer Scene could not be exhibited, both of Country, Ships, and men, all heightened by one of the brightest Days that can be imagined'.[67] Admiral Howe, now a peace commissioner as well as an admiral, arrived a few days after the Americans had declared themselves to be independent, a move commented on by Serle as 'the Villainy & the Madness of these deluded People'. The arrival of Howe was also the opportunity for the formal handover of the command of the navy in America from Vice-Admiral Molyneux Shuldham, who then requested leave to go home: 'The great Confusion in which I left my private Affairs in England when I was

---

63   NDAR, Vol.4, p.1048, Stephens to Shuldham, 18 April 1776.
64   D. Syrett, 'The disruption of HMS *Flora's* convoy, 1776', *Mariner's Mirror*, 56:4 (1970), p.423.
65   NDAR, Vol.5, p.1214, Serle to Lord Dartmouth, 25 July 1776.
66   O'Shaughnessy, *Men Who Lost America*, p.92.
67   NDAR, Vol.5, p.1043, journal of Ambrose Serle.

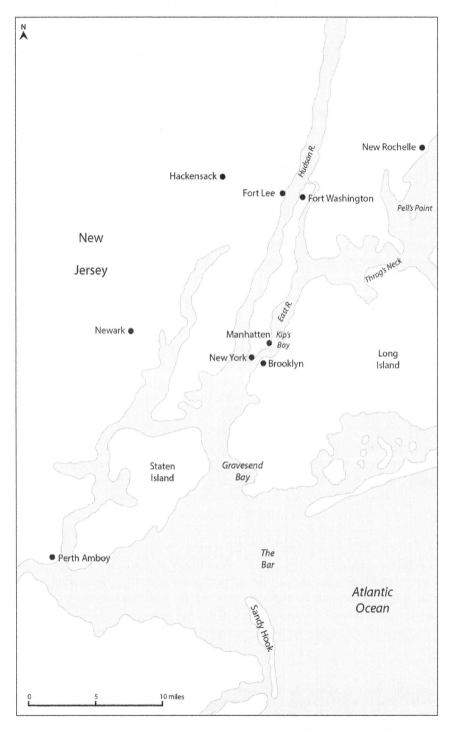

Map 4: New York area

called upon and appointed to the Command of His Majesty's Fleet in America, requiring my Return, I beg the Favor [sic] your Lordship will give me Leave to proceed to Great Britain in any Manner You shall please to direct'.[68]

The force off Sandy Hook was further augmented on 1 August when General Clinton and Commodore Parker arrived from their abortive mission to Charleston; 2,000 troops and 45 ships. The build-up was completed on 12 August with the arrival, after a passage lasting 14 weeks, of Hotham's fleet of 107 ships and the 9,000 Hessian troops: 'So large a Fleet made a fine Appearance upon entering the Harbor, with the Sails crouded [sic], Colors flying, Guns saluting, and the Soldiers both in the Ships and on the Shore continually shouting. The Rebels (as we perceived by the Glasses) flocked out of their lurking Holes to see a Picture, by no means agreeable to them'.[69] This was now the greatest expedition that Britain had ever sent to America, 3,000 miles from its home base. 'Two-thirds of the total British army and 45 percent of the Royal Navy were serving in America and the Caribbean;'[70] in terms of numbers, over 400 ships and 32,000 troops. The army could not complain about the scale of the resources committed by the navy to transporting the troops to make this concentration happen.

In August 1776, to the south of New York, General Howe (after his arrival from Halifax) had overwhelming force at his disposal. His army (which had been augmented by the arrival of Clinton and Parker from Charleston) outnumbered Washington's by 31,000 to 19,000, the British Navy dwarfed any possible American naval threat, and the American troops were in a very difficult position. Washington had concentrated his troops on Manhattan and the southern end of Long Island on the Brooklyn Heights, opposite New York. It was General Howe's responsibility, possibly taking into account the views of his subordinates, to choose where to attack the Americans and, together with his brother, decide on a landing place. General Clinton recognised that with the British holding naval superiority Washington's force could be trapped on Manhattan and Long Island if a number of ships sailed up the Hudson and landed a force at Kingsbridge. This would prevent the Americans' escape to Fort Lee on the west bank of the river. General Howe disagreed with Clinton; he would land first at Gravesend on Long Island [Map 4] and attack the Americans on the Brooklyn Heights. The troops for this operation were stationed on Staten Island, so the landings would not be 'ship-to-shore' but via flatboats from Staten Island to Gravesend. This had a number of advantages for the troops; it was easier to embark and disembark from the flatboats than it would be from transport ships and it was easier to load the

68   NDAR, Vol.5, p.1063, Shuldham to Howe, 13 July 1776.
69   NDAR, Vol.6, pp.155–156, journal of Ambrose Serle.
70   O'Shaughnessy, *Men Who Lost America*, p.92.

stores, troops, and ordnance on these small boats in the order in which the army commander wanted them to be used once on shore. Unlike Charleston, where the personal animosity between Clinton and Sir Peter Parker had been detrimental to the whole operation, the landings at New York took place under the partnership of the Howe brothers, with the admiral doing all he could to support his brother's army. The Howe brothers were close and supportive of one another. Their joint commands created the potential for successful combined operations between the army and navy, which was a crucial advantage for launching amphibious attacks against the major cities along the East Coast of America'.[71]

For the indirect assault on New York (they were first to attack the Americans on the Brooklyn Heights), Admiral Howe delegated command of the landings to Hotham, who gave the order for the boats to go ashore at 8:30 a.m. on 22 August 1776. For the landings, 75 flatboats, 11 bateaux, and two galleys ferried the men ashore.[72] The event featured in the day's log of HMS *Preston*: 'Light airs and fair weather[;] the Men of War having placed themselves in Gravesend Bay to cover the Debarkation of the Troops a number of Transports with Troops onboard anchored there also, when the Flat boats proceeded and Landed without opposition on Long Island, the debarkation continued til [*sic*] the whole amounting to 15,000 men was Landed'.[73] During the landings, five men of war made a further demonstration of the flexibility of sea power by providing a diversion with the shelling of an enemy battery at Red Hook on the Brooklyn shore.

> The Fleet assisted in this opperation [*sic*] by 5 Ships getting under way and making an appearance of attacking The Forts, on which I led with the *Roebuck*, and exchanged a few Shot with the Fort at Red Hook, but it was situated too high for our Guns to do it any damage and nothing being intended more than to make a Diversion, to keep the Enemy in their Forts, I hauld [*sic*] off again, and upon the defeat of the Rebels Ashore, the Ships Anchored by Signal from the Admiral.[74]

The landings were well executed and demonstrated the good working relationship between the Howe brothers, as well as Hotham's ability to coordinate and control the amphibious operation.

However, once ashore on Long Island Howe's army, though it gave the Americans a drubbing, did not defeat them on the Brooklyn Heights, and his

71   O'Shaughnessy, *Men Who Lost America*, p.88.
72   Willis, *Sea Power*, p.126.
73   NDAR, Vol.6, p.268, ship's log HMS *Preston*, 22 August 1776.
74   NDAR, Vol.6, pp.353–354, narrative of Captain Snape Hamond, HMS *Roebuck*, 27 August 1776.

slow follow-up of his advantage allowed the Americans to pull back across the East River into New York on the night of 29–30 August. That night, with a storm preventing the movement of the British Navy into the East River, the rebel troops were withdrawn from Long Island to Manhattan. Captain Duncan (on Admiral Howe's flagship, *Eagle*) briefly described the scene in his journal for 30 August: 'The admiral was going on shore, and was met in his barge by Colonel Sheriff, who informed him, to the surprise of the army, the rebels had quitted all their strong posts on Long Island, and deserted it entirely'.[75] Washington remarked on the apparent reluctance of Howe to engage in any energetic pursuit after the initial contact on Long Island: 'There is something exceedingly mysterious in the conduct of the enemy', a point picked up by Putnam: 'General Howe is either our friend or no general'.[76] Once again, Howe had put water between himself and Washington's army.

Having allowed the Americans to escape from Long Island to New York and Manhattan, Howe – together with the navy – needed another successful combined operation if he was to come to grips with Washington. One historian described it as 'Great Britain's last best chance to destroy the Continental army [*sic*] and crush the American rebellion [...] but the opportunity slipped away through a series of monumental mistakes'.[77] These mistakes would be Howe's; once again, he was slow to take advantage of the opportunity afforded by a successful assault on the beaches and he was not prepared to accept suggestions from his second-in-command, General Clinton. The navy on the other hand, provided admirable support as the troops went ashore.

General Howe's decision was to make this next landing around Kips Bay [Map 4], from where he hoped that he would be able to split the Americans in New York from those on Harlem Heights. However, Howe's slowness in moving meant that this did not take place until some two weeks after the Americans had evacuated their troops across the East River. As with the previous landings on Long Island, the assault on 15 September would be a shore-to-shore operation, not ship-to-shore. The navy provided the muscle power to row the 'seventy-five flatboats, galleys, and bateaux'[78] from Newtown Creek on Long Island, across the East River to Kips Bay. While the troops were being taken to their landing sites, the navy took advantage of the geography to provide another diversion. With the East River on one side of the Manhattan peninsula and the Hudson on the other, it was an ideal situation to split the enemy's attention. Admiral Howe sent four warships

75   NDAR, Vol.6, p.372, journal of Henry Duncan.
76   Hibbert, *Redcoats and Rebels*, p.124.
77   Ferling, *Miracle*, p.139.
78   Ferling, *Miracle*, p.140.

into the Hudson for that purpose. The ships did get the attention of the Americans and drew fire from the city and from the West bank of the Hudson, as Captain Wilkinson of the *Pearl* recorded in his ship's log: 'At 7 [a.m.] weighd [weighed anchor] and made sail in Company with his Majs Ships *Renown*, *Repulse*, and *Trial* Schooner. At 8 abreast of New York Town, Receiv'd a smart Canonading [*sic*] from the Town & Paulers hook [believe this is Paulus Hook on Map 4], which we return'd'.[79] While Wilkinson was playing his part in the diversion, other warships were providing covering fire for the crossing and landing. Five warships were assigned this role, among them the *Rose* (Captain Wallace).

> [A]t 6 [a.m.] came too in Kipps [different documents use different spelling] Bay York Island in 8 fm [fathom] as did HM Ships *Phenix Orpheus*, *Roebuck* and *Carisford* [*Carysfort*] to Cover the landing of our Troops, at 11 all the Boats crossing the River, began a heavy fireing [*sic*] to Clear the Rebel Trenches, at 12 [the troops] began to land.[80]

The action is also recorded in the *Carysfort's* log:

> At 1/2 past 9 Seeing the Rebels getting into their Trenches the *Phoenix* began to fire, as did the *Orpheus*, *Roebuck* & *Rose*, they being all moor'd in a line a head of us, at the distance of a Cables length from each other. After firing several Broadsides right a Shore, we hauld in the Stream Cable, and brought our Guns to bear on their Trenches on our Quarter, w[h]ere a great Number of the Rebels was assembled, on which they run off into the Woods – At 1/2 past 10 left of[f] fireing, our Troops 'being Landed & Formed, Do found we fired 20 broadsides in the Space of an hour, with Double headed, round & Grape Shott [*sic*].[81]

For the Rebels on shore the bombardment must have been terrifying, and something they had never experienced before; as one American army captain recorded in his journal, 'Our troops left their post in disorder'.[82] Bartholomew James, aboard the *Orpheus*, gave his account of the action.

> It is hardly possible to conceive what a tremendous fire was kept up by those five ships for fifty-nine minutes, in which time we fired away, in the *Orpheus* alone, five thousand three hundred and seventy-six pounds

79   NDAR, Vol.6, p.844, *Pearl's* log, 15 September 1776.
80   NDAR, Vol.6, pp.840–841, *Rose's* log, 15 September 1776.
81   NDAR, Vol.6, p.849, *Carysfort's* log, 15 September 1776.
82   NDAR, Vol.6, p.845, diary of Samuel Richards.

of powder. The first broadside made a considerable breach in their works, and the enemy fled on all sides, confused and calling for quarter, while *the army landed, but, as usual, did not pursue the victory*, though the rebels in general had left their arms in the intrenchment [my emphasis]'.[83]

In his book Willis disputes the amount of powder that James claimed to have used based on the number of rounds the ship would have had to fire to use this quantity.[84] Also, James has recognised Howe's slowness to capitalise on success which we noted after the engagement at Brooklyn Heights. As a result of the strength of the bombardment, and Washington's failure to anticipate that Howe's troops might come ashore at Kips Bay, the American Captain Richards recorded that 'their landing there being unexpected they met with no opposition'.[85] Again, the availability of sea power increased the army's flexibility of manoeuvre.

As a result of the successful landing, Howe's men entered New York almost unopposed. The inhabitants of the city, we are led to believe by some British accounts, were glad to be delivered from the Rebels: 'Nothing could equal the Expressions of Joy shewn by the Inhabitants, upon the arrival of the King's officers among them'.[86] Captain Duncan (HMS *Eagle*) went ashore at New York to be met by what he described as a 'rabble', but was pleasantly surprised:

> At the landing-place I was met by the mob, who gave me three cheers, took me on their shoulders, carried me to the Governor's Fort, put me under the English colours now hoisted, and again gave me three cheers, which they frequently repeated, men, women, and children shaking me by the hand, and giving me their blessing, and crying out 'God save the King!' They carried me to my boat, and we parted with cheering and my promising to send them some troops.[87]

Had these overly enthusiastic views been representative of those of all Americans, there would have been no conflict with the Home Country.

Washington's men in New York had largely evaded the British and gone north to join their comrades on the Harlem Heights, necessitating a further landing by some of Howe's troops at Pell's Point. Over the remaining weeks of 1776, Howe's forces drove the Americans off Manhattan and Harlem and across to New Jersey. The American Forts Washington and Lee were captured, the American army

83   NDAR, Vol.6, p.841, journal of Bartholomew James.
84   Willis, *Sea Power*, p.131.
85   NDAR, Vol.6, p.845, diary of Samuel Richards.
86   NDAR, Vol.6, p.843, journal of Ambrose Serle.
87   NDAR, Vol.6, p.846, journal of Captain Duncan.

retreated to the Delaware, and the British (against Clinton's advice) landed on Rhode Island and took the town of Newport with no opposition.

In the eighteenth century, it was normal for the campaigning season to come to an end with the onset of winter and for the troops to go into winter quarters. In December 1776, Washington famously crossed the Delaware and delivered a bloody nose to the British who had followed him from New York, causing them to leave New Jersey. The effect was far-reaching in that the British, who had intended using New Jersey as a 'market garden' for their troops in New York, now had a supply problem again. General Howe wrote to London that 'all supplies must continue to be sent from hence [Britain] & no certain dependence had of obtaining them in America'.[88] The consequence of Washington's capture of Trenton was that the navy would be further stretched to protect supply convoys for an army that was clearly vulnerable if it moved far from coastal ports. Washington had not been defeated in 1776, which had been the British hope for their massive movement of troops to America. The American commander recognised that his ill-trained army was no match for the British in a set-piece battle and that he had to avoid being drawn into one by Howe while keeping his own army intact: 'We should on all occasions avoid a general action, or put anything to risk, unless compelled by a necessity into which we ought never to be drawn'.[89]

The preparations for the 1777 campaigning season highlight the command and control problem that Britain had all through the war; how to set the aims and objectives from London while having no single Commander-in-Chief in America to execute them. As this account focuses on the navy's support of the army it does not go into Burgoyne's abortive campaign south from Canada and his subsequent defeat at Saratoga. However, the misunderstandings surrounding it deserve a brief mention. Burgoyne marched south expecting to be met at Albany by General Howe and that they would together secure New York and the Hudson. Unfortunately, Howe had other ideas; he proposed that he should take Philadelphia, which he believed was 'talismanic' for the Americans and that 'Washington would have to stand and fight to defend it'.[90] His plan spoke only in vague terms of the need 'to facilitate in some degree, the approach of the army from Canada'. The 'plan' was unlikely to end well. Readers wishing to cover Burgoyne's expedition in detail should refer to Ferling (Chapter 8), Mackesy (Chapter 6), or Black (Chapter 7). This account now moves to Howe's operations against Philadelphia.

Howe's original intention had been to march his troops from New York to Philadelphia, but this was changed to a combined operation with the troops being

---

88   Willis, *Sea Power*, p.162.
89   Syrett, *Lord Howe*, p.61.
90   Ferling, *Miracle*, p.190.

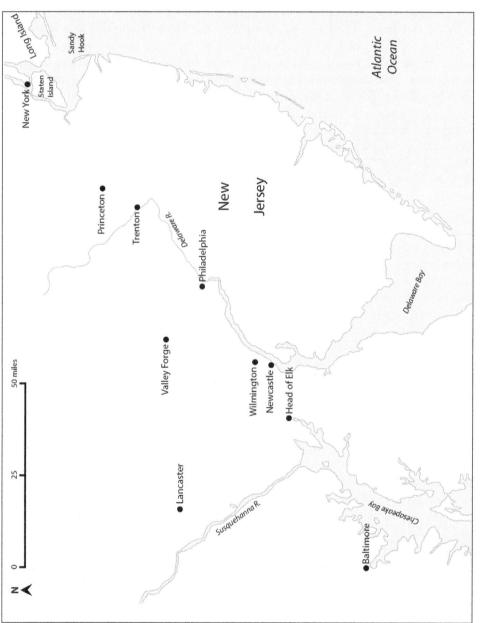

Map 5: Philadelphia area

transported by sea. The logistics involved were huge; some 13,000 troops were to be transported, together with equipment, horses, and provisions in 267 ships, but they were unable to get away until 23 July, 'the earliest Opportunity the Weather would permit'.[91] When the ships left Sandy Hook they had been destined for the Delaware River, where they would land and march on Philadelphia, but this plan changed while at sea. On 31 July, the fleet reached the mouth of the Delaware where Captain Snape Hamond in the *Roebuck,* who had been stationed at the mouth of the river for some time, joined the Howe brothers on the admiral's flagship. Snape Hamond stated his belief that the ships and transports would be safe entering the Delaware provided that they only advanced as far as Newcastle. While the admiral seemed 'to incline to the Delaware' for the landings, General Howe appeared 'from the beginning for making the landing in Chesepeak [*sic*] Bay'. The argument for changing the landing destination was based largely on the time that the army had been at sea and that this would have allowed Washington to get his army 'over the Delaware [and as a result] great opposition was expected to be given to the Troops at landing at Newcastle or Wilmington the places intended'. Following the discussions the decision was taken to bypass the Delaware and for the troops to continue their journey into the Chesapeake. The result was that the journey from New York to the disembarkation point took 47 days through the heat of summer; before the war the journey from New York to the landing place at the head of the Chesapeake had taken 'three days by the *Flying Machine*, the smartest coach to Philadelphia'.[92]

The ships had been provisioned for the expected short voyage to the Delaware, so troops were running low on rations and 'dozens of horses had perished in the dingy holds of their transports'.[93] The length of the journey, the short rations and the heat of summer must have meant a torrid time for the troops, as some accounts tell us. Their accommodation was in 'fetid, noisy, airless compartments', where they endured a steady diet of bread 'which is spoiled or full of worms' washed down with 'Stinking water with all the impurities mixed in'.[94] This might have been expected by the commanders when the decision was taken to extend the voyage from three weeks to seven, with 13,000 troops in close confinement aboard ship. During the voyage, 27 men and 170 horses perished. Ambrose Serle noted in his journal that during the voyage 'The Transports, with the poor Soldiers, were tossed about exceedingly' and on hearing that they were bound for the Chesapeake he bemoaned that 'may God defend us from the Fatality of the worst Climate in

91   TNA, ADM 1/487, f.480, Lord Howe to Stephens, 28 August 1777.
92   Urban, *Fusiliers,* p.113.
93   Urban, *Fusiliers,* p.113.
94   Ferling, *Miracle,* p.245.

America at this worst Season of the Year to experience it!'[95] On 19 August, in the Chesapeake but, about a week before the landing, Captain John Montresor wrote that 'The fleet and army [were] much distressed for the want of fresh water, having been for some time put to an allowance, but not so much so as the horse vessels, having been obliged to throw numbers of their horses overboard'.[96] There was some relief for the troops' rations; the eastern seaboard is renowned today for its seafood, and the Chesapeake seems to have been equally bountiful for Montresor's crew in 1777: 'It's remarkable in the Bay the multitude of crabs that swim nearly to the surface of the water. The Fleet caught thousands'. After reaching the bay on 14 August, Serle again gives us his view of the situation:

> Many of our Horses perished; but the Troops in general were as healthy as could have been expected, in the immense Heat of this Climate. The Thermometer in the Shade and at Sea stood frequently at 84 and 86 [degrees]. What must it have been upon Shore? – Three or four People died in our Ship of putrid & bilious Fevers, common in this Region of the World. – The Land at the Capes is very low: Not far from Cape Henry is the Dismal Swamp, a Mass of stagnated Waters & Mud of a vast Extent. These Swamps & Marshes render this Country so extremely unwholsome [...][97]

After leaving the mouth of the Delaware, the fleet crept slowly south along the coast, the wind being either calm or south-westerly, before turning into Chesapeake Bay on 15 August and reaching the disembarkation point, Head of Elk, on the 25th. The sailing of the fleet from the Delaware surprised the Americans, as Washington stated to a member of the Massachusetts Council:

> Since Genl Howe left the Capes of Delaware with his fleet on the night of Thursday forenight, we have not obtained any accounts of him nor can we fix his destination with any certainty or satisfaction by reasoning on the subject. – 'till he sailed from Sandy Hook I had no doubt in my own mind but that he would have pushed up the North River to cooperate with Genl Burgoyne; his expedition to the Capes of Delaware and departure again without further information of him have put us all into a State of conjecture as to the line of conduct he means to pursue.[98]

95   NDAR, Vol.9, p.327, journal of Ambrose Serle.
96   NDAR, Vol.9, p.768, Captain John Montresor.
97   NDAR, Vol.9, p.745, journal of Ambrose Serle.
98   NDAR, Vol.9, p.731, Washington to Massachusetts Council, 10 August 1777.

This was an example of the tactical flexibility afforded by the navy giving the British Army the advantage of surprise in its movements. Ten days after writing the above comment, Washington was still unaware of Howe's destination, although by that time he was already in Chesapeake Bay:

> From the Time, which has elapsed, since Genl Howe departed from the Capes of Delaware, there is the strongest reason to conclude, that he is gone either far to the Eastward or Southward, and with a design, to execute some determined plan. [...] The probability is in favor of a Southern Expedition; Because he has been seen, since his departure from the Capes, off Sinapuxent, steering a Southern course, – and because, had his destination been to the Eastward, his arrival there from the general state of the winds, must have announced It before this, or his Fleet would have been discovered by some of the Cruisers on that Coast. If he is gone to the Southward, he must be gone far that way; For had Chesapeak Bay been his Object, he would have been there long since, and the Fact well established. Beyond that, there is no place short of Charles Town, of Sufficient importance to engage his attention.[99]

Washington was in a quandary – what to do with his army? – while the British Navy demonstrated the enormous flexibility it gave to his opponents. The American commander recognised the options and advantages that sea power made available to Howe:

> Matters being thus circumstanced, an Important Question arises, How this Army is to be employed. If his Intentions are such, as I have supposed them, It appears to me, that an attempt to follow him, would not only be fruitless, but would be attended with ruinous consequences. The distance is so immense, that General Howe might accomplish every purpose he had in view before we could possibly arrive to oppose him, and so long a march, thro an unhealthy climate at this season would debilitate and waste a principle part of our Force. Added to this, after we had made a considerable progress, he might easily reimbark [*sic*] his Troops, and turn his Arms against Philadelphia or elsewhere, as he should think proper, without our being in a condition to give the least aid. [...] we have no Other Alternative left, than to remain here idle & inactive, on the remote probability of his returning this way, or to proceed towards Hudson's

River, with a view of opposing Genl Burgoyne, or making an Attempt on York Island, as the situation of Affairs shall Point out.

With Washington in the dark as to Howe's intentions, although the fleet was spotted sailing up the bay by the inhabitants of Annapolis on 21 August, Lord Howe took his ships up the Chesapeake towards the disembarkation point – a feat that the locals did not believe possible: 'The Shoalness of the Elk convinced the Rebels that our fleet would never navigate it, but through the great abilities of our Naval officers it was happily effected as the bottom was muddy and the ships on it were cutting channels through it for each other'.[100] The comment points out the experience and confidence of the naval officers to take their vessels into the shallow waters, as well as their initiative in cutting channels through the muddy bottom for those following. A member of the crew of HMS *Sphynx* noted the surprise of the locals: 'We [...] arrived in this river, the upper end of Chesapeake Bay, where the oldest men in this country never remembered to have seen any vessel, except small canoes. Consider what an astonishment it was to them to see a large fleet of 500 [an exaggeration] sail come up, which every body thought in the fleet impracticable'.[101] On 24 August, General Howe issued his orders for the orderly disembarkation of the troops, horses, supplies, and artillery; the first wave was to embark in the flatboats at 3:00 a.m., to be followed by two subsequent waves, all supported by six warships:[102] *Vigilant* (22 guns), *Swift* (14 guns), *Senegal* (14 guns), *Sphynx* (20 guns), *Apollo* (32 guns), and *Roebuck* (44 guns). It gives an indication of the professionalism of the naval captains that these warships were operating in only 12 feet of water.[103] Good seamanship may have been demonstrated, but so to was the opportunity for a little looting by some of the sailors: 'Two men were hanged, & 5 severely whipped for plundering'.[104]

Although Howe's army had gone ashore unopposed they were still nearly 60 miles from his objective, Philadelphia, and the troops had endured a long sea passage during the heat of summer. The condition of his men, together with his natural caution – 'Howe being Howe, he permitted almost three weeks to elapse after the landing before he went into battle'[105] – meant that he did not face Washington's troops at the Battle of Brandywine until 11 September 1777. The ensuing action was a British victory, followed by Cornwallis leading British troops into Philadelphia on the 26th of that month. Unfortunately, the Americans

100 NDAR, Vol.9, p.821, journal of John Montresor, 26 August 1777.
101 NDAR, Vol.9, p.849, letter from HMS *Sphynx*, 29 August 1777.
102 NDAR, Vol.9, p.796.
103 NDAR, Vol.9, p.811, log of *Vigilant*, 25 August 1777.
104 NDAR, Vol.9, p.311, journal of Ambrose Serle, 25 August 1777.
105 Ferling, *Miracle*, p.245.

had spent the time prior to the British arrival in fortifying the defences of the Delaware; until these were cleared the transports that would have to supply the troops could not get up the river. This would have to be done as quickly as possible as until the river was useable all the supplies had to go overland from the Head of Elk, necessitating the deployment of 3,000 troops to protect the supply waggons. The task facing the navy was considerable; the Americans had sunk *chevaux-de-frise* defences in the river, which was also defended by Forts Mifflin and Mercer, and the shallow waters and mud flats made the river difficult to navigate for large warships. The operation began on 2 October and continued well into November with ships and troops attacking the forts. In the operation against Fort Mifflin, 23 October, 'the *Augusta* [64 guns] Blew up & the *Merlin* still aground was sett on Fire By Order of Lord Howe to Prevent her Falling into the Hands of the Rebels'.[106] The Americans were firing heated shot from the fort but Lord Howe, in his report to the Admiralty, appears to have glossed over the poor positioning of the ships in the face of this threat: '[W]hen by some Accident, no other way connected with the Circumstances of the Action but as it was probably caused by the Wads from her Guns, the Ship took Fire abaft. And it spread with such Rapidity, that all Endeavors to extinguish it were used in vain'.[107] Claiming that it was an accident caused by a flaming wad from one of the ship's own guns was less embarrassing to the navy than admitting the ship was sunk by Rebel gunnery. The captain was later court martialled and acquitted as the ship's loss 'was occasioned by accidentally taking fire in Action with the Rebel's armed Vessels, not by any Neglect, or bad dicipline [*sic*] in the Ship'.[108]

Gradually, during October and November, the defences were removed and the river was opened for supplies. On 4 November, HMS *Eagle* sent 20 flatboats to Philadelphia with provisions for the army.[109] Two weeks later, on 16 November, the operation to secure a supply line up the Delaware was completed and an officer on HMS *Isis* observed 'an English flag hoisted' over Mud Fort (Mifflin).[110] The Americans recognised that 'In Consequence of the Enemy's arm'd Vessels laying at Fort Mifflin, their Provision Vessels pass unmolested up to the Mouth of Schylkill'[111] and on 23 November the first British ships arrived at Philadelphia. General Howe's troops had been 'strategically immobilized'[112] in the city while the navy spent two months clearing the Delaware to supply them. During their

106 NDAR, Vol.10, p.250, log of HMS *Camilla*, 23 October 1777.
107 NDAR, Vol.10, p.292, Howe to Stephens, 25 October 1777.
108 NDAR, Vol.10, pp.603–607, court martial of Captain Reynolds, 26 November 1777.
109 NDAR, Vol.10. p.397, log of HMS *Eagle*, 4 November 1777.
110 NDAR, Vol.10, p.512, log of HMS *Isis*, 16 November 1777.
111 NDAR, Vol.10, p.521, Brig. Gen. Varnum to Washington, 17 November 1777.
112 Syrett, *American Waters*, p.85.

time in Philadelphia, prior to the opening of the river, Daniel Wier (the British Commissary General) had written to the Treasury that 'The whole country around us is possessed by the enemy [...] We can expect no supplies or assistance from this country but must place our whole dependence on what we receive from the other side of the water'.[113] With the Delaware open and their supplies secure, the British troops experienced a quite different winter from that of their American opponents. While Washington's men had a desperate winter at Valley Forge, the British regulars had their 'most comfortable winter yet'.[114] Not only were they 'well fed' but the officers and troops were welcomed with 'open arms' by the local townspeople, many of whom would look to the British Navy for their evacuation in 1778. It is ironic that the British, having cleared the Delaware, should be well supplied from England while Washington's troops – operating in their home country and among friendly farmers – were down to their last 25 barrels of flour, without meat, and with the men 'barefoot and otherwise naked'.[115] The problem for the Americans was their poor and non-existent administration, rather than a lack of available produce in the surrounding area.

These early years of the war had shown how reliant the British Army was on the navy to support its operations in North America; denied access to local food supplies, the troops had to receive their provisions from England and their flexibility of movement could only be achieved by use of sea transport. Movement by sea, as in Howe's sailing for the Chesapeake via the mouth of the Delaware, allowed the commander to choose his landing site while confusing his opponent as to where that might be. An unintended consequence of this flexibility could be hardship for the troops if there were insufficient provisions on board to allow the change of destination, as happened in this case. Good coordination between naval and army commanders (as happened during the New York and Philadelphia operations) allowed for the rapid landing of troops, in battle order, under the heavy guns of the men of war. However, once those troops were secure in their new positions, they again became dependent on the sea for their every need. During the operations to enter Philadelphia and secure the Delaware news of Burgoyne's surrender at Saratoga reached the British. This disaster, partly brought about by General Howe's move against the American city, was the catalyst for the entry of the French into the war and a change of strategic priorities for the British.

113 Bowler, *Logistics*, p.71.
114 Ferling, *Miracle*, p.290.
115 Ferling, *Miracle*, pp.275–276.

10

'The Expectation of war increases here Every Hour'

General Howe may have felt some satisfaction at the taking of Philadelphia, but events in the north of the country had gone horribly wrong during the autumn of 1777. With no overall commander of British forces in North America and Canada, the direction of the war by Germain in London, and the painfully slow speed of communications, the scene was set for confusion. As has been outlined in a previous chapter, Burgoyne had expected to march south from Canada and join forces with Howe; the latter had informed London that he was setting out with his army to take Philadelphia. For his part, Germain was aware of, and approved, Howe's plan (Howe had outlined it to him on 30 November 1776)[1] but still expected him to be able to join forces with Burgoyne after investing that city. In his account of the war, Hibbert ascribes the 'cock-up' to the sending of a letter by Germain to Howe, outlining his instruction for the latter to join Burgoyne; the letter was sent late and allowed Howe to later claim that he had never been instructed to march to Albany.[2] In a letter to Carleton, Howe stated that any troops marching south from Canada could expect 'little assistance from hence' as he would 'probably be in Pennsylvania when that corps is ready to advance' and it would not be possible for him 'to communicate with the officer commanding it'.[3] Burgoyne would have no help from Howe. Although this account leaves it to others[4] to detail the surrender at Saratoga, 17 October 1777, it is worth citing in full Syrett's comment on the ineptness of the planning and execution of the expeditions of the two British generals.

1   Black, *War for America*, p.115.
2   Hibbert, *Redcoats and Rebels*, p.139.
3   Hibbert, *Redcoats and Rebels*, p.164.
4   Ferling, Mackesy, Hibbert, and Black all cover these events.

The 1777 campaign in America is one of the most appalling examples of strategic planning in British military history. In fact there was no plan for the campaign of 1777 but rather two uncoordinated and mutually exclusive plans. The disaster at Saratoga was the result of the failure of the government in general, and Germain in particular, to provide strategic direction to the British commanders in America and to co-ordinate the widely differing and totally exclusive schemes submitted by Generals Howe and Burgoyne.[5]

As well as being a massive blow to British prestige, Burgoyne's surrender was the cue for the French to join the conflict and take advantage of London's colonial problems. With the prospect of the French fleet facing that of Britain off the American coast, the Rebels believed that the dice were now loaded in their favour, but the French were not so altruistic as to join without giving priority to their own agenda, and that meant an America 'reliant on France'.[6]

One of the consequences of the appalling strategic planning was the virtual abandonment of the naval blockade of the American coast while ships were employed in the transport and supply of Howe's army to Philadelphia. The surrender at Saratoga further stretched Lord Howe's naval resources; not only did he have a blockade to enforce, he also had to transport and support the army's operation to Philadelphia and take on another role in relation to Burgoyne's surrendered troops. As a condition of the surrender terms Burgoyne had persuaded the American general, Gates, to allow him and his men to be transported out of America, provided they did not serve again as long as the war with America lasted. The agreement between them was a 'convention' rather than a 'capitulation'. Now the diversion of shipping from a supply role to one of troop transportation had a further detrimental effect on the provisioning of the army. The need to remove the 'convention' troops from America, as well as the need in 1778 to assist Loyalists when the British evacuated Philadelphia, conspired together to exacerbate the army's supply problems in 1778. The agreement with Gates was for Burgoyne and his men to be embarked at Boston for their move home, but this was later changed to Rhode Island[7] where Captain Dalrymple informed Burgoyne that he hoped 'that no Insult shall be offered in the mean time to any of the Ships of War, or other Ships & Vessels appointed for fulfilling the purpose of the Convention, & Distinguished by Flags of Truce'.[8] Dalrymple also informed Burgoyne that there

5   Syrett, *American Waters*, p.72.
6   Ferling, *Miracle*, p.322.
7   TNA, ADM 1/488, f.83.
8   NDAR, Vol.11, p.506, Dalrymple to Burgoyne, 4 March 1778.

was only 7,030 tons of transport available to carry the 4,000 troops.[9] Given that transport was normally allocated at two tons per man,[10] this would be a tight fit for all the soldiers with their kit and equipment.

Saratoga was an enormous blow to British arms, but its implications for the whole strategy of the war was much greater. With the entry of France (and, later, Spain) into the conflict, this was no longer limited to the North American colonies. 'Britain was being propelled into a world war by the disaster at Saratoga'[11] and the navy, on which the army in America depended for all its needs, was about to be stretched from the West Indies to India. If the blockade had been difficult to maintain before Burgoyne's surrender, it became almost impossible after it. The First Lord hoped to have between 85 and 90 ships of the line available in 1780, but as he outlined for the Cabinet Britain's navy would not have superiority, in spite of having 'a greater force than ever we had'.

> England till this time was never engaged in a sea war with the House of Bourbon thoroughly united, their naval force unbroken, and having no other war or object to draw off their attention and resources. We unfortunately have an additional war on our hands, which essentially drains our finances and employs a very considerable part of our army and navy; we have no one friend or ally to assist us; on the contrary all those who ought to be our allies except Portugal act against us in supplying our enemies with the means of equipping their fleets.[12]

The French had been quick to see the opportunity provided by British discomfort in the backwoods of the upper reaches of the Hudson River. News of the defeat did not reach London until 3 December 1777, yet by 6 February of the following year France and America – 'the United States as they call themselves'[13] – had signed treaties of commerce and alliance, 'An event [...] that pressed the seal of futility on British efforts at reconciliation and required a complete revision of British campaign plans'.[14] The treaty was for 30 years and Lord Stormont, reporting the details to London, stated that while he did not know all the terms, 'They are probably highly advantageous to France and in return for these advantages She agrees to support the Independency of the Colonies and assist them with ships of War'. At this point, Britain and France were not formally at war, though

9   O'Shaughnessy, *Men Who Lost America*, p.159.
10   TNA, ADM 111/73.
11   Syrett, *Lord Howe*, p.74.
12   Padfield, *Maritime Supremacy*, p.249.
13   NDAR, Vol.11, pp.977–979, Lord Stormont to Lord Weymouth, 6 February 1778.
14   NDAR, Vol.11, p.860.

sliding inexorably towards it. In February London learned of an arms convoy being prepared for America: 'M. de La Mothe-Piquet [usually spelt Motte], who commands five ships of the line and three frigates, sailed from Quiberon to convoy out to sea fifteen large merchant vessels departing from Nantes and richly laden for Boston. It is Mr Franklin [Benjamin Franklin was the American representative in Paris] who had these ships freighted with 25 thousand uniforms and other materials of war'.[15] The appointment of La Motte-Picquet as convoy commander was read by Stormont as 'a direct Violation of all Friendship, [and] all Good Faith' and was intended to give 'the Rebels every secret assistance', while endeavouring 'to avoid the odium of appearing the aggressor by forcing us to strike the first Blow'.[16] Lord Stormont summed up London's dilemma: 'If we attack La Motte[']s Squadron and seize the ships he convoys war is inevitable, if we suffer them to pass unmolested an almost open Trade will be carried on between France and America and the Rebels be fully supplied with Every thing [*sic*] they can possibly want'.

In order to carry out the agreement to assist the Americans with ships of the line, Louis XVI ordered the completion of the fitting out of the French fleets at Brest, under the Comte d'Orvilliers, and Toulon under Comte d'Estaing. For the ministers in London, the guessing game now began. Would the two French fleets join up and invade Britain, or would the Toulon fleet break out of the Mediterranean and sail for the West Indies and Britain's vitally important Sugar Islands? Faced with the choice outlined by Stormont, London had to act. On 10 March 1778, orders went out to Commanders-in-Chief to seize all vessels trading with the rebels, regardless of the nationality of the ships escorting them; a clash somewhere at sea was inevitable.[17] The final break between London and Paris came on 13 March 1778 when the French ambassador informed the British that his country had recognised American independence. It is worth mentioning that not all Americans welcomed the assistance of France. That country was ruled by an absolute monarch who denied his subjects the very freedoms that Americans were fighting for; on top of that, France was a Catholic nation while most Americans were Protestants. As one major in the Continental Army expressed it, 'It is painful to think that our country, instead of exerting the powers God has given her to work out her own salvation, should be under the necessity of calling in foreign troops. [...] It is a disgrace we shall not easily get over'.[18]

With the entry of France into the equation, the whole nature of the war – and the roles assigned to the navy – changed. Following the signing of the treaty between

15   NDAR, Vol.11, p.860, 23 February 1778.
16   NDAR, Vol.11, pp.1040–1041, Stormont to Weymouth, 23 February 1778.
17   Mackesy, *America*, p.160.
18   Brumwell, *Turncoat*, p.241.

France and 'certain persons employed by our revolted subjects in North America [Franklin]', the King informed Clinton (who was taking command of the army from General Howe) that 'we have come to the resolution to make an immediate attack upon the island of St Lucia in the West Indies'.[19] Additionally Lord Howe, whose objective so far had been to assist the army and maintain a blockade of the American coast, was informed by the Admiralty that '[T]he object of the War being now changed, and *the Contest in America being a secondary consideration*, the principal object must be the distressing [of] France and defending and securing His Majesty's own Possessions [...] [my emphasis]'.[20]

Having been reduced to secondary importance, forces would be removed from America to pursue the more pressing objectives: 'The main British effort was now to maintain naval control of the English Channel and to seize St Lucia'.[21] On 6 March, before war had officially broken out with France, Sandwich was advising Lord North that 'I think it should be a matter of consideration whether, if we see a war with France to be inevitable, we should not recall ten or twelve of our frigates from America'.[22] Within days of the French ambassador advising London of the French decision regarding American independence, Britain began reassigning its troops and ships: 20 frigates and sloops were ordered back to Britain; no further troops were to be sent to North America; Philadelphia was to be evacuated; 5,000 troops, four ships of the line, three 50-gun ships, two bomb vessels, and four frigates were to leave America to attack the French island of St Lucia; and the Commander-in-Chief was to have the discretion to evacuate New York and Rhode Island if he thought it was necessary.[23] Communications being slow, it was 8 May before HMS *Porcupine* arrived in the Delaware with news of the Franco–American alliance and the instructions from London. As well as refocusing the army and navy away from America, London took the opportunity to replace the Howe brothers in their respective commands; both were ready to leave and believed they needed to get back to Britain to fight off criticism of their performance in the war. General Howe had submitted his request to be relieved of command in November 1777, but this had been refused at the time. On 21 April 1778, HMS *Andromeda* arrived at Sandy Hook with the orders for him to return home and for General Clinton to assume command. Howe's leaving was rather bizarre; on the evening of 18 May, his officers put on a medieval spectacular, a *Mischianza*, in his honour: 'Mingling about the gardens were officers dressed as knights, with

19   SP, Vol.1, pp.366–367, the King to Clinton, 21 March 1778.
20   NDAR, Vol.11, p.1111, Admiralty to Lord Howe, 22 March 1778.
21   D. Syrett, 'Home waters or America? The dilemma of British naval strategy in 1778', *Mariner's Mirror*, 77:4 (1991), p.367.
22   NDAR, Vol.11, p.1066, Sandwich to Lord North, 6 March 1778.
23   Syrett, 'Home waters', p.367.

flowing capes, feathered helms and shields bearing ancient family arms. Local damsels, similarly accoutred in lavish fancy dress, gave tokens to their champions who enacted jousts in front of them. Nothing was stinted in laying on the finest music, wines and food that could be procured'.[24] There is a strong element of the surreal about 'two teams' of British officers 'dressed in striking silk costumes' in a medieval tournament between the 'Knights of the Blended Rose' and the 'Knights of the Burning Mountain;' all part of 'the most splendid entertainment [...] ever given by an army to their general'.[25] The expense of the event was 'reckoned three thousand guineas' and while it demonstrated the affection of his subordinates, it was a strange send off for a general on his way home to defend his performance as army Commander-in-Chief. His brother, the admiral, still had a role to fill in America and would not sail for England until 26 September 1778.

At this critical time, with the worldwide role of the navy expanding as a result of France's entry into the war, the command of Britain's men of war off America's coast passed through a number of hands. To say that the changes were poorly handled would be an understatement. Lord Howe was leaving and his replacement was to be Rear-Admiral James Gambier, a man considered by many to be too incompetent for the role (his sycophantic letters to Sandwich have been mentioned in Chapter 2). Howe, while wanting to leave, was wary of passing command to Gambier and the latter commented to Sandwich that when Howe left he 'condescended' to deliver the general orders to him, while sailing off with most of the frigates and leaving Gambier with a 'very inadequate' force.[26] Ever conscious of his rank and position, and any affront to them, he told Sandwich that he was 'reduced to hoist my flag on board a storeship;' it is difficult to imagine Howe or Rodney allowing this to happen and speaks volumes of the new commander's ability to assert his authority – or not. Gambier was in effect treated as a port admiral rather than a Commander-in-Chief, and he was aware of this: 'I have conducted myself in every shape to avoid it [any disagreement between senior officers], however painful and humiliating my situation has been for a long time, nay indeed ever since I have been in America'.[27] The humiliation continued, as he pointed out to Sandwich: 'Vice-Admiral Byron [who had arrived off America and was senior Gambier] informed me that he had convened with the Viscount [Lord Howe], who had made known to him my having a commission as commander in chief *during the absence of a superior officer* [...] [emphasis in the original]'. In his note, Byron required Gambier to continue 'to refit the disabled ships' and 'supply frigates to

24   Urban, *Fusiliers*, p.141.
25   Brumwell, *Turncoat*, pp.127–128.
26   SP, Vol.2, pp.308–309, Gambier to Sandwich, 6 September 1778.
27   SP, Vol.2, p.318, Gambier to Sandwich, 11 October 1778.

Rear-Admiral Parker;' in other words, Gambier was to act as a port admiral, not as a Commander-in-Chief. However, in spite of the widening of the conflict (and by April 1779 Spain had joined France in the Bourbon alliance), the lack of 'grip' over naval command continued. In January 1779, the Admiralty accepted that they had to formally replace Gambier, and Rear-Admiral Marriot Arbuthnot was chosen for a role that required decisive action in support of the army and the tact to operate closely with General Clinton: 'If the lords of the Admiralty had gone through the navy list looking for a flag officer who should not be sent to New York, they could not have come up with a better choice than Arbuthnot'.[28]

However, in the eighteenth century, things took time; Gambier sailed for England on the *Ardent* on 5 April 1779 but Arbuthnot did not arrive in America until 25 August – there was need of an interim commander. Captain Sir George Collier (of whom the King spoke so highly in Chapter 2) stepped into the breach with a more positive approach than his predecessor did. In spite of being 'ill in force' to carry out 'any enterprise, or even to supply the convoys, guards of ports and various other services which this extensive command has necessarily occasions for', he had not 'neglected to consider what might be attempted against the enemy with the little force now with me'.[29] More's the pity that he was only an interim commander. In May, Collier took his squadron raiding in the Chesapeake, capturing 'no fewer than 137 vessels and stores worth at least £1 million', and Fort Nelson was destroyed: 'The most destructive British raid of the war'.[30] We will see in later chapters that relations between Arbuthnot and Clinton were poor and he would never be able to write, as Collier had, that 'the most perfect confidence and harmony subsists between Sir Henry Clinton and myself'.[31]

Arbuthnot finally arrived to take command on 25 August 1779; with him were 3,800 troops followed by a further group of Germans and Irish on 21 September. As was so often the case, loading the convoy had not gone to plan, and the weather had not helped. Originally, it should have been ready by 20 February 1779. In April, the weather prevented him sailing and he was further delayed when the Cabinet told him to wait for more escort ships in case of attack by the French. His 215 ship convoy eventually sailed on 24 May, but many of the men were sick when they got to New York. The fever they had brought with them swept through the army putting 6,000 soldiers in hospital.

While the Admiralty had struggled to put a man in command of the navy in America, events in the colonies had not stood still. We left General Howe in

28   Syrett, *American Waters*, p.121.
29   SP, Vol.3, p.127, Collier to Sandwich, 19 April 1779.
30   Willis, *Sea Power*, pp.328–329.
31   SP, Vol.3, p.132, Collier to Sandwich, 15 June 1779.

Philadelphia but, by 8 May 1778 (having some months earlier asked to be relieved of command so that he might go home and defend his actions in America), General Clinton arrived to take command of the army. Clinton had originally been sent out, along with Howe and Burgoyne, to bolster General Gage in the early months of the war. However, as we have already noted, the 21 March 1778 decision by British ministers to evacuate Philadelphia in response to the French entry into the war was received by the new Commander-in-Chief only days after taking post. The problem now facing Clinton and Lord Howe (still in command of the navy and awaiting the arrival of Vice-Admiral Byron's squadron) was how to effect the evacuation of the city they had taken only six months previously. During their time there the British had been welcomed by many of the local citizens; they felt safe under British protection, but all that fell away when the army stated that it had to leave. Lord Howe, recognising that the Loyalists would be at risk in the city after the British left, offered transport for them, their families, and their belongs to New York; this was a rash promise as there were insufficient ships available for them and the army with all its equipment. The only solution was for the navy to take the Loyalists while the army marched to New York. On its march through New Jersey, the army would miss the transport capability of the naval ships.

> With respect to provisions, we were obliged to carry a great quantity, as our march lay through a devoured country inimical almost to a man. And as to baggage I must say it was wantonly enormous. To leave it behind would have been disgraceful. To burn it, indicated an intended flight, but fortunately we did not lose a waggon, nor suffer the least insult.[32]

On 29 June 1778 Howe's ships and passengers arrived off Sandy Hook, with his brother's army joining him the following day. The concentration at New York was giving rise to supply and provisioning problems, and many of the causes of this have been outlined in previous chapters. The army had grown in size with the shipment of reinforcements from Britain; Loyalists (both at New York and from Philadelphia) had swollen the number of mouths that had to be fed with food shipped from Britain; and the transport ships which London wanted to see returned to England were heavily involved in moving troops and civilians around the American coast. The system of supply was breaking down. The Commissary General, Daniel Wier, wrote to the Treasury regarding the shortage of provisions at New York and the number of people he was required to feed, warning that a 'French Fleet of very considerable force, lying within a few miles of us'[33] could

32   Black, *War for America*, p.157.
33   TNA, T 64/114, f.67.

prevent victualling ships from reaching the city – d'Estaing's French fleet had arrived from Toulon. As outlined in Chapter 4, supplying the army was taking up a large part of the available British sailing fleet. On 25 November 1777, the Treasury noted that 87 ships totalling 26,773 tons were employed by the victualling service, with another 43 'Oat ships' of 6,973 tons – a total of 130 ships and 34,740 tons.[34] Other letters on file also indicate the confusion in London regarding the number of people they were trying to feed. While the number of soldiers had increased at New York (November 1777) from 36,000 to 48,000, London was sending supplies for only 36,000. On 29 November, Wier advised the Treasury that while victualling ships had arrived with provisions for three months for 36,000 men, 'that number was far short of their consumption'.[35]

The lack of supplies was a problem through 1778 and into 1780, and Daniel Wier had cause to write constantly to the Treasury to ask for supplies for the ever increasing number of mouths. One unexpected consequence of Burgoyne's surrender at Saratoga was that 'convention' troops had to be fed by the British; had they been 'prisoners of war' then the responsibility would have fallen on the Americans. Here were another 4,000 mouths that were slipping through London's calculations. An example of the mismatch between the situation in New York and the understanding in London is given by Bowler for the middle of 1778. The Treasury secretary in London was convinced that the stocks available to Wier, plus those in transit from England, meant that 'there appears to be no reason to fear your wanting provisions',[36] and that there was no reason to change the contracts for 1778–1779 that had just been let for 36,000 men. It was not until 12 June, when they received Wier's letter of 12 April, that the Treasury realised the seriousness of the situation. Wier's report showed that 45,455 people were being fed and that there were only 'sixty-four days' bread and ninety days' meat left in stock'. The provisioning problems persisted, sometimes getting worse, sometimes better, with stocks frequently going down to levels well below those with which the army could sustain campaigns. At one point in 1778, Clinton, back in New York and waiting for Byron's arrival, commented that 'If he [Byron] should not arrive, and if we cannot beat them [d'Estaing's fleet] without waiting for him, I must dine with them; for I shall not have any means of dining elsewhere'.[37]

As dire as the supply situation was for the British it would be quite wrong to think that Washington's men had it any easier, in spite of being in their own country and so presumably able to draw on local suppliers. The winter was severe,

34   TNA, T 29/46, f.370.
35   TNA, T 29/46, f.440.
36   Bowler, *Logistics*, pp.116–117.
37   Bowler, *Logistics*, p.123.

making road transport difficult. On 16 December 1779, Washington described his supply situation as 'beyond description alarming'.[38] His magazines were bare and the commissaries had not the cash to replenish them: 'We have never experienced a like extremity at any period of the war'. Washington warned the states from whom he expected to draw supplies that unless there were 'extraordinary exertions' by them, his army must 'infallibly disband in a fortnight'. Although Britain had the problem of distance to contend with when supplying its troops, Washington was up against the independence of each of the states as well as the 'civil war' element of the conflict in that not all Americans were in favour of the conflict, and were not prepared to release their produce for payment in an ever depreciating continental currency.

From 1778 onwards, the British focus of the war was away from America, pulling naval resources in different directions: relief convoys would have to be sent to Gibraltar to protect the entrance to the Mediterranean; ships had to be sent to the West Indies to protect vital British interests there; the blockade of the American coast had to be continued – albeit inadequately – and the army still needed the supply and transportation services of the King's ships. The navy, in late 1777 and early 1778, was only slowly coming out of the postwar rundowns following the Seven Years War and Lord Sandwich was fighting a rearguard action for the mobilisation of the service in the face of the economising tendencies of Lord North and other ministerial colleagues. The dilemma facing the Admiralty – how to counter any invasion threat from France while also assisting the army in America – has been outlined in Chapter 4. Sandwich did not believe that the navy had the resources to do both effectively unless it was increased in size by full mobilisation. In December 1777, the First Lord sent a memorandum to North outlining his view of the navy's role in the war in light of the likely inclusion of France as a belligerent. Sandwich wanted Britain to fight a defensive war in America because he believed the real threat to the country came from Europe – France.[39] In his view, the army in America should cease offensive campaigns and pull back to protect bases from which the navy could operate against American coastal towns, denying them as bases for American cruisers. The navy would be freed from 'supporting offensive military operations'. However, these opinions were not fully in accord with those of the King as expressed to Clinton in March 1778 when that general took over command of the army. It was George's 'firm Purpose to prosecute it [the war], with the utmost Vigor', and while extra troops were to be sent to reinforce Clinton, 'if you should find it impracticable to bring

38   Brumwell, *Turncoat*, p.188.
39   Syrett, 'Home waters', p.365.

Mr Washington to a general and decisive Action early in the Campaign', then ports along the American seaboard should be attacked:

> [Clinton should] attack the Ports on the Coast, from New York to Nova Scotia, and to Seize or destroy every Ship or Vessel in the different Creeks or Harbours, wherever it is found practicable to penetrate; as also to destroy all Wharfs and Stores, and Materials for Shipbuilding, so as to incapacitate them from raising a Marine, or continuing their Depredations upon the Trade of this Kingdom.[40]

Whatever the King's wishes for a successful outcome in America, Sandwich was conscious of the need to convince Lord North of the need to mobilise the navy if it was to defend Britain and its colonies from possible French action.

> Having received the enclosed extract from Lord Weymouth, I cannot avoid pointing out to your Lordship how necessary it seems to me that further exertions should be made in order to keep pace with the French naval equipments. If they have commissioned a ship of 110 guns, surely it is time to commission the *Victory* and every line of battle ship that can be got fit for service; they will otherwise have the start of us considerably in their preparations; and if it should appear that with the assistance of Spain they have more ships in Europe ready for sea than we have, we shall either be obliged to leave our distant possessions defenceless or remain with an inferior force to guard our own coast.[41]

Eventually, on 14 March 1778, the Cabinet agreed to 'mobilise the Royal Navy'[42] and two days later a general press was ordered as well as the Navy Board being directed to use all possible speed to fit out ships for service. Only days after the Cabinet decision, 'There was the hottest press on the Thames on Tuesday night and yesterday morning ever known. The gangs took a great number of sailors, not a vessel escaped them, even those that had protections were carried off'.[43] Whatever the decision taken on 14 March, 'the stark reality of the strategic problem imposed by French entry into the American War was that in 1778 Britain's commitments were beyond the strength of the Royal Navy to maintain, while at the same time it was either politically or strategically impossible to reduce

---

40   NDAR, Vol.11, pp.1069–1070, Germain to Clinton, 8 March 1778.
41   NDAR, Vol.11, p.1050, Sandwich to North, 27 February 1778.
42   Syrett, 'Home waters', p.366.
43   NDAR, Vol.11, p.1096, *The London Chronicle*, 19 March 1778.

the scope of these commitments'.[44] The extent to which America had become of 'secondary importance' was evident from the decisions taken at Cabinet on 18 March 1778: in the event that Lord Howe had no certain knowledge of the destination of Motte-Picquet's squadron then, from the 70 ships available to him, 13 were to go to the Leeward Islands, along with 5,000 troops from Philadelphia, taking eight months' provisions with them. Twenty ships were to be sent to England; a further 3,000 men were to go from General Howe's army to Florida and a force sent for the defence of Nova Scotia.[45] The navy was left with 37 ships from the original 70 for all blockade and army operations off the American coast at the time that the French signed their treaties with the Americans. It was at this time, with Howe's army in Philadelphia (but about to be told to withdraw to New York), that ministers in London and Lords at the Admiralty entered a period of great indecision over the intentions and destinations of the French fleets at Brest and Toulon, and what the navy – on whom the army in America depended for everything – should do to counter them.

The two French fleets posed a real threat to Britain, as well as a question as to how they might affect British naval strength on the American station. D'Orvilliers, by simply remaining in Brest, would tie up any ships in a Western Squadron as well as those in the Channel Fleet; they had to watch him in case he made a move towards the Channel. In Toulon, d'Estaing might break out of the Mediterranean towards America, or he might turn north for Brest, combine with d'Orvilliers, and pose an even larger invasion threat to the Channel Fleet. In these circumstances, and with Sandwich convinced that a French move against the British coast was a greater threat than a move towards America, any reinforcement of Lord Howe was unlikely; just the threat of any movement by the French was sufficient to paralyse decision making in the Admiralty. In March 1778 Keppel, commander of the Channel Fleet, had 20 ships of the line available to him, of which 19 were more than 64 guns, and five of them were of 90 guns. However, in his note to the King, 6 April, Sandwich gave it as his opinion that:

> [T]here are not ships enough as yet in readiness to form a squadron fit to meet the Toulon fleet under Monsieur d'Estaing unless we were to sacrifice every other intended service to this object, or to send out Admiral Keppel with a proper force to meet Monsieur d'Estaing, which however seems to me a very dangerous measure, as our own coast and Ireland

44   Syrett, 'Home waters', p.367.
45   SP, Vol.1, p.364, minutes of Cabinet, 18 March 1778.

would then be subject to alarm as the Brest fleet would be superior to anything that we shall have ready for sea till Admiral Keppel's return.[46]

The concern over whether or not the Toulon squadron would sail, and if it did, where to, meant that Byron's squadron (eagerly awaited by Howe off America) would not be allowed to sail until those in the Admiralty had satisfied themselves that they were sure of d'Estaing's intentions – America was at the bottom of the pecking order. But the risk to the Channel meant that only two frigates were stationed off Gibraltar to give warning of French intentions in the Mediterranean, one of them being HMS *Proserpine*.

The preceding paragraph (and Chapter 8) outlines the dilemma facing the Admiralty and their indecision over what to do about the French fleets. Their comments indicate a natural caution, given the importance of the navy to the defence of Britain, but they are also heavily weighted towards a comparison of the number of ships on each side, important though they are in a naval engagement. Interestingly, in some advice given to the French King regarding how that country might use its navy against Britain, the writers comment on the qualities of British seamen, rather than raw numbers of ships: 'Our shortcomings, the points where they [the British] are perhaps still superior to us, are experience in navigation; experience with and inurement to long cruises and difficult patrols; the art of getting through and holding fast everywhere; and finally, a large and very promising corps of officers, among them some who have commanded squadrons and fleets'. We will see that in the years of the war following French entry, there were a number of opportunities for major fleet action, not all of which came to major engagements. The advantage accruing to the fleet to windward of its opponent could result in cautious commanders spending all their time manoeuvring, but never coming to a decisive passage of arms. However, the recommendation to the French King was that there should be such a clash: 'No small squadrons, no long-distance expeditions, large fleets, all our forces in the same waters; a naval battle at an early but well-chosen moment and for an important objective; a short, hard war'.[47]

We have seen that the French could affect British naval decisions simply by retaining a fleet at Brest, as the writers accurately summed up in their memorandum to Louis.

By keeping most of our forces assembled at Brest, we are protecting our trade and our colonies much more effectively; for we are obliging the

46   SP, Vol.2, p.23, Sandwich's Opinion, 6 April 1778.
47   NDAR, Vol.10, p.1113-1114, 17 December 1777.

English to keep forces just as large or even larger in the Atlantic and in the Channel. They dare not risk the safety of England on the outcome of a battle in which the odds are even, for invasion would become easy if they were to lose such a battle.

In suggesting to Louis that they should aim for a 'short, hard war' the writers were acknowledging that the British had important advantages in a prolonged conflict.

Our navy is by no means sufficiently consolidated as yet and is not backed up, as is that of the English, by magazines and dockyards well stocked with replacement materiel. Unlike them, we cannot always have new ships to replace those which are lost or battered by the sea. Not being so well situated geographically as they are for procuring strategic materials from the North, we are inevitably at a disadvantage in a long war.

But it was not only on the material level that the French believed the British had an advantage if the conflict were prolonged; they believed the French temperament was less well suited to situations requiring tenacity.

In support of the recommendation that our navy begin hostilities with large-scale action and not let itself be nibbled away by time and minor skirmishes, there are other arguments based on the character of our people. An enterprise which demands tenacity and perseverance becomes tiresome and boring to them, even discourages them in the long run; while one which bears the stamp of boldness and vigor lifts their spirits and calls forth those same qualities in them in response.

Later in this account, we will see how some of the French comments came to play out in the naval actions of 1778–1782.[48]

For Sandwich, with his concern that the navy should have the defence of the Channel and the British coast as its main priority, the fact that d'Estaing's fleet was at Toulon was not his main worry; it was not knowing its destination if it sailed that troubled him. On 27 April, the first positive intelligence of the Toulon fleet arrived in London; the sources were an agent in Paris, and the bankers of Amsterdam.[49] According to these reports d'Estaing had sailed on the 11th of that month with 11 ships of the line and nine months' provisions; this last information should have been enough to indicate that his destination was not within Europe

48   NDAR, Vol.10, p.1113-1114, 17 December 1777.
49   Mackesy, *America*, p.197.

– it had to be America. This was not enough for Sandwich, but the news galvanised Germain. After vigorous lobbying, he persuaded the King and Cabinet that 13 ships of the line should be sent to America. With only the two frigates watching the Toulon fleet it was not until 2 June that the *Proserpine* arrived in Falmouth with the news that the French had cleared the Straits and were headed for the Atlantic. The King's comment on hearing the news was that its heading was 'to make the passage more secure to North America. The Cabinet cannot meet too soon, nor Byron be ordered to sail'.[50] Some six weeks had been lost since the news from the bankers of Amsterdam. Byron had been chosen to take the reinforcements to Lord Howe but, as was often the case, there were to be delays before he sailed. In addition, Howe had not been informed that a squadron had not been sent into the Mediterranean to watch, and if necessary follow, d'Estaing. Luckily, the troops to be sent from Philadelphia to St Lucia had insufficient transports and were unable to sail, otherwise they would have been at sea when the French sailed from Toulon and at risk of interception. Vice-Admiral Byron was preparing to take command in India when he was told of his new destination in America. Byron insisted that his luggage (in waggons *en route* from London) would go with him. His flagship had stores for India, which had to be returned to the Victualling Office and those ships destined to go with him to America were only provisioned for Channel service, and so required the loading of another four months' supplies.[51] When Byron finally got away, his nickname of 'Foul-weather Jack' proved true and his squadron was dispersed by a storm delaying his arrival in Halifax until 8 August.

Although the Admiralty had sent Byron's squadron to augment Lord Howe's force on the American station, and they now knew that d'Estaing was bound for those shores, there was still concern at home over the possible movement of d'Orvilliers' fleet at Brest. Admiral Keppel had been recently assigned command of the Channel Fleet but was concerned that the sending of ships with Byron, as well as those he considered unfit for action, had reduced his force to the point where, if the French fleet were to sail up the Channel, 'may I ask what the King's ministers expect I am to do, with my force as I have described it?'[52] Keppel was no Rodney or Nelson; one historian has stated that his correspondence was 'permeated with a defeatism at times almost reminiscent of the letters of Admiral Byng'.[53] On the other hand, Vice-Admiral Hugh Palliser (who was subordinate to Keppel at the coming battle off Ushant) was of a much more positive disposition. Writing from Spithead a week after Keppel's letter, Palliser told Sandwich that 'I

50   SP, Vol.2, p.89, the King to Sandwich, 5 June 1778.
51   Mackesy, *America*, pp.198–199.
52   SP, Vol.2, p.55, Keppel to Sandwich, 9 May 1778.
53   Rodger, *Sandwich*, p.243.

find the language here begins to prevail that we are in want of ships for the present occasions. I take all opportunities to contradict it, and insist that we want only men, having many ships ready to receive them and more preparing for it'.[54]

Keppel was not the bold admiral that was needed to command Britain's Channel Fleet, nor of the stamp that the British people believed should command its main defence against the French, but the Admiralty were not above criticism for their apparent wish to pass some of their own responsibilities onto Keppel. In April and May of 1778, they issued him with orders that were read by him as doing just that. He (together with Byron's ships) was to take a relief convoy for Gibraltar as far as Ushant where, depending on the movements of the Toulon and Brest squadrons, he would make the decision of when or if, to detach Byron and whether they should sail for America or the Mediterranean. Keppel thought that this strategic decision should be taken in London and not by him: 'I cannot say that your instructions are such as I feel much satisfaction upon when I consider them over. It is impossible to avoid seeing that, both in case of detaching Vice-Admiral Byron's squadron or detaining him a time that may be thought too long in the event, *the blame must fall upon myself* [my emphasis]'.[55]

Keppel was also concerned that his force was too few to challenge the French and the Admiralty orders gave him a 'get out;' if he should come up against the French and discover that his numbers were inferior to theirs, then he should return to St Helens (Portsmouth). When Keppel sailed with the convoy on 13 June (Byron had left by this point), they worked their way down the Channel before turning south for Gibraltar. Having passed the Lizard they captured a French frigate which carried papers indicating that the fleet at Brest had 'twenty-seven ships of the line ready to come to sea',[56] while he had only 20. At this point Keppel's caution, and the wish not to be blamed for anything that might go wrong, determined his action: 'being so short in numbers […] obliges me to proceed as my instructions direct to St Helen's [*sic*]'. The decision to return before the French had even threatened to come out to meet him was taken badly in London; the King was 'much hurt at the resolution taken by Admiral Keppel'[57] and Sandwich, while reassuring the admiral that he was trying to send him an additional four sail of the line, wanted him to understand that London expected the fleet to take action against the French: '[I]f I return to London [Sandwich was in Portsmouth at that time] without being able to say that your fleet will be ready to sail again in a very few days, much well-founded uneasiness will appear,

54   SP, Vol.2, p.59, Palliser to Sandwich, 14 May 1778.
55   SP, Vol.2, p.77, Keppel to Sandwich, 26 May 1778.
56   SP, Vol.2, p.98, Keppel to Sandwich, 21 June 1778.
57   SP, Vol.2, p.98, the King to Sandwich, 25 June 1778.

not only among the trading part of the nation, but with every person who has the welfare of the kingdom at heart'.[58]

The opportunity for Keppel to engage with the French would come a few weeks later, following his sailing on 9 July with 24 ships, later brought up to 30 when he was joined by the additional ships sent by Sandwich. The two fleets came within sight of each other off Ushant on 23 July, and began four days of manoeuvring, which ended in an inconclusive action. The fact that 60 ships of war came together did not necessarily meant that there would be a great battle. British and French admirals had their respective Fighting Instructions, which could be very proscriptive, especially in the hands of cautious commanders. Both sides usually formed their ships 'in line of battle' sailing past each other while delivering broadsides. It took imaginative commanders like Nelson and Jervis to break the convention by steering straight through the opposing line; that was not Keppel's style. Driven by wind, the battle fleets spent much of their time trying to gain the advantage of being upwind – to windward – as this gave the initiative of choosing when and whether to close to battle. How the two sides closed was also dependent on how they used their guns; the British preferred to get close and use their 'great guns' in broadsides to smash through the hull of the enemy ships, the French tended to stand off and aim higher to take down the enemy's masts, sails, and rigging. Even if the commander of one side or the other determined on a decisive clash he would have difficulty exercising any level of control. The flag system used by eighteenth century navies had limitations once the fleets were shrouded in smoke from the powder of the guns, not to mention the bringing down of the masts from which the signal flags flew. John Jervis (later Lord St Vincent) summed up the situation with fleets of equal size, as they were that July day off Ushant: 'Two fleets of equal force, never can produce decisive events, unless they are equally determin'd [sic] to fight it out, or the Commander in Chief of one of them, bitches it, so as to misconduct his line'.[59]

In a letter dated on the second day of the engagement, Keppel wrote that the French were 'at present to windward near hull down [...] The force of the two squadrons forbids my separating; and therefore unless both are agreed to close I know not when it will happen'[60] – he sounds like a commander at the mercy of circumstance. Eventually, on the 27th, Keppel was able to use the wind to get at the French, whose object 'was at the masts and rigging, and they have crippled the fleet in that respect beyond any degree I ever before saw'. The French retired from the action allowing Keppel to claim victory: 'That I have beat the French there

58   SP, Vol.2, p.104, Sandwich to Keppel, 29 June 1778.
59   Rodger, *Sandwich*, p.239.
60   SP, Vol.2, p.127, Keppel to Shuldham, 24 July 1778.

cannot be a doubt, and their retreat in the night is shameful and disgraceful to them as a nation after the fair opportunity I gave them to form their line'.[61]

Sandwich acknowledged that the 'victory' was less than Britain might have hoped for: 'I am very sorry you had not a more spirited enemy to deal with, but I am satisfied it was impossible for you to have done more than you did to bring on a decisive action'.[62] Although separated by the Atlantic, what happened on one side of that ocean affected the other. If Germain had not won the argument against Sandwich for the sending of Byron's squadron to join Lord Howe, then Keppel would have had a five-to-three advantage against d'Orvilliers, if he had come out. In the opinion of one of the best historians of the British Navy, the sending of Byron 'on a costly wild-goose chase half across the world' was a mistake brought about 'because ministers (like modern historians) could not get America out of their minds'.[63] The French had split their fleet and, if Byron had been with Keppel (assuming d'Orvilliers had come out and not merely stayed in Brest), 'it would have opened the chance of a decisive victory before Spain could enter the war'. The war in America may have become of secondary importance but, as we saw earlier in this chapter, the King wanted it prosecuted 'with the utmost vigor' and so Byron had been sent when he might have been retained in Europe. As a result, 'a hesitant and divided government dissipated its naval strength on the strategic periphery and abandoned the initiative to the enemy'.[64]

While Keppel was making his way down the Channel before meeting d'Orvilliers off Ushant, the French fleet from Toulon was approaching the coast of America. Having sailed the southern great circle route from the Mediterranean, they approached the Delaware on 8 July and were reported by Gambier on the 28th of that month to have been seen watering 'at the mouth of Shrewsbury River near the Navesink [very close to Sandy Hook at New York], where they appear to do it with great convenience and dispatch'.[65] Prior to the arrival of d'Estaing's fleet, the British had enjoyed naval superiority off the American coast; they could attack American sea-ports almost at will, and troops could be transported and landed where the army commander wished. This freedom of manoeuvre was assumed by the King in his suggestions for the strategy of the war for 1778.

[A]s soon as the Season will permit, to embark such a Body of Troops as can be spared from the Defence of the Posts you may think necessary to maintain, on board of transports under the Conduct of a proper number

61   SP, Vol.2, p.128, Keppel to Sandwich, 29 July 1778.
62   SP, Vol.2, p.132, Sandwich to Keppel, 2 August 1778.
63   Rodger, *Command of the Ocean*, p.342.
64   Rodger, *Command of the Ocean*, p.342.
65   SP, Vol.2, p.302, Gambier to Sandwich, 19 July 1778.

of the King's Ships, with Orders to attack the Ports on the Coast, from New York to Nova Scotia, and to Seize or destroy every Ship or Vessel in the different Creeks or Harbours, wherever it is found practicable to penetrate; as also to destroy all Wharfs and Stores, and Materials for Shipbuilding, so as to incapacitate them from raising a Marine, or continuing their Depredations upon the Trade of this Kingdom.[66]

The intent was to replicate the successful raid by Captain Mowat in October 1775, although it must be said that one consequence of the success of that raid was to unite opposition against the British. Raids on civilian populations by the military, especially when they were conducted from offshore by the guns of ships of the line, always ran the risk of censure: 'Even the successes are viewed as moral failures'.[67] The arrival of the French ships changed all that, now the British would have to try to anticipate d'Estaing's moves and use their ships to counter them.

By the end of June, we saw that Lord Howe's fleet was at New York [Map 4] with his ships behind the bar at Sandy Hook, and the Admiral's brother and his army had arrived at the city after their march from Philadelphia. British moves would now have to be planned against the backdrop of a large enemy fleet operating off the coast where they had previously enjoyed freedom of movement. From the information he had, Lord Howe believed that he had fewer ships than d'Estaing, but he had a good position between Sandy Hook and the city. The bar and the entrance to the harbour made it difficult for ships of the line, with their large draught, to enter in any kind of attacking formation. The French were believed to have 11 ships of the line plus a 50-gunner and five frigates, while Howe had seven ships of the line – two of 50 guns, two of 44 guns, and three frigates. He positioned these so that they could deliver raking fire against any ships trying to make it past Sandy Hook towards Lower New York Bay. The disposition of the ships is described by Henry Duncan, Howe's captain of the flagship HMS *Eagle*.

11th July – At 2 o'clock p.m., the French fleet, consisting of twelve two-decked ships and three frigates, anchored at the back of the Hook. At this time we had only the *Preston*, *Somerset*, *Nonsuch*, *St Albans*, *Phoenix*, *Roebuck*. The *Eagle*, *Trident*, *Ardent*, *Isis*, and *Richmond* were anchored a little below the Narrows. At five, the *Eagle* and the ships with her joined those at Sandy Hook; the whole force when collected consisted of six 64-gun ships, two fifties, the *Experiment*, two forty-fours, and two or three frigates. These were drawn up in order at the Hook to receive the

---

66   NDAR, Vol.11, p.1070, Germain to Clinton, 8 March 1778.
67   Philbrick, *Bunker Hill*, p.365.

French fleet. Our ships in general were but very indifferently manned, owing to sickness and their being short of complement.[68]

The sickness in Howe's ships caused him to ask for 1,000 volunteers from the transports in New York; he got the men on the promise that they would be released when Howe returned to England. They trusted him, but not whoever might be his replacement – they did not want to be pressed. The defence of the approaches to New York was not solely down to the navy; Howe recognised that if the French were to put men and guns on the island of Sandy Hook, then his ships would be in trouble. To counter the threat some 1,800 men of the 15th and 44th Regiments, together with cannon and howitzers, were put ashore on Sandy Hook using a bridge of flat boats 'over which the army marched with great ease'.[69] The stand-off between the two fleets reached a climax on 22 July when the tide was such that there was 'thirty feet of water over the bar',[70] but d'Estaing was not prepared to risk any of his ships getting stuck there: 'At 9 a.m. the French fleet got under way, and stood off and on until 4:00 p.m., when they all stood to seaward'.[71]

For the remaining months of 1778, the British ships found themselves chasing the French. Whereas for the first three years of the war the navy had been able to focus on the blockade of the American coast (albeit with insufficient ships) and the transport and support of the army, the initiative was now with the French, and the British had to react to their moves. The navy had effectively given up the blockade to defend New York, Newport (Rhode Island), and Halifax. By 11 September, of the 85 warships of all classes under Howe's command; 79 were deployed near or at these three towns: 'Not one ship of the Royal Navy was stationed along the American coast between New York and St Augustine. Delaware Bay, Chesapeake Bay and the coasts of the Carolinas were unguarded: the blockade had ceased to exist'.[72] Three days before the French arrived off Sandy Hook, while the British were still unsure of d'Estaing's destination, Clinton sent troops in 15 transports to Newport, Rhode Island; that detachment would be at some risk if the French left Sandy Hook and sailed for Newport while Howe's fleet was till behind the bar at Sandy Hook. By 28 July, Howe had heard that d'Estaing was heading towards Rhode Island, but he was still waiting for the arrival of Byron's squadron from Britain. When the *Cornwall* (one of Byron's ships damaged in the storm) made it into New York from Halifax on the 31st,[73] with news of what had happened to

68   NRS, *Duncan*, pp.159–160.
69   NRS, *Duncan*, p.159.
70   Willis, *Sea Power*, p.238.
71   NRS, *Duncan*, p.160.
72   Syrett, *American Waters*, p.112.
73   NRS, *Duncan*, p.160.

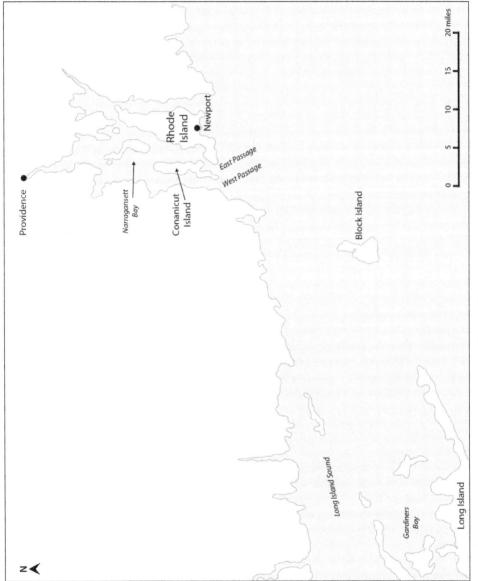

Map 6: Rhode Island

Byron's squadron, Howe realised that he could look for no assistance from that source; although outgunned by the French, he would have to sail to Rhode Island.

The Franco–American plan for Newport was for American troops under General Sullivan to make an attack against General Pigot's British garrison, while the French fleet supported the operation from Narragansett Bay. With no likelihood of assistance from Byron, Howe needed to leave Sandy Hook in pursuit of the French but he was delayed by contrary winds and it was not until 5 July that he 'weighed and got over the bar'.[74] Duncan then recorded that on the 9th, at half-past one in the afternoon, they 'saw Rhode Island; at seven anchored off the harbour. The French fleet were in it, lying near Conanicut'. Although d'Estaing had been in the bay for some days, it was not until 9 August that their attack started on the British garrison, and by that time Howe was approaching Point Judith at the entrance to Narragansett Bay. The French admiral had shown caution at Sandy Hook bar, and did the same at Rhode Island; he did not want to risk a fleet action against the British in the confines of Narragansett Bay.

Rhode Island on 9 August 1778 was one of those occasions where the very appearance of ships of the line can change a situation. The French fleet, combined with Sullivan's troops, could have been expected to overwhelm Pigot's garrison, but the arrival of Howe's ships – 13 against 12 French, though inferior in terms of guns – caused d'Estaing to prioritise the preservation of his force above that of assisting the Americans, who felt deserted by their ally. The action that followed, like that off Ushant, was inconclusive. As with all eighteenth century sea engagements, there was a heavy dependence on the wind. The day after Howe's arrival the French 'cut their cables and came to sea', but the wind 'came to the northward'. This meant that Howe, at sea, was downwind of d'Estaing as the French came out of Narragansett Bay; the French had the weather gauge, and so the tactical advantage. Howe, while at a slight advantage in the number of ships of the line (he also had frigates), was outgunned by the French; while he had only one 74-gun ship, the French had six of 74 and two of 80, giving him 772 guns against 846.[75] On the 11th, Howe tried, by a number of course changes, to get upwind of the French, but to no avail; then a storm blew up and it would not have been prudent 'to have brought two fleets to action in such weather and so late in the day, when nothing decisive could possibly be done'.[76] As Duncan recorded on the 12th, they 'Saw nothing of the French fleet'. For the rest of August, Howe's ships followed the French between Rhode Island and Boston, and back to Rhode Island.

74   NRS, *Duncan*, p.161.
75   SP, Vol.2, p.286.
76   NRS, *Duncan*, p.162.

August also demonstrated the less than perfect cooperation between Lord Howe (eager to return home) and General Clinton. The General assembled 4,000 troops with which he hoped to trap and defeat the Americans at Newport, following d'Estaing's departure on the 11 August, and for that he needed Howe's assistance. While Howe did sail for Newport, he saw the French fleet as his main objective, and so when *en route* he heard that the French had now sailed south (probably for Boston), he decided to follow them rather than continue to join up with Clinton: 'His lordship therefore pushed our fleet with the greatest expedition through between Nantucket and St George's Bank, in hopes of getting to Boston before them'.[77] Howe did not overhaul d'Estaing and, when he arrived off Boston on 30 August, he 'found the French fleet there'. On 2 September, when they 'stood close to Boston', they saw that the French 'were removed higher up the harbour' with 'no intention to come out, and it was impracticable to attack them in their present position'. That being the case, Howe sailed back to Rhode Island, arriving on 4 September. On his arrival back at Rhode Island, Clinton proposed that a joint attack by Howe's ships and 6,000 troops could defeat d'Estaing's force at Boston, but this suggestion was also turned down by Howe. Ferling is critical of Howe for failing to support Clinton at Rhode Island, and that by setting out on a 'fruitless search for d'Estaing' the admiral had 'foiled a good chance at a major victory'.[78] That Howe's trailing the French to Boston was 'fruitless' is borne out by the fact that he did not catch them; that he threw away a 'major victory' is less easily argued – would it have changed events given that the King would not grant the Americans independence? By now, the whole geographic focus of the war had moved to the southern colonies (the Carolinas) and the Caribbean. Howe sailed home for Britain on 26 September 1778, having handed over to Gambier, while d'Estaing sailed for Martinique on 4 November.

The entry of France into the war in 1778 had given the Americans hope that this would mean a defeat for the British, especially with the deployment of French men of war to the theatre, but they were wrong. Not only did d'Estaing fail to sink a single British ship of the line, but the Americans misread French war aims. Vergennes, the French foreign minister, did not have American independence as a priority; he preferred to see that country surrounded by Spain to the south, Britain to the north (in Canada), and the new, young country reliant on France for its protection. The failure of the entry of the French Navy to settle affairs had an economic consequence for the Americans. Confident that the involvement of France would mean victory, Congress abandoned its 'prudent economic measures' with the result that Americans faced 'a rapidly deteriorating currency,

77   NRS, *Duncan*, p.163.
78   Ferling, *Miracle*, p.313.

hyperinflation [and] state and national indebtedness',[79] all made worse by the fact that now that France was in the war it could no longer be counted on for a loan. As so often in life, one event leads to another. As d'Estaing had failed to defeat the British fleet, France was now at a naval disadvantage with 64 ships of the line capable of going to sea, against 90 on the British side – including those ships in Europe. France now needed Spain to join and tip the balance to 121 on the Bourbon side against Britain's 90. On 2 April 1779, France and Spain signed a treaty of alliance at Aranjuez, but the price of Spanish involvement was a high one: Gibraltar had to be returned to Spain, Minorca should also be returned, and the British should be removed from Florida. As Willis points out, American independence was not a specific Spanish war aim, but

> [B]ecause Spain agreed not to make peace with Britain without French consent, and France could not achieve peace until England recognised American independence. The Spanish would therefore ally with France and not with America, and Spain would never deal directly with American diplomats, but the American cause was still central to Spanish policy.[80]

The Bourbon alliance meant that the British had to look to the defence of their interests in the West Indies – the Sugar Islands. Sugar was the most valuable import into Britain, 'worth more than the total exports of all the North American mainland colonies combined'.[81] The islands also took more English-manufactured goods than the North Americans did. George III was adamant regarding the importance of the West Indies, and scornful of those who took a pessimistic view of any invasion threat at home.

> Our islands [in the West Indies] must be defended, even at the risk of an invasion of this island. If we lose our sugar islands, it will be impossible to raise money to continue the war; and then no peace can be obtained, [...] We must be ruined if every idea of offensive war is to lie dormant until this island is thought in a situation to defy attack.[82]

On 21 March 1778 the King had drafted orders for General Clinton (at that time in Philadelphia) to 'make a Detachment of a Body of Five Thousand Men from the Troops under your command', together with artillery, stores and equipment,

---

79   Ferling, *Miracle*, p.349.
80   Willis, *Sea Power*, p.281.
81   M. Parker, *The Sugar Barons: Family, Corruption, Empire and War* (London: Windmill, 2012), p.298.
82   SP, Vol.3, pp.163–164, King to Sandwich, 13 September 1779.

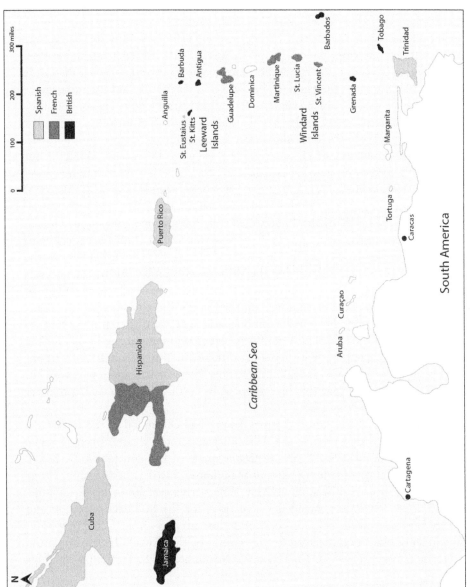

Map 7: The Caribbean

and send them under a suitable commander 'to the Island of St Lucia, and to Attack and if practicable Reduce, and take possession of the said Island'.[83] At the same time (as we saw in the previous chapter), Clinton was to start evacuating Philadelphia. Whether America became independent or not, it was big enough to stand alone, while the British islands in the Caribbean were not. They were small, each separate from the other, and frequently with a French island between them. Because of their economic importance to the European nations, they were constantly fought over. The planters, because of their wealth and the importance of their produce to the British economy, had a loud, strong voice in London; they could not be ignored. Sir Charles Middleton, the Navy Comptroller, wrote that 'The sugar islands are the best and surest markets for our staple commodities, and the most productive of all our colonies. They are the easiest source of our revenues'.[84] Before we look at the expedition to St Lucia, it is worth taking a brief moment to look at the geography of the Caribbean islands, and why this could cause problems for naval commanders on that station.

The British called them the Leeward Islands because the prevailing wind in that area was from the east, and the British islands (apart from Barbados) lie to leeward of the French islands to the south of Dominica, which is taken as the boundary between the Leeward and the Windward Islands. This distinction was important in the age of sail; a ship to windward of another had the advantage of manoeuvre. Troops could be stationed on the islands, but only in small numbers, and Europeans found the climate problematic and were dreadfully prone to sickness. When Major-General Grant was given command of the troops for the expedition he expected that within a short time of landing, only half of his troops would be fit for service. On arrival in December 1778, he had 4,945 who were fit; by April the following year this had been cut by 1,400 who were sick, a number that rose to 1,800 by May 1779.[85]

In January 1778, Vice-Admiral James Young had command in the Leewards, but on the 30th of that month, the Admiralty appointed Rear-Admiral Samuel Barrington to the position. Again, decisions made in London took time before they took effect in the far-flung parts of the empire. Barrington's flagship, *Prince of Wales*, sailed from Spithead on 10 May 1778, arriving at Barbados on 20 June. Barrington's secret orders included instructions for the St Lucia operation and required him to wait for the ships carrying Hotham and Grant from New York; unfortunately, they were delayed by the sailing of the French Toulon squadron for North American waters. Finally, on 3 November 1778, Hotham's warships

---

83   NDAR, Vol.11, p.1101, the King to Clinton, 21 March 1778.
84   Mackesy, *America*, p.184.
85   Mackesy, *America*, p.272.

(variously reported as between five and seven), together with 59 transports and 5,000 troops, left New York and arrived at Barbados on 10 December. Hotham's delay provides a further example of the problems inherent in trying to coordinate the supply of provisions from 3,000 miles away. At the time that the troops were originally ordered to St Lucia, March 1778, the Victualling Board sent three victualling ships to meet them at Barbados. With the troops arrival there delayed until December, the provisions were nine months old by the time the troops got them and found that they 'were not surprisingly rotten'.[86]

The combined operation got under way on 13 December, with ships in position for a landing the following day. By the end of the day, around 3,000 of the troops had been landed, and the rest would get their feet wet on the following day: '14 December. A.M. At sunrise, made the signal and landed the remainder of the troops'[87] under the direction of Commodore Hotham. By mid-afternoon of the 14th, 'the British Colours were flying on the Batteries at the Carenage [...] the troops having got possession of the Carenage with very little opposition and no loss'.[88] In recognition of the work done by the sailors Barrington ordered that those who had been employed on shore 'should be allowed a quarter of a pint of Rum a day each, in addition to their established allowance'. Although the operation had been short, Grant had to ask that provisions be sent to the Carenage for the troops who were now in place there: 'The roads are so difficult that it is impossible to bring any thing by Land, I must therefore beg of you to order every thing [sic] which has been carried ashore to be taken on board again, and brought round by water'.[89] Barrington supplied 10 flat boats for the purpose, demonstrating the flexibility provided by a fleet close at hand under the direction of a cooperative admiral. Grant showed his appreciation: 'I have given directions to collect some cattle and 'tis to be hoped I shall be able to give the Officers of the Navy a little fresh beef'.

Although the capture of St Lucia had gone well, the British were not out of trouble, as d'Estaing's fleet had left Boston at almost the same time as Byron left Rhode Island (3 November 1778). It was during the preparation for the landing at St Lucia that Barrington learned of the French sailing (the Leewards were their expected destination), with Byron chasing them from Rhode Island.[90] The French had 12 sail of the line and three frigates, and so considerably outgunned Barrington's force. The sensible move was to take up a defensive position at St

---

86 Mackesy, *America*, p.224, fn.2.
87 NRS, *The Barrington Papers: Admiral The Hon. Samuel Barrington, Volume 2* (London, 1941), pp.117-8.
88 NRS, *Barrington Papers*, p.118.
89 NRA, *Barrington Papers*, p.119, Grant to Barrington, 14 December 1778.
90 NRS, *Barrington Papers*, p.121, Captain Linzee to Barrington, 13 December 1778.

Lucia and await the arrival of Byron's 16 warships and frigates. At 5:00 p.m., on 14 December, the frigate *Ariadne* was observed to be flying the signal for 'seeing an Enemy's fleet'[91] and preparations had to be put in place to meet them.

> I [Barrington] immediately dispatched notice of the Enemy's approach to the General and to the Commanding Officer of the Troops at the Landing Place; and, in order to render the Transports as secure as possible, gave directions for their being warped within the Ships of War and the latter to be anchored in a line across the entrance of the Bay.

For the next two weeks the French fleet did little to worry the British ships, although they did assist French troops to land; these were subsequently beaten by Grant's men. On 29 December, after re-embarking their troops, the enemy 'weighed with their whole fleet and stood toward Martinique'. At 9:00 a.m., 'the French Commandant of the island desired to capitulate'.[92] During the action the problem of the rotten victuals in the three ships sent from England, came home to roost. Hotham's ships had obviously been provisioned on the assumption that they would be resupplied in the West Indies as, on 18 December, only five days into the operation Barrington was recording that 'I gave directions for the ships' companies to be put to two-thirds allowance of Bread, Beef, Pork, Butter and Cheese, till further order; [...] and recommended it to the General to husband the provisions of the Army also as much as possible'.[93]

In spite of the fleet also being on short rations, Grant had to make requests to Barrington for supplies to be moved to his troops on 18 December: 'I must beg of you to send boats with Provisions, Rum and Ammunition tomorrow morning' for those troops being attacked by the French landing; and again on the 25th 'to carry Rum and Provisions for six days to the Reserve and 4th Regiment'.[94] Unlike many of the other combined operations, there appears to have been a good and cooperative relationship between Barrington and Grant, which was reflected in their respective reports to London in the early days of January 1779. For his part, Barrington acknowledged 'the assistance I received from Major-General Grant and the Forces under his command',[95] while Grant was particularly effusive in his thanks: 'The Fleet and Army act with the greatest unanimity. 'Tis a pleasure to serve with Admiral Barrington, Commodore Hotham, and the Gentlemen of the Navy in general. The Commodore took a fatherly care of us from New

91   NRS, *Barrington Papers*, p.118.
92   NRA, *Barrington Papers*, p.140.
93   NRS, *Barrington Papers*, p.129.
94   NRS, *Barrington Papers*, p.130 & p.138, letters from Grant to Barrington.
95   NRS, *Barrington Papers*, p.164.

York, and brought us safe to Barbados, without the loss of a Transport'.[96] The expedition to St Lucia was a good demonstration, if on a small scale, of how well the two military arms could work together, and how the navy could add flexibility to ground forces both before and after they were put ashore.

On 6 January, Byron arrived with his squadron 'in a deplorable state' and took over command in the Leeward Islands. To his credit Byron pointed out to the Admiralty that he felt himself 'very unhappy at being so circumstanced as to be under an indispensable necessity of interfering with a command intrusted to an Officer who has done his duty with singular advantage to his Country, and much honour to himself'.[97] For the rest of his time on the station, Barrington served willingly as a junior flag officer under Byron.

Following the signing of the Franco–Spanish agreement and the sending of British ships and troops to St Lucia, the geographic focus of the war had now moved south from New England to South Carolina and the Caribbean.

96   NRS, *Barrington Papers*, p.169.
97   NRS, *Barrington Papers*, p.xxiv.

11

'The country that will hazard most will get the advantage in this war'

How easy it had all seemed in 1775, when Britain opened hostilities with its American colonies. The backwoodsmen would be no match for trained regulars and the navy would impose a blockade on the coast, while escorting victualling ships from Britain. The army, having the advantage of the mobility provided by naval transport, would be able to mount combined landings at points on the coast selected by them, and before the American commanders were aware of the intended destination. There was the risk of France taking advantage of the situation by creating problems in the Channel (and a possible invasion), but with the Bourbon powers – at least legally – uninvolved, it appeared to ministers in London that the colonists would be returned to their allegiance fairly quickly. The entry of France into the conflict in 1778, and Spain in April 1779, changed all that.

The navy was conflicted in its ability to support the army in America while it attempted to cover the various tasks assigned by London. The ability of the navy to rise to the challenge was hampered by the reluctance of the government, prior to France becoming a belligerent, to implement measures for full mobilisation. In September 1779, Sandwich wrote a long memorandum to be read to the Cabinet and delivered to the King. In this, he laid out the challenges facing the country and the navy, and the resources available to meet them; it must have made for sober reading. Some of the First Lord's comments are worth drawing out from his memorandum. The first might be a statement of the obvious: 'it is to little purpose to form plans without at the same time pointing out the manner of securing their success, [...] it will be necessary to lay down not only what ought but what can be done'.[1] He wished to inject a note of realism into any plans that the Cabinet might have for prosecuting the war.

---

1   SP, Vol.3, p.165, memorandum from Sandwich, September 1779.

The extent to which the war in America had become a secondary consideration is implied, but not directly addressed, by the priorities laid out by Sandwich in his memorandum: Gibraltar, Minorca, the Leeward Islands, and Jamaica. In addition, 'serious attention' had to be given to the problems associated with the Dutch, Caribbean island of St Eustatius because, as Sandwich pointed out:

> I am convinced that two-thirds of the provisions that we carry out under convoy from England and Ireland is, on its arrival in our islands, immediately shipped off for St Eustatius and from thence to Martinique, without which the French could not keep their fleet in condition for sea. It is idle to talk of restraining such abuses by laws; the rapacity of merchants overbears all legal obstructions, and nothing but more forcible coercion can restrain them from anything in which they find their immediate interest.[2]

The ships that would be needed to cover the geographic locations spelt out by Sandwich had to come from the ships at home, some of which were not yet ready for sea, but he laid it down 'as the foundation of the whole that the safety of these kingdoms requires that this stock [of ships] should not be drawn so low as to leave us unable to resist the united efforts of the House of Bourbon in these seas;' this was the dilemma laid out in Chapter 8 of this account. Not only might Britain have to face a combined Bourbon fleet in the Channel, but also 'We unfortunately have an additional war upon our hands' – that in America. Earlier in the war, Sandwich had pressed – without success – for mobilisation, which he now pointed out might have eased the situation in which the Cabinet now found itself:

> But still, had we been early enough in our preparations, and had not suffered them [the Bourbon powers] to go on arming and building without keeping pace with them, their superiority would certainly not have been so decided. [...] But under all our difficulties, if, as I have already said, our equipment had begun sooner or had an effectual blow been struck against the French fleet before they were joined by Spain, we should probably still have been triumphant everywhere.[3]

Was his comment on an 'effectual blow' alluding to the indecisive actions off Ushant, Rhode Island and New York? In spite of his comments on the missed opportunities of mobilisation, Sandwich tried to stay positive.

2   SP, Vol.3,p.167, memorandum from Sandwich, September 1779.
3   SP, Vol.3,p.170, memorandum from Sandwich, September 1779.

I am not yet inclined to despair; if we manage the force we have with prudence, our case does not appear to me yet to be desperate; but as we have a deep stake to play for, we ought in my opinion to husband our strength, and to employ it only on those services which are of the most importance and that have a probability of being attended with success.[4]

In other words, the limited resources would have to be well managed and assigned to tasks that had a better than even chance of being successful. Unfortunately, the characters of some of the leading actors would militate against the hoped for success.

In 1776, the British had captured Newport, Rhode Island as an alternative naval base to New York, and although the French had attempted to take it (see the previous chapter), they had left rather than fight a fleet action in Narragansett Bay. In 1779, with the French again off the coast of America, caution – or a failure of nerve – caused British commanders to pull the garrison back from Newport to New York, where they arrived on 27 October 1779. The British were constantly reacting to French initiatives, rather than setting the agenda. Arbuthnot wrote to Sandwich to explain that, as d'Estaing 'was upon this coast with 24 sail of the line', he had 'set about sinking ships on the bar of this place [Sandy Hook]'[5] to prevent the French from entering the harbour. This was a very defensive action on Arbuthnot's part given that the French admiral had previously deemed it unsafe to take his ships over the same bar to fight Howe. Additionally, Arbuthnot and Clinton believed that Rhode Island 'must inevitably have fallen if attacked' and so 'both the General and myself agreed in the measure of withdrawing the garrison'. This move meant that there was now an undefended harbour available to the French, should they desire to make a move on it, which they would do in July 1780. It must be said that in the time that Britain had held Rhode Island they had not used it as a fleet harbour and Rodney's later comment to Germain, that the leaving was 'the most fatal measure that could possibly have been taken',[6] was more to discredit Arbuthnot than a statement of the true value of the place to the British fleet. Meanwhile, Clinton was working up a plan to move south and attack Georgia, an operation in which Arbuthnot assured Sandwich that he was ready to cooperate. Unfortunately, the two commanders did not get on. One bone of contention for Arbuthnot was Clinton's position as a peace commissioner in Britain's attempts to persuade the Americans to return to the Crown. Arbuthnot felt slighted that Clinton's role would be carried out 'without taking the smallest

4   SP, Vol.3,p.171, memorandum from Sandwich, September 1779.
5   SP, Vol.3, pp.136-7, Arbuthnot to Sandwich, 30 October 1779.
6   Mackesy, *America*, p.276.

notice of the sea commander', which he considered 'so public a mark of contempt' and lack of trust in him that 'I do most earnestly beseech your Lordship to send a person to relieve me of whose capacity a better opinion is entertained'.[7] Having already told Sandwich that he was taking defensive measures against d'Estaing, and that Rhode Island was to be evacuated, the British naval commander on the American station should have had more to occupy his mind than the proceedings of a peace commission that was almost bound to fail, especially due to its insistence that the Americans would not be granted the one thing that might bring an end to the conflict – their nation's independence.

In the same manner that the British fleet had confounded Washington as to its destination when it headed for Philadelphia, so Arbuthnot was wrong in his assessment that the recently arrived French fleet was making for New York or Rhode Island. D'Estaing made the southern town of Savannah, captured by the British in November 1778, his objective. On 2 September 1779, the 33 warships, transports and 4,000 troops entered the Savannah River, completely surprising the British contingent. HMS *Experiment* (50 guns) and the frigate HMS *Ariel*, together with two storeships, were captured by the French, along with the payroll for the British troops – £30,000. (In a letter to Sandwich in February 1780, Rodney mentioned that he had received information that both of these ships had been seen entering Cadiz harbour together with 12 Spanish and two French sail of the line.[8] Navies frequently renamed captured warships and took them back to sea under their new flag). The French landings at Savannah demonstrated that this was an operational area in which they had much to learn: 'The utter chaos of these landings stand in marked contrast to the skilful efficiency of the British landings at New York and Newport in 1776, at Head of Elk for the Philadelphia campaign in 1777 and at St Lucia in 1778. It seems that the French had dreams of sea power that they were simply unable to realize'.[9] The French attack was a failure and on 10 October, they re-embarked and sailed for Europe. As with Sullivan at Rhode Island, the Americans felt deserted by their ally but, on hearing the news of the French retreat on 18 November, Clinton prepared for his own expedition to the South.

The objective of Clinton's expedition was Charleston, South Carolina, where he and Sir Peter Parker had failed in their previous assault in 1776 (see Chapter 9). Clinton had originally been against the idea of operating in the south, preferring to try to bring Washington's army to a set battle in New England, which he hoped his trained troops would win. He changed his mind after seeing the success that

7   SP, Vol.3, pp.138-9, Arbuthnot to Sandwich, 30 October 1779.
8   SP, Vol.3, p.200, Rodney to Sandwich, 16 February 1780.
9   Willis, *Sea Power*, p.316.

Collier had had in his raids up the Chesapeake River in May 1779. For the 1780 attempt, Clinton had to cooperate with Arbuthnot, but the relationship between them was no better than the previous one between Clinton and Parker. However, that was not all; as well as his differences with the admiral, Clinton also had issues with his second-in-command, Cornwallis. When the latter returned to New York in July 1779 he did not bring with him the 6,000 reinforcements that Clinton had asked for (and which he had expected Cornwallis to lobby for on his behalf) – there were only some 3,500 new men. Clinton took this as a snub by London and immediately put in his resignation, but he would have to wait some time for a reply to know whether or not it had been accepted. In the meantime, 'neither Clinton nor Cornwallis knew from one day to the next who would command on the morrow'.[10] Unsurprisingly, the two found it difficult to get along, causing problems right up to the surrender at Yorktown. Whatever the issues between them, the embarkation of the troops began on 16 December 1779 and was completed on the 21st, with the fleet of around 100 ships and 8,000 troops (different accounts give different numbers) sailing from Sandy Hook on 26 December. The journey was long and uncomfortable for the soldiers; ice in New York harbour had destroyed seven transports before they really got going and another was blown 'clear across the ocean and fetched up at St Ives'.[11] Nearly all of the army's 1,400 horses were lost at sea, along with the siege artillery, which went to the bottom with the *Russia Merchant* Ordnance vessel.[12] The fleet finally arrived at Tybee Island in the first days of February and troops started to go ashore on the 11 February on Simmons Island.[13]

The disagreements between Clinton and Arbuthnot started with the choice of landing place. The admiral wanted it to be on John's Island at the entrance to the Stono River, while Clinton got his way and landed further from Charleston at North Edisto on Simmons Island. The troops had a good distance to travel from the landing to the town, and would have to make a number of river crossings before approaching Charleston from the north from where they would make their assault. General Benjamin Lincoln commanded the defending American forces and, although he had fewer troops – some 4,300 against 11,000[14] – he had strong defensive lines from which to oppose Clinton's men as they consolidated their positions above Charleston on 29 March. In spite of the differences between Clinton and Arbuthnot, the expedition to Charleston was a successful joint operation. However, close cooperation did not rule out strict demarcation

10   Wickwire, *Cornwallis*, p.123.
11   Wickwire, *Cornwallis*, p.126.
12   Ferling, *Miracle*, p.415.
13   NRS, *The Keith Papers, Volume 1* (London, 1927), p.135.
14   Ferling, *Miracle*, p.419.

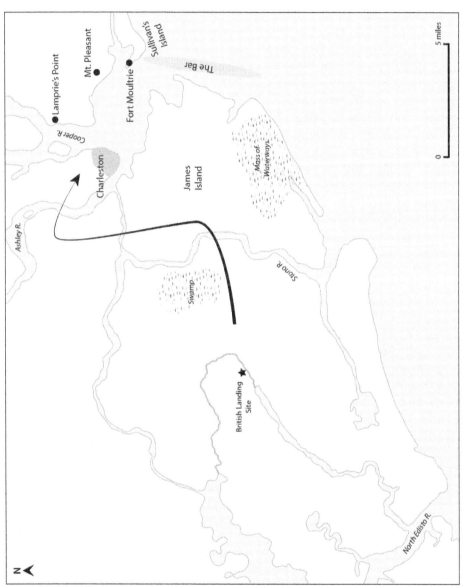

Map 8: Charleston, 1780

between soldiers and sailors, as one example demonstrates. The naval captain, George Elphinstone, based on his 'intimate knowledge of the navigation of this Country',[15] was dispatched by Arbuthnot to help and cooperate with Clinton, and to command a considerable number of naval officers and men on the route to the north of Charleston. However, these seamen, although operating together with army troops, were not to come under their control: 'I need not repeat to you my wishes that all the seamen employed in the expedition on shore should act *in toto* entirely under your command and that of the Navy officers subordinate to you'.[16] Given the close integration between the troops and the sailors, one might have expected Elphinstone's contingent to come under the command of the army.

When Arbuthnot, after lightening his ships by removing stores, sailed his force across the Bar and into Charleston's harbour, the American ships under Abraham Whipple decided that, as discretion was the better part of valour, they would retire to block the entrance to the Cooper River (Map 8) and provide a defended exit route for the rebels in the city. Had Whipple stood his ground he could have caused considerable difficulties for the British, especially as Arbuthnot was not the most aggressive of commanders. The Americans had a useful force available to them, including three of their own frigates and three from the French, giving them 260 guns afloat, plus those at Fort Moultrie which the British would have to pass. If Whipple had put his ships in line across the harbour, he could have fired broadsides into Arbuthnot's ships, which would only have had their lighter forward firing weapons with which to respond, many of the rest having been offloaded to get over the bar.[17] As it was the British ships sailed past Fort Moultrie on 8 April 'under a heavy fire from the enemy, and only one ship hurt to all appearance; [...] the *Roebuck* leading began a heavy cannonading, when abreast of the fort, which was continued by succession till the last ship passed'.[18] Cautious as ever, however, it had taken 18 days for Arbuthnot to make the move from the Bar to beyond Fort Moultrie. With the army's siege train having been lost *en route* to Charleston, the navy stepped in to provide heavy guns from their ships for the British batteries on shore. This was a considerable undertaking; as we saw in Chapter 9, a 32-pounder weighed upwards of three tons. The guns would have had to be moved from the gun-decks to the main deck, offloaded to boats, landed on shore, and then manhandled into position in the batteries – almost all the horses had died on the passage south. Arbuthnot's sailors and marines continued to assist the army in the attacks on Fort Moultrie and Lamprie's Point. On 12

15   NRS, *Keith Papers*, p.145, Arbuthnot to Elphinstone, 4 February 1780.
16   NRA, *Keith Papers*, p.160, Arbuthnot to Elphinstone, 5 April 1780.
17   Ferling, *Miracle*, p.420.
18   NRS, *Keith Papers*, pp.162-3, James Duncan to Elphinstone, 9 April 1780.

May it was all over. Charleston was surrendered to the British and yielded 'the largest collection of prisoners taken by Britain in a single engagement'.[19] It was 'the greatest defeat inflicted upon the Americans during the revolutionary war',[20] and showed how well the British Army and Navy could work together, in spite of the personal differences of their commanders; as one observer wrote, 'but 'tis pity they are not friends'.[21]

The successful campaign was an opportunity for praise to be given where it was due: in his despatch after the surrender, Arbuthnot wrote that 'The fleet has endeavoured most heartily and effectually to co-operate with the army in every possible instance, and the most perfect harmony has subsisted between us'[22]. This was published in the *London Gazette*, 15 June 1780, together with Clinton's report in which he stated that 'Your Lordship has seen how great a share Admiral Arbuthnot and the Fleet have had in every measure'. Clinton, in a letter to Germain, went to particular lengths to acknowledge the contribution of Captain Elphinstone.

> I cannot close my letter without expressing how much I am obliged hitherto to Admiral Arbuthnot for the assistance given me through Captain Elphinstone, who as yet has been chiefly employed in the naval transactions immediately relative to the Army. This gentleman's unremitted attention to us from his so ably and successfully conducting the Transports into North Edisto to this hour, with the great benefit I have derived from knowledge of the Inland Navigation of this part of the coast, merit my warmest thanks.[23]

One might be forgiven for thinking that any bad feeling had been put away after the joint success, but that was not to be. By September, back at New York and struggling with a provisioning crisis for his army, Clinton wrote to William Eden (one of the peace commissioners) that 'I have no money, no provisions, nor indeed any account of the sailing of the Cork fleet, *nor admiral that I can have the least dependence on* [my emphasis]'.[24]

The expedition to Charleston had been able to sail from New York because d'Estaing had taken his fleet home after the failed attempt on Savannah. On 10 May, two days before Charleston surrendered, Clinton received a note from

19   Ferling, *Miracle*, p.428.
20   Syrett, *American Waters*, p.140.
21   NRS, *Keith Papers*, p.143.
22   NRS, *Keith Papers*, p.142, Arbuthnot's despatch.
23   NRS, *Keith Papers*, p.143.
24   Bowler, *Logistics*, p.137.

London dated 15 March 1780, telling him that the French were on the move again; troops and 12 ships of the line were expected to sail for North America, although exactly where was not known. Once again, the British were in the position of trying to respond to the unknown movements of a French fleet. With his ships in need of maintenance, and the crews of some of his warships sickly, Arbuthnot wanted to move back to New York, which he and Clinton did on 8 June, together with 4,500 troops. Cornwallis, eager to have his own command (and Clinton happy to put distance between the pair of them), was left at Charleston to command the British troops in the south. Clinton's instructions to Cornwallis left sufficient room for his second-in-command to exercise 'virtually independent powers,'[25] he was to 'pacify South and North Carolina, maintain order in Georgia and the Floridas and then move north and take Virginia'.[26] The ill feeling between these two senior army commanders together with their poor communication during Cornwallis's move through the Carolinas and into Virginia, were partly responsible for the later situation at Yorktown. The extent to which they were failing to coordinate their plans was demonstrated by Clinton's comment after the war that 'How great was my disappointment and astonishment when I found he [Cornwallis] had come to the fatal resolution of abandoning both Carolinas to their fate and flying into Virginia'.[27] Cornwallis's activities from the time he separated from Clinton up to his move into Yorktown do not really concern this account. His troops' involvement in action against the Americans at Camden, King's Mountain, Cowpens, and Guilford Courthouse did not involve the navy. However, the decisions taken by British admirals in the Caribbean and North American waters contributed to the situation in which Cornwallis later had no option other than surrender at Yorktown.

With Clinton and Arbuthnot back in New York in July 1780 (following the news of a French squadron possibly on its way from Europe), we turn our attention to the Admiralty's requirement to cover French fleet movements towards North America and the Caribbean at the same time as they needed to relieve the garrison at Gibraltar. Five years into the war, and with the Caribbean islands now having a greater priority than America, Sandwich recognised that he needed a fighting admiral on that station. Up to that point, too many naval actions had been inconclusive; the British Navy was not displaying the superiority that the nation expected of it. The spotlight fell on Admiral Sir George Brydges Rodney, a 'King's man', a fighter, and a disciplinarian, but with a reputation for 'questionable' financial practices. To escape his many creditors and his escalating debts Rodney

---

25   Wickwire, *Cornwallis*, p.134.
26   Wickwire, *Cornwallis*, p.135.
27   Urban, *Fusiliers*, p.257.

had spent some years in France. Sandwich knew that, with his poor reputation for the misuse of public money, he would have difficulty getting Rodney's appointment past the King. The admiral's 'well-established reputation for dishonesty [...] and flagrantly misappropriating public money'[28] required that the First Lord should insert checks and balances between Rodney and the public funds. As Sandwich explained to the King, the admiral would not 'have any temptation to take advantage of purchasing stores or anything of that sort, he will have no means of doing it at present, as there will be a Commissioner on the Spot thro' whose hands all the business will be transacted'.[29] With that assurance, the King confirmed the appointment. As a result of the government's strategic reappraisal of the war at sea in the autumn of 1779, nine or ten ships were to be sent to the West Indies, together with 5,000 troops. These ships were to come from the Channel Fleet, 'making the Caribbean into a major seat of the naval war' and a 'reversal of the traditional British strategy of controlling the Western Approaches for the English Channel in great strength'.[30] The ships for the West Indies, together with the resupply vessels for the Gibraltar garrison, were to sail under Rodney. This strategic change, and the weakening of the Western Squadron, allowed French and Spanish fleets to sail to North America and the Caribbean. The questions for British ministers were when would they sail, and where to?

In choosing Rodney, Sandwich had appointed a commander who would fight, but his other character defects would cause their own issues; his need for money led to enormous problems after the sacking of the Dutch island of St Eustatius in 1781 and his strict disciplinary approach could result in subordinates lacking initiative out of fear of their commander. Rodney prided himself on his disciplinary control of his officers, as was clear in a letter to his wife: 'My eye on them had more dread than the enemy's fire, and they knew it would be more fatal. [...] I leant them to be what they had never been before, officers'.[31] His mood would not have been helped by the gout that he suffered from, and which would be his excuse for requesting to sail home after St Eustatius. Rodney's route to the Sugar Islands was not direct as he was to command the convoy to relieve Gibraltar. The plan for the deployment was that ships for the West Indies, under Sir Hyde Parker, would sail part of the way with Rodney, before detaching and making for the Caribbean while Rodney continued with the convoy to the Rock. Once he had resupplied the garrison, he was to leave for the Leeward Islands to take up command on that station. As we have seen with so many previous convoys, departure dates

28 Rodger, *Command of the Ocean*, pp.343-4.
29 NRS, *The Rodney Papers*, p.235.
30 NRS, *Rodney Papers*, pp.235-6.
31 NRS, *Rodney Papers*, p.514, letter to his wife, 27 May 1780.

were dependent on many factors, and delays caused anxiety at the Admiralty, as Sandwich demonstrated in his letter to Rodney: 'For God's sake go to sea without delay, you cannot conceive of what importance it is to yourself, to me, and to the public that you should not lose this fair wind. If you do, I shall not only hear of it in Parliament, but in places to which I pay more attention'.[32] The First Lord was probably alluding to the King in his final comment. The impressive assembly of ships left St Helens on Christmas Day, 1779; 15 ships of the line, a 44-gun ship, six frigates, and 19 transports carrying troops and recruits for the Rock and the West Indies. Also, 25 victuallers and 11 naval and military storeships, and then (off Plymouth) an additional seven ships of the line, a frigate, and nine troop transports, joined the convoy.[33] Given his irascible nature, the admiral would not have been amused to be told, only two days out, that some of the beer on his ship was bad.

> Whereas Captain Young of His Majesty's Ship *Sandwich* has represented to me that several casks of beer when got up to be issued proved sour, stinking, and unfit for men to drink and requested a survey thereon. And whereas as the hoisting them up and striking them down is very inconvenient, retards the other duties of the ship, and it may also become a nuisance by causing obnoxious stenches in the hold you are therefore hereby required and directed to survey every cask of beer as soon as complained of [...][34]

The checks that should have been made on the victuals, outlined in Chapter 3, would appear to have failed in this case.

On 4 January 1780, Sir Hyde Parker's ships for the West Indies 'parted company' with Rodney's convoy.[35] It did not take long after this for Sandwich's belief in Rodney's aggressive nature to bear fruit. On 8 January 22 sail were spotted, which proved to be a Spanish convoy under the protection of one 64-gunner and a number of smaller vessels: 'after only a token resistance every one of the Spanish ships had been captured'.[36] Those Spanish ships that were loaded with provisions were taken on to Gibraltar, where they would be well received, while the 64-gun *Guispuzcoana*, which had been escorting them, was taken over by Rodney. He sent one of his own 64-gun ships back to England as escort to those Spanish ships not taken to Gibraltar. It was mentioned in an earlier chapter that captured men of

32   NRS, *Rodney Papers*, vol.2, p.270, Sandwich to Rodney, 8 December 1779.
33   NRS, *Rodney Papers*, vol.2, p.237.
34   NRS, *Rodney Papers*, vol.2, p.297, Rodney's order book, 27 December 1779.
35   NRS, *Rodney Papers*, vol.2, p.303, Rodney to Stephens, 9 January 1780.
36   NRS, *Rodney Papers*, vol.2, p.238.

war were frequently taken into service by the side that captured them, and the ship renamed. In this case the *Guispuzcoana* became the *Prince William*: 'She has been launched only six months, [and] is in every respect completely fitted for war, and much larger than the *Bienfaisant*, […] to whom she struck'.[37]

While the taking of the Spanish convoy was an easy victory, only the one sail of the line protecting it, his next encounter on 16 January (while Clinton and Arbuthnot's force was *en route* from New York to Charleston) was much more significant. Although the admiral was given intelligence that a Spanish squadron (thought to be 14 ships strong) was waiting to intercept him before he reached the Straits, Rodney (who could have changed course further into the Atlantic and approached Gibraltar from the west or south-west) decided to fight the Spaniards. The action continued until two o'clock the following morning, by which time he had a victory to proclaim. In spite of the weather that night being 'at times very tempestuous, with a great sea',[38] the action became known as the 'Moonlight Battle'. In his history of the siege of Gibraltar, Adkins points out that the battle took place eight days before a full moon and that with so much cloud cover, it would have been very dark – but the name stuck.[39]

Of 11 Spanish ships of the line, six were 'taken' (four of them to Gibraltar), one blew up, one escaped 'with great difficulty', and another escaped 'very much damaged'. Rodney took the opportunity to send frigates to Tangier to tell the consul there that 'Great Britain was again mistress of the Straits' and he should 'hasten a supply of fresh vegetables to the garrison [at Gibraltar]'. This supply had been cut off while the French and Spanish had controlled the Mediterranean. Rodney's arrival on 18 January would have been a great relief to the army and the civilians on the Rock: the siege started on 21 June 1779 and lasted until 2 February 1783, 1,323 days.[40] One advantage that the British ships had over their Franco–Spanish adversaries was the installation of copper sheathing on the hulls below the waterline; copper bottoms. By 'coppering' the hulls the weevils which ate into wet wood, and the barnacles and weed which attached to wooden bottoms and reduced a ship's speed, were overcome; the resultant advantage was speed. Rodney restated this advantage in a letter to the Admiralty before leaving Gibraltar: 'without the copper bottomed ships the Spanish fleet so lately defeated could not have been brought to action'.[41] Not only had Rodney won a victory, he had confirmed for Sandwich that he had done the right thing in appointing him: 'the worst of my enemies now allow that I have pitched upon a man who knows

---

37   NRS, *Rodney Papers*, vol.2, p.305, Rodney to Stephens, 9 January 1780.
38   NRS, *Rodney Papers*, vol.2, p.321, Rodney to Stephens, 27 January 1780.
39   Adkins, *Gibraltar*, p.104.
40   Adkins, *Gibraltar*, p.4.
41   NRS, *Rodney Papers*, vol.2, p.362, Rodney to Stephens, 11 February 1780.

his duty, and is a brave, honest and able officer'[42] – the honesty would come into question again after St Eustatius. On 13 February, Rodney sailed from Gibraltar for the West Indies arriving at Carlisle Bay, Barbados, on 17 March 1780. He immediately got in contact with Major-General John Vaughan, in command of the troops, and told him that he was 'laid up with the gout in both feet', which may account for his tetchy comment on Sir Hyde Parker (whose ships left Rodney's convoy on the way to Gibraltar): 'I dare say you will be surprised to hear that I found neither rendezvous nor intelligence of any kind left for me here by Rear Admiral Parker'.[43] Rodney had the right to expect that Parker would position frigates so that he would have early intelligence of the French arrival, which could be passed to Rodney before he arrived on station. Unfortunately, his authoritarian style did not prevent him from belittling his own second-in-command in the eyes of the army commander.

> The unpardonable neglect of the Admiral with whom you are now acting in not leaving a frigate or two at Barbados, one of which ought to have cruised to windward of that island in order to give me the earliest intelligence of the situation of the fleet, what enterprise they had in hand, and the proper rendezvous, is such that I cannot conceive in what manner he will be able to answer it either to the public or to me. He cannot pretend ignorance of my coming into these seas.[44]

Rodney would not be an easy commander to serve.

In the early months of 1780, the British and the French were building up their naval forces in the Caribbean. On 3 February, 10 days before Rodney left Gibraltar, the French commander, *Lieutenant-Général* Luc-Urbain du Boëxic, Comte de Guichen (we will adopt the convention of calling him de Guichen), sailed from Brest for the West Indies, arriving at Fort Royal, Martinique on 22 March with 16 sail of the line, four frigates, and 83 merchant ships.[45] When Rodney arrived at Gros Islet Bay, St Lucia, the two fleets were anchored only some 30 miles apart. At this short distance, the fleets could watch each other's movements and must at some point attempt to come to action. However, the two admirals had very different approaches. Rodney, even if outnumbered, would want to bring on a fleet action and would expect his captains to engage the enemy closely. De Guichen's French fighting instructions were based on avoiding direct action if the fleets

---

42   NRS, *Rodney Papers*, vol.2, p.375, Sandwich to Rodney, 8 March 1780.
43   NRS, *Rodney Papers*, vol.2, p.400, Rodney to Vaughan, 17 March 1780.
44   NRS, *Rodney Papers*, vol.2, p.404, Rodney to Vaughan, 18 March 1780.
45   P. Trew, *Rodney and the Breaking of the Line* (Barnsley: Pen and Sword, 2006), p.57.

were closely matched; he was further hampered by special instructions 'to keep the sea, so far as the force maintained by the English in the Windward Islands would permit, *without too far compromising* the fleet entrusted to him [emphasis in the original]'.[46] These two differing styles were to play out in the waters of the Caribbean in April and May 1780.

On 13 April, de Guichen set out with 22 sail of the line and 3,000 troops in the hope of making a landing on Barbados. Rodney's orders to Captain Butchart (HMS *Fame*) demonstrate that he was conscious of the need to provide assistance to the army, as the sailing of his fleet left the island open to possible attack. As well as expecting any British ships that arrived at St Lucia to be directed to join Rodney off Fort Royal, Butchart was to:

> [A]id and assist to the utmost of your power in erecting a battery on Pigeon Island for the defence of this bay [Gros Islet] taking care that the men are not over worked and allow the seamen employed a double allowance of grog. You are likewise to aid and assist to the utmost of your power, General Vaughan or the commanding officer of His Majesty's troops in the defence of this island. [...] You are to be very attentive and keep a good look-out in order to prevent a surprise from the enemy. And to be aiding and assisting to the utmost of your power in transporting troops cannon, or any implements of war, to such places as General Vaughan or the commanding officer of His Majesty's troops may desire, and to assist in the defence of this island to the last extremity.[47]

Rodney sailed to cover the French move, and on the 16th he was 'close enough to count the enemy'. The two fleets were closely matched as Rodney had 20 sail of the line (plus a 50-gunner) against the French 22. In terms of firepower, the British had 1,494 guns against the 1,546 of de Guichen.[48] Despite Rodney's wish to bring on a general action, the result (like that at Ushant) was to be disappointing. De Guichen did what he could to avoid a full-blown fleet battle, and the British signalling system led to confusion and recriminations. Rodney was furious with his subordinate captains. As Mackesy stated, 'Only a great superiority of force could have overcome the drag of misunderstandings, inadequate signalling systems, and adherence to rule'.[49] He might have added that Rodney's stern discipline ensured that no captain would show initiative if subsequent failure meant censure. Fleet

---

46   D. Macintyre, *Admiral Rodney* (London: Peter Davies, 1962), p.112.
47   NRS, *Rodney Papers*, vol.2, p.452, Rodney to Butchart, 15 April 1780.
48   Mackesy, *America*, p.331, fn.2.
49   Mackesy, *America*, p.331.

242 ALL AT SEA

manoeuvres at that time were ordered by a flag signalling system. Signal flags, with predefined meanings, were flown from yardarms on the admiral's flagship and, taken together with the Fighting Instructions, should have directed the ships' captains to carry out the admiral's tactical plan. How and why this failed off Martinique is well explained in Peter Trew's book.[50] Rodney obviously believed that his flag signals were clear and not open to misinterpretation, as he outlined to Sandwich in an indictment of Rear-Admiral Rowley who had commanded his rear division on 17 April.

> I don't know which is of the greatest detriment to a State, a designing man or a man without abilities entrusted with command. Had not Mr Rowley presumed to think, when his duty was only obedience, the whole French rear and the centre had certainly been taken. [...] I made no hesitation to tell him that his motion without orders had saved the enemy's fleet, and that for the future he must not attempt to do the like; that the painful task of thinking belonged to me, to him *obedience* to signals and orders[51] [emphasis in the original].

It took a brave subordinate to use his own initiative under Rodney's command. There was a second opportunity for a naval engagement between the two fleets when de Guichen ventured out on 15 May 1780. Once again, manoeuvres came to naught and there was no conclusive action. On the mainland of America (only a few days previously), Charleston had surrendered but Clinton and Arbuthnot, having had intelligence of the preparation of a French fleet for North America, and carrying troops under the Comte de Rochambeau, were readying for a return to New York.

At about the time that de Guichen was preparing to leave Brest for Martinique, and Rodney was on his way from Gibraltar to take up command in the Leeward Islands, ministers in London were aware of another French squadron (under de Ternay) being prepared for an expedition to North America. The Cabinet agreed that as Sandwich had assured them that 30 sail of the line would be ready by the first of May, 'exclusive of all detachments for foreign parts', Arbuthnot's force at New York needed to be strengthened: '[I]t is agreed that six sail of the line be prepared with the utmost expedition to be sent to North America, there being reason to believe from the intelligence received that the French meditate to send thither a considerable force under M. de Ternay'.[52] The day before the Cabinet

50   Trew, *Rodney*, pp.57–85.
51   SP, Vol.3, p.217, letter from Rodney to Sandwich, 31 May 1780.
52   SP, Vol.3, pp.243–244, Minute of Cabinet, 7 March 1780.

meeting, the King had suggested this course of action to Sandwich, proposing that five ships should be sent under Rear-Admiral Thomas Graves. The King also made an interesting comment regarding the integration of captured French and Spanish warships into British squadrons; it indicates the extent to which he concerned himself with military matters and his wish for ministers to demonstrate a greater sense of risk-taking in the conflict. Normally such vessels would be subject to survey by naval shipwrights to determine the state of the captured ships before sending them to sea; George suggested waiving this step in the process to allow 'early going to sea': '[T]he Navy Board must not follow the old scrupulous method of surveying them before they are reported fit to be bought [they are naval prizes]; but if on a slight inspection they seem in good order, to run the risk and expedite their equipment. The country that will hazard most will get the advantage in this war'.[53]

Over the next few days, the force was increased from six to eight ships (after arguments from Germain for a stronger squadron) under Graves's command, who was then to become second-in-command to Arbuthnot when he arrived at New York. Once again, the best laid plans were subject to the weather and operational delays. Ordered to leave Spithead on 25 March, he was held back by weather until 8 April, before being further held up by a mutiny over pay. Two of his ships were sent off separately to the West Indies, while the final six got under way, after the mutiny had been put down, on 17 May, arriving at Sandy Hook on 13 July. By this time, Clinton and Arbuthnot were at New York, Cornwallis was pursuing his own aims in the Carolinas, and Rodney had twice attempted to bring de Guichen to battle in the Caribbean.

Three days before Graves arrived in New York, de Ternay – together with Rochambeau and his troops – dropped anchor off Rhode Island. Whatever efforts Arbuthnot had made to detect de Ternay's ships before they made landfall in North America, had not worked. We have seen that Rodney had presciently referred to the evacuation of Rhode Island as a 'fatal measure', and the presence of the French ships in Newport harbour now gave cause for concern. From this harbour, they could threaten British communications between New York, Halifax, and Britain. The West Indies may have replaced America as the main priority in the war, but something had to be done about Rhode Island. The capture of Charleston in May had demonstrated that the British had the capability to launch effective joint operations but, with Rochambeau having 6,500 troops at his disposal, an amphibious assault on Newport would require careful planning. However, the close cooperation required of land and sea commanders that was a prerequisite for successful amphibious operations was desperately lacking on this occasion and

53   SP, Vol.3, p.243, the King to Sandwich, 6 March 1780.

244   ALL AT SEA

a major cause of the ill feeling was 'booty'. Military commanders of that time expected to make their fortune from prize money. The capture of ships and towns gave the opportunity for their contents to be sold and the proceeds distributed among the officers and men, according to an accepted formula. Following the successful capture of Charleston, the two commanders failed to agree over the share of the prize, and this sullied their relationship at Newport.

Through the second half of July and early August, the two commanders swapped letters for the planning of the joint operation. On 23 July, Arbuthnot wrote to Clinton to say that if the general still intended to attack Newport then he would prevent the French warships from leaving harbour. Additionally, he would supply frigates to cover Clinton's intended landing on the east side of Rhode Island.[54] Only four days later Arbuthnot's enthusiasm for the operation had waned and he told Captain Henry Savage (sent by Clinton to Arbuthnot) that, while he was prepared to land the army and prevent the French ships from leaving, Clinton could expect nothing more from the navy; he would not allow the army to use naval guns or ammunition. The low point between them was reached when Clinton made his way overland from New York to Gardiner's Island for an agreed meeting with Arbuthnot. When he arrived at East Hampton (near the northern tip of Long Island), Clinton was given a note from Arbuthnot to say that he had set sail for the Nantucket Shoals. As Syrett expressed it, being stood up by Arbuthnot 'marked the end of the last serious attempt by Clinton to formulate a joint plan to attack and destroy the French at Newport'.[55] Although Graves's arrival with six ships had increased his advantage over de Ternay to ten against seven, Arbuthnot had no stomach for a full-blown amphibious operation. In spite of his poor support for the army, Arbuthnot's letter to Sandwich gives the impression of an eager admiral, let down by a general who failed to communicate his intentions: 'You will perceive that I lost no time after the arrival of the reinforcements [Graves's squadron] in proceeding to the face of the enemy off Newport harbour, where I anchored, and remained in anxious expectation of the General's coming in person to me'. He went on to imply that if Clinton had communicated better, then the navy would have taken 'a large transport of consequence'. He also took the opportunity to mock Clinton:

> Sir Henry Clinton's amusing me with his situation in Huntington Bay [Long Island], with his troops in transports and aide-de-camps dancing backwards and forwards with reports of intelligence with respect to the enemy, kept me in the constant hope of an *eclairissement* [sic] one way or

54 Syrett, *American Waters*, p.147.
55 Syrett, *American Waters*, p.149.

another, till time slipped from under my feet and obliged me to retire to Gardiner's Island Bay.[56]

Arbuthnot was keen to give Sandwich the impression that while he had wanted action, the army was happy to waste time to-ing and fro-ing, so causing the navy to 'loiter away' it's time for '19 days to no purpose'. The need for the commanders to support each other in this joint enterprise is missing from his letters to the Admiralty: 'I am at last honoured with a letter from the General informing me that he has *given over all thoughts of attacking the enemy* [my emphasis]'. At no point did he mention that Clinton had ridden from New York to Gardiner's Island for a meeting agreed with Arbuthnot, but which the Admiral failed to attend; nor does he indicate that he intended to give only limited support to the army, as spelt out to Captain Savage. However, keen to return home, he took the opportunity to give the First Lord the impression that it was his wish to be at the enemy.

> In the meantime the French certainly mean to leave Rhode Island immediately they are watered; [...] and every move of theirs indicates a sudden departure. Judge then, my Lord, of my anxiety! I have been out in the Sound since the 16th, at anchor, becalmed, and fogs three days, in the moment when I have it from all quarters that the enemy will certainly sail the first wind; if I can but reach the south side of Nantucket Shoal, *I think they will be lucky to escape unless a fog intervenes* [my emphasis].[57]

Maybe the French were lucky, but Arbuthnot had no engagement with their fleet.

Joint operations are the occasions when the navy is most closely involved in providing support to the army. The poor relationship between Clinton and Arbuthnot could only be detrimental to the war effort, and it had now become obvious to those they worked with, as well as to ministers in London. It was Clinton's view that, among all his other problems, he had no 'admiral that I can have the least dependence on'.[58] Both commanders were minded to resign and go home: Arbuthnot on health grounds – 'The constant fatigue of this complicated command both of body and mind is almost too much for me;'[59] Clinton because he was not receiving the reinforcements he was asking for, and so felt that he was not being listened to. Sandwich was disingenuous in his reply to Arbuthnot, on the one hand offering false praise, while on the other pointing out how badly the relationship between the commanders was working: 'It is however much to be

---

56   SP, Vol.3, pp.249–250, Arbuthnot to Sandwich, 20 August 1780.
57   SP, Vol.3, p.249, Arbuthnot to Sandwich, 20 August 1780.
58   Bowler, *Logistics*, p.137.
59   SP, Vol.3, p.250, Arbuthnot to Sandwich, 20 August 1780.

lamented that the differences existing between yourself and the commander in chief of the army *exceedingly endanger the service*, and make it absolutely impossible to continue this important business under the same direction [my emphasis]'.[60] As it was 'evident that you and he cannot serve together', the proposal was to move Sir Peter Parker from Jamaica, as he had 'passed the usual time' for service on that station, and replace him with Arbuthnot. Given that the admiral was not of an aggressive nature, it seems odd that the First Lord would consider putting him in the West Indies, which had replaced North America as the main British priority of the war. Sandwich gave a blunt summary of the situation in his letter to Sir Peter Parker, explaining the reason for his replacement: 'The fact upon which this proposed arrangement is founded is the state of things in America between Sir Henry Clinton and Admiral Arbuthnot, who are under such violent animosities against each other that the very important service entrusted to them, and on which the fate of this kingdom very probably depends, cannot go on under their joint command'.[61] It was also the First Lord's intention, by removing Arbuthnot, to remove a possible excuse that Clinton might want to use for the campaign going wrong: '[A]t the same time, it has been thought for the good of the King's service to take away from him the pretext of saying the campaign was thrown away by our keeping the command at sea in the hands of a person with whom he [Clinton] was at the utmost variance'.

Whatever problems Arbuthnot might have thought he had as naval commander on the North American station, they were about to get worse. Admiral Rodney, having heard that the French were at Rhode Island, took the unprecedented step of deciding to sail to New York and make himself Commander-in-Chief over Arbuthnot. Rodger makes the point that since the 1740s the North American waters had been divided into 'stations', each with its own commander: 'there was neither precedent nor possible justification in his orders for a commander-in-chief to abandon his own station to occupy another'.[62] Rodney and his 10 ships of the line arrived, unannounced, at Sandy Hook on 14 September 1780. Based on intelligence he had received, Rodney believed that Arbuthnot stood the risk of being 'overpowered' by the French: 'This consideration determined me to prevent so dire an accident if possible [and he was sure that] your Lordship and the rest of his Majesty's Ministers would approve the conduct of an officer who had no other view than his Majesty's and the public service'.[63] Immediately following his arrival at Sandy Hook, Rodney sent five ships to reinforce Arbuthnot at Newport,

60   SP, Vol.3, p.256, Sandwich to Arbuthnot, 16 October 1780.
61   SP, Vol.3, p.257, Sandwich to Parker, 16 October 1780.
62   Rodger, *Command of the Ocean*, p.346.
63   SP, Vol.3, p.253, Rodney to Sandwich, 10 October 1780.

and set about planning an attack on Rhode Island. However, by this time Clinton (having had his disagreements with Arbuthnot) favoured expeditions along the Hudson and was less supportive of Rodney's ideas. Once again, with no overall Commander-in-Chief with authority over the land and sea forces, the two arms were not brought together in one military plan. It had not taken Rodney long to recognise that Clinton and Arbuthnot were at odds with each other: 'I flattered myself I was come in time to attack Rhode Island; but am sorry to say the happy moment of destroying the French squadron had been lost, owing to the unhappy differences between the two commanders in chief [...] When commanders in chief differ, how much do nations suffer; it is their duty to agree'.[64]

In his letter to the First Lord, Rodney had stated that his presence at New York had 'had a most salutary effect'. He may have brought his authoritative personality, but all he did was cause chaos within the command structure. Rodney was an Admiral, and so had seniority over Vice-Admiral Arbuthnot, but his station was the Leeward Islands, not New York. The stage was set for a conflict of wills that would do nothing to further Britain's cause in America, and in which Arbuthnot's character was not likely to prevail against Rodney's. On arrival at New York Rodney let Arbuthnot know who was going to be in charge: 'You are hereby required and directed to put yourself under my command, and follow such orders as you may from time to time receive from me [...]'[65] At a time when the admiral and vice-admiral should have been concentrating their attentions on attacking the French at Newport, or supporting Clinton's plans for action on the Hudson, their energies were dissipated on disputes over seniority. Even Arbuthnot, in a letter to Sandwich, recognised that nothing positive was coming of it: 'I believe I may safely pronounce that in no one instance has the conduct of Sir George Rodney been conducive to his Majesty's service, notwithstanding the powers he has assumed and exercised on this station'.[66] Even the sending of ships by Rodney to allow Arbuthnot to have numerical superiority over de Ternay at Newport was a cause for argument between them. Arbuthnot complained to Sandwich that the 'hazarding [of] three capital ships cannot well be accounted for' given the prevailing weather during the 'autumnal equinox' and that their resulting storm damage would cause supply problems: 'I am apprehensive Sir George will be under the necessity of making use of our supplies, which I have been husbanding with a parental attention, therefore must affect me the more to find that after all my care the service has ultimately profited but little'.[67] In this one sentence, he indicates

64 SP, Vol.3, pp.253–254, Rodney to Sandwich, 10 October 1780.
65 Macintyre, *Rodney*, p.151.
66 SP, Vol.3, p.259, Arbuthnot to Sandwich, 11 November 1780.
67 SP, Vol.3, p.260, Arbuthnot to Sandwich, 11 November 1780.

the difference in character between himself and Rodney: the latter will risk the storms to get at the enemy, Arbuthnot is concerned to husband stores. From his station on board *Royal Oak*, watching the French at Newport, Arbuthnot paints himself as the more active commander, wronged by a senior: '[W]hilst I am at a distance pursuing the line of my duty to the best of my abilities, another warm in port and in the possession of comfortable ease deprives me of the privileges of my command'.

For all his bluster, Arbuthnot's attempts to do his 'duty' did not bring the French to combat, although Rodney believed his 13 ships of the line were 'fully sufficient' to that purpose. Rodney may have assumed command over Arbuthnot but he had left it 'entirely to you, Sir, how to dispose of that Squadron as to answer so desirable an End'.[68] Rodney's intention that he 'would be the Admiral' had no positive impact on the war in North America, or the navy's support of the troops. He had asserted his authority, one he had taken upon himself, and humiliated Arbuthnot, but he needed to return to the Leeward station. Before sailing he sent a letter to Clinton with a final comment on the vice-admiral: 'God bless you and send me from this Cold Country, and from such men as Arbuthnot'.[69] Prior to leaving Sandy Hook on 15 November Rodney gave his opinion on the conduct of the war in America: 'I must freely confess that there appears to me a slackness inconceivable in every branch of it; and that briskness and activity which is so necessary, and ought to animate the whole and bring it to a speedy conclusion, has entirely forsaken it'.[70]

As the first chapters of this book indicated, the issues facing the British Army in North America were not all concerned with bringing the enemy to battle. On a more mundane level the troops had to be supplied with equipment and food, and that had to be addressed whatever the arguments between admirals and generals. Through 1779 and 1780, the supply situation became increasingly serious, and there was no one cause which, if fixed, would remedy the situation. As we have seen with the evacuation of Philadelphia, it was not only the soldiers that had to be fed; there were also the Loyalists and refugees attached to the army and looking to it for succour. Sending all the provisions in just two large convoys every year meant that any delay in sailing would affect a huge number of rations. Could they not be sent in more frequent, smaller convoys? In September 1780, the Treasury requested the Navy Board '[T]o form some Plan and arrange and settle some Mode with the Lords of the Admiralty for more effectually sending out such Supplies in future, as may prevent any Disaster happening to the Troops for want

68   Macintyre, *Rodney*, p.153.
69   Syrett, *American Waters*, p.159.
70   SP, Vol.3, p.262, Rodney to Sandwich, 15 November 1780.

of Provisions, and any such similar inconveniences as are now Represented to have arisen'.[71] The proposal for more frequent convoys, escorted by armed vessels, was approved in October 1780. But, as previously noted, the biggest problem was a shortage of tonnage in which to transport the victuals, often because ships were retained in America after their dispatch from Britain. In July 1780, Clinton, who 'deluged the authorities' with complaints at the lack of logistical support he was receiving was directed to, 'pay strictest attention to the speedy dispatch and return of victualling transports'.[72] The Commissioners of the Navy had written on this topic to the Treasury in strong terms:

> We must [...] represent in the most serious manner [...] the necessity of directing the Commanding Officer of the Troops at different Stations abroad not to detain upon any account longer than shall be absolutely necessary, the transports employed in carrying the Provisions for the use of the Army [...] We must repeat and desire of having this measure as much enforced as possible.[73]

While Clinton might complain to London about the shortage of provisions, he and Arbuthnot must bear some responsibility for the problem because of their tardiness in returning ships after they had been unloaded. Clinton blamed the admiral for not providing convoys; the latter blamed the general for not having them unloaded promptly. Once again, their personal differences were affecting operations, and they were not going unnoticed. In September 1780, Captain Walter Young wrote to Charles Middleton, the Comptroller: 'I am exceedingly sorry to find such disagreements here between our land and sea officers. The army will be much distressed for provisions by some ridiculous conduct; your victuallers lay here empty for near six months, and the admiral would give no convoy because he had no admiralty orders on that head'.[74]

Sometimes the ships were held back because of a shortage of warehousing for the provisions at the ports in America. Fires at New York in 1776 and 1778, which the British had grounds to believe had been set by the Rebels, had destroyed the warehouses and as a consequence, transport vessels were used in their stead. This meant that the ships were lost to the victualling convoys and the provisions deteriorated more quickly by prolonged storage in ships' hulls. Whatever the reasons for the retention of vessels, the effect was serious for Clinton and his troops.

---

71 Syrett, *Shipping and the American War*, p.159.
72 Syrett, *Shipping and the American War*, p.162.
73 TNA, T 64/200, f.95.
74 Syrett, *Shipping and the American War*, p.170.

The contracts for the provisions for 1780 would have been let in 1779, according to the processes outlined in Chapter 3, and should have arrived in spring and summer of 1780. However, the various delays meant that no provisions arrived in New York until November 1780. The seriousness of the situation was stressed to Sandwich in a letter in September 1780: 'My Lord – The state of the provisions in America is much more serious than I could have imagined; and if any misfortune should attend the *Charon*'s convoy, or the present one lose the advantage of the first change of wind, the army will be in great danger'.[75] The Treasury had handed over responsibility for the transport of army provisions to the Navy Board in 1779, and the situation did improve through 1781 and into 1782, but by that time, the war was effectively over.

The naval support for the army had worked well during the siege of Charleston, in spite of the growing differences between Clinton and Arbuthnot. In the subsequent months, the change of focus of the war from America to the Caribbean, Gibraltar, and home waters caused the navy to direct its attentions to these theatres. As part of the reassessment of priorities, ships were withdrawn from American waters, further reducing the effectiveness of the economic blockade of the colonies. With the need to stretch the limited resources of the navy following the entry of France into the war, and the slow mobilisation of Britain's main defence against invasion, the Admiralty needed to appoint its best admirals to the command of squadrons that were 3,000 miles from the centre of government. Unfortunately, that did not happen and personal animosities took on a much greater importance than they should have, to the detriment of the war effort. With Rodney's departure from New York for the Caribbean our narrative moves to 1781, the capture of St Eustatius, and the denouement at Yorktown.

---

75   SP, Vol.4, p.369, comptroller to Sandwich, 29 September 1780.

12

'Oh God! It is all over'

1781 began with Admiral Rodney back in the West Indies. Clinton was still struggling with supply issues in New York, Cornwallis was making his way through the Carolinas, and in Gibraltar the garrison was still under siege and in need of further relief. On 1 January, the decision was made to send another convoy to the Rock under the command of Vice-Admiral George Darby. These orders were to have consequences, months later, for the war in America. Darby was in command of the Channel Fleet and had maintained a blockade off Brest until he had to take his ships home for refit on 21 December 1780 – ships kept continuously at sea through the autumn storms off Brest could suffer a great deal from storm damage. The victuallers for Gibraltar were being prepared at Cork, though this was delayed (as so often) by a shortage of ships returned from America. When his refit was completed, Darby took the advantage of a suitable wind to sail for Cork, hoping to collect the victuallers and make sail for Gibraltar. However the winds around Ireland were not in his favour 'and ten more days were lost in sight of the bleak hills of County Cork' before the transports joined him at sea.[1] The relief of Gibraltar was a priority which 'ought to be undertaken [...] but we [the Admiralty] were well aware that many other important services must be sacrificed to this very necessary measure'.[2] Darby sailed with 28 sail of the line escorting 97 cargo ships with provisions for the Rock.[3] The escort of warships was believed to be necessary because the British had received intelligence to say that the Spanish had 32 sail of the line, 'waiting with a determined resolution to dispute our entrance into the Straits'.[4] As the memorandum drawn up by the Admiralty and laid before the House of Lords stated, 'Therefore Admiral Darby had two of the greatest

1   Mackesy, *America*, p.389.
2   SP, Vol.4, p.347, memorandum, 18 February 1782.
3   O. Rutter, *Red Ensign: A History of Convoy* (London: Hale, 1942), p.80.
4   SP, Vol.4, p.347, memorandum, 18 February 1782.

objects in view that this country had to wish for, namely, the relief of Gibraltar and the bringing the fleet of Spain to a decisive action'.[5] The Spanish fleet did not materialise and the convoy made its way unmolested to Gibraltar, arriving on 12 April 1781. When they hove into view the sight of the fleet was described by an ensign of the 72nd Regiment, garrisoned on the Rock, as 'one of the most beautiful and pleasing scenes it is possible to conceive'.[6]

Although the garrison had been relieved, the sailing of Darby had consequences for the troops in North America. By escorting the convoy, Darby's ships could not cover the French port of Brest with the result that a French fleet had put to sea unopposed by the British Navy. The Comte de Grasse had been given command of the French fleet in the West Indies, *Chef d'Escadre* Suffren the East Indies, and *Chef d'Escadre* de Barras at Rhode Island. On 22 March 1781 de Grasse (20 ships of the line, including the 104-gun *Ville de Paris*) and Suffren (five ships of the line) sailed from Brest with a large convoy.[7] One week later Suffren and his squadron separated from de Grasse, while de Barras sailed from Brest for Rhode Island on 26 March. Writing after the event, the Admiralty's memorandum sought to excuse the navy for de Grasse's exit from Brest: 'Allowing therefore that the succouring Gibraltar and the hopes of bringing the Spanish fleet to action were measures to which other services must give way, nothing could be done to prevent M. de Grasse's going to his destination'.[8] However, the writer did acknowledge that things might have been done differently: 'But possibly it may be said that, as the relief of Gibraltar was a business which we had long foreseen, we ought to have been prepared in time, and have had our victuallers ready to have sailed from Spithead with Admiral Darby, by which a long delay in his getting to the Straits would have been avoided'. The excuse was that as the loading of the transports was absolutely necessary they had to await 'the return of a large number of transports from foreign parts'. One historian summed up the result in stark terms: 'while Darby's convoy sailed to save Gibraltar, across the Atlantic Britain lost America'.[9] Nevertheless, had there been different personalities commanding the British naval forces on the American and Caribbean stations, the events at Yorktown may well have been different. That is not the same as saying that America would not have been lost to the Crown. As long as Britain (through the King) insisted that Americans would not be granted independence, a British army was not going to be able to subdue that continent.

5   SP, Vol.4, p.347, memorandum, 18 February 1782.
6   Adkins, *Gibraltar,* p.187.
7   Trew, *Rodney,* p.92.
8   SP, Vol.4, p.347, memorandum, 18 February 1782.
9   Adkins, *Gibraltar,* p.185.

While de Grasse was making his way across the Atlantic and Rodney was involved with St Eustatius (of which more later), ground and naval forces were occupied in America. In his last letter to Sandwich before leaving Sandy Hook for the Caribbean, Rodney had made some suggestions based on his assessment of the situation in the colonies. Rodney proposed that Portsmouth, which 'commands the Chesapeake', should be taken as a military post. It had been occupied previously and the people had shown loyalty to the Crown but this had been poorly rewarded: 'by showing their loyalty, they were made a sacrifice to the rebels when his Majesty's troops evacuated that post'.[10] In Rodney's opinion, the Chesapeake was an ideal place for Arbuthnot's ships: 'I know no post in America where the squadron under Mr Arbuthnot (which he is ordered to keep with him in the winter months) can shelter themselves, but in the Chesapeake; or where the stationing a squadron would be more detrimental to his Majesty's rebellious subjects'. To implement Rodney's suggestion would require that the British occupied either Portsmouth or Norfolk, 'without which the squadron stationed in the Chesapeake would find it extremely difficult to get fresh water'. The first steps were being taken towards the later events at Yorktown.

As sometimes happens in time of war, a senior member of one side defects to the other; Benedict Arnold left the American side for the British and became a brigadier-general in that army. He is still reviled in America for having turned coat (Brumwell's *Turncoat* gives an excellent account of Arnold's actions). As Rodney had pointed out to Sandwich, the British ought to reoccupy Portsmouth on the James River. To that end, Clinton sent Arnold with about 1,800 troops to take the town, leaving Sandy Hook on 20 December and arriving at Hampton Roads on the 30th. A feature of the war was the tendency of the British to garrison posts that were many miles apart and so, unable to provide mutual support, they were totally reliant on the navy; Clinton was in New York, Cornwallis was moving through the Carolinas towards Virginia, and Arbuthnot was at Gardiner's Bay, on the northern tip of Long Island. Germain was critical of this piecemeal approach by Clinton, as he made clear in a letter to the general '[T]he war should be conducted upon a permanent and settled plan of conquest, always securing and preserving what has been recovered, and not by desultory enterprises, taking possession of places at one time, and abandoning them at another, which can never bring the war to a conclusion [...]'.[11]

Arnold's isolated force was at some risk from the French squadron at Newport, Rhode Island – these ships were now commanded by *Capitaine de Vaisseau* Destouches following the death of de Ternay on 15 December 1780. Throughout

10   SP, Vol.3, p.263, Rodney to Sandwich, 15 November 1780.
11   Mackesy, *America*, p.403.

the first two months of 1781, Clinton (in New York) and Arbuthnot (in Gardiner's Bay) attempted, by letter, to formulate a strategic plan for the continued conduct of the war. Given their mutual antagonism, it is not surprising that each misunderstood the other, and they were left reacting to French moves. On 19 February 1781, Washington had dispatched 1,200 Continentals under Major-General Lafayette to Virginia,[12] where they reached the head of the Elk River on 8 March. If French ships were in the Chesapeake then Arnold's force would be cut off. On 10 March, Arbuthnot learned from his frigates that the French had left Rhode Island. To avoid detection by the British, and to confuse them as to his destination, Destouches sailed due east from Newport before changing course for the Chesapeake. On the 12th Arbuthnot spoke with a merchant ship bound for New York 'who informed me that the day before he was chased by one of the French fleet consisting of ten sail of large ships, and that they were at this time 24 leagues to the southward of us'.[13] If he was to assist the British troops at Portsmouth, he needed to make all haste to the Chesapeake to arrive 'so close after them as to put it out of their power to accomplish their machinations'. On 16 March, the two fleets engaged off Cape Henry after a certain amount of manoeuvring to gain the weather gauge. Once again, the result was less than might have been expected. Destouches battered the British ships but failed to take advantage by entering the Chesapeake; Arbuthnot failed to give clear signals to his captains with the result that his ships did not give a general chase. As one historian summed it up, 'the French outmanoeuvred and outfought the British'.[14] However, Destouches failed to enter the bay and Arbuthnot, by preventing him from doing so, won the strategic victory and saved Arnold's force from being trapped by Lafayette's troops and French ships. The British admiral, in his subsequent letter to Sandwich, claimed to have been in time 'to save both Mr Arnold's forces here and also Lord Cornwallis'. The second part of his claim is more dubious. The King was certainly less than totally convinced by the action: 'I was much hurt that the action had ended without any advantage in our favour but the retreat of the French squadron. [...] Yet it has saved the troops under the command of Arnold [...]'[15] In his reply to Arbuthnot, Sandwich also alludes to the fact that the 'victory' was less than complete, especially as the French had been able to escape.

> I most sincerely congratulate you upon the defeat of the French fleet. I am convinced that everything that could be done to make the action more

12 Syrett, *American Waters*, p.166.
13 SP, Vol.4, p.167, Arbuthnot to Sandwich, 30 March 1781.
14 Syrett, *American Waters*, p.169.
15 SP, Vol.4, pp.171–172, King to Sandwich, 24 April 1781.

decisive was done on your part, and I am much obliged to you for the detail you give me in your private letter, which clearly shows the cause to which the enemy owe their escape.[16]

The French did not enter the Chesapeake, but neither was their fleet 'defeated'. Arbuthnot now slips from our narrative and on 4 July Rear-Admiral Thomas Graves took over command of the navy in North America.

With the benefit of hindsight, there is a whiff of inevitability about the way events moved towards the British surrender at Yorktown in 1781. As a result of America becoming a 'secondary consideration' in the war (after the entry of the French), troops and ships were drawn off to other stations. The relief of Gibraltar was prioritised over the speedy reinforcement of the navy in American waters, with the result that the French fleet sailed from Brest; Arbuthnot and Clinton could not work together, and the admiral did not fight his ships aggressively when the opportunity presented itself; and Arbuthnot handed over command to Admiral Graves in time for him 'to fight and lose one of the decisive battles in history'.[17] The relationship between the two army commanders, Clinton and Cornwallis, was also poor by this time. The result was poor communications between them at the time that Cornwallis was fighting his way through the Carolinas into Virginia and to the final act at Yorktown.

In November 1780, Rodney left New York, having given his views on the prosecution of the war to Sandwich, and arrived in the Caribbean in late December, many of his ships having suffered storm damage on the way. As we have already seen, Rodney's style was abrasive and on his arrival he demanded priority for the repair of his ships; as Willis stated, he 'wielded his seniority like a boarding axe'[18] to ensure that he got what he wanted. As Commander-in-Chief on the station, Rodney needed a second-in-command, but that could be a difficult appointment to fill, as many of the possible candidates would have been aware of the admiral's reputation. In a letter to Rodney, Sandwich pointed out to him that 'It has been difficult, very difficult, to find out proper flag officers to serve under you'[19] and while Sandwich gave some of the reasons, he avoided the tricky subject of the admiral's reputation. Admiral Drake was approached to take the position but his reply to Sandwich stated that 'the shattered condition of my constitution prevents my eager acceptance of your Lordship's kind offer';[20] in today's parlance that sounds like a 'thanks, but no thanks'. Rear-Admiral Samuel Hood, then in

16   SP, Vol.4, p.172, Sandwich to Arbuthnot, 1 May 1781.
17   Syrett, *American Waters*, p.184.
18   Willis, *Sea Power*, p.413.
19   SP, Vol.3, p.232, Sandwich to Rodney, 25 September 1780.
20   SP, Vol.3, p.227, Drake to Sandwich, 22 August 1780.

charge of Portsmouth dockyard, when first approached, turned down the offer on health grounds, but then reconsidered only two days later:

> Feeling myself so much better than I was on Saturday, […] and flattering myself that a warm climate will tend more towards removing my complaints than any assistance I can get at home, I hope and trust that I am not too late in signifying my very great readiness to accept my flag and to go to the West Indies at your Lordship's pleasure.[21]

Sandwich believed that he had selected one of the few men 'that might actually get on with Rodney'. As it would turn out, Hood was very critical of his commander's control of the later action against de Grasse off Martinique and of his behaviour over the sacking of St Eustatius. Something may have happened between the two men to cause Hood to write as badly of Rodney as he did; Willis states that his letters were 'full of bile',[22] while Macintyre's biography of Rodney has Hood 'taking every opportunity to blacken his character in private, while professing friendship to Rodney's face'.[23] Hood knew what Rodney's reputation was; he had sailed with him twice in his early career, and he had returned a second time to accept the offer from Sandwich to give up Portsmouth and sail as Rodney's second-in-command. Unfortunately the relationship between them did sour (particularly on Hood's side), with effects that would influence subsequent events in America. Early in January 1781, Hood arrived with eight ships of the line, four frigates and more than 100 merchantmen and storeships to replenish empty food stores. The fleet available to Rodney had now grown to 21 ships.

When the Admiralty informed Lord Howe that America had become of only secondary importance in the war the Caribbean was one of the theatres that deposed it. The sugar islands were vital to Britain's economy and the British planters and merchants, because of their wealth, had enormous influence in London. One of those islands was St Eustatius, 'the entrepôt of the Caribbean'.[24] The island was Dutch and as long as Holland was neutral in the war the merchants felt relatively sure that their trade would continue unmolested; any interference with shipping to the island stood the risk of drawing Holland, another maritime nation, into the war against Britain. While Britain wished to avoid a war with the Dutch, the greater need was to prevent Dutch ships from transporting naval stores

21 SP, Vol.3, p.229, Hood to Sandwich, 18 September 1780.
22 Willis, *Sea Power, p.438.*
23 Macintyre, *Rodney,* p.165.
24 R. Cock, "'Avarice and Rapacity" and "Treasonable Correspondence" in "an Emporium for All the World": the British capture of St Eustatius, 1781', *Mariner's Mirror*, 103:3 (Aug. 2018), p.266.

to French ports. In the summer of 1780, the Northern Powers had come together in the League of Armed Neutrality to open French and Spanish ports to naval stores from the Baltic.[25] Holland had not joined, but was expected to, and Britain could not afford to allow Holland to continue its trade in Baltic products with France and Spain. Britain needed the Dutch to provide a pretext that would allow them to open hostilities with Holland before that country joined the League; if they took action after Holland joined, Britain would also find itself at war with the other Northern Powers. The pretext was the British capture of a ship containing documents that had evidence of negotiations between the American Congress and Holland; as the ostensible issue was not neutral rights, 'the League refused its help to the Dutch'. By virtue of a fast British sloop, the *Childers*, the news of the Dutch war reached Rodney and Major-General Vaughan in the West Indies before it got to St Eustatius. The ship also carried orders for Rodney and Vaughan, which they received on 27 January 1781, to mount amphibious operations against St Eustatius. The island had been a thorn in the British side ever since France had joined the war, we have already seen (Chapter 11) that Sandwich was convinced that a large percentage of provisions from Britain found their way, via that island, to French stomachs. The governor of the Leeward Islands made a similar point to Germain in May 1780: '[N]otwithstanding every effort to prevent it, a clandestine Trade has been carried on from that Government [Dutch] to St Eustatius which has much supplied the French Settlements and vessels frequently arrive at St Eustatius cleared out from the Isle of Wight and Cork'.[26]

Frustrating as it was to see British provisions diverted to French use, the Caribbean Islands were also of importance to the American colonies as much of their raw materials and other goods came through them. Rodney was particularly galled by a trade that he could see going on, but (prior to the instructions from London) felt himself unable to stop, and in which he believed British merchants were heavily involved. After capturing the island, he wrote to the Admiralty:

> I am fully convinced our possessing St Eustatius will be the means of cutting off entirely the Enemy from supplies in this part of the World as well as securing our Government against the Treasonable Practices of such as calling themselves subjects of Great Britain and availing themselves of her protection, have had the opportunity of proving themselves the most pernicious of our Enemies.[27]

25   Mackesy, *America*, pp.377–379.
26   K. Breen, 'Sir George Rodney and St Eustatius in the American War: a commercial and naval distraction, 1775–1781', *Mariner's Mirror*, 84:2 (1998), p.194.
27   Breen, 'St Eustatius', p.194.

The first that the islanders knew of the war between Britain and Holland was the arrival of Rodney and his ships (with Vaughan and his troops) on 3 February 1781. There was no real resistance other than a single broadside – for form's sake – from the Dutch 32-gun frigate *Mars*. It was only when the British arrived that they appreciated the full scale of the trade taking place between the island and the colonies. Riding at anchor in the roadstead (the island had no harbour) were about 130 merchant vessels in various stages of loading and unloading, together with five American privateers.[28] Warehouses were stuffed with American produce for Europe and European goods for sale to America. As Rodney described it to his wife, 'All the magazines and store-houses are filled, and even the beach covered with tobacco and sugar'.[29] The taking of the island had been both quick and successful and as Rodney put in his letter to Sandwich, 'It must be felt, and severely, in all their [the enemy's] provinces'.[30] The booty was enormous, 'beyond conception;' it was in Rodney's opinion 'the richest island in the world'. For the admiral, this must have looked like a godsend, a way to rid himself of his many debts. Unusually, he and Vaughan decided to split the proceeds of the naval and army captures equally between the two services; they had the potential to become wealthy men. From the point of view of the war in America, the navy had cut off a vital supply line to the American troops but there would be other less beneficial consequences in the months ahead.

Rodney's reputation for avarice and bad debts had almost cost him the post, with Sandwich having had to vouch for him to the King. The size of the prize money available to Rodney and Vaughan was on a scale that was going to distract a man with his financial problems. On the pretext of trying to untangle the 'complicated web of neutral, British and enemy property',[31] he stayed on the island for three months, for which he was later criticised. That, however, was the least of his troubles. The merchants took him to court on the grounds that he had no right to act as he did, and the convoy taking the booty to Britain was captured by the French before it reached a British port. Unfortunately for the war in America, Rodney's distraction – it held him 'like a magnet'[32] – had operational consequences that contributed to Cornwallis's surrender at Yorktown.

Earlier in the chapter we noted that de Grasse had sailed from Brest (while Darby's convoy was *en route* for Gibraltar), but his destination was unknown; it could have been North America or the West Indies. Unaware of when the French might sail and to prevent himself being surprised if de Grasse took the latter

28   Cock, 'St Eustatius', p.266.
29   Cock, 'St Eustatius', p.267.
30   SP, Vol.4, p.148, Rodney to Sandwich, 7 February 1781.
31   Cock, *St Eustatius*, p.277.
32   Mackesy, *America*, p.417.

course, Rodney positioned Hood to windward of Martinique on 12 February. By 17 March, no French fleet had been seen so Hood was ordered to move to leeward of the island to cover Fort Royal, a move that Hood disagreed with as he felt that his ships and men needed to refit and recoup in port. The ships were short of fresh provisions and, even worse, scurvy had broken out. Rodney was not moved by the arguments and wanted Hood to cover the French ships at Fort Royal: 'However, the blockading of Martinique becomes now highly Necessary, and I am convinced by your Cruizing off Fort Royal it will be impossible for him [the French] to escape an Action should he come [...]'[33] Unaware of the criticism Hood was to level at his commander, Rodney signed off the letter 'Adieu, my Dear Old Friend'. With the near parity in numbers of ships, the British would have an opportunity to defeat the French fleet in the Caribbean, but only if the ships and men were used appropriately and if the commander had that as his fixed aim; the criticism of Rodney was that his mind was taken up with securing the safe return of the St Eustatius booty. Hood, as well as needing time in port for his ships and crews, strongly disagreed with the decision to position him to leeward of Martinique, watching Fort Royal, and tried one last time to persuade his chief.

> I most humbly beg leave to suggest, with all due submission to your better and more enlightened judgement, whether it would not be more advisable, when the whole of the very respectable force you have done me the honour to commit to my charge are watered, stored, victualled and collected together, *that it be stationed to windward*, with a proper number of frigates to look out. The chance would be abundantly more in my favour for effectually crushing any squadron of the enemy coming to Martinique, than by cruizing before Fort Royal [...] [my emphasis].[34]

That chance did come Hood's way on 29 April, but while he was still to leeward; 'I had a *long-shot* action on the 29th of last month, in sight of Fort Royal, with twenty-three sail of the line (to my eighteen)'. At a numerical disadvantage, and with 'near 2,000 men' sick, 'I thought it my duty to bear up, and made the signal at eight o'clock. I never once lost sight of getting to windward, but it was totally impossible'. The odds, as well as the wind, were against Hood but his constant criticism of Rodney for sending him to leeward of Martinique has been interpreted as a foil to deflect attention from the fact that he had not brought the French to a decisive engagement. Hood's comment on Rodney's motive was scathing: 'But

---

33   Macintyre, *Rodney*, p.171.
34   Enclosure, extract of a letter from Hood to Rodney, 1 April 1781, NRS, *Letters of Lord Hood, 1781–1783*, vol.3 (1895), p.17.

doubtless there never was a squadron so unmeaningly stationed as the one under my command, and what was Sir George Rodney's motive for it could be I cannot conceive, *unless it was to cover him at St Eustatius* [my emphasis]'.[35] The implication of Hood's letter is that Rodney had put personal interests before those of the navy and his country.

Over the next three months, the opposing fleets followed each other around the Caribbean with an opportunity for a fleet action presenting itself off Tobago in early June. Once again the French had the numbers – 24 of the line and five frigates against the British with 20 of the line – and 'for once the British held the weather gauge'.[36] However, Rodney, given the proximity of the Grenadines and the dangers of an action close to a lee-shore, did not press and the French slipped away. Once again, Hood was critical of Rodney in a letter to George Jackson, Deputy Secretary at the Admiralty.

> It is quite impossible from the unsteadiness of the commander-in-chief to know what he means three days together; [...] The truth is I believe he is guided by his feelings on the moment he is speaking, and that his mind is not at present at ease, thinking if he quits the command he will get to England at a time that many mouths perhaps may be opened against him on the top of Tobago, and his not fighting the French fleet off that island after the public declarations he made to every one of his determined resolution to do it; and again, if he stays much longer, his laurels may be subject to wither.[37]

Before there could be any withering of Rodney's laurels, events in the Caribbean moved on a step and forced some decisions to be made. In early July, Rodney and Hood learned of the sailing of de Grasse's squadron from Fort Royal. Although its destination was not known, North America had to be a strong possibility. Rodney was in a quandary over what to do; he was aware that Arbuthnot was vacating the command in New York and his replacement, Thomas Graves, was not really the man for the job. Aware that he needed to send ships to reinforce the New York squadron, the question was should he go himself, or should he send Hood? Had he sailed, he would have assumed command in North America, but he knew that Hood would be second to Graves. In the end, he decided that he was too ill and drew up orders for Hood to sail for New York. On 1 August, 'having the day before given up the command of his Majesty's fleet at the Leeward Islands to me

35   NRS, *Hood Papers*, p.15, Hood to Jackson, 21 May 1781.
36   Macintyre, *Rodney*, p.179.
37   NRS, *Hood Papers*, p.18, Hood to Jackson, 24 June 1781.

[Hood]',[38] Rodney sailed for England leaving Hood with only 14 of the original 22 ships of the line. Additionally, a fast ship was sent to warn Clinton and Graves that a French fleet was probably sailing for the American coast.

'At dawn of day' on 10 August Hood sailed from the West Indies, making a fast passage to Cape Henry (the ships all being copper-bottomed), which he reached on the 25th. From there he sent a note to Graves to let him know that he had arrived with his 14 ships. Unaware of the location of the French, he made the sensible decision to check the Chesapeake and Delaware and finding no enemy ships, he continued on to Sandy Hook, arriving on the morning of 28 August. At this point it is worth reviewing the British position in North America prior to Hood's arrival.

We left Cornwallis making his way through the Carolinas towards Virginia. With most of his march being inland, supplying his troops had been a problem, so it would have come as some relief to the men when they made their way into Wilmington, on the coast of North Carolina, to receive some fresh provisions from navy ships. On 25 April, Cornwallis left with some 1,500 men to begin the journey north. Clinton had not wanted Cornwallis to march into Virginia, he preferred that he stayed and ensured that the Carolinas were secure. Some years later Clinton wrote, 'How great was my disappointment and astonishment when I found he had come to the fatal resolution of abandoning both Carolinas to their fate and flying into Virginia'.[39] With both commanders playing a vital role in the ground war against the Americans, their lack of communication is, at least, surprising. The march north from Wilmington was not a pleasant one for Cornwallis and his men; food was short and when they did find grain, the water in the streams was too low for the mills to be able to grind the corn. On the way, men fell ill and when they reached Petersburg on 20 May, many were scarcely fit for duty.[40] Cornwallis' troops were not the only British force there; Benedict Arnold had been sent with 2,000 men, followed in March by British Major-General William Phillips with another 2,500 (he died of a fever a week before Cornwallis arrived), as well as 1,700 reinforcements sent by Clinton. Cornwallis, in Virginia in spite of Clinton's wish for him to be in the Carolinas, now had over 7,000 men in his command.[41]

Clinton may not have wanted Cornwallis in Virginia, but he had failed to exercise adequate control over his subordinate. He had sent the 1,700 reinforcements to Cornwallis, expecting him to use them to strengthen his position in the south; 'If

38   NRS, *Hood Papers*, p.24, Hood to Stephens, 30 August 1781.
39   Urban, *Fusiliers*, p.257.
40   Hibbert, *Redcoats and Rebels,* p.314.
41   Hibbert, *Redcoats and Rebels*, pp.314–315.

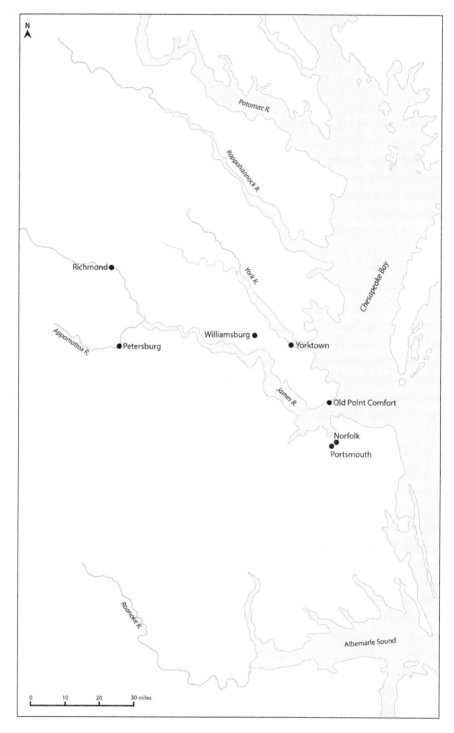

Map 9: Yorktown and Chesapeake Bay

he joins Phillips I shall tremble for every post except Charleston, and even for Georgia'.[42] In spite of that concern, he made no attempt to meet Cornwallis and insist on his own plans being followed by his subordinate. Cornwallis claimed not to have heard from his commander in some three months, and so he made his own choice to move north. In the words of one historian, 'Cornwallis's vanity and his aspirations drove him to insubordination, and to a destiny that included a rendezvous with ruination', while his commander 'acquiesced to what had transpired and left Cornwallis, and Britain's hopes in this war, to fate'.[43] Although Clinton did not want Cornwallis in Virginia, there were reasons for having troops there. Arnold and Phillips had been sent to establish a naval base at Portsmouth on the Elizabeth River, where it flows into the James. This would then be the base for raiding operations; it was also usefully situated at the mouth of the Chesapeake. Over the succeeding months, the British moved location between Portsmouth and various sites on the Williamsburg peninsula. In New York, Clinton and Arbuthnot were considering sending troops for an attack on the French at Rhode Island, for which they wanted Cornwallis to send men from Virginia. For his part, having no agreement from Clinton that he could launch offensive operations from his new base, Cornwallis (having taken command from Phillips and Arnold) had no alternative but to carry out the orders they had been given by Clinton; choose a base from which ships of the line could operate, which necessitated a move from Portsmouth to the Williamsburg peninsula. Old Point Comfort, on the southern tip of the peninsula, was Clinton's choice but that location was considered unsuitable by Cornwallis's engineers, and he decided on Yorktown, with another post on the opposite side of the York River at Gloucester. However, the defences on the landward side of Yorktown were inadequate and required a lot of heavy labouring to be done by Cornwallis's troops to put them in a position to resist the expected attack by a combined Franco–American force. The lines of fortification that had to be dug, along with redoubts for the guns, was estimated to take some six weeks and would be carried out during the heat of the Virginia summer. To add to their problems, provisions were unlikely to be available from the surrounding area and supply by sea would be problematic, given that the French fleet of de Grasse was off the American coast. Cornwallis was now in a vice. Clinton believed that he had to defend New York against the possibility of the Bourbons launching a serious attack against the city. Graves, who had taken command from Arbuthnot, had his ships within the Bar at Sandy Hook, and there were French ships at Rhode Island (de Barras sailed for Newport just after de Grasse left Brest in March). By the end of August, Washington, having left

42 Hibbert, *Redcoats and Rebels*, p.315.
43 Ferling, *Miracle*, p.510.

2,500 men to guard the Highlands, was marching south of Staten Island towards Princeton and Trenton[44] and Clinton would have been in no doubt that their aim was to hit Cornwallis. If ever the British Army in America needed effective naval support, it was now.

In the summer of 1781, the command of the navy in America was again bedevilled by the need to satisfy individual egos, rather than ensure that the right man was in the job. Rodney, for all his financial greed, had the aggressive spirit and assertiveness needed and was begged, unsuccessfully, by Sandwich to remain in post.[45] As it was, Thomas Graves was sent out to relieve Arbuthnot but, not having total faith in him, the Admiralty followed up by sending out Rear-Admiral Robert Digby, after Arbuthnot, to take eventual command. Digby sailed from home on 22 July and arrived off America at the critical time for Cornwallis and his troops but (as Willis states) 'refused to take over command. This was Graves's mess'.[46] Other historians are not as censorious as Willis is; Mackesy states that Digby 'agreed to serve for the time being under Graves'[47] (they were both rear-admirals), while Trew states that 'At Digby's invitation, Graves was again in command until completion of the business in hand'.[48] As well as Graves and Digby, Hood was also on station, having been sent by Rodney before the latter sailed home. As if the strategic challenges facing him were not enough, Graves was concerned with seniority; aware that Digby would be coming out to take command he wrote to tell Sandwich (on the day he took over from Arbuthnot) that he hoped 'it is not intended I should serve abroad in an inferior station after being superseded by a junior officer'.[49] In the eighteenth century, patronage was rife, and naval careers frequently rose and fell by whom an officer knew rather than competence. The various archives of this war hold many examples and Graves was but another among many. The Admiral was a friend of the Prime Minister, Lord North, who wrote to Sandwich on his behalf regarding the appointment of Digby, and what job might be available to Graves after he was superseded.

> Before Admiral Digby sails I cannot help mentioning once more a subject on which I have already had some conversations with you. All the friends of Admiral Graves, and all mine who are acquainted with the circumstances of the case, consider the superseding of him by Admiral Digby as disgraceful to him, and not very honourable for me, unless he

44   Ferling, *Miracle*, p.526.
45   Mackesy, *America*, p.393.
46   Willis, *Sea Power*, p.455.
47   Mackesy, *America*, p.425.
48   Trew, *Rodney*, p.124.
49   SP, Vol.4, p.175, Graves to Sandwich, 4 July 1781.

can be employed somewhere in a creditable manner. [...] I shall lose all political honour and consequence if, when a disgrace is to be suffered, my friend is chosen as the proper object of it. I wish you would consider this, and find some employment in some part of the world which may save the honour of Mr Graves and prevent me from falling into the most disgraceful and embarrassing situation possible.[50]

At a critical phase of the war (the relief of Cornwallis at Yorktown), and with the army so reliant on naval support, the command of that service was not being determined by competence but by precedence, seniority, and patronage.

In August 1781, Hood was approaching his *rendezvous* with Graves at Sandy Hook and Cornwallis was within the confines of Yorktown, which he began to fortify 'at a leisurely pace' owing to the heat and the sickness among his men. Until September 8, he was unaware of the approach of the combined armies of Rochambeau and Washington, who had marched some four hundred miles south from New York'.[51] When Hood arrived off New York – knowing that de Grasse had sailed for North America and not having seen him in the Delaware or the Chesapeake – he recognised that 'great delay and inconvenience might arise from going within the Hook with the squadron under my command'.[52] Hood could see that being 'over the Bar' at Sandy Hook, while a good defensive position, would make it problematic to get ships out to sea in a hurry. Graves's ships, however, were within the bar and at his first meeting with him Hood 'humbly submitted the necessity which struck me very forcibly, of such of Rear-Admiral Graves's squadron as were ready coming without the Bar immediately'. In other words, those of Graves's ships that were ready for sea should join Hood outside the bar. Graves 'readily acquiesced' and said they would be 'out the next day' the 29th: 'but for want of wind they [were] still within the Hook' on the 30th. At that time, Clinton and Graves were 'deliberating upon a plan of destroying the ships at Rhode Island'. Given that they had been warned on 25 August (by a schooner sent ahead by Hood to give notice of his impending arrival) of the sailing of de Grasse for North America, Graves might have been expected to have got his own ships over the Bar (before Hood's arrival) to be ready for any eventuality. Then, shortly after joining Hood, Graves received intelligence that de Barras had sailed from Rhode Island on 25 August and correctly guessed that he was probably aiming for the Chesapeake: 'A huge Franco–American trap was about to close on the

50   SP, Vol.4, p.208, Lord North to Sandwich, 14 July 1781.
51   O'Shaughnessy, *Men Who Lost America*, p.279.
52   NRS, *Hood Papers*, p.26, Hood to Stephens, 30 August 1781.

British in America, but Clinton and Graves, despite mountains of information about enemy movements, did not appear to see what was happening'.[53]

Washington's strategy in the closing months of the summer of 1781 was for Cornwallis to be trapped between the French fleet and his army. Lafayette was already at Williamsburg and was told by Washington that de Grasse was on his way and he should hold on and prevent the British from breaking out of Yorktown. Meanwhile, for Washington's plan to come together the ships of de Barras and de Grasse had to *rendezvous* in the Chesapeake and his troops had to march some 450 miles from the area of New York to Yorktown. Cornwallis, who had disembarked his men at Yorktown on 2 August after vacating Portsmouth, had been told to expect a strong British squadron to arrive between Yorktown and Gloucester by 5 October. In the next two and a half months, Cornwallis received a number of reassurances that efforts were being made to relieve him. Behind his earthworks, Cornwallis had a choice; stay or attempt to break out. In late August and early September, Cornwallis had a numerical advantage over the Americans as Washington and Rochambeau's troops had not then joined with Lafayette. He would have had to leave his sick and wounded behind at Yorktown, but he had a reasonable chance to escape. He decided not to – 'I do not think myself justifiable in putting the fate of the War on so desperate an Attempt'[54] – and, on 14 September, his decision was confirmed for him when he received a note from Clinton to say that 'the best way to relieve you, is to join you [...]'[55] As well as the reassuring notes from Clinton, he had supplies that would last him until 1 November; surely the British ships would arrive by then.

The British troops in Yorktown were now totally reliant on the navy, whose commanders would need to take bold action against the French fleet if the garrison was to be relieved. De Barras (with the siege guns and supplies for the expedition against Cornwallis) left Rhode Island on 25 August and, like Destouches in March, sailed east to avoid British ships, before setting course for the Chesapeake and a *rendezvous* with de Grasse. Having got his ships over the Bar at Sandy Hook, Graves (and Hood) 'proceeded together on 31st of August to the southward; my intention being to go to the Chesapeake, as the enemy's views would most probably be upon that part'.[56] The pieces were beginning to fall into place for the Battle of Virginia Capes between the British and French fleets off North America.

53 Syrett, *American Waters*, p.185.
54 Ferling, *Miracle,* p.530.
55 Ferling, *Miracle,* p.530.
56 NRS, *Hood Papers*, p.40, Graves to Stephens, 14 September 1781.

De Grasse, after sailing from the West Indies, reached the Chesapeake on 29 August. The British had expected him to leave some of his ships in the Caribbean before sailing north, but he had taken them all with him. After leaving one ship to keep watch on Yorktown, he entered the bay with 28 warships (once again, numbers vary from account to account). As Ferling states, he could have frustrated Graves by merely remaining in the bay and preventing the British ships from entering but that would have made it difficult for Barras (with the siege guns) to make it through Graves's ships and into the bay.[57] The French admiral elected to sail out and confront the British fleet. From the point of view of numbers, this would have been an easy decision, he had 24 ships (two ships of the line and a 50-gun ship were left to blockade Yorktown) to Graves's 19 and 500 more guns, but he would be vulnerable while exiting the bay. However, fighting strengths are not sufficient to determine the outcome of an engagement, as Syrett points out:

> Graves had nineteen ships of the line, one 50-gun ship, seven frigates, and one fireship. The British ships were fully manned and had copper bottoms, but some of them were in need of repairs and refitting. HMS *Terrible*, for example, was in no condition to take part in a battle and went into action with her pumps working. De Grasse had to leave two ships of the line and a 50-gun ship to blockade Yorktown, but he still had five more ships of the line than his opponent. Nevertheless, his 24 ships of the line were slower than the British ones because they were not copper-bottomed and were undermanned because 1,500 crew members had been left in Chesapeake Bay to man small craft, but the French ships were in a better state of repair than the British ones.[58]

The French ships were in a better state of repair because they had only sailed from France in March while the British ships had, largely, been on station off America for many months with little chance of visiting dockyards for ongoing maintenance and repair, while the advantages given to the British by virtue of copper bottoms have been touched on in Chapter 11. Ironically, on the very day that Graves and his copper-bottomed ships were to meet de Grasse, the navy comptroller included an interesting comment in a letter to Sandwich.

> An inferior fleet of coppered ships under a judicious commander will keep a superior one that is not in awe, and prevent their gaining any material advantage. [...] If coppered ships, on meeting with squadrons or convoys

---

57   Ferling, *Miracle*, p.528.
58   Syrett, *American Waters*, pp.194–5.

of the enemy, will instead of attack[ing them] wait for opportunities, they will from circumstances of negligence and weather be sure to meet with them and generally have it in their power to turn them to advantage. Such commanders as are afraid to adopt this Fabian plan are unfit to command a coppered squadron.[59]

Off the Virginia Capes the French admiral was not 'in awe' of Graves's squadron.

On 5 September, with the British squadron outside the bay, de Grasse slipped anchor and sailed his ships out to meet Graves. Leaving the narrow entrance to the bay was a vulnerable time for the French, as Hood described in a letter to George Jackson: 'they began to come out in line of battle ahead, but by no means regular and connected, which afforded the British fleet a most glorious opening for making a close attack to manifest advantage, *but it was not embraced* [my emphasis]'.[60] In an enclosure to his letter Hood emphasised the opportunity that he felt had been missed but, as we have seen from his comments on Rodney, he had form for telling others what he would have done had he had command: 'Yesterday [the 5th] the British fleet had a rich and most plentiful harvest of glory in view, but the means to gather it were omitted in more instances than one'.[61]

This battle was one in the long list of naval actions bedevilled by signalling problems. Padfield gives a good explanation of the confusion caused by the signals that were raised by Graves, at one point the signal for 'close action' was flying at the same time as that for 'line of battle'.[62] There was no standardised system of signalling; commanders-in-chief issued their own or, as in Graves's case, reissued those of the previous commander – Graves adopted those of Arbuthnot. In the action that followed, the British ships sustained more damage than the French did and continued to stand out to sea until they sailed for New York on 13 September, arriving on the 19th. Graves was much criticised (especially by Hood and Rodney) for a lack of aggression. Hood, after the event, suggested that the whole squadron should have sailed into the bay – it had been vacated by de Grasse for the battle – 'they might then not only have succoured Lord Cornwallis, but have destroyed the enemy's ships there'.[63] Hood may have been right in his assessment but when Barras joined de Grasse, around the 11 September, the French had their siege guns and the numerical advantage of 36 ships to Graves's 18.[64] The French could have sat outside the bay and bottled up the British fleet. After manoeuvring around

59   SP, Vol.4, p.62, Middleton to Sandwich, 5 September 1781.
60   NRS, *Hood Papers*, p.28, Hood to Jackson, 16 September 1781.
61   NRS, *Hood Papers*, p.31, enclosure 1, 6 September 1781.
62   Padfield, *Maritime Supremacy*, pp.262–267.
63   NRS, *Hood Papers*, p.29, Hood to Jackson, 16 September 1781.
64   Padfield, *Maritime Supremacy*, p.268.

each other for some days, the two fleets separated, the French to the Chesapeake, the British to New York. After a 'Council of War' with his various commanders, at which a report stated that 'the [French] large ships appeared more numerous, and to be in divisions',[65] Graves took the decision that 'Upon this state of the position of the enemy, the present condition of the British fleet, the season of the year so near the equinox, and the impracticability of giving any effectual succour to General Earl Cornwallis in the Chesapeake; It was resolved that the British squadron [...] should proceed with all possible despatch to New York'. In taking the decision to break off and return to New York, Graves was conscious of the fact that he was effectively deserting the troops at Yorktown, though he tried to put the best gloss on Cornwallis's situation: 'I fear much for our ships in York River in the Chesapeake, as well as for the Earl of Cornwallis. His post is a good one, and I understand he has 7000 veteran troops. We cannot succour him, nor venture to keep the sea any longer'.[66]

Graves was unfortunate in that he would later find himself in command of the battle that effectively determined the fate of Cornwallis at Yorktown. He had been sent to North America not because he was the right man to lead the British Navy at a critical time, but to hold the fort until Digby arrived to take command after the resignation of Arbuthnot. Hood, who had criticised Rodney's actions in the West Indies, gave it as his opinion that had Rodney 'led his Majesty's squadron from the West Indies to this coast, I will venture to pronounce that the 5th of this month would have proved a most glorious day for England'.[67] Graves may not have been the man for that battle, but he was commanding the only British fleet in the Americas and could not afford to lose this asset: 'Naval strength was the key to the balance of power among the European empires in the Americas, the Mediterranean, and the Pacific. The loss of a fleet would have had catastrophic implications for Britain. Its survival was more important than that of the army at Yorktown [...]'[68] Given the importance to Britain of its navy it is unreasonable to lay the blame for the loss of America on the shoulders of this one man, as some have done: 'He had lost no engagement, no ships, none was lost on either side. He had merely lost America'.[69] Graves had been cautious by not attacking the French ships as they exited the Chesapeake on 5 September but, bearing in mind the problems of naval signalling systems of that time, 'the advantages of randomly engaging a superior enemy were always likely to be outweighed by the loss of

65   NRS, *Hood Papers*, p.35, enclosure 5, 13 September 1781.
66   SP, Vol.4, p.183, Graves to Sandwich, 14 September 1781.
67   SP, Vol.4, p.189, Hood to Sandwich, 16 September 1781.
68   O'Shaughnessy, *Men Who Lost America*, p.313.
69   K. Breen, 'Graves and Hood at the Chesapeake', *Mariner's Mirror*, 66:1 (1980), p.53, citing Michael Lewis (1957).

cohesion'.[70] By the time that Barras had joined de Grasse, the French had 36 ships to the British 18 and only more ships would have rectified the situation: 'For this deficiency Lord Sandwich and the ministry in London must primarily answer'.[71]

Wherever the blame lay for the failure to gain a victory over the French ships, Cornwallis' situation at Yorktown had not been improved. With six weeks' worth of provisions, he was earnestly hoping that Clinton's intention to join him (as mentioned in the letter received on 14 September) would provide the needed relief. However, with Washington's colonial army between Cornwallis and a land route to Clinton in New York, the relief of Yorktown was dependent on ships: 'The crucial factor, as indeed throughout the war, was naval force: that side would triumph which could reinforce and supply its own army while denying the same to the enemy'.[72] At New York Clinton had 4,000 troops that he wanted to send to Cornwallis (he knew that there were 12,000 Franco–American troops *en route* to lay siege to Yorktown), but he needed the navy to transport and land them. To effect an amphibious operation at Yorktown, in the entrance to the Chesapeake, would require the British to have naval supremacy over the French. When Graves arrived at New York on 20 September, following his meeting with de Grasse, he told Clinton that he was prepared to assist in a relief operation, but that he must first refit his ships. However, before leaving the Chesapeake he had expressed the view that 'nothing by Sea can be got up to Lord Cornwallis'.[73] Events were to prove him right. On 24 September, a meeting of the senior commanders agreed that the loss of Cornwallis' force would be serious, and all efforts should be made to send a force that would leave New York on 5 October. Then the delays began. Graves first postponed the leaving date until 8 October, then again until the 12th. To Major Frederick Mackenzie (he had been in America with the 23rd Regiment since the start of the conflict and was now on Clinton's staff), the delay demonstrated a lack of concern on the part of the navy. 'If the Navy are not a little more active, then it will be too late. They do not seem to be hearty in their business or to think that the Army is an object of such material consequence'.[74]

On the day that the senior commanders met to see what they could do to assist Cornwallis, Admiral Digby arrived with his three ships from England. London had decided that Graves was not the man to be Commander-in-Chief of the Navy at this sensitive time, but their choice for the role, Digby, did not take command on his arrival.

70   R. Middleton, 'Naval resources and the British defeat at Yorktown, 1781', *Mariner's Mirror*, 100:1 (2014), p.39.
71   Middleton, 'Defeat at Yorktown', p.40.
72   Padfield, *Maritime Supremacy*, p.259.
73   TNA, CO 5/103, ff.170–171.
74   Urban, *Fusiliers*, p.273.

I found the fleet here fitting after the action for an expedition to endeavour to relieve Lord Cornwallis. It was determined that Lord Cornwallis could not at that time quit his post at York[town], and that nothing but the co-operation of the fleet with the army to relieve him and co-operate with him afterwards could save him. *This was a strong inducement to me not to damp the undertaking* at that period, as it was necessary the fleet should be got fit for sea without loss of time. But I must own from all the information I have been able to collect I look upon it as a desperate undertaking, [...] *I shall with cheerfulness serve under Rear-Admiral Graves* [my emphasis].[75]

The Admiralty had sent Digby because they considered him the better person to take command of the navy in North America and, while there is an argument for saying that changing command during the planning of an operation is to be avoided where possible, Digby appears to have made the assessment that this was an expedition likely to fail and he preferred Graves's name to be associated with it rather than his own.

With the fate of Cornwallis dependent on the navy commanders taking decisive action, Major Mackenzie would have had his views on the inactivity of that service reinforced if he had been privy to the rest of Digby's letter to Sandwich. Where he might have been expected to give some views on how he intended to exercise his new command, he used the rest of his letter to complain about perceived slights by Graves to his authority as the new commander.

I could wish he [Graves] had treated me with a little more attention respecting my command; [...] I can't help being hurt and disappointed at Admiral Graves's putting them [fireships] in commission after my arrival, in a clandestine way, without ever consulting me or mentioning it to me, [...] I am sensible that his seniority gives him a right to appoint to regular vacancies directly under his own eye, but when he takes the advantage to appoint a captain after I am in port to a prize, not condemned, not surveyed, not valued, without ever consulting me, it appears so irregular and unreasonable that I must again repeat that I trust your Lordship will supersede the appointment with one of my officers.

Digby, sent out to command at a critical time, was more concerned with the perceived usurpation of his rights of patronage, and how that would be viewed by those who relied on him for promotion and prize money. The First Lord replied

75   SP, Vol.4, p.193, Digby to Sandwich, 11 October 1781.

that 'it is impossible for this Board to set aside any of his [Graves] appointments while his flag was still flying;'[76] and it was flying because Digby had elected to leave Graves in command and serve under him. The navy, as Mackenzie had noted, was not being 'hearty' in their efforts to relieve Cornwallis. On the day that Digby wrote to Sandwich, Cornwallis, whose position was now under bombardment from the surrounding Franco–American troops, wrote to Clinton: 'I have only to repeat what I said in my letter of the 3rd that nothing but a direct move to York River, which includes a successful naval action, can save us'.[77] Four days later, on 15 October, Cornwallis could see that his situation had deteriorated to the point where relief was unlikely and hazardous: 'I cannot recommend that the Fleet and Army should run great risk in endeavouring to save us'.[78]

There was now no way to save the beleaguered garrison at Yorktown and so, on 19 October 1781, a day which 'dawned beautiful and unusually warm',[79] the British troops surrendered. The expedition to save Cornwallis and his troops sailed too late, leaving New York on the day of the surrender. Graves sailed with 7,149 troops, 25 ships of the line, three 50-gun ships, and eight frigates, but the French had 36 sail of the line. On 24 October, *en route* for the Chesapeake, Graves learned from three men who had escaped from Yorktown and were picked up at sea that 'Lord Cornwallis had capitulated on the 18th inst. [*sic*], the day before the fleet sailed from Sandy Hook'.[80] When the British fleet arrived off the bay they confirmed that 'de Grasse's squadron was much stronger than their own, [and] they could do nothing but return to Sandy Hook, where they arrived on 2 November'.[81] Willis argues that there had been a point when Cornwallis could have extricated his force using the ships that were available to him at Yorktown and that he was not 'entirely reliant upon the navy for his rescue'.[82] At his disposal were 'sixty-eight ships including the 44-gun *Charon*, the 32-gun *Guadeloupe*, the 24-gun *Fowey*, and seven sloops and brigs ranging from ten to sixteen guns'. Additionally, he had 32 troop transports, victuallers and a shoal of small boats. While these would not have enabled him to break out of Chesapeake Bay through the French ships, Willis argues that he could have taken his men up the York River, which the British controlled as far as West Point, 18 miles away. The opportunity would have had to have been taken during August or early September but Cornwallis 'had no eyes for his ships;' all the ships' guns were landed and used in the fortifications

76   SP, Vol.4, p.205, Sandwich to Digby, 4 December 1781.
77   TNA, ADM 1/489, f.473.
78   Cornwallis to Clinton, TNA, ADM 1/489, f.491.
79   Wickwire, *Cornwallis*, p.1.
80   TNA, ADM 1/489, f.488.
81   Syrett, *American Waters*, p.217.
82   Willis, *Sea Power*, p.452.

while the sails were used to make tents for the sick and wounded. Once this had been done then he was totally dependent on Graves and his fleet.

From the point of view of this narrative, Yorktown was the end of the war. While thousands of British troops remained at New York and other towns on the coast of America, the war against the Rebels was over. On 4 November de Grasse sailed for Martinique, followed a week later by Graves to take up his position in Jamaica, leaving Digby to take command in North America. Clinton sent in his resignation, which was accepted in February 1782 and Carleton took over the army command. On 11 November, Hood left Sandy Hook for Barbados with 17 ships of the line. It was not until 27 November that the news of Yorktown arrived in London, causing Lord North's exclamation, 'Oh God! It is all over'. In March 1782, the North government resigned, to be replaced by one pledged to end the war. After Yorktown, the main function of the navy in American waters was to supply the troops in their scattered posts along the American coast, and then to transport them home when the war was finally declared to be over. Too late to change events in America, Rodney defeated de Grasse (and took him prisoner) at the Battle of the Saintes on 12 April 1782; for once a British fleet had numerical superiority over the French.

The surrender at Yorktown covered only the army of General Cornwallis; it was not a surrender of the thousands of British troops at New York, Charleston, and other posts on the American seaboard. In the same way that the surrender of Lee's Army of Northern Virginia in April 1865 was not a total Confederate surrender, both effectively ended their respective wars by handing a major defeat to a war-weary public; but in both cases peace came later. In spite of North's view that it was 'all over', the King had not yet given up hope. In the Commons, he urged that the war 'to restore my deluded subjects in America' be continued despite the 'late misfortune' at Yorktown.[83] Rodney's defeat of de Grasse at the Saintes was troubling for the French especially as Austria and Russia had recently signed an alliance that might threaten French interests in eastern Europe. The Americans moved more quickly than their French allies by agreeing a separate peace with Britain (in spite of promises to France to do no such thing) if their claim to independence was recognised; it was. Peace with America was signed by Britain on 29 November 1782; Washington signed the order to cease all acts of hostility on 9 April 1783; and the final act, the Treaty of Paris, which included France and Spain, was signed on 3 September. The evacuation of troops and Loyalists was a huge logistical operation, requiring hundreds of transport vessels; Carleton (now commanding in America) had to make Loyalists leave their personal possessions behind because of the shortage of ships. In an earlier chapter,

83 Ferling, *Miracle*, p.541.

we saw that contractors could command large sums for the hire of vessels when the Admiralty was taking all that were available. For the New York evacuation, they were forced to charter at the rate of 13 shillings 'ready money per ton',[84] and even then, it could not hire all the vessels that it required. On 25 November some 20,000 British troops, together with thousands of civilians were 'withdrawn from the city of New York, in good order, and embarked without the smallest circumstances of irregularity or misbehaviour of any kind'.[85] The war had ended as it had begun, with the army dependent on the navy for the transport of its men, their equipment, and all provisions.

84   Syrett, *Shipping and the American War,* p.240.
85   Syrett, *American Waters,* p.226.

13

'Their Command of the Sea gives them Advantages'

The heading to this chapter is a quotation by the American Lieutenant-Colonel William Tudor to John Adams in August 1776[1] when he was preparing defences at New York against the expected amphibious landing of British troops. The Colonel was correct in the context of the flexibility of manoeuvre that it gave to British generals, but the extent of the reliance of the British on their use and command of the sea was to play a part in their failure in America. The British Navy had shown itself to be a power to be reckoned with at the end of the Seven Years War but, following the peace, the navy (ships and men) had been drastically cut back to reduce the expense on the exchequer. In 1775 Britain found itself falling into a war that it had not expected, against people who were 'subjects of the Crown', and were over 3,000 miles from London. Right from the start the British Army was in a fight that it would be difficult to win: there were too few troops on the ground; it quickly found itself confined to the environs of Boston; it could not feed or supply itself from local resources; orders and direction from London were subject to a sea voyage of six weeks in each direction. Those directing the war soon realised that the army was totally reliant on supply by sea: 'Without sea power the American War of Independence simply could not have been fought at all'.[2] As the war progressed, it quickly became apparent that the army had enormous difficulties operating at any distance from a defended sea port. In his account of the importance of logistics to the British in the war, Bowler made the point that a defeated American army could 'melt back into the countryside' but the British did not have that opportunity.

---

1   NDAR, Vol.6, p.227, Tudor to Adams, 18 August 1776.
2   Holmes, *Redcoat*, p.18.

Its only hope was to fall back on a fortified port. If the navy was not there with its usually overwhelming power, the army might still be lost, as Yorktown demonstrated. A British army without lines of communication with the sea was, by a continuous *petite guerre* as well as by the natural process of attrition, bound to weaken while the American force opposing it grew stronger.[3]

This was not a war that Britain wanted or had prepared for, and with which eighteenth century administrative systems could not cope. While the navy had in place the systems and procedures for victualling and the fitting out of ships for extended sea service abroad, the army was less well served. In the early years of the conflict, the Treasury had the responsibility for the troops, but it would be sorely stretched in the American war. The sheer size and complexity of providing all of the army's needs, when the number of troops grew from around 10,000 to nearly 100,000 in a period of three or four years, and to do that across sea lanes 3,000 miles long, while accounting for winds and tides, was more than just a formidable task. Armies of the time were used to living off the land. If they were on the move, they threw out bands of foragers to find, take (and sometimes purchase) their needs as they moved through enemy territory; if they were garrisoned then they attempted to control a large enough area around their post to provide the provisions they required. This was difficult in the colonial context of America where the 'enemy' was nominally subject to the Crown and included a considerable percentage of the population who were Loyalists and disagreed with the aims of the Rebels. In the same way that not all Americans were Rebels, so there were some British commanders who were not fully in favour of the need for military action against the colonists. Frequently this was demonstrated by reluctance to forcibly take the provisions they needed from the locals, as they appreciated the need to retain their loyalty, and forcing them to supply provisions might work against that. Once the army was confined to Boston, the sea became the only sure way of provisioning the troops: 'Logistical considerations, therefore, moored the redcoats to the coast, or to rivers, in the same fashion that a ship was tethered to the docks'.[4]

Given the constraints of the administrative systems with which they worked, the navy did a reasonable job of supplying the troops. The men did not starve, although they did have to go on short rations at times. Convoys were often subject to delays before leaving Cork, Portsmouth, Plymouth, and other British ports because of slow delivery by contractors or contrary winds. It is easy, in the age of motorised ships, to overlook the extent to which sailing ships were dependent

3   Bowler, *Logistics*, p.240.
4   Ferling, *Miracle*, p.565.

on the weather. The wind that took a ship from Cork to Spithead would be the wrong one to allow the same vessel to leave Spithead and sail down Channel for the Western Approaches. The contracting system with which the Navy and Treasury Boards had to deal was struggling to cope with the huge volumes of foodstuffs and equipment that were needed. Contracts that were let in London for butter from Cork had to have quality assurance procedures in place that could take account of the distance and time between the office in which the agreement was drawn up, and the port from which the products would leave for America. While far from perfect, the survey system that was put in place, together with the use of identifying marks on the casks to indicate the supplier, went a long way to ensuring that the contents met the specifications of the contract. That does not mean that there were no cases of poor, even putrid, foodstuffs within the victualling casks. However, as some of the figures in Chapter 3 demonstrate, the percentage of condemned product was small; an enormous achievement when the volumes involved are taken into consideration. However, what might have been considered 'good and wholesome' in 1776 would be unlikely to receive the same accolade today.

Although the army did not starve, it frequently lacked the quantity of supplies that commanders believed they needed in reserve to allow them to mount operations that were likely to last some months. While this is a valid criticism of the supply chain, the army has to bear some responsibility for the shortages. As we have seen, commanders were constantly at fault for failing to provide accurate and timely reports of the number of mouths that needed feeding. While the army commander might move troops to various posts and extend a place of safety to Loyalist civilians, while promising to feed Indian tribes who helped him, these numbers rarely made it back to London in time for supplies to be sent in the required quantities. Contracts at the Treasury and the Navy were let on the basis of the troop numbers available to the clerks in London, adjusted by their understanding of the food already in the stores and warehouses in America. Where these figures were wrong it would take three months for letters and notes to make the round trip between Britain and New York. However, troop numbers, as we have seen, were not the only problem; provisions had to be transported, and that meant having ships on hand or available for contract. A constant complaint from London was the holding back of transport ships in American ports – vessels that should have been returned so that they could make further supply voyages to the troops. What was seen as a simple problem by the clerks at the Navy Board was not viewed in the same light in America. Ports had insufficient warehousing (if it had not also been burned down as it was at New York) causing transport ships to be used as floating storeships. In addition, the army needed to be able to conduct operations at various points along the American coast, and for that, the troops needed sea transport. Again, ships that were expected back in Britain by those planning the provisioning convoys were held back for other purposes by the army. The shortage of available transport vessels for hire by the Treasury and Navy Boards drove up the cost of leasing. For the first years of the conflict the Treasury struggled to supply victuals and transport ships to carry out their commitment to the army, before they convinced the Navy Board of the need to take on the role in 1779: 'While the Treasury learned, the army suffered'.[5] The supply problems reached their peak in 1778, but that was also the period when France entered the war, when America became 'secondary' to other priorities and when the army had successfully spread itself down to the Carolinas with the capture of Charleston – so exacerbating the issue of ships for transport and the feeding of Loyalists.

The navy may more fairly be criticised for its operational support of the troops, although here again it was constrained in ship numbers as a result of political decisions. In the hope that the war could be limited to America, and with a wish not to provoke France into becoming a belligerent, Britain was slow to put full mobilisation of the navy in place. The Admiralty found itself, particularly after the entry of France, having too few ships to service all the priorities of the government; they could not maintain an economic blockade of the American coast, provide all the ships needed for the support of the army, protect the Sugar Islands, and relieve Gibraltar, while also ensuring that the Channel was safe from a French invasion.

The Americans had little or no armament industry; all their firearms, ammunition, and powder had to come from overseas. It is a measure of the failure of the blockade, and the ingenuity of the Rebel privateers, that Washington's army had the arms to defeat the British. Had France not joined the war then the British admirals may have received sufficient ships to tighten the blockade, but the Bourbons saw their opportunity and, after their defeat in the Seven Years War, it is no surprise that they took it. However, when it came to participation in combined operations, the navy showed how well it could contribute. New York, Kips Bay, Head of Elk (Philadelphia), and Charleston in 1778 stand out as particularly successful. The way in which captains handled their ships, the organisation of landing boats, and the use of naval guns and crews on shore demonstrated admirable cooperation. Unfortunately, poor relationships between admirals and generals had a detrimental effect on the support delivered by the navy, offsetting any 'vast Advantages' that it should have afforded. The plan to attack Newport in 1780 was largely scuttled because of the poor communication between Clinton and Arbuthnot, which culminated in the admiral failing to attend a meeting with the general, after Clinton had ridden across a large part of Long Island for that purpose. The 1776 attempt to take Charleston was blighted

5   Bowler, *Logistics*, p.260.

by the failure of Clinton and Parker to join their headquarters on one warship, preferring to send letters between ships in the same anchorage. It is a sad fact that while the nature of the war (operating 3,000 miles from home and with painfully slow communications) required the best men for the job, those chosen were often assigned the post for reasons other than competence; seniority trumped ability, as well as the need to assuage personal egos. Patronage was rife in the army and the navy; one needed interest – 'that rich mixture of patronage, influence, family and regimental connection'.[6] Holmes was commenting particularly on the army, but his point is equally relevant in a naval context. The obsequious letters from Gambier to Sandwich, together with Arbuthnot's poor relationship with Clinton and Rodney, did not smack of strong leadership. Their bickering and preoccupation with their own status and egos would not have instilled confidence in the Admiralty in their choice of commanders.

As the introduction to this book makes clear, this is not a blow-by-blow account of military actions, be they on land or sea, nor does it include every occasion on which those various armies and navies faced off against each other. The bibliography includes many ideal sources for readers who wish to delve into that level of detail. In the same way, the direction of the war by the commanders in the American theatre and the politicians in London is only touched on briefly, or to the extent that they affected the support of the army. However, the failure to appoint one man as commander-in-chief of all British forces involved in America has to be mentioned. Too often the navy and army commanders were more inclined to pursue their own objectives rather than combine towards one aim, whether at the level of a combined operation or the use of transport ships. The North American, Jamaican, and Leeward Island stations were three separate naval commands, with each commander-in-chief following his own agenda. There was some recognition of the need for a more holistic approach to the use of the navy in American and Caribbean waters in an exchange between Rodney and Sandwich: as this took place only a few months after his success at the Moonlight Battle, Rodney obviously saw himself as the man for the job. Having laid out what he thought the French might do in the West Indies, he declared that

> With the remainder of my squadron I shall hold myself in readiness, as they are all copper bottomed, to assist either America or any of his Majesty's colonies that may be in want of my assistance. [...] At the same time I think America may want my assistance. I have desired Mr Arbuthnot [Commander in North America] to send me expresses of the

6   R. Holmes, *Sahib: The British Soldier in India* (London: Harper Press, 2006), p.189.

situation of affairs, and hold a large squadron of copper-bottom ships ready to sail to his assistance.[7]

Rodney could see that there might be a future need for his squadron to support Arbuthnot against the French, but without overall command, he had no authority over that admiral; each had a commission to command in their own theatre. When Rodney did sail to New York a few months later he did little more than cause disruption and ill feeling. In his reply, Sandwich appeared to acknowledge the benefits of having one admiral with overall responsibility, but he did not go as far as implementing the idea.

> I am very glad that you tell me you shall hold yourself in readiness to assist in America, or wherever the enemy may endeavour to make their impression; for that is the only measure that can give us security. It is impossible for us to have a superior fleet in every part; and *unless our commanders in chief will take the great line as you do, and consider the King's whole Dominions as under their care*, our enemies must find us unprepared somewhere, and carry their point against us [my emphasis].[8]

With the distance between America and Britain, and the nearly three months for the sending of a letter and receiving a reply, having one commander with the authority to dispose of the available ships to 'consider the King's whole Dominions' would seem to be a logical appointment. Sandwich went on in his letter to make clear that a move by Rodney into Arbuthnot's command area would please the First Lord, while demonstrating a lack of confidence in Arbuthnot's capabilities against the French: 'I own I think that they [the French] are now gone to America, and am pampering myself with the idea of the glory you will acquire by pursuing them with your coppered ships and rendering their designs abortive'.

Not appointing a naval *supremo* for North America and the Caribbean once the French had joined the war demonstrated a lack of vision at the Admiralty and prevented the most effective use of the ships available.

Following the surrender at Yorktown, the Admiralty came in for serious criticism over its inability to support Cornwallis following the failure to defeat de Grasse off the Chesapeake. Sandwich and others had to defend their positions before Parliament. One accusation was that the navy had failed to have sufficient ships available to meet the French fleet. The Admiralty's counter was that where the enemy could 'choose at what particular points they are to direct their efforts',

7   SP, Vol.3, pp.224–225, Rodney to Sandwich, 31 July 1780.
8   SP, Vol.3, p.231, Sandwich to Rodney, 25 September 1780.

the British had to allot their available ships 'to the defence of such posts as we think are most likely to be in danger and are of such importance as to require our particular attention'.[9] At the time, Gibraltar was considered so vital that Rodney had to take a fleet of warships and relief vessels to the Straits, before heading for the Caribbean. One consequence of relieving Gibraltar was the opportunity for the French to leave Brest. The reinforcement of Graves was also hindered by the late departure of Digby from Ireland as a result of contrary winds. However, the force available to Graves would have been larger but for decisions taken in the Caribbean. Rodney, before leaving for home, sent two ships to Jamaica to cover a convoy with orders to sail immediately after for New York; they were both delayed by Sir Peter Parker. When Rodney sailed for home he handed command to Hood and ordered him to sail to join Graves for the expected meeting of the British and French fleets; unfortunately Rodney took six ships with him, leaving Hood with 14 of the 22 that had constituted Rodney's squadron. Additionally, Graves was criticised by Hood for not having all his ships together after being warned of the approach of the French:

> Had Rear-Admiral Graves have kept *all* [emphasis in original] his ships collected together and ready to have joined me upon my appearance off New York, as he promised to do, he might have been upon Grasse's heels, at the time he was putting his troops on shore, and with five ships more than he had on the 5th of September, including the *Warwick*, *Chatham* and *Assurance*.[10]

The end result was that Graves was outnumbered off the Chesapeake as a consequence of the eight ships (six with Rodney and two in Jamaica) from the Caribbean being diverted, not having all of his own ships together, and the late arrival of Digby's ships. While a single commander for American and Caribbean waters could have done little to speed Digby's arrival, he could have ensured that the other eight ships were not diverted by the commander in Jamaica and the commander in the Leeward Islands. It was the view of the Admiralty that, allowing for the need to relieve Gibraltar, they had taken the steps to sufficiently reinforce Graves had these not been thwarted by 'accidents': 'Had not the intended measures of Government been frustrated by various accidents, Admiral Graves would have been superior to the French fleet at the time of his action with M. de Grasse'.[11]

9   SP, Vol.4, p.344, memorandum for House of Lords, February 1782.
10   SP, Vol.4, p.199, Hood to Digby, 31 October 1781.
11   SP, Vol.4, p.342, memorandum, 6 February 1782.

282   ALL AT SEA

But ship numbers were not the only factor in naval engagements; the resolution of the admiral and his intent to bring on an action, without being dictated purely by the question of numerical superiority, had a direct bearing on events. Rodney had the aggression, but his 'Moonlight' battle took place off the coast of Spain and the Battle of the Saintes was in April 1782, after Yorktown. The admirals who commanded the American station did not demonstrate the aggressiveness of Rodney or Hawke (at Quiberon Bay in 1759), although Lord Howe did later go on to fight and win a fleet action against the French during the French Revolution – the Glorious First of June. The British public, as well as the troops in America, expected the fleet to demonstrate the superiority they had won during the Seven Years War; they did not expect admirals to put up the smoke screens of who had the most ships or heaviest guns. George III wrote to Sandwich on this point, believing that determined action could make up for inferiority in numbers: 'This country, with such numerous enemies, must be ruined unless what we want of strength is made up in activity and resolution. Caution has certainly made this war less brilliant than the former; and if that is alone to direct our operations, [...] without much foresight it is easy to foretell that we must be great losers'.[12] While the contractors, clerks, and administrators in London, Cork, and other ports had done their best to ensure that the army in America did not starve, the admirals were causing the King to question their fighting spirit. Although the aggression shown was not always what was expected, the politicians cannot escape their responsibility for failing to provide the number of ships needed for the number of tasks the navy was expected to fulfil. In the aftermath of Yorktown, when the Admiralty had to refute 'the charges brought against Government for their not making a proper use and distribution of their marine force during the year 1781', the following extract was drafted for Sandwich to deliver in a speech to Parliament. It serves as a final statement of the navy's less than glorious support of the army when called on to engage in fleet action with the French off the American coast:

> In former wars British valour and knowledge in naval matters carried our glory to the highest pitch. We did not then *minutely measure the force we attacked* [my emphasis]; this is a new doctrine now entertained, and often inculcated by gentlemen of very respectable situations, but one that I must ever most cordially reprobate. If British admirals of the present day are unequal to cope with those of our antagonists, if our naval superiority in the hour of engagement cannot now be supported, if English sailors have lost that national pre-eminence which the history of past times has

12   SP, Vol.4, p.55, the King to Sandwich, 3 September 1781.

bestowed on them with no less glory than truth, then indeed I shall think this country on the brink of ruin. Time has been, and will I hope again return, when British courage has been estimated on a more enlarged and comprehensive scale.[13]

13   SP, Vol.4, p.360, draft speech, February 1782.

Bibliography

Abbreviations in footnotes
NDAR: Naval Documents of the American Revolution
NRS: The Navy Records Society
SP: *The Private Papers of John, Earl of Sandwich*
TNA: The National Archives at Kew

Archives
The National Archives, Kew, Admiralty Papers (ADM): ADM 1/487–489; ADM 1/4132–4133; ADM 111/72–73.
The National Archives, Kew, Colonial Office Papers (CO): CO 5/92; CO 5/103.
The National Archives, Kew, Treasury Papers (T): T 29/45–46; T 64/106; T 64/108; T 64/114; 64/200.

Printed primary sources
Navy Records Society, *Journals of Henry Duncan, 1776–1782* (London: Navy Records Society, 1901).
Navy Records Society, *Letters of Lord Hood, 1781–1783*, vol.3 (London: Navy Records Society, 1895).
Navy Records Society, *The Barrington Papers: Admiral The Hon. Samuel Barrington*, vol.2 (London: Navy Records Society, 1941).
Navy Records Society, *The Health of Seamen: Selections from the Works of Dr James Lind, Sir Gilbert Blane and Dr Thomas Trotter* (London: Navy Records Society, 1965).
Navy Records Society, *The Keith Papers*, vol.1 (London: Navy Records Society, 1927).
Navy Records Society, *The Private Papers of John, Earl of Sandwich*, 4 vols. (London: Navy Records Society, 1931–39).
Navy Records Society, *The Rodney Papers, 1763–1780*, vol.2 (Aldershot: Navy Records Society, 2007).
Navy Records Society, *The Vernon Papers* (London: Navy Records Society, 1958).
Partridge, R. (ed.), *Memoirs of Sergeant Bourgogne, 1812–1813* (London: Constable, 1996).

Books

Adkins, R. and L., *Gibraltar: The Greatest Siege in British History* (London: Little, Brown, 2017).

Baker, N., *Government and Contractors: The British Treasury and War Supplies, 1775–1783* (London: Athlone Press, 1971).

Barnett, C., *Engage The Enemy More Closely: The Royal Navy In The Second World War* (London: Penguin, 2001).

Bicheno, H., *Rebels & Redcoats: The American Revolutionary War* (London: HarperCollins, 2003).

Black, J., 'Naval power, strategy and foreign policy, 1775–1791', in M. Duffy (ed.), *Parameters of British Naval Power, 1650–1850* (Exeter: University of Exeter Press, 1998).

Black, J., *War for America: The Fight For Independence, 1775–1783* (Stroud: Alan Sutton, 1991).

Blake, N., *Steering To Glory: A Day in the Life of a Ship of the Line* (London: Chatham, 2005).

Bowler, R.A., *Logistics and the Failure of the British Army in America, 1775–1783* (Princeton, NJ: Princeton University Press, 1975).

Brumwell, S., *Turncoat: Benedict Arnold and the Crisis of American Liberty* (London: Yale University Press, 2018).

Bunker, N., *An Empire on the Edge: How Britain Came to Fight America* (London: Bodley Head, 2015).

D'Este, C., *A Genius for War: A Life of General George S. Patton* (London: HarperCollins, 1996).

Duffy, M., 'The Establishment of the Western Squadron as the linchpin of British naval strategy', in M. Duffy (ed.), *Parameters of British Naval Power, 1650–1850* (Exeter: University of Exeter Press, 1998).

Ferling, J., *Almost a Miracle: The American Victory in the War of Independence* (Oxford: Oxford University Press, 2009).

Gordon, A., *The Rules of the Game: Jutland and British Naval Command* (London: John Murray, 1996).

Gwyn, J., *Ashore and Afloat: The British Navy and the Halifax Naval Yard before 1820* (Ottawa: University of Ottawa Press, 2004).

Hibbert, C., *Redcoats and Rebels: The War for America, 1770–1781* (London: HarperCollins, 1992).

Hoffer, P.C., *Prelude to Revolution: The Salem Gunpowder Raid of 1775* (Baltimore, MD: Johns Hopkins University Press, 2013).

Holmes, R., *Redcoat: The British Soldier In The Age Of Horse And Musket* (London: HarperCollins, 2001).

Holmes, R., *Sahib: The British Soldier in India* (London: Harper Press, 2006).

Macdonald, J., *Feeding Nelson's Navy: The True Story of Food at Sea in the Georgian era* (London: Chatham, 2004).

Macintyre, D., *Admiral Rodney* (London: Peter Davies, 1962).

Mackesy, P., *The War for America, 1775–1783* (Lincoln, NE: University of Nebraska Press, 1993).

Middlekauff, R., *The Glorious Cause: The American Revolution, 1763–1789* (Oxford: Oxford University Press, 2005).

Morriss, R., *The Foundations of British Maritime Ascendancy: Resources, Logistics and the State, 1755–1815* (Cambridge: Cambridge University Press, 2011).

Mostert, N., *The Line Upon The Wind: An Intimate History of the Last and Greatest War Fought at Sea Under Sail, 1793–1815* (London: Jonathan Cape, 2007).

O'Shaughnessy, A., *The Men Who Lost America: British Command during the Revolutionary War and the Preservation of the Empire* (London: Oneworld, 2014).

Padfield, P., *Maritime Supremacy and the Opening of the Western Mind: Naval Campaigns that Shaped the Modern World, 1588–1782* (London: Pimlico, 2000).

Parker, M., *The Sugar Barons: Family, Corruption, Empire and War* (London: Windmill, 2012).

Philbrick, N., *Bunker Hill: A City, a Siege, a Revolution* (London: Bantam Books, 2014).

Reed, R., *Combined Operations in the Civil War* (Annapolis, MD: Naval Institute Press, 1978).

Rodger, N.A.M., *The Command of the Ocean: A Naval History of Britain, 1649–1815* (London: Allen Lane, 2004).

Rodger, N.A.M., *The Insatiable Earl: A Life of John Montagu, 4th Earl of Sandwich* (London: Norton, 1993).

Rodger, N.A.M., *The Wooden World: An Anatomy of the Georgian Navy* (London: Norton, 1986).

Rutter, O., *Red Ensign: A History of Convoy* (London: Hale, 1942).

Syrett, D., *Admiral Lord Howe: A Biography* (Stroud: Spellmount, 2006).

Syrett, D., *Shipping and the American War, 1775–83: A Study of British Transport Organization* (London: Athlone, 1970).

Syrett, D., *The Royal Navy in American Waters, 1775–1783* (Aldershot: Scolar Press, 1989).

Trew, P., *Rodney and the Breaking of the Line* (Barnsley: Pen and Sword, 2006).

Tuchman, B.W., *The First Salute: A View of the American Revolution* (New York: Ballantine Books, 1988).

Urban, M., *Fusiliers: How the British Army Lost America but Learned to Fight* (Croydon: Faber and Faber, 2007).

Van Creveld, M., *Supplying War: Logistics from Wallenstein to Patton* (Cambridge: Cambridge University Press, 2004).

Wickwire, F. and M., *Cornwallis and the War of Independence* (Northampton: History Book Club, 1970).

Willis, S., *The Struggle For Sea Power: A Naval History of American Independence* (London: Atlantic Books, 2015).

Articles

Armstrong, B., '"Zeal, Intelligence and Intrepidity": naval irregular warfare and the War of 1812 on the Lakes', *Mariner's Mirror*, Vol.103, No.1 (Feb. 2017), pp.30–42.

Bonner Smith D., 'The capture of the Washington', *Mariner's Mirror*, Vol.20, No.4 (Oct. 1934), pp.420–425.

Bowler, R.A., 'The American Revolution and British Army administration reform', *Journal of the Society for Army Historical Research*, Vol.58 (1980), pp.66–77.

Breen, K., 'Graves and Hood at the Chesapeake', *Mariner's Mirror*, Vol.66, No.1 (1980), pp.53–65.

Breen, K., 'Sir George Rodney and St Eustatius in the American War: A Commercial and Naval Distraction, 1775–81', *Mariner's Mirror*, Vol.84, No.2 (1998), pp.193–203.

Broomfield, J.H., 'Lord Sandwich at the Admiralty Board: politics and the British Navy, 1771–1778', *Mariner's Mirror*, Vol.57, No.1 (1965), pp.7–17.

Cock, R., '"Avarice and Rapacity" and "Treasonable Correspondence" in "an Emporium for All the World": the British capture of St Eustatius, 1781', *Mariner's Mirror*, Vol.103, No.3 (Aug. 2018), pp.265–278.

Cock, R., '"The Finest Invention in the World": the Royal Navy's early trials of copper sheathing, 1708–1770', *Mariner's Mirror*, Vol.84, No.4 (Nov. 2001), pp.446–459.

Fyers, E., 'The transport of troops by sea', *Mariner's Mirror*, Vol.6, No.11 (1920), pp.322–328.

Jones, G., 'The voyage of the 23rd Foot to New York in 1773', *JSAHR*, Vol.38 (1960), pp.49–56.

Knight, R.J.B., 'The introduction of copper sheathing into the Royal Navy, 1779–1786', *Mariner's Mirror*, Vol.59, No.3 (1973), pp.299–309.

May, W.E., 'The Gaspee affair', *Mariner's Mirror*, Vol.63, No.2 (1977), pp.129–135.

Middleton, R., 'Naval resources and the British defeat at Yorktown, 1781', *Mariner's Mirror*, Vol.100, No.1 (2014), pp.29–43.

Rowbotham, W.B., 'Soldiers' and Seamen's wives and children in H.M. Ships', *Mariner's Mirror*, Vol.47, No.1 (Feb. 1961), pp.42–48.

Spencer, F., 'Lord Sandwich, Russian masts, and American independence', *Mariner's Mirror*, Vol.44, No.2 (1958), pp.116–127.

Syrett, D., 'HM Armed Ship *Vigilant*, 1777–1780', *Mariner's Mirror*, Vol.64, No.1 (1978), pp.57–62.

Syrett, D., 'Home waters or America? The dilemma of British naval strategy in 1778', *Mariner's Mirror*, Vol.77, No.4 (1991), pp.365–77.

Syrett, D., 'Living conditions on the Navy Board's transports during the American War, 1775–1783', *Mariner's Mirror*, Vol.55, No.1 (1969), pp.87–94.

Syrett, D., 'Lord George Germain and the protection of military storeships 1775–1778', *Mariner's Mirror*, Vol.60, No.4 (1974), pp.395–405.

Syrett, D., 'The disruption of HMS *Flora*'s convoy, 1776', *Mariner's Mirror*, Vol.56, No.4 (1970), pp.423–427.

Syrett, D., 'The fitting out Of HM Storeship *Elephant*, July 1776', *Mariner's Mirror*, Vol.74, No.1 (1988), pp.67–73.

Syrett, D., 'The methodology of British amphibious operations during the Seven Years' and American Wars', *Mariner's Mirror*, Vol.58, No.3 (1972), pp.269–280.

Syrett, D., 'The organization of British trade convoys during the American War, 1775–1783', *Mariner's Mirror*, Vol.62, No.2 (1976), pp.169–181.

Syrett, D., 'The procurement of shipping by the Board of Ordnance during the American War, 1775–1782', *Mariner's Mirror*, Vol.81, No.4 (1995), pp.409–416.

Yerxa, D.A., 'Vice-Admiral Samuel Graves and the North American squadron, 1774–1776', *Mariner's Mirror*, Vol.62, No.4 (Nov. 1976), pp.371–385.

Unpublished Thesis

DeVaro, L.J., 'The impact of the Gaspee affair on the coming of the revolution, 1772–1773', unpublished PhD thesis, Case Western Reserve University, January 1973.

Published Theses

Canfield, D.T., 'Understanding British strategic failure in America, 1780–1783', thesis for a Masters of Strategic Studies, US Army War College, 2012.

Pearson, J. T., 'The failure of British strategy during the Southern campaign of the American Revolutionary War, 1780–1781', thesis for Master's degree, Carnegie Mellon University, 2005.

Online Resources

Armstrong, F., 'An act of war on the eve of revolution', *Naval History Magazine*, Vol.30, No.1 (Feb. 2016), available at http://www.usni.org/magazines/navalhistory/2016-02/act-war-eve-revolution (accessed 16 March 2018).

The Gaspee Committee, www.gaspee.com (accessed 20 March 2018).

Naval Documents of the American Revolution, http://ibiblio.org/anrs/ndar.html (accessed 26 January 2017).

Index

From Reason to Revolution – Warfare 1721-1815

http://www.helion.co.uk/published-by-helion/reason-to-revolution-1721-1815.html

The 'From Reason to Revolution' series covers the period of military history 1721–1815, an era in which fortress-based strategy and linear battles gave way to the nation-in-arms and the beginnings of total war.

This era saw the evolution and growth of light troops of all arms, and of increasingly flexible command systems to cope with the growing armies fielded by nations able to mobilise far greater proportions of their manpower than ever before. Many of these developments were fired by the great political upheavals of the era, with revolutions in America and France bringing about social change which in turn fed back into the military sphere as whole nations readied themselves for war. Only in the closing years of the period, as the reactionary powers began to regain the upper hand, did a military synthesis of the best of the old and the new become possible.

The series will examine the military and naval history of the period in a greater degree of detail than has hitherto been attempted, and has a very wide brief, with the intention of covering all aspects from the battles, campaigns, logistics, and tactics, to the personalities, armies, uniforms, and equipment.

Submissions

The publishers would be pleased to receive submissions for this series. Please contact series editor Andrew Bamford via email (andrewbamford18@gmail.com), or in writing to Helion & Company Limited, Unit 8 Amherst Business Centre, Budbrooke Road, Warwick, CV34 5WE

Titles

No 1   *Lobositz to Leuthen. Horace St Paul and the Campaigns of the Austrian Army in the Seven Years War 1756-57* Translated with additional materials by Neil Cogswell (ISBN 978-1-911096-67-2)

* indicates 'Falconet' format paperbacks, page size 248mm x 180mm, with high visual content including colour plates; other titles are hardback monographs unless otherwise noted.